D1143802

THE REFORMATION IN
BRITAIN AND IRELAND

THE REFORMATION
IN BRITAIN AND
IRELAND

An Introduction

W. IAN P. HAZLETT

t&t clark

T&T CLARK LTD

A Continuum imprint

The Tower Building, 11 York Road
London SE1 7NX
UK

15 East 26th Street
New York, NY 10010
USA

www.continuumbooks.com

Copyright © T&T Clark, 2003
Reprinted 2005

All rights reserved. No part of this publication may be reproduced or transmitted
in any form or by any means, electronic or mechanical, including photocopy,
recording or any information retrieval system, without permission in writing from
the publishers or their appointed agents.

British Library Cataloguing-in-Publication Data
A catalogue record for this book is available from the British Library

ISBN 0 567 08280 6 (Paperback)
0 567 08409 4 (Hardback)

Typeset by Waverley Typesetters, Galashiels
Printed and bound in Great Britain by MPG Books Ltd., Bodmin, Cornwall.

Contents

List of Illustrations

Cover image. Map of the British Isles with all ecclesiastical sites by Abraham Ortelius, engravings by Franz Hohenberg, in *Theatrum orbis terrarum* (Antwerp 1580).

I: Page from the first edition of William Tyndale's English translation of the New Testament.

II: Page from the English Geneva Bible.

III: Page from the first complete Bible in Welsh, 'Morgan's Bible'.

IV: Page from the first Irish Gaelic translation of the New Testament.

V: Page from the Common Gaelic translation of the Scottish *Book of Common Order* by John Carswell.

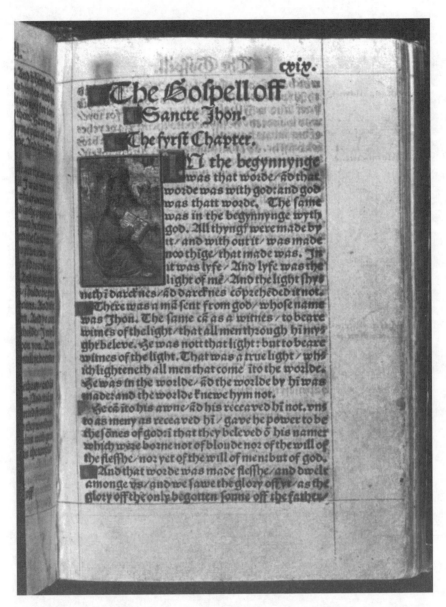

I Beginning of John's Gospel in the first New Testament in English translated directly from the Greek by William Tyndale, printed at Worms in 1526. This illustration is from one of the three surviving complete copies, the other being in Stuttgart. Between 3000 and 6000 copies had been printed.

Source: British Library, C.188.1.17, folio CXIV recto.

1 Aul an Apoſtle of Ieſus Chriſt, by the wil of God, to the *Saintes, which are at Epheſus, and to the faithful in Chriſt Ieſus:

2 Grace (be) with you and peace from God our Father, & (from) the Lord Ieſus Chriſt.

3 *Bleſſed (be) God euen the Father of our Lords Ieſus Chriſt, which hathe bleſſed vs with all ᵃ ſpiritual bleſsing in heauélieᵒthings in Chriſt,

II Paul's Epistle to the Ephesians, Ch. 1, vv. 1–3, in the 1562 edition of the English Geneva Bible (1560). Note the innovation of verse numbering in the left margin. The Preface to the Reader declared: 'To our beloved in the Lord the brethren of England, Scotland, Ireland.'

Source: Glasgow University Library, Special Collections, DT c.13, folio 81 verso.

Aul Apoſtol Jeſu Griſt trwy ewyllys Duw, at y Saint ſydd yn Epheſus, a'r ffyddloniaid yn Ghriſt Jeſu.

2 Grâs [ſyddo] i chwi a thangnedŵyf oddi wrth Dduw ein Tâd, a'r Arglwydd Jeſu Griſt.

3 Bendigedig [ſyddo] Duw, a Thâd ein Harglwydd Jeſu Griſt. yr hwn a'n bendithiodd ni â phôb bendith yſprydol, yn y nefolion [‖ leodd] yn Ghriſt:

ethau.]

III   Paul's Epistle to the Ephesians, Ch. 1, vv. 1–3, in the first complete Welsh Bible translation published by William Morgan in 1588, here from the 1620 edition. The Dedication was to 'Elizabeth, Queen of England, Wales and Ireland'. Morgan's Bible incorporated a revised version of the original Welsh translation of the New Testament published by William Salesbury and Richard Davies in 1567.

Source: Glasgow University Library, Special Collections, Dr. b. 11, signature Q2 verso.

Ol abſdal Ióſa Cſioſd tſē
toil Dē, cum na nóm atá
a Nepheſuſ, aguſ cum na
dſuinge cſeideſ a Nióſa
Cſioſd;

2. Gſáſa maille ſib aguſ ſioc-
cám ó Dhia aſ natḡ, aguſ ón otiḡeſna Ióſa Cſioſd.

3. * Glóiſ aguſ moladh do Dhia,
eadon datḡ aſ otiḡeſna Ióſa Cſioſd,
noc do bẽnuid ſin lē gac uile bẽna-
cadh ſbioſadálta, ſna neitib nẽmda, a
Gcſioſd:

IV   Paul's Epistle to the Ephesians, Ch. 1, vv. 1–3, in the first Irish Gaelic translation of the New Testament published by William O'Donnell in 1602, here from the 1681 edition. The Preface was addressed 'To the Christian People in Ireland'.

Source: Glasgow University Library, Special Collections, Bm-f.13, p. 264.

DO CHVM
GACH VILE CHRISDV-
idhe ar feadh an domhain go himlan &
go hairidhe dfearaibh Alban & Eire-
and, don mheid dibh ler bhail briathra-
dífle Dé do ghabhail chuca na gcroid-
headhaibh & na nindtindibh, ata Eóin
Carfuel acur abheandachta agas
aguidhe an fpirad naomh dho
ibh odhia athar trid.
IOSA CRISD
ARDTIGH-
EARNA.

(✳✝✳)

V   From John Carswell's translation (1567) of the *Book of Common Order* ('John Knox's Liturgy'), the first ever printed book in Irish or Scottish Gaelic, of which only three copies have survived. This illustration is of the Epistle to the Reader: 'To every Christian throughout the whole world, and especially to the men of Scotland and Ireland, to such of them as desire to receive the true Word of God in their hearts and minds, John Carswell sends his blessing, and prays that they may receive the holy Spirit from God the Father, through Jesus Christ our Lord.'

Source: diplomatic reprint of the original, edited by Thomas Maclauchlan, *The Book of Common Order translated into Gaelic anno domini 1567* by John Carswell (Edinburgh 1873), p. 17.

Preface

The subject matter of this book represents a thoroughly revised, amplified and updated version of a series of public *Kerr Lectures* delivered at the University of Glasgow and published here for the first time.

The *Kerr Lectureship* – originating in 1887 within the former United Presbyterian Church[1] – is now vested in the Church of Scotland and operates intermittently at Glasgow University. Privileged to have been nominated to the lectureship (though it has usually been devoted to 'doctrine' or 'biblical studies' rather than 'Church history'), I chose, in consultation with the Kerr committee, the topic: 'The Reformation in the British Isles'. Foreseen were outlines of, and reflections on, the diverse courses, tributaries, hindrances and outcomes of the general European Reformation as exemplified among the various peoples of England, Ireland, Scotland and Wales. Whatever was distinctive in each case would be viewed as subordinate to that which was common, namely the general religious turmoil and political evolution throughout Europe of the era. Such a relatively unconventional aim was determined chiefly by the deficit of accounts, even basic ones, in which a reasonably balanced, fourfold story is related. Traditionally, England and Scotland (the Lowlands) inevitably steal the limelight, sometimes under the rubric of something like 'the Reformation in Britain'.

This handicap also relates to the fact that since the nineteenth century in particular the various Reformation histories pertaining to Britain and Ireland have been mostly individuated. They have been composed on *separate* national-ethnic, political, and ecclesiastical lines. This normative practice has been understandable, if not particularly forgivable. It reflects what happened elsewhere in the Europe of nation- or kingdom-states, submerged nations, and religious confessionalization. The stress on the 'national' and particular tended to induce disconnection from the 'international' and general. Boldness suggests that they who know only the Reformations in England, Scotland, Ireland or Wales do not really know the Reformations in England, Scotland, Ireland or Wales.

The intention of this reworked version is threefold. Firstly: to provide synoptic accounts of the events, processes and personalities associated with the contentious irruption of the Reformation into the four contiguous regions comprehended by the descriptor: 'Britain and Ireland', alternatively known as the 'British Isles'. It is hoped that this survey-element will meet the recognized need among students, teachers and general readers for a convenient, comparative and synthetic presentation of seemingly diverse, yet obviously related histories – modern atomizing trends notwithstanding. Provision of serviceable access in the form of a general textbook and initial reference work is the main keynote. This book also takes into consideration various manifestations of resistance, opposition, revival and conservative counter-reform within the old Church and its membership. Obviously, the text does not offer a comprehensively detailed narrative. There exist already many and near-exhaustive versions of what unfolded in England and Scotland. Recently Wales has been better provided for, whereas an authoritative general account of the special situation in Ireland is still awaited, although there has been a modern flurry of specialist studies. Various well-known and not so well-known histories or studies concerning all four countries will be often alluded to in the text or found in the Bibliography. A concern of this portrayal is, however, to pay an unconventional degree of heed to the inevitable inter-relatedness of developments in the different scenarios. This was due partly to individual networking, partly to governmental policies, and partly to mutual proximity.

Secondly: to extend the declared purview into the *early* seventeenth century. One reason for this is that the Reformations in the 'three kingdoms' were of a chronologically 'long' nature. Another reason is that following the promotion of James Stewart as sole pan-insular monarch in 1603, political preconditions were in place for attempts to impose a uniform religious and ecclesiastical settlement on the entire region. This was enhanced by a new sense of 'mission' grounded in apocalyptic awareness and divine mandate. However, the seventeenth century actually sees the completion of the transition to multiple confessional orthodoxies and religio-political 'identities': Protestant, Catholic, Episcopalian, Presbyterian, Calvinist, Puritan, Anglican and so on. This was to condition future historical memories and vocabulary.

Thirdly: to familiarize readers new to, or not advanced in, the subject with some of the ways and means, past and present, of writing about the Reformation in the respective lands. They will also be made alert to various formative myths and legends, ancient and modern. The broad, essential outcomes of recent research in the field are highlighted along with some critique of them by the author. Accompanying this are some critical reflections on the difficulties of separating the observer from the observed. Who makes and shapes history – the actors or the tellers?

The original lectures were given to a combined public and mainly undergraduate audience. Deriving from this original context, the style and tone is necessarily somewhat hybrid. The content is then partly introductory, partly reportage, partly discursive, and partly occasional analysis of certain ideas, events or accounts of them by historians and others. Nonetheless, the nature both of the content and of the method represents an experimental approach to a topic whose treatment has for too long been 'set in its ways'. The chief hopes are to whet or revive interest, and to open up new perspectives – though anything 'definitive' or magisterially synthetic relating to the broad objective is still a long way off in the future. However, in anticipation I have devoted more attention than is wont to developments in Ireland, Wales, and the Gaelic half of Scotland in the firm belief that the impacts of the Reformation there need to be liberated from conventional postscripting and marginalization. Modern research into those traditionally Cinderella domains of Reformation history, seen as barren ground, has made remarkable progress. Studies based on the 'centres' of the Reformation, whether on the Continent or in the British Isles, can result in obvious distortions and naïve generalizations. The complex rippling of impulses throughout perceived peripheral territories as well as the large hinterlands and localities, where the majority of people lived, has only begun to be illuminated in recent decades.

In the redrafted, published form of the material, I have included some notes and a selective Bibliography of work done in the last thirty years or so on the Reformation era in each of the four countries. This reflects the varieties of approach and interpretation. Useful general reference material is also added. Main primary sources, whether in their original format or in later edited collections, are mostly cited in the Notes.

Chapter 1 contains general theoretical reflections that were not part of the original lecture series other than in an allusive way. This chapter has been added here to recall and emphasize two things. Firstly, the practice of church history, the study of Christianity in its various expressions, has never been immune from changing ideas of what 'history' is or should be. Accordingly, past and present studies of the Reformation, for instance, are governed by conceptual genetic codes of one kind or another. Secondly, church history is not a wholly autonomous and free-standing activity, a rigidly circumscribed discipline. The history of the Church or of Christianity, regardless of how it should be defined, has never been plausibly separable from general history, political, social, economic, religious, cultural and ideological. The abortive, ahistorical programme of 'dialectical theology'[2] within neo-Protestant orthodoxy in the first half of the twentieth century, with its radical scepticism about finite, temporal data and frameworks, underlined the point – the truths of (Christian) history, it affirmed, can only be appropriated with certitude by faith, not by mental contemplation of so-called objective historical facts. Such historical pessimism, part of a wider 'frenzied flight from history'[3] at the time, ran into the sands.

Yet the interdisciplinary discipline of church history, open to everyone, retains distinctive ultimate concerns that not everyone might acknowledge. These are with the nature of manifold Christian communities and Churches that perceived themselves as *viatores* or migrant cities of God within terrestial and mundane environments. Such an optic need not imply a ghetto-like preoccupation with the 'internal', such as piety, polity, or 'pure' theology, though neglect of these undoubtedly diminishes understanding of the Church's external manifestations and impact. For the tale is one of Two Cities and their interaction, smooth or rough. In the Reformation era the religious controversy was primarily fuelled not by differences of opinion about how to tackle religious abuses, or by the need to legitimize the redistribution of wealth, or by the forces of 'lay liberation' from clericalist control – in the way that tends to be represented in reductionist historical accounts. Rather, it was rooted in colliding concepts of God, human nature, the world, salvation, the Gospel, faith, grace, authority, sanctity, church, ministry, and worship – a collision which inevitably soon became assimilated to other conflicts in the 'public' domain. Toning down or even bypassing questions of ultimate belief and doctrine enhances neither knowledge nor understanding, and will only necessitate future reinventions of conceptual wheels.

The focus of church history – the study of the 'church in history' – therefore implies a bipolar way of looking through the multisided prism of historical perception. The task is hardly straightforward, since it obviously involves dimensions that are hypothetical, non-rational and supernatural. 'Ecclesiastical history' or 'the history of Christianity', and so 'Reformation history' is nonetheless an inseparable part of a larger, unbounded historiographical enterprise. It goes without saying, however, that not everyone would acknowledge such a bipolarity. There is also little doubt that the core 'religious' history of the Reformation era is increasingly less prioritized by some (though not necessarily on principle). Its inner world and preoccupations are perceived as intangible and opaque, or as alien and even inimical to modern predispositions, and so dispensable. As suggested, this pragmatic attitude engenders much modern writing about the Reformation that is confined to the study of power struggles, social unrest and realignment, and 'cultural' transformations within the dimension of the earthly One City. The official Church Reformation's politically conservative, imperialist and counter-cultural impulses help account for this – though it shared such instincts with the Catholic Church that it wished to reconstruct, not just restructure.

For all that, the essence of the Reformation's historical appeal is relatively unique. Whereas most major (enduring) historical changes are gradual and piecemeal, the fascination of the Reformation consists in the relative suddenness with which it was at least adopted in certain regions of Europe – even though there had been talk about the need for a

'Reformation' since the fourteenth century. Not since the fourth century, in the Roman Empire, had there been such a global attempt to change (or radically modify) religion, culture and civilization within a generation or two. Modern people can be just as perplexed by this as many sixteenth-century contemporaries were. One example was the disillusioned dominie and priest in Scotland, Ninian Winzet, who was one of the very few defenders there of the old order. In 1559, he pondered on the phenomenon of what earlier Catholic apologists elsewhere had termed 'New Christians':

> I wondered how it might be that Christian men professing, teaching, and preaching Christ and his Word for so many years, should in the space of a month or thereabouts be changed in a completely opposite sense on so many lofty matters with such enthusiasm. At Easter and certain Sundays afterwards they taught with great apparent zeal, and ministered the sacraments to us, in the Catholic manner. And by Whitsun they change their beliefs with an about-turn.[4]

The *Kerr Lectureship* refers to the bearing of 'modern thought' on 'evangelical theology'. It can hardly be gainsaid that the religious Reformation was in one or other way 'evangelical', at least in its self-understanding and articulation. What will be said in Chapter 1 – and alluded to thereafter – about the impact of modern thought on Reformation historiography should reasonably meet that *Kerr* criterion.

There is, however, a continuous semantic problem. Unfortunately, the word 'evangelical', like the word 'Catholic', is in general fraught with difficulty, especially in English-speaking parlance. In this, the word 'evangelical' has party-theological connotations reflecting dissensus within Churches of Reformation provenance. It is regrettable that each of these words is often used as the other's antonym, leading to permanent misconception. In earlier generations, things were less ambiguous when, in relation to the Reformation, 'Protestant', and 'Papist' or 'Roman' were used. The last two designations (and increasingly the first) are now tainted, culturally incorrect, and even subject to censorship, tacit or explicit, by some modern editors. In the Reformation context, 'evangelical' properly refers to the normative primacy of the Word of God in Scripture for preaching, teaching and practice as stressed in the Protestant Reformation (which however claimed to be also properly Catholic). 'Catholic' conventionally refers to the view that also ascribed normative status, conjoint with Scripture, to inherited extra-biblical (unwritten apostolic) tradition and observances, as stressed in the Roman Catholic Church (which also claimed to be properly evangelical).

The current practice of substituting 'Protestant' and 'Roman(ist)' with 'Evangelical' and 'Catholic' – derived as it is from long-standing German practice – can then exaggerate the degree of religious polarization considerably. One can hardly deny that historical Roman Catholicism, for all its indictable or imputed blemishes and accretions apart from unwritten apostolic traditions, was also inherently evangelical – 'preaching Christ and his Word', as in Winzet's quote above. Nor is it doubted that Reformation Churches, for all their adhesion to perceived 'pure' and 'original' Christianity (New Testament, and testimony from the Church Fathers compatible with Scripture), also retained many Catholic non-biblical traditions and usages. Apart from the primary doctrines of the faith as articulated in the Oecumenical Councils of the early Church, these included infant baptism, Sunday worship, Christian weddings and some liturgical customs, as well as some bad practices like the victimization of dissidents and heterodox thinkers. The fact is that both Roman and Protestant Churches *claimed* to be simultaneously evangelical and Catholic. The universally divisive issue in the Reformation era was the value and authority to be ascribed to extra-biblical, church tradition(s), and by whom. Everything else flowed from this question of legitimacy and validation. The various paths taken by the Reformation, including those in Britain and Ireland, reflect even inner-Protestant divergences of opinion on the matter, since to some extent that specific debate cut across the perceived 'Catholic–Protestant' divide.

I am indebted to two members of the *Kerr Lectureship* committee who particularly encouraged the project. These are firstly, Dr Henry Sefton, involved in his capacity as Master of Christ's College, Aberdeen; secondly, Professor Joseph Houston, at the time Acting-Principal of Trinity College, Glasgow, the remnant of the former Free Church College linked to the Faculty (now School) of Divinity in the university. The indexes (except the subject index) were prepared with characteristic care and exactitude by the Revd J. Ainslie McIntyre, MA, BD, whose adjunctive copy-editing suggestions were also much appreciated. Finally, the astute critique and valuable suggestions of a well-informed proofreader, Father David White in Devon, have been a greatly appreciated bonus.

IAN HAZLETT
Glasgow, St Patrick's Day, March 2003

CHAPTER 1

History, Church History and Reformation History

In attempting to explain the past, one soon realizes that much modern historical 'narrative' – or at least 'writing' – is not what it is generally understood to be. Envisaged normally is a distilled, ordered presentation of trends, events and changes, making them generally comprehensible, digestible and significant. Increasingly, other perspectives and considerations have now been interposing themselves. One can cite a variety of current ways of doing broadly 'religious' history in terms, for example, of nation, ethnic group, class, region, (popular) culture, *mentalité*, gender (female), media, spirituality, roots, post-modernism[1] etc., all of which jostle for legitimacy or even ascendancy. Many writers, therefore, practise new kinds of history, or even histories of 'their own', and so of hitherto neglected veins or invented ones. As a corollary, 'confessional', 'denominational', 'ecclesiastical', 'religio-political', and 'biographical' ways[2] in the broadly religious sphere tend to be frowned upon as inadequate, unimaginative, shackled and exclusive. They are predicated as 'traditional', 'clericalist', or redundant, emanating from one or other kind of self-selecting 'establishment'. Hence they are largely circumvented by historians considered as progressive. In this respect, modern historiography has undergone apparent emancipation. Yet if the new special fields and perspectives are divorced from the other spheres and seen as self-determining, even almost parthenogenetic, then they too will engender blinkered accounts as well as new chimerical legends replacing old ones. In respect of the sixteenth century, when the demarcation between spiritual and secular was conceived wholly differently from now, historiographical reshuffling risks missing the point. Reformation religious agitation – Protestant, Catholic, Christian Humanist or Anabaptist – and the Reformation 'era' inhere mutually. The former was not just an 'aspect' of the latter.

Another consideration bears on the very nature of history and the means of 'doing' it. The modern zeal of professional historians, also within

1

Reformation studies, for massive micro-studies of smaller regions, towns, dioceses, parishes, personnel categories, etc. within limited time-periods, signals the large Russian-novel approach to history. But who, even among academy historians, has the time to read and digest worms'-eye views of seismic movements and myriad occurrences? Anyway, what kind of truth does the strictly empirical approach in matters of faith and religion reveal? Leopold von Ranke (1795–1886) is considered the progenitor of modern historical narrative. His famous, though often misunderstood, confession to the pursuit of 'history as it really [i.e. *essentially*] was'[3] – an adage authorizing the primacy of (documentary) detail, 'facts' and 'context' – can be both a golden goose and a bottomless pit. To some it intimates an El Dorado of historical discovery, illumination and reality, 'scientific' objectivity, neutrality and disinterestedness. If not 'truth', then multiple relative 'truths' can be distilled. For others, the massively detailed accounts derived from slagheaps of archival data, and presented in a manner whereby content has priority over literary form, do not so much resurrect history as suffocate and inhume it. For some others, such an intrinsically inexact science has occasioned sinuous, unsettling and even unwelcome debates about facticity, historicity, veracity, meaning and hermeneutical criteria.[4]

Ranke's objective was in no way inherently subversive of religion, a domain in which the notion of 'facts' challenges conventional understanding. His influence did enable (some) history in the post-Reformation religious context to be written that was neither manifestly 'Catholic' nor 'Protestant', even if such impartiality was already aspired to by some historians in the sixteenth century.[5] Conviction history gave way to thesis history. Ranke's exhortation was primarily methodological, the preliminary to the search for meaning, 'significance', or the 'essence' of the matter inherent in the evidence accumulated – not in arbitrary or self-referential constructs of the interpreter's mind. The interpretation of the later historian must be tempered by the original 'context'. Also, the forests of detail point to something beyond. For Ranke, the causation and motion of history was of extrinsic determination – and by Providence ultimately. This operates in a 'top-down' manner, by way of institutional and hierarchical authorities. The evidences, testimonies, and relics of such history are therefore the 'hieroglyphics of God', in need of decoding. Ultimately, Ranke's conception embodies a Christian Humanist merger of Aristotelian (God the prime mover or first cause) and Platonist (truth is veiled) epistemologies married to a Judaeo–Christian vision of the ultimate fulfilment of history in the future – teleology. His study of the Reformation in its political context was grounded in such a concept.[6]

The techniques advocated by Ranke subsequently ignited a massive explosion of archival and source-research that obviously remains active. The new combination of (re)sources, craft and letting history speak for itself, became the breeding ground of the 'monograph' on a 'special subject'. The ultimate effect has been that general accounts, as well as comparative or synthetic narratives by a single author, have waned in estimation. They are replaced by multi-authored bumper volumes, or by more modest 'introductory surveys' or 'compendiums'. Definitely 'useful', the latter in particular function as gateway 'text-books'[7] initiating readers into the past.

The basic procedure and probing attitude urged by Ranke has been common to the chief schools and notions of history that emerged subsequently,[8] and to the modes and philosophies that helped shape Reformation studies as well. These modern ways of presenting and interpreting history, particularly the sensitivity to context, came into being largely in reaction to aspects of eighteenth-century Enlightenment rationalism, utilitarianism and 'universalism'.[9] Typically, Enlightenment writers had claimed high moral and cultural ground based on the 'iron cage of Reason', aesthetics and the sovereignty of the autonomous conscience. This provided the basis for adopting judgemental postures and for discounting any claims based on divinely revealed truth. Such an approach to history operated with the criteria of 'reasonableness', 'progress' and 'virtue', so that past eras, developments, personalities, episodes, etc. were evaluated in accordance with criteria of what was seen as sensible and good (civilized) or irrational and bad (barbaric). This was particularly inauspicious for the critique of 'Christianity' in the hands of seminal Enlightenment thinkers like Voltaire and David Hume, including many of their subsequent epigones. The optical lens of their theories of knowledge, ethics, culture and religion caused them, understandably, to excoriate, or dismiss, much in historical and dogmatic Christianity including the Reformation (and Counter-Reformation).

However, among church historians and other historians at the time, attempts were made to save for the Enlightenment something of the Reformation, since it was considered as somehow less obnoxious than Catholicism. By means of conceptual recycling it was asserted that the 'good', or the 'reasonable', in the Reformation was its major part in helping humanity escape from medieval church totalitarianism and its 'crafty theologians'; it contributed significantly to the evolution of the human spirit, the 'sentiments of mankind', higher religion, freedom of conscience, etc. Notable representatives of this position were Edward Gibbon (1737–94), J. L. von Mosheim (1693–1755), J. S. Semler (1725–91), and in Edinburgh, William Robertson (1721–93). The last three were also prepared to grant that the providential hand of God guided such a phase in human and spiritual growth, and so did not rule out ultimate supernatural influence. In general then, the Age of Reason sanctioned a cherry-picking attitude to the Reformation.

Examples of significant and often overlapping post-Enlightenment developments in attitudes to history that have exercised conscious or unconscious influence on the broadly modern writing of history and church history, have been, to start with: *Romanticism.* Sceptical of rational analysis or empirical enquiry, it revolved round notions of freedom from classical norms, of empathy, the self, the transcendent and the imagination. An early articulation of Romanticism (though the word was invented later)[10] was by the philosopher-theologian, J.-G. Herder (1744–1803), who in turn had been influenced by the critique of reason proposed by the philosopher Immanuel Kant (1724–1804). Kant had restricted much in the perception of 'truth' to 'truth claims', limited by experience and cognition. This helped open the door to the Romantic Movement, which encouraged greater *inner* consciousness of individual, ethnic, national and religious 'identity', especially with reference to 'feeling', 'genius', 'personality', 'spirit', 'belief', 'grandeur' and other non-rational factors. It soon suggested a fresh way of discerning history.

Two of its major keynotes were *international pluralism* and *individualism.* The former was understood not in our contemporary sense of 'multi-culturalism' *within* nations or societies, rather of distinctive national cultures and separate identities coexisting *externally* with each other in harmony (it was imagined). Historically, each of these cultures is to be considered in relation to the conditions in which they existed (context), all part of one humanity evolving in various ways and at different paces. This ruled out assessment in terms of absolute relativism, value equivalence, or putatively universal canons of reason and ethics. Though sympathetic, judgement was, as it were, reserved or provisional. The seemingly affirmative and tolerant attitude to diversity was, however, not so applicable *within* the perceived orthodox 'national' or 'cultural' context. Here, ideas of norma-tive identity encouraged chauvinism, exclusivism, coercive homogeneity, discrimination, etc. This signalled a mirror image of older Christian ideas of mandatory uniformity and unity.

As for the second keynote of Romanticism – individualism – this considered events and movements primarily in terms of specific persons. They alone have real existence, even if they also behave in non-rational and largely intuitive ways. Romantics (or 'Romantic idealists') stressed the unique value of individuals, so that personal biography of select 'particular people' was highlighted. This found some resonance in existing traditions of Christian theology and Christian philosophy. The former saw individuals as bearing the image of God, or to a greater or lesser degree harbouring seeds of the divine *logos*. The latter, in the form of 'philosophical realism',[11] reckoned that 'universals' only exist in 'individuals'. This accordingly enhances the status of individual human 'beings', whose cause, or 'ground of being', is God.

The combination of these ideas with Romanticism greatly stimulated the biographical approach to history and church history. There already was an analogous tradition of Christian hagiography, just as in the history writing of classical antiquity there had been a stress on roles of Great Men in shaping the course of history.[12] The nineteenth-century genre (e.g. Thomas Carlyle) concentrated on heroes, larger-than-life personalities, and geniuses, whose 'lives' predominate at the expense of ignoring the less well-endowed common man. In Reformation studies, biographical –

near hagiographical – preoccupation with the main original Reformers ensued, though a very useful outcome was editions of complete or collected works of such individuals. An extension of this personalized method issued in notions, often caricatures, of the collective individuality (or 'spirit') of nations, cultures and spiritualities; for example, German creativity, English moderation, French rationalism, Italian extroversion, Scottish ardour and so on. This was seen as somehow 'natural'.

In the train of Enlightenment- and Romanticism-fatigue there emerged a variety of other ways of conceiving and writing history. A major one derived from *Historicism*. The practical prototype of it was represented by Ranke. Its parent was the philosopher, G. W. F. Hegel (1770–1831), who maintained that the 'phenomena' of history are the revealing vehicles of truth or 'the World-Spirit'.[13] Contrary to the vision of Hegel, historicism as practised by later historians is effectively the way of Ranke stripped of his a priori belief that history echoes the pulses of God. Like in Ranke, this secularized, sub-Hegelian version also asserts the primacy of historical *context* in understanding and assessing the past. However, it crucially rejects evaluation derived from (non-existent) universal, timeless truth 'out there', religious or philosophical. It holds rather that truth, or truth-claim, being wrapped in time and particular histories (Hegel), is *exclusively* contingent – it has no validity or relevance beyond that. This departure from Hegel and Ranke opened the door to relativism; values determined and assessed by context *only*. Objective 'truth' is not determinative or attainable; rather, what is encountered are subjective, inconstant, provisional, and so 'just' historical truths. Interpretation is therefore bound to notions of 'change' and 'development' – ideas that in particular posed a challenge to the understanding of the history of Christian doctrine.

Wedded however to Romanticism and ideas of 'destiny', historicism can reinforce nationalist or patriotic attitudes to history with their appeals to eponymous heroes, ancient myths and poetry. The invocation of mythological and mystical origins had already a venerable lineage. Employed in the Old Testament and classical antiquity, it was revived in the era of the Renaissance and Reformation.[14] Its function was to help validate contemporary social, political and certain religious attitudes and 'changes'. This may legitimize aggression or positive discrimination in the name of 'struggle' for and 'rediscovery' of identity. Moreover, the step is not long to sanctioning cultural and religious colonialism in the name of 'superiority', 'mission', or 'election' (as in Protestant Ireland). A nation or a culture is not defined by appeal to universal principles, rather to its unique, proper 'spirit' or *Volksgeist*. 'Faith, fatherland and culture' can then be conjured up as the essence of nationhood, nationality and religion (as in Catholic Ireland or Orthodox Greece and Russia). In post-Reformation England, the definition of English patriotism became inseparable from Crown, country, liberty, Bible and Protestantism.

The convergence of Romanticism, notions of heroic origins, and historicism had a perceptible influence on Reformation studies. For example: Martin Luther mutated from being a universal Christian prophet into a German national hero, and John Knox from a prophetic and apocalyptic apostle of 'pure worship' and social justice to the patron saint of Scottish Presbyterianism, or at worst, the 'thundering Scot'. There was also a reaction against cosmopolitan and universal perspectives in favour of more focus on the local and the indigenous. The idiomatic consequence was that 'the Reformation in Germany, England, Scotland', etc. became 'the German, English, or Scottish Reformations', etc. As mentioned above, the trend also did strange things to notions of identity: Englishness became equated with Anglicanism, Scottishness with Presbyterianism, Irishness with Roman Catholicism, and strangest of all, Germanity with Protestantism. Such notions help explain why, in writing about Scotland, P. Hume Brown could write: 'it was by *natural* affinity that Scotland adopted the special form of Christianity which had been formulated by Calvin'.[15] This suggests that the adoption of Calvinism by other areas or communities throughout Europe was somehow unnatural.

Since radical historicism is usually linked to scepticism about interventionist divine providence, it has alternative recourse to ideas of autonomous and inherent 'laws of history', inexorable, impersonal, determinist, irresistible and predictable (Hegel during one phase, Comte, Marx, Toynbee, etc.). Such laws and patterns are freestanding, unattached to abstract moral criteria and divine supervision that have no objective reality whatsoever. In the place of God as direct agent or ultimate mover, substituted are impersonal, amoral determinism and inevitability. Individuals recede in actual importance. They are powerless to influence the mechanical course of history, which is guided by 'abstract' forces. Humans cannot be 'divine instruments'. In some Reformation studies influenced by forms of this paradigm, Luther, for example, is depicted as a pawn in the power of the absolutist princes, early bourgeois capitalist revolution, German patriotism, and – initially at least – the common man. In the British Isles, the Reformation can be presented as a subordinate, though intrinsic part of English or British centralism, patriotism, expansionism, land hunger and the *Drang nach Westen*, culminating in the colonization of America. In Scotland, Knox can be depicted as a tool in the strategic power of the English government and Scottish 'robber barons', with all their ulterior and inevitably unworthy motives.

Then there has been *Positivism*. Issuing ultimately from Enlightenment theories of knowledge and its hallowing of sense-experience (Francis Bacon, David Hume), this method adheres to strictly scientific empiricism. Its founder was Auguste Comte (1798–1857). Positivist history is the study of humanity's emergence from childhood and youth to adulthood – the 'positive' (or scientific) phase. The stuff of historical study is confined to actual and given reality, strictly observable phenomena, calling for pragmatic, hard-headed and common sense treatment. 'Brute facts' and experience are sovereign. Like historicism of the contingent and relativist kind, this way of thinking claimed liberation from the abstractions of theology and metaphysical philosophy as criteria of assessment. In other words, it saw itself as 'ideology-free'. However, unlike historicism, which had an interest in the historical and developmental functions at least of philosophy and religion, and retained a concern for 'relative truth', positivism diminishes the relevance of these even in the historical context. They are passed over as fanciful distractions, since first causes and ultimate ends are outside the bounds of empirical science, which is confined to tangible 'phenomena'. Also eschewed is the significance of imponderables derived from individual human personality and genius. Consequently, the scientific and disinterested later observer, with mind uncluttered, and someone concerned solely with evidence-bases, knows and 'understands' things better. Inductive rather than deductive, positivism's keynotes are therefore 'description', 'verification' and 'explanation' of quantifiable 'data'.

Seductively 'neutral', it too can engender value-judgement in the form of moral relativism – 'whatever is, or was, is right', or 'might is right'. This usually has fostered greater attention to the 'winners' rather than the 'losers' in history.[16] The 'outcomes' are what matter. Positivism can excuse or even laud dubious actions, even when they were grounded in appeal to the irresistibility of arbitrary divine commands as perceived by the participants.

In its more polemical form, positivism – combined with historicism – berated religion and metaphysics as temporary historical aberrations, unscientific or irrational hindrances to human progress. It tends to put those in the same pre-scientific category as 'superstition'. Hence it was confessionally 'anticlericalist', though the past in general was still worthy of study and even reverence. An even more radical form was represented by the English materialist writer, H. T. Buckle, in the first half of the nineteenth century. With truly Jacobin aplomb, he argued that history is to be rejected, putting his faith in scientific progress[17] – an ancestor of the 'history is bunk' idea that has some popularity today.

The prevalent modern form of positivism puts historical sciences on a methodological par with 'social' sciences (following Comte) in the search for the security of intrinsic 'laws' or at least 'patterns', 'trends', and 'trajectories'. This method has been widely employed in the English-speaking world. Being rigidly confined to description and (interpretative) explanation of finite evidence, such historical writing claims no competence in relation to *ultimate* causes and ends, though it does seek (or invent) general, determinative, quasi-scientific 'models'. Accordingly (judge-mental) marginalization of metaphysical, theological and spiritually trans-cendental factors remains characteristic of it. It is secularist historiography *par excellence*. It is not deterred by critiques based on relativism, or 'perspectivism' – the idea that 'facts are precisely what there is not, only interpretations' (Nietzsche).

To be fitted into the picture is *Darwinianism*. This also encouraged more attention to winners (the strong) at the expense of losers (the weak) with its notion of natural selection, competition and survival of the fittest. The vanquished, and their after-history, are downgraded, resulting in their relative submergence on the continuing historical plane. In theology, the concepts of orthodoxy and heresy can be fitted into such a paradigm in accord with the doctrinal 'truth' factor. In overall Reformation history, Anabaptists, varieties of radicals as well as other dissenting elements (depending on the context, Catholic or Protestant) – and so the losers – were largely excluded by confessional or establishment historians until recent times. The conquered tended to be written out of the story, or demonized, after their defeat.

More enduring has been the Darwinian biological or botanical analogy, with the mapping of 'genesis', 'origins', 'evolution', 'adaptation', 'transformation', 'mutation', etc., now commonplace concepts in historical writing. This merged well with long standing cyclical and organic paradigms of 'rise' and 'fall', 'growth' and 'decline'.[18] The Darwinian conception accelerated, especially in the study of Reformation ideas, the quest for 'precedents', 'forerunners', 'sources', 'transmission', 'formation', 'development', 'effects', 'influence', etc. – all commonplace vocabulary in modern historical writing as well as in various analytical text-critical editions of literary sources. While it is obvious that Darwin influenced many Church historians' analytic procedures, his apparent relegation of history to chance, and of humanity to an element in the laws of nature seemingly unrelated to any beneficent divine plan, was wholly incompatible with the Christian understanding of history.

A radical challenge to the writing of history was posed by *Marxism*: 'the materialist conception of history' (Engels); 'modes of production determine human life and history' (Marx). Aspects of life including religion are seen as self-justifying 'ideologies', by-products ('epiphenomena'[19]) emanating essentially from given socio-economic needs and processes, especially decline; they have no independent causal capacity. This materialist view of history is an extreme form of historicism, since the formative *context* is the environment, labour, capital, class, the market, exploitation and conflict of 'interests' – all amoral forces. Much of the vocabulary underlying Marxism is derived from the idealist philosophy of Hegel, such as the dialectical conflict of interests, alienation, processes, revolutionary liberation, ultimate end (teleology) and so transcendence. In Marx, the sovereignty of 'matter' substitutes that of the 'world-spirit', or 'God', or 'nature'. As suggested above, Reformation history in modern times has obviously not been immune from Marxist analysis with varying degrees of rigour. Examples are: religion and the Peasants' Revolt, the social–political profile of Luther, and certain approaches to the Reformation in towns and cities as a symptom of early bourgeois capitalism or class conflicts.[20]

Lastly, and most ambitious of all, there is *Holistic* or *Total History*. Derived from the social sciences (Durkheim, Weber) and their positivist origins, this initially shifted attention away from specific political, ecclesiastical, diplomatic, economic and biographical histories to the overall systems and structures of society. It seeks understanding in the positive and negative effects of the 'synergistic' processes of markets, states and bureaucracies on society and populations. Identified in particular with the French *Annales* school, this embodied a concern with 'total history' (Lucien Febvre,[21] Marc Bloch,[22] Ferdnand Braudel) based on amassing and tracking socio-economic 'facts', 'processes' and 'laws' as the building blocks of the total picture of 'society'. Synthesis is its goal, and it seems to aspire to a 'god's-eye view' of the world. Its undisputed contemporary appeal (to academics) and methodological success is largely explained by the alternative it offers to both 'traditional' and Marxist historiography. And it represents a counter-force to the pessimism of relativism and of Nietzschean perspectivism (the latter includes the view that language and grammar distort and falsify reality, though no other option is available). Modern total history, then, pursues what is seen as a legitimate quest for enduring, fixed realities behind the flux of experience and the artifices of language. As the history of 'men in time', it also signals liberation from total dependence on conventional documentary evidence. It transposes archaeological techniques to the history of all ages.

As for internal religious history, however, rather than supplementing it, total history in practice often inclines to relegate, marginalize or relativize it. For example, the Reformation may be *primarily* projected as a phase in European religious development meeting the needs of the early modern rising bourgeoisie, whether in Nuremberg, Norwich or Ayr. It thereby runs the risk of being explained in a reductionist manner as 'an adaptation of Christianity to social evolution',[23] a transitional religious artefact, as it were. Misunderstandings at the time, particularly in urban contexts, can corroborate this analysis. For the Reformation stress on the pure Gospel could be perceived as the common good transposed into theological keys, beneficial for civic integrity and development, free from the disruptive meddling of external and foreign church authorities.

One influential style has issued from the methodology and interests of this school, but not wholly sharing the reductionist hypothesis. Its concern is not so much with the social 'background' of Christianity at any given point, as with the all-pervasive socio-cultural matrix of late medieval and early modern Europe. Historiographical realism is its keynote. Not losing sight of the ecclesiastical and theological top strata as well as official church activity, it claims to disclose substrata of 'dechristianization' – close to what the Reformers characterized as 'superstition'. It examines 'community' rather than 'church'. It tries to capture mentalities, mainly 'popular' and 'ordinary', and not just the minds of professional and extraordinary formation, or of political elites. Close attention is paid to actual religious life (or the 'real' life of apparent believers) rather than the formulaic, official and handbook religion of the institutional Church. Notable names in this school of wide appeal have been Gabriel Le Bras, John Bossy and Jean Delumeau.[24]

In general, the enterprise of total history, or 'intersecting histories' (*histoires croisées*), has been normally unable to beget individual holistic or synthesizing minds, so that the 'whole' and the 'totality' remain elusive and subjective. Lucien Febvre, who also made a major contribution to the study of the Reformation movement in France, paradoxically expressed hostility to the 'spirit of specialization' and to 'the superstitious respect for facts'. And with Olympian grandeur he advocated 'history without intellectual frontiers'.[25] This aspiration may be realizable by the occasional genius or extraordinary talent, but not, however, by most vocational historians, few of whom see themselves as frontiersmen. Anyway, the danger of added-value 'inter-disciplinary' models is that they can paradoxically become exclusivist, generate new myths, and so baffle inquirers. Rather than being illuminative, 'total context' runs the risk of being an obscuring and even tyrannizing veil masking a black hole of mystery.

However, not all concern with socio-economic contexts implies a dumbing down or relativization of religious and theological dimensions. Within Reformation studies the view of church history as the record of human response to the ongoing incarnation, responses embodied in 'the changing vestures of the faith',[26] has been advanced by historians linked to the school of Harold Grimm (1901–83)[27] in particular. There are echoes of the Two Cities perspective in this. There are also common avenues linking Grimm's concerns to those of writers like Bernd Moeller, Steven Ozment and Heiko Oberman. The call is to explore the 'real social history of the Reformation' and to construct 'a social history of Reformation ideas' in respect of transmission, diffusion, marketing, reception, effects and so on. Accordingly, 'social historians of the Reformation need to learn to read tracts and sermons and vernacular translations as well as tax rolls and visitation protocols'.[28] Studies emanating from this methodological source, rediscovering theology as it were, have enhanced the understanding of Reformation responses and processes in recent decades.

Inevitably, some of the above paradigms have accelerated the desacralization of history and the elimination of transcendental dimension from the landscape of interpretation, such as divine intervention, providence and revelation. As we saw above, aspects of the Enlightenment had instigated this process.[29] Along with increasing anticlericalism and laicization, such a trend has had a heavy impact on the practice of 'church history', stripping it of sustainable autonomy, absorbing it within One City affairs. Since the time of Eusebius of Caesarea (AD 264–340), ecclesiastical history had understood itself as the demonstration of the continuing interaction between the will of God and human obtuseness, derived from the primary biblical format of 'salvation history' or Providence in action. This was in opposition to established notions of history as fate, chance, accidents or a series of dice-throws. The Christian Roman philo-sopher, Boethius (*c.* AD 480–524) articulated the formative view: 'Some sages say that Fate rules both weal and woe of every man. But I say, as do all Christians, that it is the Divine Purpose that rules them, not Fate.'[30] In addition, consequent on the impact of Augustine (AD 354–430), teleological consciousness was sharpened, so that the goal of history, the eventual establishment on earth of God's kingdom or city, was the guaranteed outcome. This determined the nature of the Christian writing of history up to the sixteenth century and beyond. Luther reiterated the standard view when he wrote: 'Histories are nothing else than a demonstration, recollection and sign of divine action and judgement', although, more sceptically, some 'histories are extremely unreliable and God's work is shamefully obscured'.[31]

The recession, eclipse, or secularization of these previously normative ways of thinking means that nowadays few historians – even Christian ones – would depict, for example, the Reformation of whatever variety as a chapter in the history of salvation or divine providence, at least not explicitly.[32] If there is still 'Christian historiography' outside avowedly confessional parameters, no widely accepted replacement has been found for the bipolar, Eusebian–Augustinian model of world history into which topics like the Reformation might fit.[33] Inevitably, faith history – of a religious kind – is a soft target for censure in the ex-Christian world.

Modern Reformation historians are none the less impelled by the quest for all-revealing sources, evidence, and records (just as Eusebius, the inventor of source-based history of any kind, had done 1700 years before them). The early Protestant and Counter-Reformation historians, like Johann Sleidan, Matthias Flacius, Jean Crespin, John Foxe, John Knox, Henry Bullinger on the one side, and Caesar Baronius, Nicholas Sanders, etc. on the other, were also orientated to sources and evidence. With the notable exception of Sleidan,[34] their specific aim, however, was to assert and verify religio-theological beliefs, and so was frankly 'confessional', powered by religious conviction.[35] In contrast, the majority of modern historical writers function according to eclectic conceptual criteria, and are muted or discreetly non-committal on theology, so that questions of doctrinal validity largely evaporate, are held in reserve, or are left to others.

There is, however, a cleavage, occasioned by two forms of reductionism. As indicated, due to ideological preconceptions some modern 'Reformation' (era) historians (neo-positivist) will not permit the evidence to have any significance beyond secular and societal parameters, and so devalue and even excise serious religious and theological factors as extraneous or obtrusively alien (though 'piety' or 'spirituality', being phenomenological, is exempt). A minority of others (partly historicist, partly Darwinian) applies a kind of DNA fingerprinting approach to history. They pursue the complex history of thought, ideas and doctrines in terms of context, origins, sources, evolution, transmission, linkages, effects and influences, and maybe include evaluation. Neither method, however, offers a magic sponge to make history or the truth come alive either, since abstraction, elusiveness, illusion, delusion, source contamination and selectivity can notoriously vitiate the 'results' as well.

As the novelist, Thomas Mann, once remarked: the narrator of history is 'a whispering conjurer in the Imperfect tense'.[36] Since, however, modern historians are no longer narrators of a 'story' or chroniclers, rather combine-harvesters of 'material', architects of complexity and purveyors of theses and hypotheses retrospectively, neither their product nor prose necessarily enhances the diction, dispels the mystery or makes the past transparent. The laudable explosion of activity can engender disintegrative implosion or conjure up unscalable mountains of history: ''Tis all in pieces, all coherence gone.'[37]

To avoid falling foul of a chronic pessimism, which legitimate but frustrated historiographical aspirations might actually induce, one can, all the same, take temporary refuge in the selective bird's-eye view of history in order to make some or any coherent sense of it, even if subjective and provisional. The good thing about such a broad scan over the forests and mountains of research, as well as lurking methodological landmines, is that it is soon compelled to make everything within the chosen frame immediately, even if arbitrarily, intelligible. Admittedly it runs the risk of falling into the modern heresy of subordinating content to form. It is arguably necessary, none the less, if a general sense of history is to survive in wider culture. Thereby one, newly oxygenated, can escape momentarily the endless pursuit of pieces needed to complete the great, eternally expanding jigsaw puzzle. And it is not necessarily confined to national, geographic, confessional or any other 'disciplinary' frontiers, real or hypothetical. Anyway, such pragmatic exercises may rouse the interest and stimulate the appetites of mentally less constrained, less self-censoring audiences outside the tiny professional and privileged circuit. As Lucien Febvre stated in his famous essay: 'The average man will only understand . . . history if he is taught by means of results and not if he is lectured to by learned men.'[38]

As for the topic of this book and the original lectures, an important reason for choosing it was to alert non-specialist, though reasonably informed listeners and students, to specific developments in modern historiography of the Reformation in these islands. These developments are (often unwittingly) impregnated to various degrees with the approaches outlined above. Apart from various caveats, I had one axe to grind. This was – as intimated earlier – to underline that the modern striving for a 'holistic' presentation of a historical set of waves like the Reformation, taking account of contingent political, social, economic and cultural dimensions, can ironically downgrade and even eliminate the conceivably primary religious and theological ones. As the Erlangen church historian, Bernd Hamm, has stated: 'The stimulating *centre* of the Reformation was its theology, and the structural centre of this was the doctrine of justi-fication.'[39]

The danger of added-value 'inter-disciplinary' models of historical work is that they can paradoxically become exclusivist, generate new myths, and so baffle inquirers. 'Context' then, rather than being illuminative, runs the risk of being an obscuring, even tyrannizing veil masking an ocean of enigmas. The other problem with modern all-inclusive and inter-disciplinary works, highly commendable though they are, is that they necessarily appear in multi-authored format, reflecting the specialist interest, or the particular 'discipline', of various authors.[40] The editor at the helm might well attempt to tie everything, or something, together in a synthesizing final chapter. However the overall effect is that of an encyclopedia or 'reference work', announcing comprehensiveness of material or 'aspects', and so a multiplicity of understandings and inter-pretations. They are collective 'projects'. One can admire the erudition, insights and value of the various contributions, but it is hard to develop affection for such books as a whole. They lack the uniquely internal imprint of a single guiding mind and the influence that this can radiate. A recent induction into the Reformation, devoted to balancing the 'total context' with the essence of the shift in theological paradigms at the time, honestly admits the elusiveness of a 'single vision of the movement or its long-term consequences'.[41]

Following the immense diversification and avalanche of historical research in the nineteenth and twentieth centuries, quantitatively and qualitatively, it is no surprise that it has now become almost mandatory to invalidate single-handed portrayals. An anonymous Reformation authority has allegedly affirmed: 'The solo flight through the pages of the past, whether undertaken by the theologian, or intellectual, social or constitu-tional historian, no longer merits licensing by historical science.'[42] No more Eusebiuses, Gibbons, or Toynbees, no more Grand Narratives. The literate, non-specialist general public is left, then, to feed on the crumbs of 'popular history'.

The forgotten example of T. M. Lindsay

One of the first (and almost last) attempts in the English-speaking world by a single author to present a primary source-based history of the Reformation in contrast to the conventionally derivative 'history of the Protestant Reformation' was by the Glasgow church historian, Thomas M. Lindsay.[43] Anticipating the interdisciplinary aspirations of our times, his six books in two volumes, *A History of the Reformation* (1906–7), were remarkable for various reasons. The work prefigured by many years modern textbooks of value on the Reformation that attempt to project a balanced spectrum of Renaissance and Christian Humanism, theology ('religious principles'), Protestant Reformation manifestations in the whole of Europe including England and Scotland (though excluding with apologies Eastern Europe),[44] the Catholic Reformation, as well as Anabaptism, various radicals and dissidents. However much Lindsay's treatment of these topics may be dated and slated in light of modern research, his book significantly included two unusual chapters – on 'socio-economic conditions', and on late medieval 'family and popular religious life' or 'non-ecclesiastical religion'. This was an innovation for Reformation historiography in English. (It might be pertinent to point out that unlike any other church historian in the nineteenth or twentieth century one can think of, Lindsay himself was also involved actively with contemporary social and agrarian agitation.)

His book can be characterized as a relatively novel quest for the historical and a (partly) demythologized Reformation using the methods and some preconceptions of recently developed scientific and critical historiography. Lindsay's work is accordingly transitional in significance. While committed in the last analysis to an old idea of the Reformation as a recovery of smothered religious truths, it not only contains echoes of the approaches of empiricism, historicism and Romanticism, but also anticipates future developments such as the notion of 'history from below'. He is still, however, concerned with the question of authentic Christianity, which he articulates not so much in 'theological' or 'dogmatic' terms, as 'religious', 'spiritual', or 'experiential' ones.[45] A churchman and believer, Lindsay employs phenomenological and empirical approaches while retaining a theistic interpretation.

To illustrate his tones and the influences behind them: 'No important fact has been recorded for which there is not contemporary evidence' (vol. 2, p. vii). 'I have read and re-read most of the original contemporary sources' (vol. 1, p. vii). 'This . . . has been written with the intention of describing a great religious movement amid its social environment' (ibid.). Further, he admits to a dilemma in the area of ethical evaluation: 'While the morality of one century can be judged by another, the men who belong to it must be judged by the standard of their contemporaries, and not altogether by ours' (ibid.). The neoteric concern for a contextual, global and holistic approach is aptly described with: 'The religious revival was set in a framework of political, intellectual, and economic changes, and cannot be disentangled from its surroundings without danger of mutilation. All these things add to the *difficulty* [my italics] of description' (ibid.). Lastly, his interest in pre-Reformation popular and domestic piety, 'which few have cared to investigate', resulted in his adoption of the controversial view that the religious Reformation at base level represented in certain respects continuity rather than discontinuity: 'The evangelical revival was not a unique phenomenon . . . there was continuity in the religious life of the period' (vol. 1, p. viii). 'Reformation theology represents the [authentic] piety of the medieval Church.' This is a variation of the traditional Protestant historical thesis, represented notably in the sixteenth century by John Foxe in his *Book of Martyrs*, and Matthias Flacius,[46] one of the Magdeburg Centuriators. Their view was that the Reformation had its medieval 'precursors', that the 'true' and 'hidden' church is traceable in the foggy landscapes of medieval Catholicism. For Lindsay, however, such witness was found not only in high-profile 'heretics', dissenters and medieval reformists, but also among nameless ordinary people.

Accordingly, along with his novel consideration of social, economic and cultural contexts, Lindsay still subscribed to the traditional idea of the primacy of the religious factor in the 'Reformation', of which Luther was the chief embodiment. But he gave the standard view a new twist. For in so far as there was positive response to Luther, this was because his teaching 'was no startling novelty, but something which [people] had always at heart believed . . . they accepted it as something they had always felt' (vol. 1, p. ix). In his contribution on Luther to the *Cambridge Modern History* (1904) edited by Lord Acton, Lindsay expressed the relationship between Luther and the pre-existing tradition of authentic piety in the following poetic manner: 'The river comes from a thousand nameless rills and not any single selected fountainhead.'[47]

The driving force of the Reformation was 'religious experience . . . its beginnings were not doctrinal but experimental . . . doctrines are never the beginnings of things . . . religious experience finds very inadequate description in that or any other statement of doctrine' (vol. 1, pp. 434ff.). Yet while Lindsay properly highlights Luther's universal religious significance, he also romantically entitles a subsection (vol. 1, p. 252): 'Luther the representative of Germany'.

Lindsay's point of departure, that the Reformation was primarily religious, would still command support nowadays among those sceptical about monodimensional secularist interpretations. More controversial would be his understanding of a religious reaffirmation, arising phoenix-like, and more especially that it was 'popular'. By this term he meant that unalloyed Christian piety existed continuously among some people in the shadow of church-sponsored liturgies, devotional practices and mandatory good works. The word 'popular' is currently understood to mean mass, majority, or extensive support, not the meaning ascribed to it by Lindsay. For him, the transmission and survival of true faith is not contingent on numbers, institutional forms, or legal sanction – and this is a familiar idea in Christian apologetics. Consequently, the modern zeal for 'proving' that the Reformation only commanded 'minority' support among the 'people' is theologically naïve, even if historically beyond dispute, since it reveals a defective grasp of Christianity's self-understanding.[48] Moreover, such an opinion-poll approach to historical interpretation tends to result in a view of history as 'it ought not to have been', and with underlying moralizing tones.

Lindsay's concept is undoubtedly influenced by his personal, partially counter-cultural position. This had two aspects. Firstly, he belonged to the nineteenth-century Scottish Free Church and evangelical tradition with its stress on experiential and affective piety. Secondly, he shared much of the critique, after post-Calvinistic orthodoxy, of confessional and formulaic theology (as in the Westminster Confession) with its notions of limited atonement and restrictive grace. After all, he functioned within the after-effects of the excommunicated 'heretic' in Scotland, John McLeod Campbell.

For whatever reasons, the relatively holistic vision of Lindsay surveying church, theology and spirituality in *both* socio-economic *and* political contexts was not to be significantly advanced in Reformation historiography until the last third of the twentieth century. He did not, however, apply the new procedure to his treatment of the Reformations in England and Scotland, for which reputable socio-economic histories at that time were non-existent.

CHAPTER 2

Introducing the British Isles
and their Reformations

At the outset, it should be stated that while the expression 'The British Isles' is evidently still commonly employed, its intermittent use throughout this work is only in the geographical sense, in so far as that is acceptable. Since the early twentieth century, that nomenclature has been regarded by some as increasingly less usable. It has been perceived as cloaking the idea of a 'greater England', or an extended south-eastern English imperium, under a common Crown from 1603 onwards. The influential English historian, Edward Gibbon, in speaking of 'England', referred to 'the extraneous appendages of Scotland, Ireland, and Wales'.[1] The historical and political basis of this deep and widespread perception was derived not just from raw English aggrandizement, crude English colonialism, or simple defence interests, but also from wider European Renaissance ideas of monarchy and increasingly proactive, centralizing regal government.[2] The Anglo-British Isles originated ultimately in the wider Norman Conquest, was later boosted by Tudor expansionism and territorial consolidation,[3] and then mutated into an Anglo-Scottish condominium driven by Stewart all-'British' ideology.

Nowadays, however, 'Britain and Ireland' is the more favoured expression, though there are problems with that too. For the sake of convenience and without any coded undertones I have, however, opted simply to use both expressions interchangeably. There is no consensus on the matter, inevitably. It is unlikely that the ultimate in non-partisanship that has recently appeared, the (East) 'Atlantic Archipelago' will have any appeal beyond captious scholars.

Necessary is a word of explanation about the structure of the material. A certain sequence is followed: England, Wales, Ireland and Scotland. Scotland's fourth position is due to two reasons. Firstly, it was the last area of the British Isles (and one of the last in Europe) where the Reformation was legally enacted, that is, between 1560 and 1567, even though its Reformation movement originated in the early 1520s. Secondly, Scotland was politically a wholly separate jurisdiction and so an independent entity.

The nations and peoples of England, Wales and Ireland were politically linked through the English Crown, whose dominions they constituted. Although there were two Parliaments, one in London and one in Dublin, these were two Parliaments subject to the same sovereign (or 'lord') and Crown, which was English (though there was a notional Irish Crown from 1541 onwards). This meant that anything which royal policies wrought in England was also enacted in the Welsh principality, and usually in the Irish 'kingdom', too, from the time of Henry VIII. Accordingly, Reformation (and Marian recatholicizing) legislation in England and Wales was on the whole replicated in Ireland. This then is the reason for taking the Reformation in England, Wales and Ireland together, since in legislative terms they constituted the spheres of authority of the English and then Anglo-Irish Crowns. The same 'type' of official Reformation ensued.

Consequently, bearing in mind the disproportionate size and importance of England within this triangular relationship, it is self-evident that until 1603 at least, the immediate influence determining religious changes in Wales and Ireland was the English Reformation rather than any significantly indigenous pressure for reform. This is at least the conventional view. In contrast, since Scotland remained a separate kingdom with its own Parliament in the Reformation era, it has a different legislative history in religious as in temporal matters. Yet as long as the chief Continental Atlantic powers, France and Spain, remained Catholic, Reformation England was in reality the major external guarantor of the Scottish Reformation, despite mutual unresolved ecclesiastical and credal differences.

Therefore until 1603, when the English and Scottish Crowns were united (but neither the Parliaments nor the Churches), developments occurred within quite a different formal framework of political authority as well as within a different cultural and ecclesiastical atmosphere. To a considerable extent then, one is faced with somewhat different histories, even if the magnetic pull of England is vigorous, and if the issues are common. These histories emerge as even more variegated when one encounters the diversities within the four nations as such.

While one speaks legitimately of the 'Reformation in the British Isles', or the 'Reformation in Britain and Ireland', or possibly even the 'British Reformations', much less sound is the notion of a 'British Reformation', implying an easily recognized, distinctive and essentially monochrome package. In the sixteenth century 'Britain' did not exist in the way it does nowadays (or used to), when it refers to the joint entity of England, Wales and Scotland, under a single government and Parliament within a wider 'United Kingdom' that includes part of Ireland, and in the context of a common superculture or mutual self-interest. In the Reformation or 'early modern' era, 'Britain' was an antiquarian and slightly affected, increasingly fashionable way of describing the largest of the islands in the British Isles.

The concept of a politically and culturally united 'Britain' was gestating. This was a fruit of European Renaissance Humanism, with its interest in history, antiquity, and national origins and identity, fanned by perceived glories of the past and heroic inceptions. It was not until later centuries that 'Britain' or 'Great Britain' became normal usage, to the extent that by the eighteenth century, 'Scotland' metamorphized as 'North Britain', and even Ireland was baptized by some as 'West Britain'.

Nonetheless, it was in the course of the sixteenth century that 'Britain' came to be increasingly employed as a positive concept serving to advance politically unionist or pan-British notions (even if ultimately anglocentric).[4] The inhabitants of the mainland often came to be referred to as 'Britons'. This notion would help transcend (at least notionally) the actual and problematic divisions within the British Isles, or their apparently natural disunity. The concept was rooted in the idea of a united, free, and powerful Britain, which was reckoned to have existed before the Normans, before the Anglo-Saxons, and before the Romans. It was in a sense rooted in the world of Arthurian legend and a kind of Asterix mentality. This re-discovered (or invented) heritage of submerged virtue, valour, and values could serve to reunite Britain and embrace Ireland as well, in everyone's mutual interest. Crucially, the Protestant Reformation was grafted on to it, for it too was presented as the true, original Christian faith of antiquity. Such a religio-political entity would be a far safer bulwark against foreign and Catholic aggressors and powers, notably the Spanish and the French.

In reality – it has been argued – such a mythological device was employed ultimately to make increasing English Protestant preponderance and domination acceptable. Thereby a virtue out of a (perceived) necessity was made. And since the Reformation was one of the essential and formative elements of the package, there were centrally directed and concerted, if abortive, attempts to impose either an episcopalian or presbyterian type of church Reformation on the entire British Isles. Accordingly, the concepts of being 'British' and 'Protestant' underwent symbiosis. Despite the strictures of some, there is nothing uniquely perverse or at least unusual in this development. After all, in the early Church, Christianity and *Romanitas* gradually became interchangeable, as were 'Christendom' and 'European' in the medieval Church, or as Byzantine Greek, Russian, Serbian and Bulgarian national identities became virtually inseparable from Orthodoxy.[5]

In the forefront of growing 'all-British' thinking were some Scots, like the firmly Catholic John Mair or Major (*c.*1467–1550),[6] Sorbonne theologian, Principal of Glasgow and then St Andrews universities, and also George Buchanan (1506–82), Scotland's chief Reformation Christian Humanist. It is no accident that Buchanan was the tutor of James VI (1566–1625), the first bearer of the united or 'triple crown' of England, Ireland and Scotland in 1603, and so British Isles unionist pioneer. It is also of note that a leading contributor in a later century to the developing common British ideology was another Scot, David Hume (1711–76).

As has been already indicated, in the sixteenth century the British Isles remained a politically divided conglomeration, with two Parliaments in the English Crown imperium, at London and Dublin, and a Parliament at Edinburgh (usually) in the Scottish kingdom. However, these formal political divisions concealed even more complex ethnic, cultural and linguistic divisions. Taken as a whole, all this diversity and heterogeneity was typically European. If one looks at the Continent in the same era, it is evident that official political divisions do not often correspond to cultural, ethnic, linguistic or even geographic entities. Neither 'Germany' nor 'Switzerland', the homelands of the Protestant Reformation, embodied any greater political or cultural cohesion; on the contrary, they were in some respects even more ineluctably diverse than the British Isles. All this complexity was the legacy of the constant ebbs and flows of ever-changing European history. As already mentioned, what made more urgent the need for a united British Isles (even if under English Protestant hegemony)[7] was the increasingly centralized and so powerful unitary kingdoms of Catholic France and Spain, not to forget the Spanish Netherlands. Their proximity to the vulnerable British Isles helped to concentrate minds and sink differences, especially in view of the new religious bifurcation, and the commitment of the Spanish empire in particular to the Counter Reformation. 'Security' therefore was a paramount issue. This of course is no reason to disparage the Reformation in the British Isles as ultimately 'political'. A political dimension can be ruled out nowhere, whether in Protestant or Catholic contexts.

In early sixteenth-century Britain and Ireland one did not have to look far to be aware of significant internal dissimilarities. The 'English', still something of an emerging nation, were ethnically a mixture of old British Celtic, Anglo-Saxon, Scandinavian and Norman French elements. Government, power and wealth was firmly located like now in the south-east, and much energy was required to control independent-minded forces and barons in the English north and west. The conclusion of the Wars of the Roses in the fifteenth century had not guaranteed automatic internal stability and cohesion.

Wales was an old British Celtic area in the west, with its own language, Cymric or Welsh, and a subdued 'principality' subject to the English Crown. Yet even Wales was not wholly homogenous, for in the south-west of Wales in this era there was an increasing immigrant population from southern Ireland. In addition, there was an Anglo-Welsh population, speaking English only, which inhabited largely the towns.

Scotland was more obviously a country consisting of two distinctive peoples and two main languages. The Lowlands, the east coast and the towns were populated mainly by people of Pictish, old British Celtic, and Germanic origin, which spoke Scots English (Scots, Lallans). The Highlands and most of the west were populated by Gaels who spoke 'Irish' as it was then called and continued to be until the nineteenth century, when the increasing taint of politico-religious incorrectness associated with the word caused it to be substituted by 'Scottish Gaelic'. Among the Scots Gaels, as among the Irish Gaels, there was also an absorbed Scandinavian stream going back to the Vikings and Danes. The kingdom of Scotland as known in the sixteenth century goes back to about 1054, the time of Malcolm Canmore, based on an earlier Pictish–Gaelic united kingdom achieved by Kenneth mac Alpin. Significantly for Reformation development in the country, and future political development, mobile urban, east coast and lowland Scots tended to relate economically and culturally to England and countries of the North Sea rim. Gaelic Scots tended to relate more naturally to Ireland, Ulster in particular, which was within easy reach of the southern Western Isles and the Firth of Clyde.

And if there were different Scotlands, so also were there even more different Irelands. In the twelfth century (1171), Gaelic Ireland, or part of it, with a mandate from the papacy, was seized and settled in part by the Anglo-Normans, so that the King of England (and 'France'), Henry II, became the 'Lord' or sovereign of Ireland, with a colonial 'parliament' in Dublin. Thereby Ireland was pulled by the hair into the European mainstream. Real Anglo-Norman power in the lordship of Ireland never extended in reality beyond the east coast, and an area composing the hinterland of the city of Dublin, the 'Pale'. Beyond the Pale were various old Anglo-Norman–Gaelic earldoms, kind of buffer territories or march lands, and beyond that more conspicuously Gaelic territories, which for all their famed disunity were powerful enough never to be conquered fully until the mid-seventeenth century. There were in addition some ghettoized towns of Anglo-Norman or 'Old English' origin, like Kilkenny, Cork, Limerick and Galway. Centuries before the Reformation, which is often treated as a scapegoat for all sorts of ideas now seen as unacceptable, the Anglo-Normans or 'English' had a strong 'image of themselves as a conquering people chosen by God to civilize the barbaric Irish'.[8]

As a whole, however, Irish and Scottish Gaeldom presented a potentially considerable power bloc in the broad northwest of the British Isles, being part of a wider western Celtic crescent. One of the most fateful and somewhat understated achievements of the Tudors was to be the containment and permanent paralysing of this sleeping giant, possible natural allies of foreign invaders.

All areas of this patchwork-quilted British Isles were potentially unstable, internally and externally. Wars, civil wars, dynastic instability, baronial bad behaviour, insubordination, blood feuds, local tumults and skirmishes were endemic. This could become more serious if other European powers became directly involved. In terms of international diplomacy, Scotland was an ally, client and satellite of France. England tended to be within the sphere of influence of Spain, especially following the marriage of Catharine of Aragon to Henry VIII. As one can imagine, this became a serious problem once the Reformation emanating from central Europe began to make headway in England and Scotland.

To recapitulate on these diversities: there were two Crowns, and soon to be at least a nominal third Crown when Ireland was declared a kingdom in 1541 by Henry VIII. There were three Parliaments, in London, Dublin and Edinburgh. There were four nations, English, Welsh, Scots and Irish, though Ireland was divided ethnically, politically (and ecclesiastically) into Anglo-Norman or Old English, and Gaelic Irish zones. There were ten languages in use: Latin, English, Welsh, Scots, Scottish Gaelic, Norn, Irish Gaelic, Cornish, Manx and French spoken in the Channel Islands and of course Calais, which till 1558 was part of 'England'.

The only thing of which there was one kind was religion, since the island participated in the cosmopolitan *corpus Christianorum*, or Christendom. This had the form of the traditional Roman Catholic faith. It certainly was a transcendent and unifying factor. However, the Reformation was to undermine radically this ancient religious cohesion, in fact if not intentionally. There were five church provinces. First, the Scottish Church was composed of one province and thirteen episcopal dioceses. This included two archbishoprics created in the fifteenth century at St Andrews and Glasgow, that is, in the east and the west, though the former enjoyed a *de facto* precedence. The Anglo-Welsh Church composed two provinces consisting of twenty-three dioceses, including two metropolitan archbishops at York and Canterbury. The four sees in Wales formed part of the primatial Canterbury province. Not unexpectedly, during the Papal Schism in the late Middle Ages (1378–1417), Scotland and England were on different sides. The Scots aligned themselves with Avignon and conciliarism, the English with Rome and papalism, something which had a definite 'after-effect' in the Reformation. Ireland had two provinces and metropolitan archbishops at primatial Armagh and at Dublin, covering thirty-five dioceses; among these there were two other titular archbishoprics, Cashel in the southern secular province of Munster and Tuam in the western secular province of Connacht. In Ireland there was marked diocesan inflation.

In traditional treatments of the Reformation in the British Isles, England and Scotland receive, not unexpectedly, most attention, chiefly because happenings there are seen as (relative) success stories in a grand format. Wales has usually been relegated to a footnote of the English Reformation. The Reformation in Ireland has been seen as only a pseudo-Reformation, since it was an overall failure in terms of even nominal conversion of the majority of the population. Despite this though, a politically strong Protestant phalanx, largely imported, and backed by Anglo-Scottish and certain Continental European interests secured control of the country, if not its religion, in the end.

One can, however, contend that the course of the Reformation in the four countries is to some extent four different and equally interesting tales, since each nation presented different problems and challenges. Yet there are familiar problems. Firstly, the hegemony of England and Scotland in traditional historiography, understandable though it is, needs to be addressed and modified, so that a more instructive global picture beyond automatic legislative change in Wales and Ireland can be arrived at. Recent studies in and on these countries, and greater overall awareness of the 'billiard ball effect' among all four, have helped to illuminate matters and diminish partial visions. This should also advance understanding of the subsequent permanent disruption of the Church in the British Isles, when the notions of 'British Christianity' (or 'British Church'), and 'Irish Christianity' (or 'Irish Church') became ambiguous or even meaningless. This ensued from the eventual fragmentation and *de facto* pluralism that emerged and was deplored by everyone.

Secondly, the conventional practice of treating the English and Scottish Reformations apart is not always helpful. A certain English isolationist ethos (or self-preoccupation) and a traditional Scottish affinity with the Continent have helped to reinforce this. This can obscure the fact that in both the short and the long terms, the English and Scottish Reformations had definite bearings on each other's development, and so on that elsewhere in the British Isles. The tradition of historiographic apartheid is an old one, but so also is the notion at least of a more integrated approach. It was an Episcopalian Scot, Gilbert Burnet (1643–1715), onetime Professor of Divinity at Glasgow University and then appointed Bishop of Salisbury by King William III, who tentatively made such a plea in his influential *History of the Reformation of the Church of England*, published over the period 1679 to 1714. Arising out of his account of Henry VIII's frustrated intention in 1541 to pressurize his nephew, James V, into manufacturing a break with the papacy in Scotland similar to that which had occurred in England (Henry did not want Scotland to be part of a pan-European crusade against him),[9] Burnet inserts a long digression on Scotland and religious developments there. He justifies this with the following reasons:

> Its neighbourhood to England, and the union of these kingdoms, first in the same religion, and then under the same princes, together with the intercourse there was both in this and the next reign between these nations, seem not only to justify this digression, but rather to [require] it as a part of the history, without which it should be defective. And it may be the rather expected from one who had his birth and education in [Scotland].[10]

In reality then, Burnet's interest in Scotland in this context is essentially a concession to his own background. Despite his insight into the sense and value of treating the English and Scottish Reformations in some way together, the account of the Scottish side does not, even throughout his book, attain any status more than a 'digression' from the main plot. Subsequent generations were not able to advance on this in any pro-grammatic way.

In the interest of differentiation throughout the course of this survey, important requisite distinctions have to be made between the following: first, the Reformation 'movement', second, Reformation 'legislation', and third, the Reformation 'process' of implementation and inculcation.

Further, preceding the 'movement' one can identify 'beginnings', and following the process of enforcement and re-education, one can speak of 'settlement', even if there was no absolute guarantee of permanence. Accompanying these distinctions is 'resistance' to the Reformation by Roman Catholics, as well as resistance to certain kinds of Reformation by Protestants. Both can be either active or passive. On the Catholic side, resistance or opposition eventually went on the offensive encouraged by Europe-wide 'Counter Reformation'. In the British Isles this was contained, but not eliminated. On the Protestant side, dissatisfaction with various 'settlements' handed down by legislators, particularly within the English spheres of influence, generated a (puritan) determination to regard perceived half-measures as only provisional, and so work for their supplanting. In Scotland, too, the 'Anglican' model provoked resistance for similar, but also other reasons.

Something else to be borne in mind is that authentic religious commitment and zeal of the pro-Reformation kind was mainly found among a small, if activist and influential fraction of the various populations. This should come as no surprise, since, historically, movements for religious change and reform are rarely spontaneous mass movements. The provenance and sphere of activity of this 'forward' element in the sixteenth century was usually academic or urban, and if rural, then among some gentry who combined the new piety and theology with asset-enhancement at the old Church's expense. Most people simply went along with what their rulers, chiefs or town councils told them to do. On balance, however, the conservative majority seems simply to have preferred the old ways, partly out of comfort, and no doubt partly out of conviction, in so far as such a thing can be assessed. This was no less true in England or Scotland than it was in Ireland or anywhere else in Europe; it is just that the historical outcomes were various. Moreover, in respect of England and Scotland, there is little evidence to suggest that most ordinary people were bothered much about whether their Church was governed by bishops or by presbyteries. This sort of thing was essentially only a problem for the various elites, at least in the initial phases of conceptual challenge and dispute.

Within the wider European field, the Reformation in the British Isles tends traditionally to be viewed as peripheral, derivative, or at best 'distinctive'. This was partly because it was adopted too late to have any influence elsewhere in Europe,[11] and partly because it produced no especially creative theologians or thinkers of the first rank (any with such potential were martyred). Oddly, the Scottish Reformation is often perceived as embodying unadulterated 'presbyterian Calvinism' – an a posteriori inference conditioned by events around 1690 rather than 1560. The general assessment is reinforced by axiomatic judgements viewing the establishment of the English Reformation in particular as essentially an 'act of state'[12] or an abortive 'half Reformation', or at best a quintessential '*via media*'. Selective highlighting of secondary rather than primary features, that is, stressing purely contingent, national and other peculiar characteristics at the expense of fundamental and normative features shared with the Reformation at large, reinforces such devaluation. Anyway, concentrating on perceived Continental 'centres' and 'norms' would hardly reveal the truth of the historical impact of the entire European Reformation. The assumption throughout this book is that the Reformations in Ireland and Britain were typically European and so ambivalent responses to the breakdown of the religious and theological consensus. The issues and fundamental problems were at bottom the same everywhere, be it Iceland, the Channel Islands, Swiss cantons, the Scottish Highlands and Islands, German imperial free cities, the Irish Pale, London, Normandy or East Frisia. This was inevitable once the definition of 'the', or a 'true church', her essence and face, was put on the agenda, as it had been initially by Luther and Zwingli.

Conversely, all the various regions and territories produced relatively distinctive solutions (or results or outcomes) in secondary matters. The legislative and effective Reformations in Zurich, Geneva, Basle, Strasbourg, Wittenberg, Hesse, Hamburg, Lüneburg, Nuremberg, Montbéliard, Scotland, England, Denmark, etc. were not clones or replicas of each other. Even in theological formulae (if not necessarily substance) they could vary from each other – indeed the 'Reformed' tradition in particular welcomed local confessional diversity.[13] Unlike the Catholic Reformation, the Protestant Reformation was not a Procrustean remedy and programme implemented internationally. This was because there was no supranational authority of an ecclesiastical institutional kind in the Reformation world equivalent to the papacy or the Council of Trent, even though doctrinal consensus was an unattained ideal. Even within particular 'traditions' neither Wittenberg, Geneva nor Canterbury ever exercised or claimed to exercise an authority like that, despite the fondness of some historical writers and commentators for such convenient paradigms of equivalence. This helps explain why the outcomes of the Reformation not only in Europe in general, but also in England and Wales, Scotland, and Ireland, were consistently variable and lacked a single organ or authority with efficacious executive powers. Rather than a common Church, the most that was achieved was a fraternal association of Churches with many common basic interests.

CHAPTER 3

England: Modern Accounts

For all the imputed moderation often attached to the English Reformation, much of both the traditional and recent literature about this defining episode in English history has been overtly or implicitly polemical and impassioned. This is not unique or unusual. It is just that one must stress that English Reformation historiography has been no more exempt from these (dare one say extremist) tendencies than that anywhere else. Self-consciously modern minds tend to associate the writing of 'conviction history' with the past or one or other form of confessionalism, especially since such history is viewed as committing the cardinal sin of not being 'objective'. In recent decades, however, controversy over the English Reformation has intensified with the formation of fresh battle lines, determined often by new kinds of 'convictions'. This has generated a 'Niagara'[1] of publications. The illuminating survey by Rosemary O'Day on English Reformation historiography,[2] past and present, exposes the frequent acute interaction between the ideological or credal predisposi-tions of the historians and the object of their study in this respect. Who, quite frankly, is to be believed? Consequently, understanding the English Reformation is a bit like negotiating a labyrinth: how can one both gain access to the core and make an exit safely?

Until about the 1960s, ways of writing about the English Reformation were predictable. They could be confessionally conditioned, in a Protes-tant, Catholic, Anglican or Anglo-Catholic sense. They could also be ideologically conditioned in other ways. An important example of this was the influential 'Whig' school.[3] By Whig is meant 'liberal', and at least secular Protestant, or cultural Protestant. Its analysis sees the Reformation as a significant stage in the evolution of religious, political and national 'progress' and 'freedom'. This way of thinking, still widely found in many quarters of public opinion today, understood the Reformation as the midwife delivering England from the Dark Ages, papal and ecclesiastical tyranny to the threshold of modernity. Consequently, the Reformation was projected as a turning-point in the progress of civilization and the human autonomous conscience. Such a Whiggish Protestant view, whose paternity was in a mixture of the Enlightenment and Romanticism, was often grafted on to a strong sense of English national, constitutional and social pride. Examples were influential writers like James A. Froude[4] and Benjamin Kidd.[5]

Paradoxically, adapting perceptions of the Reformation to philosophical and cultural trends such as those can also result in contrary images that denigrate the Reformation and present it as a chimera. An example was William Cobbett (1763–1835), the socio-political reformer and non-Catholic Catholic Emancipationist. He was no historian (considering academic historians as Establishment quislings), but published a compelling and popular history of the Reformation in England and Ireland.[6] Based on public lectures, this was essentially a diatribe of contempt from the point of view (that is, his point of view) of the Catholic and Protestant proletariat, the monumental victims of a modernity that had been spawned by the Reformation. The book introduced social history of the Reformation with a big bang. His 'caricature of the English Reformation ... had a profound impact on later interpretations of the Reformation because it presents [it] as the brainchild of a lustful monarch and his capitalist courtiers, and as the originator in England [and Ireland] of the oppression of the poor by the rich'.[7] Influenced in part by High Tory and Romantic conceptions articulating aversion to the social misery and degradation accompanying the Industrial Revolution, and by nostalgia for a lost world of harmony and happiness, Cobbett presented pre-Reformation society as near-Utopian. It had been an Eden in which there were indeed poor classes, but which were lovingly cared for by a selfless Church. The English Reformation embodied original socio-economic sin – symbolized in the destruction of the monasteries, subsidizing married clergy by tithes, the creation of the *nouveaux riches* – and so the ultimate cause of deprivation and oppressive Poor Laws and other post-lapsarian evils like social exclusion. There are traces in this conception of the interface between Enlightenment and Romantic thought as represented by the social-historical ideas of Rousseau.[8] In Cobbett accordingly, Henry VIII, Cranmer and Elizabeth I, incarnations of *amour propre*, are demonized. Are there not distant echoes here as well of the theologian of the German Peasants' Revolt, Thomas Müntzer, with his radical and populist critique of the princely and theologians' Reformation in Germany?

Attributing the perversion and evils of society to a confused conjunction of the Reformation and the Enlightenment rationality is found, for example, in a later Victorian historian, W. N. Massey. For him, the stability of earlier society was rooted in faith and obedience, now cast down by the impact of Reformation dissidence and sedition: 'To believe and obey are the guiding perspicuities of men. And the principle of the Reformation was to subvert authority and substitute reason as the arbiter of questions of the utmost moment to the temporal as well as to the eternal welfare of the great human family.'[9] Needless to say, Catholic historians usually welcomed such corroboration of their analysis from such quarters.

If Cobbett and those propagating diluted versions of his thesis had had access to broader historical vision, they might have been aware that the fifteenth-century crossroads of late medieval religious sensibility, the Renaissance, and the growth of the cash economy had already provoked 'a furious chorus of invectives against cupidity and avarice'. Also, that 'hatred of rich people', especially the new rich, was general. Reformation and Counter-Reformation preachers and moralists, like Franciscan Observants among others before them, simply sang the same song of calamity about the 'unconverted world'.[10]

An example of a more recent 'ideological' interpretation that has some roots in earlier social critiques of the Reformation is the discreet, semi-Marxist one that informs elements of the 'Total History' approach (see Chapter 1). This tends to understand the Reformation as an epipheno-menal manifestation of economic decline, occasioned by inflation, price-rises, and accompanying social unrest. In this way of thinking the Reformation can be seen as a self-justifying credal identity which came in on the back of the rising middle-class or bourgeoisie, which always profits when the majority artisan, labouring and peasant classes fall on hard times. Irrespective of the validity of such a hypothesis, a positive outcome of it has been to encourage research into certain groups like the landed gentry (old and new), which profited from the confiscation of the monasteries and church patrimony, merchants, who profited from the woollen and cloth trade at the expense of farmers – since arable land was turned over to sheep – and lawyers, the *sine qua non* of any rising middle class. At the time of the Reformation all these classes in England did make capital gains. They also tended to be strong supporters of the Reformation (at least the Henrician kind), though many others were not, like most of the Old English landed gentry in Ireland. However, the Achilles' heel of this analysis is that the people most authentically committed to advanced Reformation religious ideas and their propagation were not usually those concerned with financial capital gains or with enhanced real estate. On the contrary, they tended rather to appeal to the ancient Christian traditions of asceticism, modesty and restraint – not exactly something to make their general ideas universally 'popular'. However, the paradoxical link between this, the new spirituality of glorifying God through secular vocation, and dedication to wealth generation, was proposed by the 'Weber thesis', associating 'Calvinism' with early capitalism.[11] This concept is still reflected in recent studies.[12]

Mainstream recent trends

Since the 1970s, English Reformation historiography has revealed four identifiable schools, connected with the names of Geoffrey Elton, Geoffrey

Dickens, Christopher Haigh and Patrick Collinson. Elton's primary interest was in the functioning of power at the dirigiste 'top' of the new English unitary church–state or state–church. He was concerned with the process of policymaking among the lay rulers, and in the organs of implementation and enforcement.[13] This is undoubtedly a crucial area of study, for we will never really understand how a Reformation was adopted anywhere by looking only at the thought of churchmen and theologians. The thoughts and problems among those in power in the secular domain are what really count when it came to the point of deciding whether to adopt and implement the Reformation in any country. Accordingly, for Elton, the real architect of the new order in England was not so much Henry VIII, who instigated the new situation, as the Principal Secretary of State, Thomas Cromwell. Similarly the Elizabethan Reformation is not so much the achievement of the queen, as of her Principal Secretary, William Cecil, later Lord Burghley, and so on. In relation to new religious formats that became permanent, administrative implementation *de haut en bas* by executive officials and of course bishops,[14] was determinative.

Though he has no strong religious axe to grind, Elton evaluates the religious changes positively – he sees them as having been a good thing at least for the new England. There is an undercurrent of the Calvinism–Capitalism (Weber–Tawney) paradigms in Elton's thought. That is: alertness to the relevance of the relationship between broad Calvinism, the new bourgeois Protestant asceticism, intensifying market economy, religious reform and social reconstruction along the south German and Swiss model – though he disassociates this from the faded orthodoxy of the notion of the 'rise of the middle class'. On the whole, however, that suggestive aspect of his thought has not been systematically developed in relation to England by researchers from his stable. Discordant in Elton, and something that has had wide influence, is a dismissive attitude to the prophetic spirit and keen conviction theology. This seems to derive from 'a deep antipathy to the puritan ethic'.[15] For him, passionate religious commitment, and not just of the Protestant kind, is the source of tiresome 'intrusions' from 'zealots' who make life difficult for everyone by being unreasonable. Edward VI and Mary are 'bigots', Bishop Hooper and John Knox are 'passionate extremists' and 'firebrands', and the Marian exiles are 'dedicated fanatics'.[16] Similarly dismissive are writers like Susan Brigden, who, like many of her compatriots, tends to employ 'Scottish' as a synonym for hydrophobic utterance.[17]

In some contrast to Elton is Geoffrey Dickens. His personal stance can be characterized as latitudinous Protestant Anglican, and so not confessional in the narrow sense. He is primarily concerned with the religious and subjective side of the Reformation and its spread in England. He has a twofold perception: of course the Reformation was imposed from the top (like everywhere else in Europe), but accompanying this were perceptible pressures and aspirations from below and outside the corridors of power in church and state.[18] These emanated in some measure from a pre-existing tradition of popular religious dissent, as in Lollardy.[19] Accordingly, Dickens affirms that to understand what was happening, we have to look beyond elite figures and sources like monarchs, secretaries of state, archbishops, bishops, monasteries, liturgies, confessions of faith, etc. Routes into the minds of lesser officials, clergy, monks, artisans, peasants, teachers and so on have to be explored. Therefore Dickens calls attention to the wider social dimensions of the Reformation movement.

He has, however, issued a warning that some of his disciples have not heeded. This was that not all answers would be found in tracking down the religious inclinations of this clerk, or that blacksmith, this merchant or that baker. Such an exclusively socio-biographical heuristic approach will not reveal all. Concentrating on the half-hidden and semi-articulate makes no sense if it is divorced from the educated utterances and writings of the thinkers, the theologians and the preachers.[20] One problem in Dickens is uncertainty about where the 'below' actually begins. Below whom? – the king, the royal councillors, members of Parliament, the bishops, the ordinary clergy, below the squirearchy or town councillors? Who is below, and who is above? For in a semi-feudal society like England, almost everyone was above and below somebody else.

Dickens has also been criticized for underestimating the strength of residual and even reviving Catholicism in Reformation England. Notwithstanding, his main book still retains the status of being the standard work, especially in view of its good awareness of the European context and of religious and theological issues. This cannot be said of many works on the English Reformation in recent times. Along with the studies of David Loades, Dickens' position is also replete with insights on the teleological significance of the Reformation for Anglo-British evolution.

A third school has made the subject of the English Reformation hot to handle. This school is characterized as 'revisionist', and may be seen as an attempt to undermine or at least revise the influential interpretations of Elton and Dickens. The main names associated with this trend are Christopher Haigh, John Joseph Scarisbrick, Richard Rex, Eamon Duffy, and with important qualifications, Patrick Collinson. While these writers as a group are not at all tarred with the same ideological brush, they all reject the contrasting paradigms of Elton and Dickens. Elton's was: coercion by the government and acceptance by the people. Dickens' was: legislation by the government as response to public opinion in the political nation.

The revisionists propose new models. They have to acknowledge government coercion, but rather than acceptance, they envisage grudging compliance, or minimal prudential conformity. A response-to-public-opinion scenario does not seem to them to fit the facts. This means that what the state Reformation induced was reluctant obedience rather than conversion. This view has some merit, although some of its more radical proponents present it in a manner suggesting that the only Protestants in England were a handful of government officials with their hands on the levers of power. Scarisbrick, for example, almost writes Protestants out of the script altogether, so that for him the church Reformation before Elizabeth (1533–1603) had little to do with Protestantism. Haigh's position is not so negationist, although his perception has the same tendency. He is reluctant to ascribe any autonomous reality to the 'Reformation in England', so that the 'English Reformation' is, as it were, reduced to a nominalist icon or semantic conceit. The English state Reformation, a political story, accidentally coincided with the Continental Reformation and was not to the people's taste.[21] Is there a hint of Little England populism in all this? To be fair to Haigh, while he maintains that in England there was a series of statutory reformations by instalment, he does recognize that there was also a genuine evangelical movement. He holds that it was chiefly among a well-educated minority of Christians, and that its situation was very tenuous until the Elizabethan period. Nor is he averse to affirming that 'we cannot quite write [anticlericalism and Protestantism] out of Reformation history altogether'.[22]

The revisionists – perhaps better designated as 'realists' – are on the whole convinced that ordinary people were either hostile or indifferent to the Reformation. Some like Duffy stress that far from being decrepit and unpopular, late medieval English Catholicism was both vigorous and popular, and that the contrary traditional image was the received propaganda of Lollards and early Reformation historiographers.[23] However, as we shall see below, there is a danger that this insight contains the seed of new myths suggesting that hardly anyone wanted the Reformation, or that what ordinary people 'wanted' was actually relevant! Anyway, post-revisionist studies indicate that in the Henrician era, sluggish response to religious change was not universal, that the church realignment managed by Henry also stirred up strong passions against traditional religion and for the new theology.[24]

Some revisionists shy away from 'elitist' sources of the state, church and theology. Instead they have recourse to micro-study of parish, diocesan, borough, court and guild records, as well as allegedly telltale private wills and testaments. This is occasioned by the Rankian concern to discover 'how things really were' (see Chapter 1 above), as if to say, in such mundane records one will find the (decisive) truth of the matter, especially in regard to the real opinions of ordinary people. The most recent and immensely valuable study in this genre by Duffy undoubtedly reveals realities of the utmost pertinence about the disruption of the cosy certitudes of traditional parish life by Reformation legislation, especially during the reign of Edward VI.[25] The essential conclusion is that there was lots of transitional pain with little or no gain.

Yet the wider significance of the analysis of such a community remains contestable. Firstly, it is doubtful that much faith can be put in such records as regards people's religious preferences, for those can conceal as much as they reveal. Anyway, they are not usually written by the 'people' themselves. Evidence of discontent with the top-down church changes

and prudential minimal conformity does not prove prior blissful content-
ment with the old order and unquestioning commitment to it. Secondly,
it is hard to believe that such records tell us all that much about ordinary
people, since people with their names in such records can hardly be
regarded as especially ordinary. The vast majority of the population in
the sixteenth century still would not have had their names written down
anywhere, not even in marriage or baptismal registers. Thirdly, random
micro-studies can hardly provide grounds for generalizing about a whole
country. Fourthly, there is as yet no serious comparative research involving
the rest of the British Isles and the Continent. This would magnify
difficulties greatly. Lastly, since such sources seem to be used largely to
induce scepticism about any popular pro-Reformation movement, it must
be stressed that the lines between natural feet-dragging, uninformed
apathy or antipathy, and educated or intuitional active resistance are often
very blurred. The comment of the Glasgow historian, John Thomson,
about the religious temper of English late medieval Christianity is arguably
relevant for the early Reformation period too, namely that 'most people
were neither passionately devout nor vehemently critical'.[26] Consequently,
the assessment of Herculean historiographical recasting is in abeyance;
its fundamental premiss must be called into question, namely that fragmentary revelations intimate the actual truth of the matter.[27]

Next, a much more positive form of revisionism or reassessment was
initiated by Patrick Collinson[28] and followed by others like Diarmaid
MacCulloch[29] concerning astigmatic perceptions of Elizabethan Protestantism and 'puritanism'. This has contributed significantly to the long
overdue correction of false and unjust notions that had become embedded
in the language of many indigenous English writers on the Reformation
in England. Accompanying it is a weeding and tidying up of the concepts
and language used about the theological, religious and ecclesiastical
landscapes in the later sixteenth century. In addition, Collinson's work
has helped to modify the traditional preoccupation with the Henrician
1530s among historians of the English Reformation since the early
eighteenth century.

It is well known that as time went on, the Reformation Church of
England under Elizabeth Tudor and after her, James Stewart, suffered
from serious and unresolved internal tensions, particularly in the areas
of church–state relations, church polity, ministry and lay religious education. The now discredited, 'history-from-distorted hindsight' approach
estimated that the problems were caused by alien, unEnglish, Calvinist
puritan impatience with the exemplary, moderate Anglican *via media* of
the English Reformation. Largely through the work of Collinson, Peter
Lake and MacCulloch, but also of others before them who prepared the
ground, like Basil Hall and Buick Knox, there is something which is now
much better understood, and importantly, accepted. This is that while all
church puritans were Calvinist, not all church Calvinists were puritans, or
as they were often called at that time, 'precisionists'.

In other words, it was possible and indeed common to be a Calvinist in the broad sense without having to be a puritan, a presbyterian, a congregationalist, or a militant biblicist. For until the middle of the seventeenth century the Reformation Church of England shared the broad reformed consensus in soteriology, justification, and sacramental theology. It was only later that there were relapses, and then only partial, into semi-Pelagian ideas, soon to be known as Arminianism.[30] The Reformation Church of England's constitutive theology was then radically Augustinian and firmly reformed, tempered by a Lutheran and adiaphorist attitude to externals and secondary matters. This is precisely what annoyed the puritans, who were influenced by the more prescriptive, and restrictive, south German and Swiss ecclesiastical models.

It is now therefore conceded that the developed theological profile of the English Reformation Church, whether it be described as Calvinist or reformed consensus, or as somehow latitudinarian and broad church, did not reflect any *via media* between Catholic and Protestant theology. If there was a *via media*, it was between various shades of Protestant doctrine. Such a phenomenon was not at all unique to England, granted that during the time of Henry VIII in the 1530s and 1540s, there had been a groping for an elusive mean between Romanism and Lutheranism. Attempts at mutual theological accommodation took place on the Continent.[31] Universally after 1541, and after the launching of the Council of Trent in 1547, such possibilities decreased and virtually vanished.

Recent studies have shown that in the later sixteenth century the biggest market in Europe for the works of John Calvin, in Latin or in translation, was England. Further, that in the Elizabethan Church, possibly even more popular than Calvin was Henry Bullinger, successor of Ulrich Zwingli in Zurich. The problem was that while many English Calvinists were content with the traditional episcopal form of the Church, and with a state Church, many other Calvinists would have preferred a Church more specifically modelled along actual Genevan lines (or intentions). For them, the favoured concept was that articulated by the first Presbyterian theoretician, Theodore Beza (1519–1605), Calvin's successor. Such English Calvinists were indeed puritans, but not all puritans were unanimous on the matter, just as in France, some Calvinists argued for church government by presbytery, others for a congregationalist polity.[32]

Finally: as already indicated, work on the English Reformation in recent decades has made a merciful shift from a long obsession with the Henrician 1530s. This realignment of the field has been caused partly by revisionist concerns; partly by less hagiographical writing about Catholics in the Reformation era, particularly those who survived; partly by more serious study of neglected English Anabaptists and radicals; partly by more sensible study of Catholic, Reformation and puritan theological writings; partly by attempts to understand the role of social and economic factors, particularly at the popular level, and partly by Reformation women studies. There have been fine monographs on certain committed Catholic bishops in

Henry's time, like John Fisher[33] and Stephen Gardiner,[34] thereby breaking an old preoccupation with high-profile lay Catholics like Thomas More. In addition there have been major new studies of Thomas Cranmer,[35] Archbishop of Canterbury throughout the critical Henrician and Edwardine eras. Apart however from Nicholas Ridley,[36] John Hooper,[37] Edmund Grindal,[38] Matthew Parker[39] and Robert Ferrar,[40] the majority of bishops in the early and mid-Reformation era remain relatively neglected by modern researchers. The recent work by Carleton has helped make good the deficit.[41]

Although apart from London, England at this time had no cities to match the development or status of certain Continental cities and their pivotal role in the Reformation, there have been important recent works on English towns and the Reformation. Examples are the work on London by Susan Brigden, on York by Dickens, on Bristol by Martha Skeeters, and on Norwich by Muriel McClendon. These have added to the wider industry of the 'Reformation in an urban context' on the Continent. This has stimulated further specialist studies, many of which are now helpfully available in one volume.[42] They do provide a very useful balance to many other studies of English towns in this era of what one might call a neo-Marxist kind. For in work of this genre, even in towns where the Reformation was an event, it is treated either as a non-event, or as an ephemeral manifestation of social change and class struggle. Among others, Collinson has blown the whistle on studies on early modern English towns of such a socio-economic reductionist character.[43] Notwithstanding, a diagnosis of the Reformation in England that ascribes only symptomatic character to the religious issues involved, side-effects of secular mutations, is still expressed in one-dimensional terms. Recently and in a positivist spirit, T. Betteridge has written ingenuously: 'The English Reformation, a simple struggle between two coherent doctrinal camps, Protestant and Catholic, was a result and not the cause of the social and cultural conflicts that were the English Reformations.'[44]

In conclusion, contemporary writing on the English Reformation as a religious phenomenon reflects broadly what has been happening elsewhere. It is no longer largely in the hands of the theologians or 'ecclesiastical historians'. In a sense, one can speak of the laicization of Reformation history, though in some cases this tends to secularization. There is a salutary side to this, but it may mean that controverted theological and spiritual questions, which were centre stage at the time, are avoided, phased out, or marginalized. Steven Ozment's remark about many modernist approaches to Reformation history is apt, namely that they 'keep theologies of elites at arm's length',[45] though historians not theologically tutored have been doing precisely that since the eighteenth century. The 'quagmire of doctrine'[46] is to be shunned. Anyway, the 'abstract principles'[47] of Reformation theology could not really have had a serious mass appeal. This has reinforced a tendency that already existed in modern writing on the English Reformation. For example, huge tranches of twentieth-century pupils, students and scholars were nurtured on A. F. Pollard's view that the English Reformation movement was 'not in essence doctrinal', rather an episode of church–state relations.[48]

The long-term effects of this relative secularization, 'deconstruction', or at least 'de-theologizing', on the understanding of the English or any other Reformation remains to be seen. There are people of various agendas who seem consequently to find comfort in the notion that the English Reformation, or at least the one instigated by Henry VIII, was somehow 'not really religious'. Oddly, this perception has always tended to evade the paradox that despite a proclivity for behaving badly, Henry VIII was one of the most theologically literate European monarchs of the entire early modern era. His fame in this respect rested on his contribution to anti-Luther controversial theology.[49]

By way of retrospect, the tendency to downgrade the authenticity of the English Reformation had predictable precedents in the older Roman Catholic view that necessarily interpreted it as rank heresy embraced by people clearly in no state of grace. It was precisely with the aim of refuting such understandably disparaging views that Gilbert Burnet undertook in his seven-volume *History of the Reformation of the Church of England* (1685) in the Grand Narrative tradition, an attempt to make good England's lack of a 'Sleidan'[50] in the Reformation era. This was still apologetic, though archive-based historiography. The political and religious aspects of the Reformation were kept in balance, something previous historians had failed to do. The 'magisterial' nature of the English Reformation is portrayed in a commendable, though critical light. Burnet's book was more specifically a response to a seventeenth-century reprint of a work hostile to the English Reformation published posthumously by an exilic Catholic and political activist, Nicholas Sanders (or Sander) (*c.*1530–81) in 1585.[51] Burnet deplored the influence of this on the Continent, where the Reformation in England is perceived 'as one of the foulest things that ever was'.[52] 'The short history' of such an interpretation, writes Burnet, 'being, that it was begun by the lusts and passions of King Henry the Eighth, carried on by the ravenousness of the Duke of Somerset under Edward the Sixth, and confirmed by the policy of Queen Elizabeth and her council to secure her title. These things [are] generally talked and spread abroad in foreign parts.'[53]

Yet Burnet was not concerned with whitewashing Henry VIII's persona, or writing 'a panegyric on him',[54] since he makes the good biblical and theological point that God does not shun using unregenerate princes as instruments of his purposes. Be that as it may, disparagement of at least the Henrician Reformation, on whatsoever the grounds, has never been a Catholic prerogative. After all, Luther had uttered: 'What Squire Harry wills must be an article of faith both for life and death',[55] and 'Henry VIII is also now an enemy to the Pope's person, but not to his essence and substance . . . [he retains] the soul of the Pope.'[56]

CHAPTER 4

Reformation in England

Henry VIII's Church: accident or design?

Were one asked to explain graphically the essence of not so much the English Reformation as the English Reformation Church, the Church of England, one should recommend a trip to Zurich. On display there, in the Swiss National Museum, is something that helps illuminate the pith of the new English Church. The museum's silver collection contains four inscribed items from the sixteenth century of English interest. They were originally gifts either to the Zurich Council or to the city's Church and reformer, Henry Bullinger (1504–75), Zwingli's successor. Three of the pieces were mementoes of gratitude from members of the English Protestant community who had been refugees in Zurich during the Catholic restoration in England under Mary Tudor (1516–58) in the period from 1553 to 1558. These three donors, including the eminent John Jewel (1522–71), subsequently became Elizabethan bishops. The fourth item is from Queen Elizabeth (1533–1603) herself to Bullinger, in acknowledgement of services rendered. These services included not only his role in having English refugees looked after in Zurich, but his contribution to the defence of the Church of England and its Reformation in the larger European arena, and in particular his published response to the excommunication of Elizabeth by Pope Pius V in 1570.[1] In 1568, Pius had issued a Bull (*In coena Domini*) denouncing state control of the church anywhere. Generally speaking, Elizabeth was no more fond of theologians than most other people were, but she had an unconcealed admiration for Bullinger, the patriarch of Reformed Protestantism after Calvin's death in 1564, as a defender of her Church and queenship abroad.

These pieces of silverware were more than just tokens of thanks. They also symbolized general sympathy with the Zurich Reformation, and in particular, with the exemplary 'magisterial' nature of the Zurich Church, which was of course very much a state Church.[2] In other words, there was a correspondence between on the one hand, the religious and church authority assumed by the Zurich government at the time of the Reformation, and on the other hand, that expressed in England by the Royal Supremacy, exercised in part through Parliament. Some Lutheran princes in Germany shared the same concept. This revolution had been expressed in England by the 1534 Act of Supremacy of Henry VIII (1491–1547), whereby the headship of the earthly English Church was transferred from the pope to the (imperial) monarch, whose powers will resemble those of Emperors Constantine, Theodosius and Justinian in the Early Church.[3] The corollary was that the (Christian) civil authority arrogated to itself also the role of arbiter of doctrine. England now had a 'resident Royal Pope'.[4]

In short, there is a striking similarity between the English Church constitutional model and that of the Zwinglian Church constitution. This should be emphasized, as it has been customary to perceive the Reformation English Church in this respect as something unique, unparalleled and special. Zurich was hardly a conscious model in Henry VIII's mind at the time, but the ideological and theological analogies, as well as the common sources can hardly be denied. For example, a qualified 'caesaropapism', that is, the real ruler of the earthly Church is not so much the supreme earthly bishop, like the Bishop of Rome, or even an ecumenical council, but the given Christian secular sovereign, who has such an office from God. This then implies the right to be guardian and even arbiter of doctrine and practice. Further, the idea leads to a blurring of the distinction between church and state, due to a concern to integrate the Christian commonwealth much more effectively. Such an arrangement then will lead to a 'reformation' of both church and society; it will diminish the independent jurisdiction of the Church; it will hold the clergy responsible to civil law and so abolish clerical immunity from the civil courts; it will laicize and rationalize social services and education.

It is no accident that in Henry's reign there were government-encouraged attacks on the clerical cult of Thomas à Becket (*c.*1118–70). The martyred Archbishop of Canterbury was a potent symbol of the Hildebrandine or Gregorian notion of the independence of the church from the state, and even of the claim of church authority over the state. The Tudor royal supremacy effectively repudiated such a concept, just as it was by the magistracies in Zurich, Strasbourg and elsewhere, even in Geneva. Henry VIII saw himself not only like Christian Roman Emperors such as Constantine or Theodosius (though he was hardly likely to submit to the latter's spiritual disciplining by an unlikely Ambrose of Milan in the Church of England), but also like the Israelite kings who reformed religion. Protestant reformers, particularly Zwingli and Bullinger seemed at least to provide him with plenty of theological corroboration. If one may call this a 'Zwinglian' church–state model, later in the sixteenth century and thereafter it came to be called 'Erastianism', after Thomas Erastus (1524–83), physician and philosopher-theologian in Heidelberg and Basle. His writings gave classic expression to the doctrine in the later Reformation era, though the seminal roots of the idea were found in the medieval thinker Marsilius of Padua (*c.*1280–1343).[5] As we shall see subsequently, the concept and its ramifications in church government were to become highly controverted in England and especially Scotland.

Till now we have highlighted the comparison with the Swiss precedent. But there is also a notable contrast, at least in relation to the circumstances of implementation. This is: that while the Swiss model was initially twinned with Reformation theology, the English one was not, or not particularly. It is true that firm Catholics like Bishop John Fisher[6] (1469–1535) and the ex-Lord Chancellor, Thomas More (1478–1535) repudiated fatally the royal supremacy on grounds of conscience. Yet it is also true that Henry's Principal Secretary, Thomas Cromwell (*c.*1485–1540), had clear Protestant leanings. But apart of course from the Defender of the Catholic Faith himself, Henry, one must stress that among the high profile supporters of the royal supremacy were Catholic bishops like Stephen Gardiner[7] (*c.*1483–1555), Catholic jurists like Christopher St German, and political theorists like the Catholic humanist, Thomas Starkey (*c.*1499–1538). In other words, one did not actually have to be a Protestant to support the royal supremacy and its elimination of the pope from church management. Were therefore Henry and his aides just bad Catholics?

Bearing in mind the prior Swiss analogy, Starkey in particular provides a clue to solving this riddle. He had studied in Italy, and was steeped in Renaissance Humanist learning. His reasoning about the validity of an autonomous and sovereign state church derived from his study of Aristotle, Plato, Paul, the early Church (after AD 325) and Marsilius of Padua. As alluded to above, Marsilius' highly influential *Defender of Peace* had in particular prefigured such ideas.[8] These were notions that helped shape Zwingli's thinking on the topic. Therefore the Swiss magisterial and the English royal-parliamentary reformations were not, constitutionally speaking, intrinsic to Reformation theology as such. Rather they were semblable responses to prior concepts mediated by Humanism. From the start, the Swiss response was clothed with Reformation theology. Henry's royal supremacy was not. But soon it too began to be coloured in that way. One fruit of Thomas Cromwell's enlisting of Humanist writers to provide ideological ammunition and apologetics for the transfer of supreme authority in the English Church from the pope to the king was an abridged English translation (1535) of *Defender of Peace.*[9] Further, Archbishop Thomas Cranmer[10] (1489–1556), and Bishop Edward Foxe[11] (*c.*1494–1538) did their best to accommodate the royal supremacy to Lutheran and Reformation theology. Luther's influential *Address to the Nobility* (1520) undoubtedly helped provide theological scaffolding as did subsequent ideas of the Reformers on the 'rights of the civil magistrate'. The English schism then began to look a bit like not only a Swiss church–state arrangement, but also the Reformation of the German princes. The ideology, then, was not conjured up *ex nihilo,* it was a pre-existent model or paradigm which Henry and his advisers availed of.

Reformation, or at least reform, under Henry embodies the first of three legislative phases constituting the English Reformation. The other two were under Edward VI, and Elizabeth I. As is well known, the immediate pretext of Henry's course was his need for a divorce from Catherine of Aragon (1485–1536).[12] This was partly because he was in love with Anne Boleyn (1507–36), and partly because he felt he needed a male heir to help secure the dynasty and national peace. Pope Clement VII refused, not least because he had no wish to offend the most powerful man in Europe, the King of Spain and the Emperor, Charles V (1500–58). Catherine of Aragon was Charles' aunt, and he was hardly likely to be unmoved by such a humiliation of this kind. Once Henry persuaded Archbishop Cranmer to grant the divorce, the die was cast. Scholars soon provided 'new' theories of kingship and sovereignty to make it all respectable. Central to this was the notion that the King of England presided not just over a kingdom, but an Empire, an *imperium*. This implied exemption from summons or subordination to any foreign court, such as the papal curia. This imperial sovereignty also contained the responsibility for religion – the *sacerdotium* – in the 'Erastian' sense. Henry therefore ought not to be seen as a bandit or a plunderer bent in self-glorification. Rather he was a very skilful adapter to pre-existing or reconstructed political, religious and legal theories, especially if they were congenial.

The king's new status as 'supreme head on earth' of the Church of England depended in some measure on a sector of opinion that was sympathetic to reform and reformation in its conservative Erasmian, or Protestant forms. Two of the highest office holders in the land were of a Protestant persuasion, albeit relatively discreet, namely the Archbishop of Canterbury, Cranmer, and the chief Secretary of State, Cromwell. Their views were not of course sufficiently representative to enable any kind of sweeping programme of change to be introduced. Anyway, for all his willingness to interfere with the Church's constitution and institutions, there is little evidence that Henry was enamoured of Protestant theology as such. In fact, he had made a name for himself as a spokesman of traditional doctrine in his famous defence of the seven sacraments against Luther in 1521,[13] which earned him the title of 'Defender of the Faith' from pope Leo X.

However, a church reform programme issued in the so-called 'Reformation Parliament'. This programme cannot be described as particularly Protestant, rather at the most, as having Protestant tendencies. Obvious abuses and out-of-favour institutions were tackled. And so monasteries were dissolved and their lands confiscated. A limited iconoclasm was sanctioned, since the associated cult of the saints fostered financial improvidence among the populace. By order, an English Bible was placed in all parish churches. This was the *Great Bible* (1540) edited by the ex-Augustinian friar and future Bishop of Exeter, Myles Coverdale[14] (1488–

1568), not to be confused with Coverdale's own translation of the Bible earlier. The Great Bible incorporated rather most of the biblical translation (1526–36) of William Tyndale[15] (*c*.1494–1536), England's chief Reformation activist and polemicist on the Continent, eventually betrayed by a fellow countryman and martyred at Antwerp. Included in the Great Bible was an important preface by Thomas Cranmer.[16] It expounded the doctrine of *sola scriptura*, not however in the restrictive (proto-puritan) biblicist sense as advocated by Tyndale. For the archbishop, concerned to demonstrate that the English reformed Church was not 'new' or revolutionary, but claimed continuity with the early Church, demonstrated how normative the Bible was for the thought and lives of the Church Fathers. There is a tendency to characterize this orientation to the patristic tradition as typically 'Anglican'. However, Cranmer was representing the thinking in writings of Reformers with which he was very familiar, namely Philipp Melanchthon and Martin Bucer. They made much use of the 'patristic argument' to buttress Reformation ideas, and as Cranmer was to do most vividly in his evangelical eucharistic apology of 1550, *A Defence of the true and catholic doctrine of the sacrament*.[17]

The placing of the English Bible into the public domain is not quite to be seen as an invitation to the nation to read the Bible, since the vast majority of the population was illiterate. For subsequently Parliament passed an act forbidding unlicensed people from the lower orders to read any Bible at all. Such restrictiveness was in accord with Catholic tradition. Further, holy-days were reduced – they had proliferated so much that employers complained that they were bad for productivity. Indulgences for souls in purgatory were condemned. And in the area of doctrine the *Ten Articles of Religion* were sanctioned in 1536.[18] They were reinforced in 1537 with a commentary along increasingly evangelical lines, *The Institution of a Christian Man*, otherwise known as the *Bishops' Book*.[19]

The religious and political background to the *Ten Articles* is of interest. Because of the schism he had presided over, Henry's position in the international stage had become vulnerable and precarious. It gave the traditional enemy, France, another reason to intensify hostility. It marked the beginning of the process by which England's traditional and best ally, Spain, became transformed into her most dangerous enemy. And since Charles V could never forgive what Henry had done to his aunt, the power of the Empire, particularly its Netherlands base, could also be turned against England. No wonder then that Protestants among Henry's advisers drew his attention to the possibility of alliance with the power-bloc of German Protestant princes and the Free and Hanseatic cities, the Schmalkald League. Its Lutheran dominant members operated a policy of alliance based on common religious confession – this is why the Swiss were not members due to the Eucharistic issue. Accordingly, English diplomats and churchmen were dispatched to Wittenberg to negotiate with the Lutherans, who insisted on English acceptance of essential Reformation doctrines. After difficulties with Luther in particular about

Henry's divorce and the execution of Anne Boleyn, the outcome of this was an agreed document, the *Wittenberg Articles* (1536), drafted largely by Philipp Melanchthon.[20] Representing the English Church were Nicholas Heath[21] (*c.*1501–78), Edward Foxe and Robert Barnes (1495–1540). Although Henry was invited to become supreme general of Protestant forces in Europe, the negotiations floundered on his refusal to accept the *Augsburg Confession* (1530). Nonetheless, English theological links with the *via media* approach of that Confession through these negotiations were now firmly established. Enough, however, was agreed upon to keep the possibility of alliance in the future open. Also in 1536, an English translation of the *Augsburg Confession* and its *Apology* was published in London by the English Lutheran in the circle of Cromwell, and Bible translator, Richard Taverner (*c.*1505–75).

The *Ten Articles* embody the limits of how far Henry was prepared to go in the area of doctrine. The result is that these articles are a masterpiece of ambiguity; they embrace, for example, a concept of double justification, by faith and by consequent works. Their immediate aim was, as they declare: 'to eschew outward unquietness occasioned by diversity in opinions'.[22] This is evidence, surely, that even if Henrician England was no hotbed of Protestantism, the Catholic theological consensus had fragmented. Henry had forbidden all preaching until these articles were devised. After that, the clergy were instructed simply to read out the articles, and not expound them.

Lastly, in this Reformation programme, the Latin Mass was significantly left untouched, though an innovative English *Litany* was permitted in 1544. Further, the various measures were laced with social, economic and educational pleas about the individual and common good, to which proper religion should be harnessed. Here, then, we see tentative steps towards the implementation of reformation not only of church and religion, but also society, so characteristic of the south German and Swiss Reformations.

Before concluding remarks on the religious complexion of Henry's reign and policies, further mention should be made of the dissolution of the monasteries, and the confiscation of huge areas of monastic lands – church lands, by the Crown. Valuation figures were set by the *Valor Ecclesiasticus* of 1535. Firstly, if technically sacrilegious, the dissolution was not brutal. Most of the 12,000 or so monks and nuns were provided with pensions for life. Nor were religious vows and the regular religious life forbidden as such. Secondly, all the assets were not just confiscated by Henry and the Crown. About half of them were to be leased or sold off, not just to nobles, squires and small farmers to increase their estates, but also to the young upwardly mobile class of city lawyers and business men, now given a golden opportunity to become landed gentry. The political value was obvious. Such beneficiaries, now with enhanced or new real estate, were inevitably guaranteed supporters of the broad features of Henry's church arrangements, in which they had a personal stake.

In general, the interpretation of developments in Henry's reign is problematic, even with hindsight. In a sense, it must have been even harder for contemporary analysts who did not have access to the documents and papers that we now have. Under Thomas More's chancellorship, England's first six Protestant martyrs were burned, largely of the Lutheran persuasion. In the European context, this was nothing unusual. In 1535 twenty-five Anabaptists were executed, and there was nothing exceptional about that either. However, in the same year, Catholics like John Fisher and Thomas More, as well as six Carthusian priors were executed. Henry had a macabre sense of theatre and symmetry in his execution policy, apart from using it as a means of ridding himself of obsolescent wives. For once, on the same day, he had six figures executed, of whom three were Protestant and three were Catholic. The king thereby demonstrated that the royal supremacy was lord of the individual conscience. He was after all, by virtue of his imperial office, now 'next to God'. And if the English schism or church reform may not be described as an adoption of *the* Reformation because of a still seemingly conservative theology, the restructured Church had in public perception somehow betrayed the old Church and faith. How else can one explain the Catholic rebellion in the north of England 1536–7, the Pilgrimage of Grace? For all his religious conservatism, Henry was not prepared to tolerate such popular Catholic militancy, and so suppressed the rising in an appropriately sanguinary manner. This helped create the Catholic image of the king as a heretic.

The last decade of Henry's reign (1538–47) is often interpreted as backtracking, a conservative and non-papalist Catholic reaction guided by him. In reality, it was more of a political attempt to steer the English Church along pre-Council of Trent Catholic reform lines within an Erastian context. This resulted in doctrinal intervention of a catholicizing kind by the King, the ungrateful disposal of Cromwell by execution – a month after he had been created Earl of Essex; the marginalizing of Cranmer, the resignation of famous preaching bishops like Hugh Latimer, the execution of the leading English Lutheran theologian, Robert Barnes, and the exile of a client of Cromwell who was a key teacher of Lutheran theology at Cambridge, the Scot, Alexander Alan, or Alesius[23] (1500–65). Alesius was in England from 1536 to 1539.

However, the international scene at this time should be considered. The bad news for England was that France and the Habsburg empire had negotiated peace, leaving England as a lesser power vulnerable to joint attack by the Empire, France and Spain, the three superpowers. This was due to England's suspect religious image. There was also talk of an international crusade against heretics and schismatics. Further, English exports were firmly locked into the Antwerp market, in the Imperial heartlands. Accommodation with the big powers was now much more relevant than any speculative alliance with the remoter Schmalkald League of German Protestant states. Further, France's ally, firmly Catholic Scotland, never mind *de facto* Catholic Ireland, completed the encirclement. To make matters worse, the pope formally excommunicated Henry in 1538. Diplomatically stranded, Henry had to placate Catholic Europe. Hence the enactment and proclamation, with draconian penal provisions, of more Catholic doctrinal articles in this period, the *Six Articles*,[24] and as an answer to the *Bishops' Book* of 1536, the *King's Book*[25] (1543), as well as discreet Protestant emigration. There was in England, of course, strong internal Catholic loyalism, but the international climate was arguably more decisive.

Ultimately, Henry remains his own man. Four years before his death, in the middle of this apparent recatholicizing process, he married his sixth wife, Catherine Parr (1512–48). The most notable thing about her was that like Margaret of Navarre, she was a moderate Protestant and lady of letters, and arranged for a Humanist and Protestant education of Henry's young children, Edward and Elizabeth. His own immediate circle was in his latter years composed of those with marked evangelical sympathies. Decisively, in his dying days Henry entrusted the protection and the rule of his boy-successor, Edward (1537–53), to leaders of the Protestant political party, namely Edward Seymour (*c*.1500–52) and John Dudley (*c*.1504–53). There have been suggestions that Henry admired them more because of their military part in chastising his least favourite enemies, the Scots. Studies however suggest that this political development was not just adventitious.[26] Rather, that the ageing Henry's own theological development was moving in a more pro-Reformation direction anyway. Whatever the truth is, the enigmatic Henry seems to have been consciously preparing the political ground for an explicitly evangelical Reformation after his demise. On his dying, then, he also sanctioned, or at least condoned, valediction to the 'Henrician Settlement'.

The abortive Protestant Surge under Edward VI

The birth pangs of what only in later generations was called the 'Anglican'[27] Church were painful. One of the strongly formative episodes was the more manifestly Protestant direction followed by the English Church guided by Thomas Cranmer during the reign of Edward VI (1547–53). Edward had become the monarch at the age of 9 in 1547. He was the son of Henry VIII and Jane Seymour (1509–37), sister of Edward Seymour – a link helping the latter's rise to power in Edward's minority. High church Anglican historians, like Bishop Walter Frere, deplored the period as 'the lowest depth to which the English Church has ever sunk'.[28] Some modern revisionists like Eamon Duffy have revived this tradition by finding it corroborated at parochial level, at least in the periphery of the king-dom.[29] One must wonder about the bishop's world of values. It is true that in the name of an offensive against idolatry – iconoclasm – the Edwardian regime removed and destroyed inanimate objects like statues, altars, holy pictures and other graphic paraphernalia from churches. Many churches were physically restructured to make them more suitable for reformed worship. In this process, medieval (visual) aesthetics gave way to the Humanist and Reformation exigencies of homiletical rhetoric and corporate, congregational participation. Yet how this can be viewed as more horrific than the destruction of scores of actual human beings that occurred in the subsequent Marian regime is puzzling. Aside from this, can one designate the king and his archbishop as English ecclesiastical yobs?

Edward's minders were Protestant, as were those who exercised effective political power in his name, firstly his uncle, Edward Seymour (*c.*1500–52), Duke of Somerset and Lord Protector or President (executed in 1552), and secondly, John Dudley (*c.*1505–53), Duke of Northumberland and Earl of Warwick. Edward's youth provided a providential opportunity to train and educate a Protestant prince and a godly king. His rigorous education in biblical studies and the classics was the best that Renaissance and Christian humanism in England could offer. His tutors[30] included Richard Cox, Chancellor of Oxford, and John Cheke[31] (1514–57), Professor of Greek at Cambridge, and others, all of whom were committed Protestants. This was reinforced by the teaching of court preachers, such as Hugh Latimer[32] (*c.*1485–1555), ex-chaplain of Anne Boleyn and ex-Bishop of Worcester, and even Martin Bucer, the Strasbourg exile. These men inculcated Edward with Reformation theology. Further, they advanced the vision of Thomas Cromwell: by means of a conservative social gospel rhetoric,[33] they urged the reform of society, which was referred to as the 'Commonwealth'.[34] For example, legal, social and economic ills were highlighted, such as those that had ensued from land enclosures, currency devaluation and inflation. Also cited was the exclusion of the talented poor from the universities. The Tudor 'civility' programme was therefore not to be confined to the Celtic or Gaelic hinterlands.

Under this political and intellectual regime, the royal right of church government was exercised in such a way that official religion in England was to experience a quantum leap by attempting to align itself in form and substance more explicitly with the Reformation. The result was, to rephrase Jerome's words on the apparent Arian takeover of the early Church in 360: 'The whole of England groaned and was astonished to find itself Protestant.'[35]

At the level of church and theological leadership, an impressive array of talent from home and abroad was recruited. One who received the call was the Scot – in French detention at the time – John Knox (*c.*1514–72). After spells in the Church of England ministry at Berwick and Newcastle (both centres of exilic Protestant Scots), he was offered the bishopric of Gloucester (ironically Bishop John Fisher's old see), which he did not accept, becoming a court chaplain instead. Knox's relatively influential role in England was due largely to the favour he enjoyed from the Duke of Northumberland, who advocated a more advanced Reformation than that which Cranmer and others were prepared to countenance at the time.[36] By continuing to refuse further offers of preferment, Knox retained relative freedom of speech. The ex-Cistercian, and theologically fastidious, John Hooper[37] (*c.*1495–1555) was then appointed as bishop in Gloucester. His *Declaration of Christ and his Office* articulates his thinking on the essence of evangelical episcopacy.[38] Committed, but more moderate Protestant bishops like Cranmer and Nicholas Ridley[39] (*c.*1500–55), bishop successively of Durham and London, were initially given a free hand, but on becoming alienated from Northumberland, Cranmer's role became less proactive.[40]

Very important for the future was the invitation to four Contintental theologians of note to settle in England. One German, one Pole and two Italians came, all of whom were associated with major Reformation centres like Strasbourg, Zurich, Basle and Emden in East Frisia. The two Italians, the ex-Capuchin, Bernard Ochino (1487–1564) and the ex-Augustinian, Peter Vermigli Martyr (1500–62) were made professors in Oxford. The ex-Dominican, Martin Bucer[41] (1491–1551), Strasbourg's exiled Reformer due to the *Interim,* was made Regius Professor of Divinity at Cambridge where he established a special relationship with a future Archbishop of Canterbury, Matthew Parker[42] (1504–75); the aristocratic Pole and ex-priest, Jan Laski (John à Lasco) (1499–1560) was made superintendent of the Strangers' church in London. These were all crucial appointments, since these men helped to educate a generation of students who were to shape future English Protestantism. Indeed a blueprint for the reformation of English Church and society, *On the Kingdom of Christ*[43] (*De regno Christi*), was drawn up in 1551 by Martin Bucer in consultation with the government and a group of progressive social-economic reformers known as the 'Commonwealth Men'. This work was to be consulted by several other Reformation Churches in the future other than the Church of England. It embodied a remarkably nice balance, being theologically broad, ecclesiastically conservative and socially progressive. It was based on the premiss and article of faith that enhancing secular society belongs to the service of Christ, that it is a waste of energy committing so many resources to pious concern about the dead, for this is within the domain of God. Such a goal of Christian service presupposes, however, that the Church and its ministry be put on a sound footing. Accordingly, in this blueprint, Bucer expatiates on the ministries of the Church in the domains of teaching, sacraments and pastoral care, as well as liturgical and moral discipline.[44] The Church was to be the medium by which the kingdom of Christ would be established on earth, so that not just individuals, but also society would be transformed – something that had not occurred in Strasbourg and was not to occur in England either.

Bucer's earlier links with England had consisted famously in the dedication of his erudite *Romans Commentary* of 1536 to Thomas Cranmer and the English Church. This work was a major thesaurus of ecumenical or conciliatory Reformation and biblical theology. Furthermore, he had also dedicated the 1536 edition of his massive *Gospels Commentary* to Edward

Foxe, the Bishop of Hereford. Bucer's other major contribution to the English Church was his part in the quality assessment of the English liturgy, the *Book of Common Prayer*, in other words, his *Censura* (1549).[45] Then in 1548 his *Congratulations to the Church of England* was devoted in fact to presenting the case against mandatory clerical celibacy.[46] In addition he contributed decisively to the *Ordinal* of 1550, the service to be used for the ordination of ministers. It represents the transition from the traditional role of clergy offering a sacrifice and saying Mass for the living and the dead to one of 'preaching the Word of God and administering the holy sacraments'. Bucer also collaborated with Archbishop Matthew Parker in compiling a patristic anthology on matters relating largely to ecclesiology, rites and observances – in an attempt to garner the best and most profitable elements of church tradition. Purely a manuscript collection at the time, the material has been published in modern times,[47] and underlines the extent of Bucer's involvement with the English church leadership as well as his characteristically Catholic churchmanship.

It was partly with people like Bucer in mind that Geoffrey Elton wrote that the edifice of the new Christian society in England was being erected with 'bricks manufactured in South Germany'.[48] By this was meant the attention that was paid not only to theology and liturgy, but also to economic, social, educational and legal issues as integral to the Reformation programme – so typical of Upper Rhine and Swiss projects. Elton rightly dismisses the view that Protestant social theology in Edward's reign was primarily adaptive to new socio-economic pressures, or was determined by *raisons d'état*. Rather it was subject to the primacy of spiritual and pastoral concerns. In other words, the concept was of faith active through love and social responsibility (not just charity). The righteousness of faith had secular implications for the common good, wealth creation, labour, social welfare, education and civic consciousness. Arguably, laymen understood this better than the vocational churchmen. For until the input of Bucer's *De regno Christi*, English theologians were unable to construct a globally coherent programme. In reality, they rarely progressed beyond exhortation to moral rectitude. Anyway, how far what might have been deliverable in south German, Imperial Free or Swiss urban republics could be replicated in a large semi-feudal kingdom like England, remained to be seen.

In the meantime, church and religious reform was hurried through, at least in law.[49] In an Erastian manner, the government appointed Protestant bishops. Parliament declared the right of congregations to receive Communion in both kinds at the Eucharist. Chantries were dissolved, their endowments seized and redirected to social and educational purposes.[50] This was a sharp attack on Catholic piety, since chantries were endowed by the wealthy to say Masses for the dead in order to expedite their sojourns in purgatory. There was state-sponsored (riot free) iconoclasm, much deplored by art historians and pre-Raphaelite romantics. Yet this process was viewed as a means of enhancing worship by detaching it more from creaturely distractions, however beautiful they may have been. Purifying edification was preferred to soul-clouding aesthetics, and the Old Testament at least seemed to provide exemplary justification. Edward was in many ways the new Josiah. However, others understood the Tudor destroyer as the new Solomon, the rebuilder of the Temple.[51]

Other legislation followed (including measures to enhance the identification and enumeration of subjects or citizens such as the compulsory registration of births, marriages and deaths). Clerical marriage was legitimized (1549).[52] The Latin Mass was abolished. Parish worship was restructured by *Acts of Uniformity* (1549, 1552), providing for editions of the English liturgy, the *Book of Common Prayer* (1549). Its preface was decidedly apologetic, defending both the Reformation and set forms of prayer. The 1552 version of this was decidedly reformed, with its radical departure from the Roman Canon of the Mass, which had been still the substructure of the 1549 edition. Furthermore, a communion table, symbol of a fellowship meal, now replaced the traditional altar, symbol of sacrifice. Worship now was not just a devotional spectacle, but an event requiring cognitive understanding of the Word and congregational participation. A *Book of Homilies* (1547), twelve sermons composed chiefly by Cranmer,[53] was issued for compulsory use by the clergy when preaching, most of whom had no training in the art. Now that the confessional box was abolished in the reformed church, the pulpit became the major instrument of exhortation and persuasion, the means of achieving religious reformation and conformity among both clergy and people, as well as the means of disseminating and realizing religious policies on specific issues. The homilies endeavoured both to wean people away from traditional Roman Catholic ideas of piety and to immunize them against Anabaptist Gospel-holiness and experiental enthusiasm.

The Scottish Lutheran theologian based in Germany, Alexander Alan, or 'Alesius', made the *Book of Common Prayer* (1549) available to a wider European audience with its translation into Latin (*Ordinatio ecclesiae*).[54] It was published in Leipzig in 1551. Alesius had already published in 1548 a Latin version of the *Order of Communion*. The intent was probably conciliatory in the fraught religious situation in Europe during the 1550s, when the Reformation was forced on to the defensive.[55] The less discontinuous form and face of the English Reformation Church was perceived as having mediating possibilities elsewhere.

In England, the forms of ministry were reduced to the classical, hierarchical three of the early Church: bishop, presbyter and deacon. Finally, the Royal Council issued the markedly Protestant *Forty-two Articles* (1553) of doctrine, composed by Cranmer, though vetted by the more openly evangelical royal chaplains.[56] They had not been presented to either Parliament or the Church's Convocation. Substantively, they clearly marked the lines of demarcation between the English Church and both Catholic and Anabaptist theologies. Internally, the new Church of England remained hierarchical in form and 'liturgical' in worship, but mutation was evident in its vernacular Protestant rite and increasingly reformed theology.

Effective implementation was impeded by various serious problems climaxing in the death of the king, so that much remained in cold storage. There was the outbreak of two foreign wars, against the Scots and the French, there was a series of bad harvests and concomitant disease, and there were two rebellions. 'Kett's Rebellion' in East Anglia and Norfolk was largely social and economic, but the 'Western Rebellion' in Devon and Cornwall was more religious. The sudden imposition of the *Book of Common Prayer* – a 'Christmas play' – offended traditionalist sensibilities in that peripheral region, not least because it found Cranmer's south-eastern English no more comprehensible than the Latin Mass![57] The *Book* was therefore thrown into bonfires on many occasions.

It follows then that while England's national Church in 1553 was Protestant, one cannot seriously speak of a nation of reconstructed and sanctified Protestants. There was no manifest evangelical pandemic, the commonwealth remained more ungodly than godly.[58] It is hard to think of anywhere in Europe where significant conversion to communal right-eousness occurred anyway. Wrong conclusions should not be drawn from Martin Bucer's pessimistic analysis of the English Reformation. In August 1550 he wrote to Calvin that 'most people were happy to reject the papacy and let Christ reign in heaven, but not so keen to let him reign on earth through his Word, sacraments, and discipline'. In May of the same year he had written to the Reformer of Württemberg in south-west Germany, John Brenz, that 'things are for the most part carried on by the means of ordinances, which the majority obey very grudgingly, and by the removal of the instruments of the ancient superstition . . . Of those devoted to the service of religion only a very small number have as yet entirely addicted themselves to the kingdom of Christ'.[59] Since Bucer had persistently lamented over similar problems at Strasbourg during his long ministry there, one should hesitate about ascribing a distinctively English quality to popular lukewarmth about the Reformation. Anyway, the recent study by Catharine Davies on the boom in vernacular anti-Catholic and anti-Anabaptist polemical literature as well as didactic and devotional works (both official and unofficial) during the Edwardine era suggests two things. Firstly, there was a demand, and secondly, there was no lack of popular interest, passion and agitation, even if not universal.[60]

This 'mid-Tudor' national crisis, as it is called, clearly hindered Reformation progress. And that the dawn was false was underlined when Edward himself died and was succeeded by his elder half-sister, Mary (1516–58), daughter of Catherine of Aragon and Henry VIII, and a com-mitted Catholic. If Edward's mission as the new Josias and Solomon had been to make the Church of England a purified and true church, Mary's mission was to reintegrate it with the Church of Rome, and undo all the measures implemented by her brother and father. She embarked on such a course with crusading zeal. Accordingly, from the beginning of Mary's reign in 1553, Protestantism in England was on the run and had to take cover due to the process of Roman Catholic restoration. The zig now became a zag.

Morphology of English Reformation manifestations up to 1553

Before looking at the religious volte-face under Mary, it is worthwhile delineating the broad contours of the Reformation movement and process up to the time of Edward's death in 1553. Opinions differ about this. The impact and interaction of various influences and strands is still not very clear. One can point to various plausible ingredients or at least put a marker on them. For example: the significance of Lollardy, the pre-Reformation tradition of underground popular dissent derived from the life, works and reform ideas of John Wycliffe in the fourteenth century. Like Waldensianism in France, it now came out of the shadows and merged with the new Protestantism.[61] One can cite anticlericalism or at least, endemic antipapalism. Among educated circles one could consider the dissolving influence of Erasmian Christian humanism. Hard to deny is the diffusion of Lutheran and Zwinglian ideas – in 'stations of high tension' like the universities, London law schools and Hanseatic business centres in particular – as well as Anabaptist notions among elements in the artisan class.[62] Broadening literacy must also have been a factor, though in this era there was never anything like the new media war of pamphlets and tracts that there had been in Germany.

It is not possible to freeze the frame. Hence the apt remark of Dickens, that the English Reformation is a 'hugely documented, but in some respects still obscure story'.[63] A provisional rough consensus suggests that there was little broad popular support for the Reformation outside London and some counties in the far south-east until well into the reign of Elizabeth. Outside the south-east, there were many towns with Protestant groups, especially ports like Bristol and Hull and industrial inland towns like Leeds, Halifax and Coventry.

Some writers hold that the Reformation movement was either inexplicable or unreal. That it was not inevitable is justified by referring to the relatively wholesome state of the pre-Reformation English Church. This view is represented by (among others) John Thomson. He stresses that the English bishops were not notably corrupt, that parish religion was flourishing, that there was no special resentment against monasticism, and that there was no marked anticlericalism or antipapalism.[64] Responding to this evidence, one has to say that Reformation attitudes do not necessarily depend on a pre-existing degenerate church and Christianity, even if this acts as a catalyst. The Reformation, far from being about the 'deformation' that some modern writers are still tempted to affirm, was about a different kind of Christianity, based on knowledge and personal assurance rooted in faith, and not on trusting submission to tradition and a priestly Church, however worthy it might be. The fundamental issue then was not just the assured or unassured quality of the church. Rather, the reconfiguration of the divine–human relationship is what mattered to conviction Protestants, however few they might have been.

As mentioned before, many revisionists cite the apparent preference of the population for 'traditional religion'. By this one suspects that what is really meant is traditional culture. Such writers do not always appreciate two things. Firstly, the Reformation proper entailed a revolution in doctrine and spirituality. Secondly, to convert people to this effectively was a formidable challenge, involving the arduous tasks of preaching, catechizing and discipline. This in turn required expensive training in ways and means which took generations to establish. Leaving it to a few charismatic individuals, or to lukewarm clergy to read out prescribed sermons, would hardly work. Further, resistance to this process or just plain apathy was not unique to England. It was just as widespread in Lutheran Germany and elsewhere, as some studies demonstrate.[65]

Evidence of apathy and resistance has therefore led to the suggestion that Reformation theology simply had no intrinsic appeal to ordinary people. This axiom is questionable, particularly in respect of such concepts as unmerited, classless and even-handed grace, and especially of the idea of the democratically equal share in sin and its consequences, irrespective of status. Either penance or money could not, in Reformation thinking, cancel the common inheritance of sin. This was a liberating idea. The instructive *Biographical register of Early English Protestants* by John Fines, indicates an appeal of the Reformation across the entire social spectrum. The 3000 or so names listed there have been interpreted by some like Dickens as the 'tip of a Protestant iceberg', and as indicators dispelling the myth that the Reformation was a 'sordid monument of middle-class self-interest'.[66]

In this cursory look at Reformation contours, the role of non-religious factors is elusive. For example, the bearing of rural and social discontent, price rises, inflation, devaluation, population growth, unemployment, begging and vagrancy, superstition, land enclosures, rebellious youth, disease and food shortages, secularization, the growth of the book industry and literacy and so on. All these things belong to the picture, but we cannot freeze it, so that we are left with speculation and surmise. One thing seems certain however. The Reformation movement in England, as elsewhere, attracted the more physically and mentally mobile classes of lay people. For example, merchants of the London–Antwerp nexus, or traders with the North Sea and Baltic Hanseatic cities, also seamen and boat people, entrepreneurial craftsmen and artisans, teachers, students, lawyers, and rebellious teenagers. It was from the affluent among such people that the English Bible translations of the martyred William Tyndale were paid. Leading merchants in London like Richard Hilles[67] also acted as go-betweens in the networking of English Protestants and the

Reformation churches in Strasbourg, Frankfurt and Zurich – all in the course of doing business.

The Catholic Queen, Mary, 1553–8: the Reformation's best ally?

When Mary Tudor became queen in 1553, a long-term Habsburg plan came closer to realization. The English monarchy came within the grasp of the Spanish royal family, since Mary's mother, Catherine of Aragon, had been a daughter of Isabella and Ferdinand, Queen and King of Spain (from 1479). This dynastic link with Spain was cemented when Mary married Philip of Spain in 1554, who soon thereafter became King of Spain (from 1556) when his father, Charles V, abdicated. Not unexpectedly, popular English sensibilities became apprehensive about the potential subordination of England to the Spanish interest, especially since Spain was now a world power with American colonies. Apparently much less unpopular was Mary's declared intent to rid England of heresy and restore Catholicism, to which she had steadfastly adhered in the face of years of hostile pressure. She planned then to restore the Roman papal supremacy and repeal the schismatic and heretical legislation of the previous twenty years.

Protestant bishops were imprisoned, and the universities were purged of heterodox teachers and books. However, since an English monarch did not have absolute power, and had to work with Parliament, Mary soon encountered obstacles. These were in respect of restoring papal jurisdiction and supremacy, and restoring confiscated wealth and land to the Church. While Parliament was willing enough to go along with the restoration of the former religion, it rejected the idea of restoring papal supremacy, preferring to retain the royal one. Therefore Mary was constrained, against her wishes, to accept the headship of the Church. Nor did the devotion to Catholicism by the English Parliament extend to a willingness to return assets to the Church that had been impropriated under Henry VIII. Members of Parliament had profited handsomely from this.

Accordingly what was restored was not so much pre-Reformation Roman Catholicism, as the essence of the Henrician church settlement purged of Protestantizing elements. This is what both Mary and even Pope Paul IV had to accept, at least in the interim. Only then was Cardinal Reginald Pole[68] (1500–58) allowed to come to England from Italy, where he had been for the previous twenty-three years, to become Archbishop of Canterbury. No hard-line traditionalist, he was an evangelical Catholic 'moderate', identified with the reform initiatives of Pope Paul III. As archbishop, however, his energies were devoted to ecclesiastical reorganization and discipline rather than to Catholic re-education. Aided by bishops like Stephen Gardiner[69] (c.1483–1555) and particularly the heavy-handed

Edmund Bonner[70] (*c.*1500–69) in London, this policy – and perhaps herein lay the fatal error – was essentially conservative, rather than imbued with the spirit of Tridentine revival Catholicism.

The legal basis of the Catholic restoration was enacted during the first two years of Mary's reign. Edwardian religious enactments were repealed, and all anti-papal legislation since 1529 was abrogated (excepting the royal supremacy). By the autumn of 1554, England was formally readmitted to the Roman religious obedience and so became subject again to the full panoply of canon law. Mary's Counter-Reformation programme was embodied in the *Injunctions*[71] issued in the spring of 1554. The only specific heresy mentioned was 'sacramentarianism', the denial of the objective real presence of Christ's body in the eucharistic elements; this was targeting 'Zwinglianism' in particular. And the particular new irregularity attacked was clerical marriage. In a somewhat uncatholic, never mind unchristian manner, she urged that provision be made for (compulsory) divorce of married clergy, even after they have been deprived of church office. The *Injunctions* also strongly urged banning and censorship of Reformation literature and publicity. This confirms that if, as many maintain, Edwardian Protestantism was superficial, there was nonetheless a lot of Protestant literary diffusion and colportage around.

There began in 1555 the state-sponsored, but not so popular persecution of Protestants in England and Wales,[72] though not Ireland. The terror began by bringing Archbishop Cranmer, Bishops Hugh Latimer and Nicholas Ridley to Oxford for a show trial, resulting in their being burned alive in 1556. Two other bishops, John Hooper, and the less frequently mentioned Robert Ferrar[73] (*c.*1500–55) in Wales, met similar ends as did sixteen ordinary clergy including the northern evangelist, John Bradford[74] (*c.*1510–55), the biblical translator, John Rogers (*c.*1499–1555), and the very popular evangelical preacher and family man, Rowland Taylor, Cranmer's domestic chaplain. English historians tend to boast that religious persecution in Marian England was modest compared to certain places on the Continent. Yet England was the only place in Reformation Europe where bishops and clergy were executed, including the English Primate. But the statistics tell another tale. There were about three hundred religious executions in Marian England, mainly in the Dioceses of London, Norwich, Chichester and Canterbury, areas with good communication links to the Continent. Of these, well over two hundred were lay people, and so the overwhelming majority. Among them, the majority was from the artisan and skilled working class. This is important when one recalls attempts to identify the Reformation movement largely with the well-educated, clerical and academic minority, in order to deprive it of any 'popular' credibility. Lastly, Mary, showing that she was aware of one of the intellectual sources of advanced Protestantism in England, ordered the bones of Martin Bucer to be disinterred and ritually burned at Cambridge, and then scattered on the Thames in London.

Those among the Protestant clerical leadership who were not killed went into exile, such as John Ponet[75] (*c.*1514–56), bishop of Winchester, and, like John Knox, a proponent of resistance theory. Foreign Protestants, whether theologians or artisans, were expelled. It is estimated that about 800 Protestant activists either were deported or exiled themselves to the Continent, settling in Switzerland, Germany, and some even in Venice. These were the so-called 'Marian exiles'. With hindsight one can say that both the blood of the martyrs and the future return of the exiles was to be formative of much in later English (and Scottish and Irish) Protestantism, particularly its theologically Calvinist flavour. The diaspora leaders studied under or worked with notable Reformers like Henry Bullinger and Peter Martyr in Zurich, Calvin in Geneva, Jan Laski in Emden, etc. Though there was dissensus among the exiles on liturgy, ceremonies and church government due to differences between moderates and militants (future puritans), especially in the important exilic church at Frankfurt, they continued to disseminate Protestant literature in England. Since most of this was in English, arguably there were more Protestant books in the vernacular circulating in England during Mary's reign than there ever had been before!

Apologists of the Marian persecution suggest that since the 300 or so martyrs included a 'majority' of 'Anabaptists', they would have been executed in time by a Protestant Church of England anyway. Others (e.g. Dickens) reject this, pointing out that in the five years of Edward's reign, only two 'Anabaptists' were executed.[76] Further, it is claimed that the name 'Anabaptist' was not applied in fact to any of the Marian martyrs. It has also been suggested that the Marian persecution was due largely to a couple of experts of the Spanish Inquisition who had been recruited to make sure that things were done properly. However, David Loades' studies of Mary show that the primary propellent of persecuting zeal was Mary herself.

Mary's general and particular policies were, however, to run into difficulties. Their efficacy remains a matter of debate among historians.[77] Firstly: religious executions gained no popular support; in fact they often had to be done at night because of popular sympathy with the victims. Little did Mary realize that with every execution Protestant credibility and moral status increased in public opinion.

Secondly, the persecutions created an underground reformed church, autonomous and wholly detached from state religion, not unlike the contemporary Scottish 'privy kirk'. The blood of the martyrs was obviously seed for such churches.[78] Organized in conventicles, such communities developed new skills and ecclesiological concepts, such as autonomous, non-episcopal government and discipline, lay participation, gathered congregational fellowship, theological articulation, and sharp antipathy to all aspects of Roman Catholicism. Many future developments and tensions were to derive from this.

Thirdly, in 1555, the new pope, Paul IV (Peter Carafa), wished the restored English Catholic Church all the worst. This was partly because it did not accept papal supremacy, partly because of his pathological antipathy to the Spanish interest, which now included England, and partly because of his animosity to Cardinal Pole. The pope tried to recall Pole to Rome to face trial on charges of holding, or at least publicizing, Lutheran views on justification.

Fourthly, in their concern to restore Catholic institutions and practices, Mary and Pole neglected to follow this up with necessary Catholic evangelism and teaching to secure the minds as well as the hearts of the people. The Injunctions had urged such catechizing and re-education. Foreign observers and diplomats in England at this time nearly all report that the English were only pretend Catholics – not that London can be taken typical of the whole country, of course. But symptomatic of this was the refusal of Mary and Pole to accept the offer of a Jesuit mission. Restoration, therefore, rather than revivalist reaffirmation was the keynote of Marian Catholicism. It looks as if it was unreformed rather than reformed Catholicism that was welcomed at the popular level – an interpretation suggested by the comment of the future Elizabethan bishop and Church of England apologist, John Jewel. He noted that under Mary, the nation had relapsed into 'a wilderness of superstition'.[79]

Lastly, in the course of a Habsburg–French war into which England was drawn on the Spanish side, Mary underwent an all-time low in the public opinion polls because of the loss of Calais to the French. Calais was no imperial outpost like the modern Rock of Gibraltar; it had been part of 'England' for the previous six hundred years and returned two MPs to Parliament. Even the *Book of Common Prayer* had been translated into French for the francophone English citizens of Calais.[80] It has been said the loss of Calais did as much as anything else to make England Protestant, since it was a consequence of the pro-Catholic and pro-Spanish policies of an English government.

The austere Anglo-Aragonese Catholicism of Mary and the hispanicization of the royal court (rather like the gallicization of the Scottish court of Mary Stewart a few years later) embodied the limitations of the 'popularity' of the Catholic restoration. If 'in the country', the traditions of old 'merry England' and Epicurean Catholic culture went hand-in-hand, evidence for this in the sombre Catholic puritanism of the royal entourage was not copious. Things of course might have turned out differently had Mary lived longer or had an heir. She and Pole died on the same day in 1558. When her half-sister, the basically Protestant Elizabeth Tudor,[81] daughter of Henry VIII and Anne Boleyn, succeeded her, everything that Mary stood for began to be dismantled.

Further remarks are apposite on the impact of the Marian persecutions on English Protestantism, which had now been baptized with fire, and so was of a new character. The persecution had supplied it with an inspirational typological arsenal. This involved a sense of divine censure for having accepted too readily previous religious compromises under Henry and Edward, and for having accepted idolatry for too long, whether images or the Mass. Other biblical motifs that English Protestants now applied to themselves were exile, captivity, eschatological and apocalyptic expectation, and deliverance.

In this connection one can reintroduce John Knox, for he above all articulated controversially this feature of the new English Protestantism. It was in the company of the English (and Scottish) exiles in Frankfurt and Geneva that Knox developed his ideas of resistance and deposing a perceived tyrannical ruler by force in the *First Blast of the Trumpet against the Monstrous Regiment of Women* (1558) – a work that he composed at Dieppe in France. Though he primarily had England in mind, Knox's vision of England and Scotland at this time was of countries subjected to a satanic trinity of Catholic rulers, all in thrall to the papal Antichrist. To make matters worse, these rulers were also female (in contravention of natural and divine law) and all called Mary. These were: in England, Mary Tudor, and in Scotland, Mary of Guise, the Regent, and her daughter, Mary Stewart, the queen. This tract was to backfire on Knox, for in his polemic against female rulers he did not reckon that another woman would soon govern England. Embarrassingly for him she would be a Protestant. Elizabeth was in no way amused about his views on either women in power or the legitimacy of insurrection against lawful authority, and so had him banned from the country. The climax of his philippic had been inflammatory, pleading for the removal of Mary as a religious duty:

> Insofar as the nobility and estates have most heinously offended against God, placing in authority such as God by his Word hath removed from the same . . . in token of true repentance . . . they ought without delay to remove from authority all such persons as by usurpation, violence or tyranny do possess the same.[82]

Knox's tract was a *coup de théâtre* of propaganda of both a sublime and low kind for modern tastes.[83] Identifying himself with Ezekiel, the Watchman to the House of Israel, he mingles three considerations in order to foment a divinely required revolt in England. These were cultural, socio-political, and religious. The cultural was male chauvinism, hostile to female rulers. The socio-political was assimilation to foreign (Catholic) powers. This engendered feelings of nationalism and racism. The religious was infidelity to God and his commandments and which provokes God's wrath and vengeance. Hence the trauma of the Marian regime. England and Scotland have wrongly permitted females to rule. It is bad enough, Knox asserts, that Scottish national integrity is threatened with the marriage of the Scottish queen to the King of France, but much worse is Mary Tudor's marriage to the King of Spain. Its people are odious, not even proper Europeans, more Jewish and Arab in origin, despisers of Christ, he points out. Knox's call is to true believers, the men of the Covenant, to rise up and liberate England from foreign assimilation and subordination, Catholic idolatry (the Mass), papal tyranny and the prospect of an indefinite Babylonish Captivity, all seen as a consequence of Mary Tudor's policies. It is remarkable that a Scot like Knox should have become the voice calling for the vouchsafing of English national 'identity' grounded in 'faith and motherland'.

While much in Knox's tract, particularly that which seemed to incite revolt against lawful authority, was greeted with general disapprobation (and dismayed Calvin), in reality it expressed what many were thinking. It soon, though, provoked a riposte from within English Reformation circles.[84] One element in the *First Blast* was to be crucial for the near future. This was the linking of the Reformation, in England in particular, but also Scotland, to national and patriotic sentiments. This ideological symbiosis was to be, as we shall see, almost decisive in determining the future wide political and public support for the Reformation, especially in Elizabethan England. Also, it was to fuel Anglo-British determination to advance the Reformation in Scotland, and no less so in Ireland. One might therefore argue that subsequent comprehensive support for the 'Reformation' was anchored more in political than in religious factors – even if such a distinction in those times was not so discernible or permissible as it is now.

The forging of the Protestant realm of imperial England under Elizabeth and James

A. *General remarks*

Altogether, what happened in Elizabethan and Jacobean England was that an apparent synthesis occurred between Protestantism and patriotism, or nationalism.[85] Ultimately this helped provide the ideological basis for a further mutation into imperialism and colonialism. This colonialism was disguised as bringing the light of 'civility' to barbarous societies, whether in Gaelic Ireland and Gaelic Scotland, and subsequently Indian America and elsewhere. In the eyes of many Englishmen, Protestant England had a divine mission to the world, she was the new Israel, and her people were among the elect of the Covenant, marked out for a special vocation. There are some famous slogans epitomizing this attitude, notably that of a Marian exile, John Aylmer (1521–94), future Bishop of London. In his *An Harborowe* [haven, refuge], he remarked in 1559 that 'God is English'.[86] Even in the sixteenth century this was seen as a semi-joke, but many people were inclined to believe it. This resulted in the idea being a bizarre ingredient in the rapid gestation of the Elizabethan Protestant and political culture.

Since the idea was not completely new, one cannot blame the Reformation for this. It was said in the fourteenth century, during the papal schism, that 'now the Pope has become French, Jesus has become English'.[87] English ethnocentricity therefore pre-existed the Reformation.

In 1500 the Venetian ambassador noted that 'the English are great lovers of themselves, and of everything belonging to them; they think that there are no other people than themselves, and no other world but England'.[88] But a word of caution: even in Elizabethan times not all English people shared such naïve beliefs. Further, in itself the idea was not exclusively English either. There was an ancient French tradition of the same thing, and indeed the English version of it is seen by some as being derived from France. There, the monarchy and the race were seen as having a divinely ordained special status within Catholic Christianity and European Christendom, symbolized in the unique title borne by the mystically redolent French monarchs, 'The Most Christian King'.

Another general point to be made in this respect is this: before the time of Elizabeth, the Reformation was perceived by many in England with distaste on the grounds that it was 'foreign'. The great change that happened between Elizabeth and James is that most people now stopped seeing Catholicism as the 'old religion' of England, or the religion of Old England. Rather they came to see it as foreign, un-English, and even anti-Christian. Catholicism meant the prospect of tyranny exercised by a 'foreign power', meaning not just the papacy, but big powers like Spain. Those who continued to adhere to the old faith, whether in the North of England, parts of Wales and Scotland, and in Ireland came then to be seen as people with treason in their hearts, since their consciences were bound to a foreign power. This then gave rise to the continuously fraught situation whereby the population of the British Isles was divided into what we might call the conforming loyalist majority, and the nonconforming, suspect and possibly rebellious minority deprived of civil rights. The iconography in many parish churches of England, Wales and Ireland conveyed the message: where the crucifix used to be, there was now the coat of arms of the English monarchy. Here we have then not just the religion of the state, but state religion. Being Christian meant being Protestant English, or Anglo-Irish, or 'British'. And if this potent new ideology was to be really effective, the Scots too, previously enemy aliens, had to be somehow brought into the new covenant – a process facilitated by the clever and successful use of the semi-mythological concept of 'Britain' (see Chapter 2). This device had already worked well in the Welsh context.

Arguably, however, the concept was in reality the veil behind which the new and progressive English Empire was being generated and made acceptable, just as Roman imperialism and Catholic Christianity had been intertwined in the fourth and fifth centuries, and continued in Byzantium. And when Rome fell in the West, the cultures of converted barbarian Europe entered into the partnership. The sixteenth-century Anglo-Protestant motif initially functioned in the British Isles, or at least southern Britain and Ireland, and then beyond. Its ultimate symbols were to be the Union flag in one hand, and the Bible in the other. And it only worked because significant elements or classes in the other nations consented, and gained in status from it. As Loades has recalled: 'Nothing succeeds like success.'[89]

B. *The Elizabethan Settlement, its fortification and its undermining*

To turn to the Elizabethan Reformation itself: constituting the third and last phase of the Tudor legislative Reformation in England and Wales (and at least technically, Ireland), it is normally referred to as 'The Elizabethan Settlement'. But as we shall see, one of its chief attributes was elemental lack of settlement, due to the continuing cohabitation of Catholic structure and Protestant theology – the 'cuckoo in the nest'.[90] It is usually dated as 1559–63. A better finish date would be 1571, when the provisional quality of the earlier arrangements evaporated. If Henry VIII had been portrayed as 'next to God', and Edward VI as a young 'Josiah', Protestant opinion saw Elizabeth as a 'new Deborah'. Her reign sees the effective protestantization of England, even if one cannot speak of a serious evangelization of the population along solid Reformation principles. But as Claire Cross has neatly put it: 'The Elizabethan Settlement was not the climax of the English Reformation, but only the end of the beginning.'[91]

If the real builder of the Henrician Church was Thomas Cromwell, the face of the Elizabethan Church was reconstructed by the queen's Principal Secretary, William Cecil, later Lord Burghley (1520–98).[92] He was Elizabeth's chief adviser for nearly forty years. Although Cecil had conformed externally to the Catholic Church under Mary, he had strong Protestant credentials. In King Edward's time he had studied at St John's College, Cambridge, a nursery of Reformation ideas, and had also attended lectures by Martin Bucer there. Cecil favoured a general rather than a 'precisionist' Reformation. His Erastian ecclesiology and his lay spirit gave him an aversion to a clericalist church, believing that the 'religion of Christ'[93] was too important to be left to the clergy. And as a royal mandarin, he realized fully that implementing the Reformation in England meant practising the art of the possible on a large national and territorial scale. Unity, comprehensiveness and uniformity were his goals, just as they were also the queen's.

The legislation of the Elizabethan Settlement, effectively Cecil's achievement, was embodied in the Acts of Supremacy[94] and Uniformity[95] (1559), the third *Book of Common Prayer* (1559)[96], and the confession of faith, *The Thirty-nine Articles*.[97] This last, based essentially on the Edwardine *Forty-two Articles*, was passed by the Church in 1563, but not sanctioned in their English form by Parliament until 1571. One thing omitted from the Edwardine article on the Lord's Supper was a Zwinglian component rejecting the Lutheran doctrine of the ubiquity of Christ's body, and denouncing reference to the 'real and bodily presence'. Added, however, were clauses to the effect, firstly, that the 'eating' of Christ's body is only in a 'heavenly and spiritual' manner (and so not physical or carnal), and secondly, that the wicked and unbelievers do not (objectively) receive the body of Christ in the Eucharist. One detects here the influence of aspects of the sacramental theology associated with the nexus of Bucer, Melanchthon and Calvin, most likely reinforced by the new Archbishop of Canterbury, Matthew Parker.[98]

The elements of compromise in the statutory instruments derived from certain religio-political realities at that time in England. The conventional understanding was that the 1559 enactments were simply the outcome of a difficult struggle between a conservative, essentially Henrician queen and a fervidly Protestant Commons.[99] The actual situation is now better comprehended:[100] there was a pro-Catholic minority in the House of Commons. The majority in the Lords was conservative and so pro-Catholic. And the English episcopate in 1559 was still explicitly Roman Catholic, since it derived from appointments made earlier by Mary. The queen herself is best described as strongly Erastian and broadly Protestant.

Any doubts about the queen's commitment to essential Reformation tenets and ideals are dispelled by her *Injunctions* of 1559, even if over a half of them replicate the Edwardine ones.[101] The text refers to the 'suppression of superstition', the 'planting of true religion' and to pilgrimages, relics and the use of images as 'abhorrent to God', being non-scriptural. The public are encouraged to read and believe the Bible, the antidote to 'the vice of damnable despair'; the 'living Word of God', the means and source of secure faith, consolation, hope and salvation, being 'the only stay of man's conscience'. Clergy are defined not as priests, but as 'ministers of Word and sacraments', and the holy Catholic Church is defined not primarily in terms of episcopal hierarchy but as 'the whole congregation of Christian people'. Praying for the dead is conceived not as supplicating intercession for them; rather, living Christians should pray that they themselves, along with those who departed in the faith of Christ, thereby setting a good example, might share in the resurrection and eternal life.[102] Elizabeth's special concern for religious peace and harmony is reflected in the exhortation to mutual charity, 'the knot of all Christian society', and to the shunning of 'contentious disputations' on religious topics. Words of abuse are banned and actionable, such as 'papist', 'papistical heretic', schismatic', and 'sacramentarian'.

The 1559 enactments embody a diplomatic degree of assuagement of the Protestant programme under Edward VI in the interests of widening their appeal. They were not primarily grounded in *via media* aspirations in the area of fundamental Catholic–Protestant discord, now exacerbated by the Council of Trent. Rather, in the area of doctrine there are concerns for wider Protestant concord throughout Europe. Overall, they were determined chiefly by pragmatic considerations in order to achieve what was deliverable. The supremacy was redefined from being 'Supreme Head on earth' to 'Supreme Governor'. This was partly to meet Catholic objections, and partly a concession to Calvinist aversion to the word 'Head', that being reserved for Christ. The Catholic bishops were inevitably soon deprived, harassed, and replaced by Protestants, many of whom were returned exiles from the Continent with a well-developed Reformation consciousness. This, however, did not give a green light to change the legislation in a more advanced Protestant direction. Arising from this general situation, the official liturgy and confession remained moderate. They aimed to express reformed theology without utterly alienating the Catholic or traditional party. Yet they did also issue from a pre-existing irenic tradition of a 'third way' associated with Bucer and Melanchthon, now mediated by Archbishop Parker. In view of the context, the Church of England's creed was just as 'political' as the *Confession of Augsburg* (1530), one of its ultimate sources. Some notion of 'comprehensiveness' was not to be abandoned.

Although the *Thirty-nine Articles* do not at all embody a middle road between Catholic and Protestant dogma, here and there certain matters are left imprecise. As time went on, this frustrated increasingly Protestant opinion, particularly in the areas of the extent of the atonement, grace, church government and discipline. Initially, the more advanced Protestants were prepared to acquiesce in episcopacy, on the grounds it was expedient for the Church in the interim, that is, for her provisional well-being (*bene esse*), even if episcopacy does not pertain to its essence (*esse*). Eventually, however, there was agitation for the restructuring of the Church along presbyterian lines in particular.

Up to 1571, subscription to the Articles was required just by members of Convocation (a Church of England assembly of bishops and representatives of diocesan clergy). Thereafter subscription was required of all ordained clergy and benefice holders. The Act of Parliament required subscription to the doctrinal articles only, so as to cater for the scruples of puritans who dissented from the article (35) on episcopal church order. However, a final revision by Convocation required subscription to all the articles in the hope of enforcing universal episcopal authority through the church courts. This situation only papered over the cracks of dissensus on church polity and discipline. In 1583, the Archbishop of Canterbury, the Calvinist but anti-presbyterian John Whitgift (*c.*1530–1604),[103] attempted to strengthen uniformity even more with a subscription formula embodied in his *Three Articles*.[104] These reaffirmed the royal supremacy, the exclusive use of the Prayer-book in worship as scripturally based, and the validity of all thirty-nine articles. In 1604 Convocation and James I (but not Parliament) sanctioned the *Three Articles*. Subscription to all the *Thirty-nine Articles* and the royal supremacy was mandatory for all clergy – the laity were required not to attack them.

Another early symptom of discontent was the problem of clerical vestments, giving rise to the 'vestiarian controversy' that came to a head in 1566. Its origins seem to have been in the Edwardine period, when progressive Protestants among the English clergy like Bishop John Hooper called for the abolition of clerical vestments, since they were unbiblical. Continental theologians in England like Laski supported him,[105] but others like Bucer and Vermigli (Peter Martyr) took a less strict line. The queen wanted clergy to wear the white surplice, specified in the 1559 *Injunctions*. The view of church leaders was that while this was indeed a matter of adiaphora, inessential things of secondary importance, it ought to be worn for the sake of decorum and uniformity. The white surplice should be worn as standard liturgical dress, as prescribed in the *Book of Common Prayer*. Anyway, the queen's express wish could not be treated indifferently in view of her office in the Church. Many clergy and people, however, were hostile to what they saw as the 'rags of Rome', which understandably reminded them of stage props in the recent persecution. Others were concerned that distinctive clerical dress implied a reversion to the idea of clergy as a spiritual 'class apart'. Following prescriptive guidelines issued by Archbishop Parker – *Advertisements* – nearly forty ministers in the Diocese of London were suspended for not wearing the prescribed dress. The matter also became an issue of obedience to royal authority in the Church. The affair subsided though some clergy were deprived.[106]

The controversy was a further sign of the problems to be caused by the prescriptively biblicist drift in the Church of England, characterized as 'puritanism'. For while the vestments controversy may seem petty, irrelevant and laughable to modern eyes as much sartorially ado about nothing, it was a firm indicator of how the problem concerning the operation of the scriptural principle was unresolved. Should things not forbidden by the Bible be permitted? Should only those practices and beliefs sanctioned by Scripture, or clearly inferred from it, be permitted? Is the Word of God dependent on, or free from such regulations? The English debate mirrored the earlier dissensus over the issue on the Continent, initiated by Andrew Carlstadt in Wittenberg in the early 1520s. Moreover, as we shall see below, in England the vestments affair was to be inextricably linked to increasingly divisive debates on three other matters that caused cracks within the Church of England. These were, firstly, the exercise of moral discipline in the Church; secondly, wider religious education as envisaged in 'puritan' lectureships and biblical studies courses for clergy – called 'prophesyings' (or in Scotland, 'exercises'); thirdly, aversion to church government by bishops in favour of a presbyterian hierarchy of representative church courts of presbyters, lay and ministerial. Crucially, in all these areas, royal authority was marginalized and 'biblical' authority elevated, so that in the English church-political context, they acquired damaging stigmas.

Meanwhile, the *Thirty-nine Articles* and the *Book of Common Prayer* were soon supplemented by a revised re-issue of the 1547 *Book of Homilies*, a supplementary second *Book of Homilies* (1563)[107] and by a *Catechism* in 1570. The Dean of St Paul's and ex-Marian exile, Alexander Nowell (*c*.1507–1602), drafted the latter. Authorized by the Church earlier in 1562, it was influenced considerably by the *Genevan Catechism* and the *Heidelberg Catechism*. Its text replicated a third of the former. Its hallmark was a combination of unambiguous reformed theology with strong exhortation to obey the authorities, and to accept the royal supremacy in church affairs. One of the two most frequently republished books in England up to 1640, the *Catechism*'s aim was inculcation of Reformation ideas and the Elizabethan religious settlement among the laity, learned and unlearned.[108]

In the fields of church law and discipline, obviously there was need for revision and amendment following the new 'magisterial' Reformation of the English Church. This had resulted in the abolition in 1535 of the study of Roman canon law at English universities. An earlier draft proposal composed partly by Cranmer was adopted in 1570,[109] the *Reformatio Legum Ecclesiasticarum* (The Reformation of Ecclesiastical Laws).[110] This – being 'human' rather than 'divine' law – was never to have the same authority over consciences exercised by the previous Roman canon law. Despite this, church courts continued to have teeth, though this gradually became weakened in the face of increasing evangelical freedom, dissent, or simple libertarianism.

To reinforce these foundational and ecclesiastical documents, the Reformation in England and its Church was provided with further literary corroboration. To cite the major examples: First, there was the Latin *Apology of the Church of England* (1562, English translation by Lady Ann Bacon) composed by the ex-Marian exile, John Jewel, Bishop of Salisbury.[111] Derived from his 'Challenge Sermon' of 1559 defending the Elizabethan church settlement against Catholic criticisms of 'innovation' and 'schism', the *Apology* was a vindication of the basis of the authority of the Church of England with an international audience in mind. It embodies prototype 'Anglican' apologetics: the Church of England is compatible not only with Scripture, but also best patristic theology and practice in the early Church. The *Apology* is accordingly an exposition of the principle of 'Catholic and reformed'. There is in fact nothing especially 'Anglican' about such an argument, since it had been used earlier in the century by Continental Reformers like Melanchthon and Bucer in defence of the Reformation, especially on the basis of the *Augsburg Confession*. Despite its adhesion to monarchical episcopacy, the *Apology* was acclaimed in Zwinglian Zurich.[112] By 1568, Continental English Catholics had published forty-one tracts of attempted refutation.[113]

Second, between 1592 and 1600 there appeared the *Laws of Ecclesiastical Polity*, by Richard Hooker (1544–1600), a London minister.[114] This work was a defence of the threefold ministry and episcopacy against doctrinaire presbyterian theory, with its notions of ministerial parity, lay eldership, conciliar church government, preaching exercises for clergy and consistorial discipline. Arguing from a combination of Scripture, tradition, natural law and reason, Hooker asserted that church government is a matter indifferent and that indeed episcopacy is not essential to the constitution of the Church by virtue of any divine prescription in Scripture. The Bible does not prescribe one immutable church polity. However, reason and tradition suggest that it is appropriate and convenient (*bene esse*); the proper authorities (royal supremacy) could rightly insist on such a polity on pragmatic grounds. The same reasoning was used to justify certain 'unbiblical' rites and ceremonies. In respect of episcopal theory, it has to be stressed that neither Jewel nor Hooker advocated episcopacy by divine law. That line of argument was to come later in the Church of England,[115] advanced originally by John Bridges, Dean of Salisbury in his *A Defence of the Government Established in the Church of England* (1587) It was subsequently articulated most authoritatively by a former Dutch reformed clergyman in England, Adrian Saravia[116] (*c*.1532–1613), a 'Catholic Calvinist'. It was to clear the way for subsequent fundamentalist episcopalianism.

Presbyterian manifestations in England – curiously nearly always described by atheological modern historians as 'extreme' – were most pronounced in London and the south-east, where Continental influences were strongest.[117] It created many problems for the Established Church, since presbyterian advocates came from within it. Its theory – mandatory presbyterian church government by divine law and so parity of ministers – was represented on the Continent by Theodore Beza (1519–1605), Calvin's successor in Geneva, and in England by notably Walter Travers[118] (*c*.1548–1635), Thomas Cartwright[119] (1535–1603), John Field[120] (1545–88), Thomas Wilcox (1549–1608), and during his stay in England, by the Scot, Andrew Melville[121] (1542–1622). Since the queen was firmly opposed to such untraditional notions, which took no account of the royal supremacy, the movement was frustrated at every turn, though it remained dormant until the next century. Several specific controversies, however, upped the ante. Firstly, the 'Admonition Controversy' (1572 *et seq.*), and secondly, the 'Marprelate Tracts' (1587–9).

In 1572, John Field and Thomas Wilcox, both Church of England curates, boldly submitted an 'Admonition to the Parliament' severely criticising the state of the English Church, which was characterized as half reformed.[122] The document was highly controversial, since it criticized the entire hierarchical and liturgical structure of the Elizabethan Settlement. It demanded a Church constructed around three authentic marks, namely preaching, the sacraments and discipline. Requisite, therefore, are ministerial parity, the office of the eldership (seniors), stricter adhesion to Scripture in all matters of faith, worship, and order, and the abolition of 'all popish remnants'. The better practices of the reformed Churches in France and Scotland are cited. Many leading church puritans prudentially distanced themselves from the petition, and its authors were imprisoned for a year, though not subsequently deprived. However, the episode provoked a series of controversial literary exchanges involving John Whitgift, the Cambridge vice-chancellor, a defender of the ecclesiastical *status quo*, and Thomas Cartwright, who argued the presbyterian case. In 1570, Cartwright had been dismissed by Whitgift from the Divinity Chair in Cambridge following his lectures on the Book of Acts, in which he demonstrated that in comparison to the original Church, the Church of England was lamentable.[123] In the controversy, which lasted until 1577, there were irreconcilable concepts of Church. The one was magisterial, comprehensive, territorial, hierarchical, externally part of the fabric of society, if spiritually imperfect. The other was spiritually autonomous and sovereign, free from individual hierarchy and so conciliar, clericalist, and kept worthy and sanctified by the exercise of discipline. The outcome was that Cartwright was effectively silenced; he moved to the Continent, and on his eventual return he took no part in public life. Nonetheless, the seeds of opposition he had spread continued to propagate.

The second phase of turbulence caused by the pro-presbyterian party among the Puritans was connected with the appearance of the 'Marprelate Tracts' (1587–9). A couple of years earlier there had been abortive attempts by presbyterian parliamentarians to have the English Church restructured along more Genevan lines. This led to the publication of seven (anonymous) tracts by 'Martin Marprelate'.[124] The authors, one of whom may have been an MP (Job Throckmorton), and their assistants were laymen. The English bishops ('Antichrists') were lampooned with superb prose satire and ridicule, and episcopacy was discredited 'root and branch'. The apocalyptic imperative made bishops redundant. The only good bishop is an ex-bishop. The tractarians also constructed an alternative genealogy of the English Reformation, excluding earlier, magisterial martyr-bishops. Their amused popular reception provoked further Establishment clampdowns that did not do the presbyterian or the puritan opposition any apparent good. Proto-presbyterial gatherings for preaching and exegetical exercises by clergy – such a group was called a *classis* – were terminated. In reality, however, the ideological battle was only being deferred, for the Marprelate authors aspired to a national presbyterian Church. Hooker's *Laws* emanates from this context.

The flames of controversy were further fanned by the publication of controversial writings by Continental thinkers on the related topic of the exercise of church discipline. The ideas of Thomas Erastus[125] that were inimical to consistorial discipline (whereby joint committees of ministers and elders exercised individual and collective moral supervision with the power to excommunicate) were published posthumously in London in 1589.[126] The work's appearance was encouraged by the anti-presbyterian though Calvinist Archbishop of Canterbury, John Whitgift, and argued that such discipline should be left to the secular authorities. The following year saw a response published by Beza in Geneva and London simultaneously.[127] The outcome of this debate was that ideas of presbyterian church government and autonomous church discipline of community morals became inextricably linked. Government by royally appointed bishops along with moral discipline exercised by the episcopal courts and the secular authority was the preference imposed by the state Church – so much so that 'Erastianism' came to be a synonym for 'episcopalianism'.

If Jewel and Hooker were the chief intellectual apologists of the English episcopal Church and moulders of the primitive Anglican face, Protestant religious commitment in the wider public domain was given a decisive boost by John Foxe[128] (1516–87), a returned Marian exile. An historian of (true) Christianity from its origins, he saw the potential of writing in the vernacular. The result was his epic *Acts and Monuments*, or *Book of Martyrs* (1557–83), illustrated handsomely with woodcuts.[129] This *tour de force* helped to shape the national Protestant mentality, and became a classic of English literature.[130] Its understandably anglocentric concentration on the lives and deeds of the martyrs of all social classes under Mary made it especially appealing and 'relevant'. It became a bestseller. It was a valuable apologetic and propaganda tool, since it provided a view of the whole of church history from a Protestant viewpoint. Its edifying value was recognized. The government ordered copies to be placed in cathedral churches, and many parish churches made a copy available as well. Foxe also directed a series of translations of the almost forgotten Luther into English, notably the Reformer's commentaries on Galatians (with a preface by the Bishop of London, Edwin Sandys), some psalms, as well as some of his sermons. Translations by others of further Luther selections soon followed. These had no significant impact on English theology as such, but at the level of piety, spirituality, edification, pastoral care and general knowledge of Luther, they were influential.[131] They introduced, or reintroduced, to English piety the subjective and experiential dimension of Luther's message about the consoling nature of the Gospel *pro nobis* [for us]. This contrasted with the formalism of the statutory Church, and with the imperative of personal abnegation in Calvinist religious sensibility to the chief end of glorifying God. Not least, no longer did many late sixteenth-century English Protestants have to ask: 'Martin who?'

Lastly, though it is of primary importance, the fourth significant book determining the formation of Protestant England (if not the Elizabethan Settlement) was the English *Geneva Bible*, originally a production of the English Marian exiles in Geneva between 1557 and 1560.[132] Among clergy and the literate laity it was the preferred text for biblical study. Its superior and congenial format – notes, verse numbering, attractive print, etc. made it the household Bible. The Church Establishment was uneasy about this, since many of the notes in the Geneva Bible were seen as too 'Calvinist', or in the terms of some, 'presbyterianizing' (though such criticism refers more properly to editions based on the 1565 revision). Attempts by some bishops to produce another alternative and less puritan English Bible enjoyed no great success. The popularity of the Geneva Bible endured well beyond the official *King James Bible* of 1611. One hundred and forty editions were published, and it became the officially sanctioned Bible in Scotland. The matter demonstrated that what was of central importance was not so much an accessible Bible, as whose Bible?

The real counterblast came from English Catholic circles abroad. In 1582, a Catholic-inspired English New Testament, with strongly anti-Reformation notes, was published at Rheims, the work of Gregory Martin. It was a translation of the Latin Vulgate. This *Rheims New Testament* was supplemented by the Old Testament in 1610, the work of other exilic translators, and published at Douai. Both translations formed what became known as the *Douai Bible*. The preface to the New Testament is highly controversial and apologetic, constituting a lucid and scholarly statement of Catholic opposition to the Protestant (and Erasmian) attitude to and use of Scripture.[133] Attacked in particular is the idea of the democratization of the Bible, a sure recipe for rampant subjectivism and disorder. Instead, the people should only be exposed to it through the prism of the leaders of the Church and their sanctioned interpretative authority grounded in reason and tradition. The classic Catholic point is made that moral regeneration does not seem to follow from unlimited scriptural knowledge. Reading this preface alongside various Protestant prefaces provides a strong authentic indicator of what the substantive issues in the religious Reformation were.

C. *A failed Reformation or a failed Reformed Church?*

How then can we assess the Reformation in England after 1560? Was it a half Reformation? Was it a Reformation of gloss rather than serious substance? Did it result in a hamstrung reformed Church, disabled by State control and political subordination? The answer to these questions depends on how one looks at the situation, or on what is meant by 'Reformation'.

For example, it can be held that the greatest boost to the Reformation as a popular religio-political movement in England was the excommunication of the Queen by Pope Pius V in 1570. Not surprisingly, the English bishops appealed to Zwinglian Zurich for support and vindication of the magisterial English Reformation. Henry Bullinger obliged with his *Confutation of the Pope's Bull*,[134] published in Latin, English and German. This confirmed England's status among the comity of European Protestant states.

The crossing of the Rubicon occasioned by the Bull accordingly secured the long-term success of the English Reformation. For it was more than just personal excommunication. If it had been only that its consequences might not have been so tragic. For the papal Bull, *Regnans in excelso*, also announced that Elizabeth had no right to be queen, and that as her subjects owed her no allegiance she should be considered as deposed. Further, that those who did obey her were also to be excommunicated. This was certainly inflammatory, especially in the immediate context. In 1569 there had been the crushed northern Catholic rebellion. Moreover, there was the potentially minatory presence now in England of the deposed Scottish queen, Mary Stewart. Mary was not only Catholic, but had a good claim to the English throne, since her grandmother was a sister of Henry VIII. Elizabeth tolerated Mary's confined presence in England for eighteen years. But after the third plot involving Mary to assassinate Elizabeth, and have Mary made queen with the aid of a foreign invasion, the ex-Scottish queen was executed in 1586. That is, just two years before the Spanish Armada set off. Finally, the Bull arguably did more than anything else to weaken the loyalty to the Crown of the bulk of the still mainly Catholic population of Ireland, fuelling ideas of legitimate rebellion.

The Bull of excommunication was largely determinative of this whole scenario: it gave the English government grounds for seeing all Catholics as possible traitors. Severe penal legislation was now passed against them, and was to afflict English and Irish Catholics for generations to come. This was hard, for many Catholics actually wanted to be obedient to both Queen and pope – but that, theoretically, was no option any more. Also, occasional actual Catholic plots at home and abroad against Elizabeth, apart from Mary Stewart's ones, did not help the public image of Catholics, just as it did not help instinctively loyalist Catholics either. The 'Gunpowder Plot' of 1604 and its association with Spanish interference represented the last fling of English political Catholicism until the era of James VII & II. The Oath of Allegiance (1606) introduced by James VI & I was designed to ensure Catholic loyalty to the Crown,[135] but papal denunciation of the Oath and assertion that heretical rulers may be deposed or murdered, placed Catholics in an invidious position. And so in England and Ireland a Catholic semi-underclass was created, which Protestant public opinion regarded as a threat to both religion and national security. The official name for them was 'recusants', those who rejected the religious laws of the kingdom and who inevitably became objects of discrimination as well as intermittent persecution.

In short, an effect of the papal Bull was to accelerate the sea change synthesizing Protestantism, dynastic stability, national defence, cultural identity and chauvinism into an indivisible reality. The *Gestalt* of the Protestant nation gained its greatest firming up from the failed Spanish Armada, or 'Enterprise of England' in 1588. This underlined the necessity of extending the new English Empire throughout the British Isles. The union of the English and the Scottish Crowns in 1603, when the firmly Calvinist James VI (1566–1625), King of Scots, also became James I of England and Ireland, inaugurated the era of striving for a Protestant religious uniformity throughout the British Isles under a single monarch. This was a perfectly respectable medieval concept originating ultimately in the early Church under the Emperor Constantine. Accompanying this was a policy of anglicization and modernizing 'civility'. From the English point of view, global and infrastructural reform on all fronts and hinterlands was necessary to secure the English Reformation and English defence. It was also seen by some as part of God's plan for Britain as a new Israel.

On the international plane, solidarity was expressed by moral and material English support for foreign Reformations in Scotland, France, the Netherlands, Geneva and the Rhineland Palatinate. England was now part of the so-called 'Calvinist International'. This culminated in the design of James to form a pan-European Protestant coalition, headed by himself. In this overall sense then, the Reformation hardly failed in England, in view of the wider cultural and religio-political consequences.

As for the English Church itself, and the process of popular religious re-education, judgements are more uncertain. The grand vision of Elizabeth and James, church uniformity and comprehensiveness, was never realized. The reasons for this were twofold. Firstly, not all Catholics were absorbed, since some retained an autonomous existence, especially the further away from London they were, though this element contracted in time, except in Lancashire.[136] And some gentry Catholics, chiefly in the more comfortable south-east, were kept in the faith by Jesuit and other seminarian missioners of the Catholic International, operating from English Catholic bases at Louvain, Douai (1568, a seminary funded by the pope and the King of Spain, and linked to the university there), Rheims, Rouen, Valladolid, Seville and Rome where an English College was established in 1579 by William Allen (1532–94).

These exilic centres were crucial for maintaining the flow of intellectual capital to surviving Catholics in England and elsewhere in the British Isles. As mentioned above, it was at Douai–Rheims that a Catholic translation of the Bible into English was achieved (1582–1609), largely the work of Gregory Martin, assisted by Allen and Richard Bristow, the College's rector.[137] English Catholic writers and apologists had already operated at the new Catholic university in Douai (founded by Philip of Spain in 1562) including the ex-regius divinity professor at Oxford, Richard Smith[138] (or Smyth) (1500–63) who had been defending the Catholic cause in England and Scotland since the 1530s.[139] His forte was biblical studies, especially hermeneutics, an area where it was vital to confront Protestant conceptions.[140] He is to be distinguished from the later Richard Smith (1566–1655) at the Douai college, himself a polemical writer of note in the field of Scripture and English church history.[141] Strongly Tridentine, and a subscriber to the Roman Catholic Church's new concept of mission centralized in Rome – the *Propaganda Fide* – the latter Smith, as 'Bishop of Chalcedon', operated in England in the 1620s as pretended ordinary bishop of English Catholics. This role caused controversy within the English Catholic community.

Notable English Jesuit leaders[142] were, firstly, Edmund Campion (1540–81), who was executed for treason. Douai-trained, he had helped spear-head the initially abortive Jesuit mission to England in 1580/1.[143] Secondly, there was Campion's companion, Robert Persons (or Parsons) (1546–1610), an influential literary publicist, though he constantly backed lost causes. As one of the most outspoken advocates of foreign invasion in order to restore Catholicism on the grounds that the (spiritual) end justified the means, Persons helped fuel Elizabethan Protestant sentiment that Catholicism was traitorous or potentially so.[144] During Elizabeth's reign, over a hundred priests or missioners (123) were executed, not technically for being Catholic, but for treason.[145] Included among them was Robert Southwell (d. 1592), Jesuit and poet.

As elsewhere in Europe, the Counter-Reformation in Protestant territories was also weakened by some internal factors. For example, of the 800 or so English priests trained in seminaries abroad during the Elizabethan era, only about 450 are known to have returned.[146] The others either had no wish to return, or were redirected to work elsewhere. Further, within post-Tridentine Catholicism there were different concepts of 'mission' to Protestant lands. Jesuits tended to focus their energies on maintaining the Catholic faith in the aristocratic domain, and so often acted as Big House chaplains. The Roman *Propaganda Fide*, however, envisaged parochial ministry to ordinary people in ordinary places as well as re-conversion of the lapsed. In England, this led to tensions between regular and secular priests. Even the regulars were not of one mind. Whereas the Jesuits had political ambitions, the Benedictines were apolitical.[147]

If the continuing Catholic bogle haunted the Protestant nation and Established Church, the second source of instability was, as earlier indicated, the energy of puritan godliness, presbyterian aspirations, and the desire for a more thorough Reformation. The government was also opposed to the widening of theological access by enabling the discussion of the Scriptures among ordinary clergy and ordinary people, especially the artisan and commercial classes. Such a facility allegedly generated contentiousness and disruption. Apart from the dissolution of the quasi-presbyterian *classes*,[148] a notorious example of government policy was the placing of the Calvinist and Settlement-sceptic Archbishop of Canterbury, Edmund Grindal (*c*.1519–83), a Bucer disciple, under house arrest by the queen in 1577. For he had defended 'prophesyings', that is, parish and diocesan Bible-study seminars, against the monarch's wishes.[149] In other words, he was disobedient to the Supreme Governor of the Church.

The Establishment also became anxious about gathered separatist assemblies.[150] These saw the Church of England as a Church of unmitigated apostasy, hopelessly unreformed and unreformable, Romish, non-scriptural and anti-Christian. Among their leaders were activists and polemicists like Robert Browne[151] (*c*.1550–1633), Robert Harrison.[152] Henry Barrow[153] (*c*.1550–93) (all gentlemen and university graduates), John Greenwood[154] (d. 1593), and the ex-presbyterian converted to separatism, John Penry[155] (1559–93). The last three were hanged in 1593 for sedition. Separatism does not seem initially to have been significantly popular,[156] but government repression was determined and at least temporarily successful. A statute of 1593, *An Act to retain the Queen's Subjects in Obedience*, stipulated the expulsion from the kingdom of nonconforming sectarians, and capital punishment in the case of refusal to leave and obstinacy. Most of those who left found refuge in the more tolerant Calvinist Netherlands. The fact that around this time sixty-six 'Barrowists' were imprisoned, the largest element of whom were tradesmen, suggests a perceptible growth in grassroots popularity of radical dissent.[157]

Though usually described as 'Separatists', these dissenting radicals represent the English version of the continuing tradition of classically Anabaptist ecclesiology in all essentials – they bear little resemblance to the small number of theologically heterodox radicals who were prosecuted in the Edwardine era. And like the Donatists in the early Church, basic to their alternative, voluntarist and purist ecclesiology was the incompatibility of the true church and the civil power, a radical separation of the spiritual and secular spheres: 'What has the Emperor to do with the Church?'[158] A Christianity of holiness and believers' baptism cannot be regulated by civil law. They rejected wholly the concept of church and society held together in the bosom of legislative 'Christendom'. Accordingly they ridiculed the Elizabethan Settlement with its statutory Church.[159] The Separatists were equally opposed to both episcopalian puritans and presbyterians, since both shared the notion of Christian society and governance coextensive with the secular body politic. In the next century, the inner-puritan division was to translate into the struggle between Presbytery and Independency (congregationalism).

Inevitably, many attending Church of England services did so under private protest or with mental reservation, as 'lukewarm Laodiceans' or 'indifferent neuters' or even as 'nullifidians'.[160] Was it significantly different under the old regime? Were most late-medieval Catholics model conviction Christians, attending Mass Sunday after Sunday? In Reformation England, external conformity was all that was required. The new situation, however, was not helped by the fact that there was no coherent national strategy for popular evangelization led by the bishops. The lack of financial resources and so inadequate training for the preaching and pastoral ministry, not to mention unevangelical diffidence and unapostolic timidity help explain this.

Aristotle, who was not an Englishman, once said that 'some people fail to realize that an imperfect-looking nose that is either hooked or snub is still an excellent nose' (*Politics* V, 9). Some people reckoned this could be applied to the Church of England. But as long as people were captive to the concept of mandatory uniformity and conformity, an internal time-bomb would tick. Dissensus prevailed over the pursuit of Bible study by the laity, church government, church–state relations, liturgy and discipline. And later in James' reign, there was a corrosion of the English Reformed consensus on justification, predestination, and grace.[161] Some of the university theologians were now representing semi-Pelagian or allegedly 'Arminian'[162] views about grace and free will that seemed to be at variance with orthodox Reformation theology. The local provenance of this thinking was Pierre Baro (1534–99) and Lancelot Andrewes (1555–1626) at Cambridge, and Antonio del Corro (1527–91) at Oxford.[163] The Calvinist theological establishment tried to counter this. For example, the Church's predestinarian, though not officially sanctioned *Lambeth Articles*[164] (1595); the predisposition of the moderate Calvinist monarch, James VI & I; the Church of England's participation in the international Reformed Synod of Dordrecht (or Dort) in Holland in 1618/19; and the republication in 1618 of the strongly Augustinian work by Thomas Bradwardine[165] (d. 1349), *On God's Cause against Pelagius*, with a preface by George Abbot[166] (1562–1633), the Calvinist Archbishop of Canterbury (1611–33). All this failed to check the contraflow. In the church and national Protestant mind, such a trend was perceived as a Catholicizing relapse, a Trojan horse undermining the Reformation, and which sought political corroboration in notions of autocratic or absolutist monarchy.[167]

Once the new king from 1625 onwards, Charles I, and his favourite, George Villiers, Duke of Buckingham, began to favour the 'Arminian' party with patronage, counter-cultural and counter-theological policies became identified with the 'Crown'. This challenge, as well as all the other serious hypertensions and haemorrhages in the Established Church, contributed to the mayhem and violence engulfing English, and indeed British Isles Christianity and society in the imminent Civil War and Revolution. After that, as before, the reformed Church of England abided officially by the principle of 'no change' in doctrine – a good Lutheran confessional principle.

CHAPTER 5

Reformation in Wales

To understand the Reformation, or a particular Reformation anywhere, obviously modern observers have to abandon present-day realities and perceptions, just as the study of any historical topic requires us to put our minds into the fast-backward mode. We are subject to the 'historicist' imperative (see Chapter 1). It is inadequate, for example, to see 'the Reformation' as just a reconstruction of the Church and theology. For where the Reformation did materialize, it was usually accompanied with conspicuous changes in society. In addition, its occurrence and development may have been determined, or stimulated in part by prior 'non-religious' factors. A modern reformation of the Church would take place differently, since currently the Church is only a segment of society. In contrast, the sixteenth century was still essentially a 'medieval' world where Church, the body politic, and society were still co-extensive, traditionally described by the word 'Christendom'. If, then, there were a dramatic 'reformation' of the Church in our times, the impact on society would be mostly marginal. In the sixteenth century, however, religious and ecclesiastical revolution had implications for education, social welfare, economics, politics, culture, the family, law, science, art and leisure.

Accordingly, were momentous changes in the contemporary church and theology on the agenda, Churches would only have to persuade their members, allowing for some legal complications in the few cases of 'established' or 'national' Churches. But in the sixteenth century, the 'Church' had to convince the secular sovereign power – monarch, prince or city council – and at least the majority of the ruling elite and its insti-tutions. The more centralized a society was, the easier this was, such as in the German duchies or principalities. There, a Reformation could almost occur by fiat. The more complex a society was in terms of governance, the more difficult it was to make the Reformation plausible and acceptable. Examples of this were the German and Swiss free cities or urban republics, oligarchies whose power depended on a large measure of consent from the other strata and institutions of society; or France, with its monarchy, it large episcopate, its aristocratic estates-general, its judiciary, its Paris *Parlement*, its regional *Parlements* and the special authority of the Sorbonne; or England, with its monarchy, its bicameral Parliament, its episcopate, its two ancient universities, its London law schools and so on; or Scotland, with its informal monarchy, its corporatist traditions, its Parliament, its lordships, its Gaelic clan-system, its three ancient universities and its episcopate; or Ireland, with its two, and soon to be effectively three or even four national/ethnic groups, its old colonial Anglo-Irish Parliament, earldoms, Gaelic petty kingdoms and clan-system, English and Irish language episcopates, and its multiple legal systems.

It is necessary, therefore, to emphasize that there was virtually nowhere outside the near-absolutist German duchies where the Reformation could be implemented just by persuading a sovereign ruler and his immediate circle. To succeed in the more complex political societies, it had in the event to be wedded to non-religious forces and factors. In the previous chapter, we saw how in Elizabethan England major trends with which the Reformation effectively went hand-in-hand were popular patriotism, nationalism and chauvinism, soon to mutate into imperialism. In Scotland, too, independence and liberation from diplomatic and even administrative subservience to the French was something the Reformation was able to capitalize on. Most spectacularly of all, in Holland, Protestantism and liberation from Spanish rule were inextricably fused, just as in Ireland, resistance to the Reformation increasingly went hand-in-hand with rebellion not so much against the Crown as against colonialism. In the Swiss cantons, intrinsically very conservative societies, the pro-Reformation forces had a special legal and psychological barrier to overcome. For the old Germanic law system held as axiomatic the idea that 'good law is old law'. This then made it inevitable that the Reformation was resisted on the grounds it was innovation, and therefore not good. Swiss Protestants therefore had to use every weapon in the arsenal of Christian Humanism to demonstrate that Reformation Christianity was not new; rather, it was the restoration of ancient original Christianity that had been smothered under the innovations and human traditions of the papal Church. Therefore it was the latter which was bad, and the former good. Such argumentation was soon transposed to a British context.

Metamorphosis: a makeover for Wales

The viability of the Reformation in Wales depended on an accompanying package of constitutional change (union with England), religious realignment (break with Rome), social revolution (appropriation of church patrimony), historical reorientation (ancient-British monarchy and Celtic Christianity redivivus), and cultural affirmation (use of Welsh language in worship). This occurred in a unique and remarkably successful manner, and secured at least acquiescence in the Reformation.

First of all then, what was Wales? It is probably the least well known of the four nations. Anyone brought up in Ireland, Scotland or England learns next to nothing about Wales and her history. It used to be associated with mining, male-voice choirs and rugby prowess, but now that even all those three are in decline, Wales may generate even more obliviousness. Its lack of high profile may well be linked to the fact that unlike the English, the Irish and the Scots, the submerged Welsh have not behaved (so) badly, and therefore have not hit the historical headlines.

Ethnically, Wales seemed to be the most homogenous area of the British Isles. The bulk of its people were descended directly from native pre-Roman Britons, but in the 400 years since its conquest, there were incursions of Anglo-Norman, English, and Irish settlers and immigrants, some of whom became assimilated. Somewhat analogous to Ireland (though not at all to the same extent) there were 'Englishries' and 'Welshries'. Flint county was divided into English and Welsh areas, some towns were divided into English and Welsh sectors and there was even a Flemish community at the port of Haverfordwest. Nor was 'Welshness' confined within the borders of Wales, since there were pockets of Welsh residents in Herefordshire and Shropshire.

The Celtic Welsh majority were the only identifiable survivors of the Anglo-Saxon invasions of Britain. They were separated from these barbarians by Offa's Dyke, somewhat further east than the present border of Wales. The name 'Wales' derives from the Anglo-Saxon description of the Welsh as 'welisc' or 'wealh', which means 'foreigner', just as 'welsch' is used still in some German-speaking areas to refer to those nearby who speak French.

In medieval times, Wales, like Ireland and parts of Scotland, became subject to the Anglo-Norman *imperium,* a process which reached its climax in 1282/3 when Welsh resistance was effectively overcome by Edward I. Wales was recolonized by an alien ruling minority, symbolized by the three hundred Anglo-Norman castles there. The Anglo-Norman principality in north and west Wales, necessary as the bridgehead to Ireland, became the property of the Anglo-Norman Crown. The rest of Wales was subdivided into semi-autonomous frontier or marcher lordships. Warfare remained endemic. With the new English Tudor expansionism married to the Reformation, Wales, too, became yet again subject to integrationist pressures. On the eve of the Reformation, the country was subject to the Crown, but not to Parliament, since it was not part of England as such. Royal authority was exercised directly in the principality, and indirectly in the marcher lordships.

Welsh Christian tradition was very long and unbroken, being rooted in Romano-British and Celtic antiquity. Norman rule put an end to much of what had remained of the indigenous Celtic Church, at least outwardly, thereby enforcing greater conformity with Roman Church practices.[1] Not only that, the Norman Church modernization programme made the four dioceses of Wales part of the province of Canterbury. These dioceses were Bangor and St Asaph in the north, and St David's and Llandaff in the south. This meant that all reforms in the English area of that province automatically applied to the Welsh Church. In other words, there was no autonomous Welsh Church. It is more correct before and after the Reformation to speak of an Anglo-Welsh Church.

Historians sometimes have a weakness for making reasons for change into a theory that applies across the board. Such theories can then be employed to explain the Reformation in large number of places. The unusual thing about Wales is that very few of the internal building blocks constituting current Reformation theories pre-existed there, excepting aristocratic and squirearchical cupidity. This may in turn help to explain why in most Reformation historiography, Wales is either simply not mentioned or relegated to a passing reference or footnote in connection with England. The country seems to have had hardly any of the 'usual' domestic preconditions attending a Reformation movement. It was a remote, largely agrarian and upland country. There was no capital city, no centre of government, no university, a relatively impoverished Church, local government was semi-feudal, it had a very limited urban and middle class (something normally crucial for Reformation interpreters), no printing press initially, no serious anticlericalism or widespread dissent, no tradition of social satire, and no excess of law and order. It did have an ancient European language and a sophisticated bardic culture much older than anything English. It had a mixture of folk-Catholicism or 'community Christianity' and paganism, a greedy self-seeking nobility and landed class, and most of its higher clergy were English, and so absent. Welsh clergy of talent were usually relocated in England. But in 1542, by which time the Welsh Church as part of the Archdiocese of Canterbury had been subjected to the Henrician settlement, it did have a Protestant martyr, Thomas Capper, burned at Cardiff for proclaiming Protestant ideas during one of Henry VIII's Catholic moods.[2]

Among what has been mentioned, there are some elements that could help breed Reformation sympathies, but no surplus of the classical ones. Yet Wales has confounded all the paradigms of historians by transforming within a century into a Protestant nation, if not quite a nation of Protestants. This would not have been predictable. Why Wales, for example, and not Lancashire or the bulk of Ireland? The story has been rescued from oblivion almost single-handedly during the last thirty-five years by Glanmor Williams. His approach cannot be called revisionist, since there was little before him to revise. His studies on the Welsh Reformation are among the best on the Reformation anywhere in the British Isles even if like some others, he tends to view the Reformation largely as an outgrowth of 'Renaissance Humanism' at the expense of the constitutive theological and spiritual revolution. Sensibly, he is committed to the view that the religious Reformation in Wales was in reality a 'long' one: 'The Reformation as a body of doctrine and belief could not come of age for most people until the eighteenth century had made many of them literate.'[3] And he remarks that by the beginning of the seventeenth century in Wales, 'the task of transforming the collective Christianity of the Middle Ages into individual believers with a strong sense of personal responsibility had hardly begun'.[4]

At the time of the Reformation, the Welsh bard and religious traditionalist, Thomas ab Ieuan ap Rhys, expressed allegedly majority opinion when he wrote:[5]

> We have been changed by the faith of the Saxons (= the English),
> Our hearts are not inclined towards it.

Another bard, Siôn Brwynog, spoke in around 1550 of the 'icy coldness' of the new faith, and the 'bitter blow' of witnessing the removal of the altars and sensual adjuncts of Catholic worship.[6] Such an opinion prevailed for some time, although Protestant doctrine did have strong bardic utterance in the work of Gruffudd ab Ieuan Lylwelyn Fychan[7] (*c.*1488–1553). This being the case initially, how and why did the Welsh dragon change its religious colour? Four factors amalgamated: the Renaissance, Celtic Christianity, the Reformation and a concept of the (Anglo-) Welsh or British monarchy.

Received popular and even educated opinion has traditionally dismissed the Reformation in Wales as the consequence of an English government fiat, leading to 'a sullen acceptance of the ordinances of the government'.[8] That is the convenient way of seeing things. In fact, however, while the English government obviously wanted and needed a Reformation in Wales, it was not brought about by a crude exercise of power. Rather, to make religious and political changes palatable to the Welsh, history and myth had to be rewritten. The chief political change that accompanied the Reformation in Wales was the union with England in the years from 1536 to 1543. This entailed complete administrative integration with Wales. The Welsh were accorded full political rights and parliamentary representation. English common law was now extended to Wales.

Why did all this meet with no obvious resistance? It was done in part by ideological massaging and flattery. Pre-eminent in this was the appeal to the Welsh origins of the quasi-messianic Tudors, who now possessed the English Crown. Henry Tudor, the father of Henry VIII, had come from Pembroke. His accession to the English throne in 1485 had already made English Crown rule more acceptable in Wales. The reason for this was that the Crown was now seen by the Welsh not as English, but 'British'. This was perceived as the restoration of the pre-Anglo-Saxon authentic British kingship of the legend of King Arthur, which had been hijacked by the English monarchy in the thirteenth century. The original mystic kingship had somehow survived in Wales, and now the myth was incarnated. It was no accident that Henry VII named his eldest son Arthur, and declared him Prince of Wales, the future title of male heirs to the throne. As it happened, Arthur died young. In view of this background, it was therefore easy to sell the idea of extending English parliamentary jurisdiction to Wales.

Since this was when Parliament was embarking upon 'Reformation' legislation, the ecclesiastical changes had to be sweetened for the Welsh in two ways. Firstly, the venal landed gentry class was made even richer as a result of the scramble for confiscated monastic land and property following the dissolution.[9] Even church tithes were allocated to wealthy laymen. This property revolution obviously enhanced loyalty to the Crown and to the formal Henrician settlement. As in Ireland, however, it did not necessarily entail mass conversion of the beneficiaries to Protestantism, though by the Elizabethan era the majority of the gentry adopted or conformed to the new faith. This made it virtually impossible for the traditionalist peasantry to avoid following suit, even if it meant following their exploiters. Bishop Richard Davies (*c.*1501–81) saw that lay material gain at the expense of the Church did not stimulate spiritual gain or facilitate true religion: 'The lust for the world's goods has drowned Wales today and impoverished every special quality and good virtue.'[10]

In the Henrician era, the chief episcopal pioneer and enforcer of reform in Wales was the enigmatic and somewhat maverick figure of William Barlow (d. 1568), Bishop of St David's from 1536–48, and an English ex-Augustinian.[11] He was fundamentally a zealous Protestant – 'a fervent eager beaver of the Protestant persuasion'[12] (if sometimes tempered by prudence) – and had spent some time on the Continent. After surviving the demise of his patrons, Anne Boleyn and Thomas Cromwell, he became a scarlet pimpernel in the Marian era. His polemical ardour resembles that of John Knox, but he lacked the latter's courage, constancy and fortitude as well as contempt for lay, profiteering pseudo-Protestants. He spearheaded the campaign in south-west Wales against Catholic religious icons perceived as idolatrous. From Barlow were also heard familiar Tudor tones about the need to advance 'civility' in Celtic societies, soon to be a major theme in the world of Gaeldom in Scotland and Ireland. As the episcopal blunt instrument of the Henrician Reformation in Wales (rather like his compatriot and fellow ex-Augustinian, Archbishop George Browne in Ireland), his activity and rhetoric in St David's highlighted the chief flaw of a statutory top-down reformation: without re-education, unforced persuasion and consent, it was insecure.

This became a priority on the eve of the Edwardine era, and so inaugurated the second phase of making the Reformation palatable in Wales. Apologetics for the new religious situation were managed in various ways by Welsh Protestant Christian Humanists, who had been mostly educated in England. They advanced the following argument: in the past, the captivity of Welsh Christianity to the Roman papacy, and bondage to the English had gone hand-in-hand. Now, in the context of equal rights with the English, and so Welsh emancipation, the Reformation meant the restoration of the original, allegedly Rome-free Celtic Christianity of antiquity. One sees the Erasmian – and Lutheran – contours of that argument: true Christianity is the original Christianity of antiquity, before it fell foul of the papacy and tyrannical human traditions masquerading as divine authority.

A famous exposition of this view is in the preface to the Welsh New Testament of 1567 translated by Richard Davies and William Salesbury[13] (see below) – the 'Epistle to the Welsh Nation',[14] composed by Davies. The Reformation is neither innovation nor heretical nor English, it argues. Rather it is the restoration of the golden age of original British Celtic Christianity that has been dormant in authentic Welsh tradition and identity, and was now being adopted by the English themselves.[15] Indeed, the *Epistle* reprises an old thirteenth-century myth that the ancient Britons were the first Gentile people to receive Gospel truth, namely from Joseph of Arimathea soon after Christ's resurrection. The general argument – the Reformation was the resuscitation of the originally transmitted apostolic faith – was accepted by many Christian Humanists and Protestant apologists in England and Wales, including Archbishop Matthew Parker,[16] Bishop John Jewel, who applied it to the Elizabethan Reformation and Church,[17] and publicist cleric, John Bale[18] (1495–1563). This was no mere antiquarianism. The motivation was apologetic, being in part a response to popular indignation and offence at the government campaign against the shrines and images of late medieval piety, for example, in Wales those of Derfel the Mighty in Merioneth, St Winifred's Well at Holywell, of the Virgin in the Rhondda, or of St David, etc. As elsewhere in Protestant Europe, the restorationist keynote, the 'retrospective repossession of history',[19] was essential to the credibility of the Reformation in general and to the justification of iconoclasm in particular. The repristination of perceived original pure religion, biblical and early Christian, was the objective.

A further component in the strategy arose out of a cultural reality that was also a matter of major concern to Protestant Christian Humanists. In Wales, about 90 per cent of the population were monoglot Welsh speakers, English speakers being mostly in the towns and eastern border areas. In Edward VI's reign, the English *Book of Common Prayer* was simply installed in Welsh churches by gormless English officials or sycophantic, anglophile Welsh agents. This was no more comprehensible than the Latin Mass. Nicholas Robinson, the Bishop of Bangor (1566–85), wrote to William Cecil saying that the poor progress of the reformed religion in Wales was due in part to 'the closing up of God's worde from [the people] in an unknown tongue [English]'.[20] Welsh Refomers, mindful of Erasmus' preface to the Greek New Testament where he pleads for the Scriptures in the vernacular, [21] went on the offensive. They convinced Parliament that the Reformation in Wales could not be inculcated through the medium of a foreign language, English. The leading Welsh Humanist scholar and religious reformer, William Salesbury (*c*.1520–*c*.1600), saw the issue of religious texts in Welsh as an evangelical imperative: 'The Welsh must have the Scripture in their own tongue, unless they wish to abandon completely the faith of Christ, unless they wish to have nothing at all to do with him, and unless they wish entirely to forget and extirpate his will.'[22] Such an aspiration was made realizable by a fact of strategic significance – all the early Elizabethan appointments to Welsh bishoprics were of men who were natives conversant with the language, namely Richard Davies, at St Asaph (1560–1), and then St David's (1561–81), Rowland Meyrick, at Bangor (1559–66), Thomas Young, at St David's (1560–1), and then Hugh Jones, at Llandaff (1567–74) after the demise of the last Marian bishop.

In consequence, central religious texts, including the Bible were eventually made available in Welsh, not in a desultory way, but as the consequence of official policy. An Act of Parliament in 1563 had stipulated that the Welsh hierarchy and neighbouring Bishop of Hereford should set about providing for Welsh translations of the Bible and that the *Book of Common Prayer* in Welsh be placed in all parish churches[23] – though the bigger game plan was transition to English-only, in line with the Crown's anglicization and uniformity policy.

The long-term effect of this was, as Glanmor Williams has put it, that 'more than anything else, the Reformation kept Wales Welsh'.[24] The Welsh Bible was to help the Welsh language from degenerating to a patois, and did for the written language and its culture what Luther's Bible did for German.[25]

The process of providing Welsh religious texts was initiated earlier by Sir John Price (Prys) of Brecon, one of the emerging Protestant Humanist elite. A member of the gentry class, he had bought the priory in Brecon after the dissolution. In 1546 he published the first Welsh printed book, *Yny Lhyvyr Hwnn* [In This Book].[26] This was a primer with the three traditional requirements constituting minimal Christian knowledge, namely the Apostles' Creed, the Lord's Prayer and the Ten Commandments, along with other items. In the preface, Price denounced the clergy for failure to give religious instruction, the source of widespread ignorance. But Bishop Robinson of Bangor complained that the trouble was that most of the clergy were themselves undereducated, and too old to be sent back to school. In Price's primer, evident is the typical Reformation mutation. By this, untutored implicit faith in the good offices of the Church cedes to explicit individual faith based on personal knowledge and understanding of the Word of God in Scripture.

The contribution of William Salesbury was more than that of a Christian Humanist concerned to make core biblical and devotional texts available in Welsh. For he was also committed to specifically Protestant doctrine. In 1550 he published two works of controversial theology. The first, in Welsh, was a justification of clerical marriage (legalized in 1549), and cited the precedent in early medieval native Welsh law – the 'Law of Hywel'. The second, in English, *The Baterie* [apparatus] *of the Popes Botereulx* [buttress] *commonlye called the High Altar* (1550),[27] was an attack on the Mass as sacrifice and as a rite for both the living and the dead. This coincided with the order of the Edwardian government Council to remove and destroy altars from churches.

In 1551, Salesbury published a Welsh version of the New Testament readings for the Communion service in the *Prayer Book* – *Kynniver llith a ban*. And in 1567, in co-operation with Thomas Huet and Richard Davies, one of about twelve former Marian exiles on the Continent, he published the first complete Welsh New Testament, translated from Erasmus' Greek text.[28] A Welsh businessman in London, Humphrey Toy, paid for the project. Moreover, in the same year they also published the Welsh *Book of Common Prayer* – *Llyfr Gweddi Gyffredin*.[29] While these were milestones in Welsh history, the immediate impact was not one of great success. This was largely because Salesbury's classical bias resulted in him Latinizing Welsh orthography, so that clergy read badly, and the people heard wrongly.

As in Ireland, there was procrastination over the appearance of the whole Bible in the vernacular. This was due to tensions between 'policy' and ultimate objectives on the one hand, and pragmatic evangelical considerations on the other. When the entire Welsh Bible did emerge, it was regarded as highly successful. It was published in 1588 by a vicar, later bishop, and former student of St John's College, Cambridge, William Morgan (*c.*1545–1604).[30] It included a revised version of the Salesbury–Davies New Testament. Written in authentic contemporary Welsh, it was acclaimed by Welsh bards and authors like Morris Kyffin, and theologians as a masterpiece of textual scholarship and Welsh prose.

When one talks of the Welsh Bible, it is 'Morgan's Bible' that is meant. Welsh was the thirteenth vernacular European language into which the entire Bible was translated and it was 'the only non-state language of Protestant Europe to become the medium of a published Bible within a century of the Reformation'.[31] Yet, ironically, the publication of this Bible was accelerated (relatively) due to the activities of a native Welsh, increasingly radical puritan in England, John Penry[32] (see Chapter 4). In 1586, Penry persuaded a Welsh puritan Member of Parliament, Edward Downlee, to present a petition to Parliament: *The Aequity*. This urged the promotion of biblical and evangelical preaching in Wales, necessary to pre-empt Catholic revival. That struck a chord in London at a time when there was talk of a Spanish 'Enterprise of England'. Penry's writings on Wales did not fail to make such a point.[33] Not only that, the authorities, equally concerned about puritan anti-episcopal agitation, seemed to have decided not to leave enhanced Welsh evangelism to the puritans. For the final facilitating push to have the Welsh Bible completed, published, and distributed to every church came from Archbishop Whitgift, who had ultimate spiritual responsibility *ex officio*.

A further important work that secured an, if not the, Anglican future for Wales was the translation by the writer, Morris Kyffin, of John Jewel's *Apology of the Church of England* in 1595.[34] Moreover, Welsh-language homiletics were given a boost with the (belated!) translation of the Tudor

Book of Homilies in 1606 by Edward James, vicar of Llangatwg-iuxta-Neath.[35] Yet a Protestant work in Welsh towards the end of the century claimed that the new Church of Wales by that time was less than half-reformed in regard to ministry, evangelism, piety, and religious education and moral improvement. This, allowing for an element of unrealistic expectations, is alleged in the preface to the translation (1595) of Miles Coverdale's *A Spiritual and most Precious Pearl* by Huw Lewys, a vicar.[36] The spiritual torpitude of the population is deplored, as is the laziness of the bishops and clergy.

Catholic expiry, and balance

The Reformation package for a new Wales was composed of various elements: union with England and loyalty to a British Crown along with full legal and political rights, a reformed Church, Scriptures, liturgy and preaching in Welsh, an appeal to Celtic Christian antiquity, an enriched landed class of magnate, squires, and justices guaranteeing the external Reformation in the localities, and special provision for Welsh students at Jesus College, Oxford.[37] None of these things in themselves of course made Wales Protestant nor even especially Christian by conviction. They did make Wales politically and culturally reformed, locking it into Protestant England and Britain. It shared the same developments as Elizabethan England, whereby Catholicism, sedition, obscurantism, political subservience and foreign threats came to be seen as the same thing. However, in the spiritual and religious spheres, the arduous task of instructing the people through teaching and preaching remained. As with many other places, it is not possible to speak of a popular religious revival, chiefly due to lack of material and human resources.

During the Marian period, many tears do not appear to have been shed on the passing of the Protestant order, whose success even under Edward was only nominal. Catholic bardic utterances were not slow to welcome Mary's policies. As in Ireland, it is hard, however, to know if the 'natural propensity' of the bulk of the people towards the old faith was due to conviction Catholicism, or to hostility to religious ideas and practices perceived as 'English' – especially as most Reformation bishops in Wales up to 1553 were English imports. Nor is there evidence that the three Protestant martyrdoms in Marian Wales provoked as much public sympathy as similar executions in England did. These martyrs were Robert Ferrar (*c.*1500–55),[38] an ex-Augustinian, married, and moderate Protestant Bishop of St David's, executed in Carmarthen,[39] Rawlins White, a fisherman, executed in Cardiff in 1555, and William Nichol, executed in Haverfordwest in 1558.[40]

Subsequently, however, even limited Counter-Reformation activity in Wales met with no significant uptake due to lack of resources. Yet Flintshire and Monmouthshire remained, like Lancashire in England, relatively strong centres of residual Catholicism and attracted Catholic refugees from elsewhere. Recusant gentry families, particularly in border areas, continued for several generations to harbour the old religion, and hinder the spread of protestantization.[41] The Catholic Somerset Earls of Worcester provided support for the Catholic interest. Some Jesuit activity was organized from Cwm, on the border of Monmouthshire and England, and where a small Welsh Jesuit college was established. There was some Counter-Reformation or Catholic literature produced in Welsh. From Douai there emerged in 1568 a catechetical book, *Athrawaeth Gristnogawl* (Christian Doctrine), and translated by Morys Clynnog[42] from the Latin original of a Spanish Jesuit, John Polanco. Clynnog also hoped that Catholic restoration in Wales would occur by foreign invasion. In the area of spirituality, a notable tract on loving God appeared in 1585, *Y Drych Cristianogawl* (Christian Mirror), possibly composed by a Douai alumnus and Catholic tractarian, Robert Gwyn,[43] and reputedly printed in Wales. And again emanating from Douai, Roger (or Rhosier) Smith's translation of some books from the Catholic catechism, *Summa doctrinae christianae*, by the German Jesuit, Peter Canisius, appeared in 1609. Lastly, in the 1620s, Thomas à Kempis' *De imitatione Christi* was translated by a squire and Catholic convert, Hugh Jones of Gwenynog. These men, and the people they wrote for, were Wales' first reasonably numerous dissenters and nonconformists.

Any signs of organized resistance, as in north Wales, provoked firm responses. The consequence was that Wales did have two Catholic religious martyrs. One was a schoolmaster and anti-Reformation song writer, Richard Gywn (or White), executed in 1584 at Wrexham, the other a Douai-trained priest, William Davies, executed in 1593 at Beaumaris.[44] But in general the Counter-Reformation's complacency about Welsh popular Catholic loyalty as well as papal indifference impaired what internal resistance campaign there was.[45] On the whole, however, Welsh Catholic resistance, whether at home or from exiles abroad was haphazard and desultory, and all the odds were stacked against it as long as the Crown and state remained Protestant. Only a quarter of Welsh priests trained at Douai or Rheims returned to Wales, a reflection rather than a cause of failure.[46] Tensions between the Jesuit Order and Rome concerning overall Counter-Reformation missionary strategy and priorities did not help either. Remaining committed Catholics in Wales were slowly deprived of oxygen. Anyway, the new Catholicism, Tridentine and rigorously conscientious, may not have been to everyone's taste.

As elsewhere, apart from committed religious activists or firm believers, the bulk of the people was inert, gradually conforming and drifting into the ambit at least of the Protestant Established Church.[47] From the point of view of the Crown however, enough had been achieved, despite the ineptitude of many clergy (as in England and Ireland), the depletion of church finance, the temporal preoccupations of many bishops, and a dearth of apostolic and evangelical vocation and charisma among them.

Paramount was the defence of the English Protestant kingdom on the western hinterland of mainland Britain, as well as progress in integration and uniformity, outwardly at least. Thereby the assimilation of Wales in government and religion, in form and face at least, was achieved without demolishing its essential cultural distinctiveness – or maybe that was the reluctant price to be paid?

CHAPTER 6

Reformation in Ireland

The anomaly

In turning to Ireland one encounters a major paradox. This is not so much to be defined in terms of the country being a unique exception to the *cuius regio eius religio* principle (the religion of the ruler obtains), though the permanence was relatively unique. For under the Catholic Mary Stewart, Scotland experienced an analogous discrepancy for seven years from 1560 to 1567, as did France under the (initially) reformed Henri IV for five years from 1589 to 1593, never mind Protestant areas of Germany from 1530 onwards under the ultimate authority of the Catholic Emperor, Charles V and his successors. The incongruity of the Irish situation was that although the Reformation is conventionally perceived in terms of failure, an aborted event or a non-event, or a surviving runt kept alive by a life-support machine sponsored by the British 'state', it nonetheless made a practically irreversible, if debatable impact on the country. The miscarriage is reflected in the fact that the majority of the population dissented, and so did not conform to the confession of the central political authority, its local representatives and followers. In terms of ultimate development, this majority was to be around 75 per cent, not as large as it might have been due to Protestant immigration after 1603. Notwithstanding, the notion and expression of the 'Irish Reformation' is usually eschewed as a solecism – though other areas of Europe where the Reformation failed even more comprehensively have oddly engendered such expressions as the 'Spanish Reformation', the 'Italian Reformation', and perhaps more understandably, the 'French Reformation'. Conventionally the Reformation in Ireland has been evaluated as a 'policy' from the 'top' and from 'outside', and so unpopular and alien.

Irrespective of one's semantic choice in speaking of the Reformation in Ireland, the topic has had low status in modern general or secular histories of Ireland. It traditionally does not go much beyond its association with the Tudor and Stewart attempts to pacify, rule and legislate, as well as resistance to them. Apart from the well-known legislative programme, one normally has to look to older ecclesiastical and confessional histories of contrasting kinds to gain substantive information (and misinformation) on Reformation-era churches, activity, theology and piety in Ireland. In the early twentieth century there were some studies on the Reformation there, such as by Myles V. Ronan (Roman Catholic and antipathetic),[1] George V. Jourdan (Liberal Protestant and affirmative),[2] and Henry Holloway (Anglican Protestant, non-polemical).[3] The general received Catholic perception was reinforced by works such as James MacCaffrey's *History of the Catholic Church from the Renaissance to the French Revolution.* Volume Two surveys – with commendable realism, however – the Reformation in Ireland in the context of the entire 'British Isles' (the author uses this expression). Little further progress was made until the 1970s and this stagnation was reflected in most of the literature in the interim. One example is the otherwise admirable and widely praised textbook used in schools and various colleges all over Ireland that appeared in 1967: *The Course of Irish History.*[4] Derived from a series of lectures on southern Irish television (RTE), it was reprinted many times in subsequent years. Its 404 pages contained one and a half pages on the Reformation and Counter-Reformation, without any indication about the substantive issues involved. The further 'revised and expanded' editions of 1984 and 1994 did not change matters.

Such monumental reticence and historical script-editing suggest a reflexive censorship grounded in a philosophy of civil reductionism, vaguely benign and 'non-controversial' though the intention might have been. It is attributable ultimately to a concept of Church-controlled religious education in public schools that has traditionally prevailed in Ireland, Catholic or Protestant. This concept has ensured that religious education is essentially edification rather than imparting knowledge and encouraging understanding of alternatives. Such education has been religious, not about religion, which as a topic of informed discussion has been marginalized in mainstream culture as an almost taboo subject. Unfortunately this side-stepping is also reflected in the Oxford *New History of Ireland,* throughout which there is plenty on Churches, churchmen, religious politics, popular religious movements, etc. but little on formative religious thought or theologies. This exemplifies how the modern 'holistic' approach is often exclusive, influenced by a largely, if usually undeclared, semi-'positivist' philosophy of history (see Chapter 1).

To compound matters, general histories of the Reformation in Europe have rarely anything more than a word of two on the Reformation in Ireland either. A recent writer, Samantha Meigs, was right to complain about this in her recent book, *The Reformations in Ireland.* She is understandably so convinced of this, however, that included among some examples cited are the *Handbook of European History* edited by Brady, Oberman and Tracy (see below, Bibliography I). Here she finds 'only three references to Ireland'.[5] There are in fact three albeit modest pages (including bibliography) on Ireland in that volume, far more than one might normally expect. Despite the strictly imposed word-limit of the chapter within which those pages occur, the unusual little window opened there was included at the suggestion of one of the editors.[6]

'A full and impartial *History of the Reformation in Ireland* is still a desideratum in our literature.' James Seaton Reid, the Ulsterman who was Professor of Church History in the University of Glasgow, made this Rankian observation in the middle of the nineteenth century.[7] It is still essentially true, but in recent times much of the forbidding undergrowth has been gradually cleared away. New developments in historiography since the 1970s have contributed to the putting of the Reformation in Ireland on to the main agenda of Reformation history. This has released the presentation of the matter in Ireland from being a conventionally blinkered history of intruded Protestantism and reactive, reconstituted Catholicism. The development is also related to the (partial) breakdown of 'national' and 'denominational' and 'confessional' accounts of history, the New British/Irish history, and to the rediscovery of sixteenth-century pan-European, cosmopolitan Renaissance and Christian perspectives, etc.

Accordingly, there has been much specialist research in recent times into the apparently unpromising and stony ground of the all-Irish experience of the Reformation. Most of this research, mainly historicist in flavour (with positivist tendencies), is confined to one-dimensional political, social, economic, institutional, and religio-cultural contexts and conflicts. Consequently, it is shaped by a strong sense of distinctiveness and by perceptions of power struggles, a tragi-comedy of errors, fiascos, and ultimately heroic resistance. Except in association with 'identities' of various kinds, consideration of theologies, pieties, spiritualities and religious sensibilities, whether of the elite or of the people, still tend to be evaded or approached diffidently, though there have been some pertinent and excellent contributions in that direction.

It is on the face of it extraordinarily ironical that a recent writer (Raymond Gillespie), who stresses that he is no theologian, should call for the rehabilitation, or even introduction of 'religion' as a subject of paramount relevance in the study of early modern Ireland.[8] His own religio-historical method (though applied more to the seventeenth century onwards) is linked to the genre of the history of mentalities – the subjective appropriation, or the sub-Christian misappropriation and functioning of inherited religio-theological ideas and dogmas. In other words, addressed is the all-pervasive, non-rational, religious reality of people's lives. Consideration of this, he argues, should be rescued from folklorism and other twilight zones to enable the diminution of huge blind spots in the eyes of rigidly historicist and positivist historians. This would not, of course, provide all the elusive answers. Rather, it might shed more light. Most people of all levels in sixteenth-century Ireland, like everywhere else, were not existentially mono-dimensional. On the contrary, they were also consciously concerned with the moods, judgements and actions of God, even if only tacitly.

Gillespie's plea can be endorsed by recalling that the Reformation intended to offer a corrective to the traditional understanding of the divine–human relationship. This envisaged human co-operation with God by means of works generating the merit that inclines the Deity to be favourable. The alternative conception, in the fundamental area of the means of appropriating salvation (faith or grace alone, unmerited pardon, works are consequential, not conditional), was not rooted in Renaissance or Christian Humanism (or 'English heresy'). Rather it represented a radicalization by Luther of pre-existing streams and tensions within traditional Catholic doctrine. Such acutely Augustinian ideas were anything but an intended precursor of the Enlightenment, 'modern man', and personal religious subjectivism, as the writings of any of the Reformers amply testify. They urged subjection to the objective *divine* Word rather than to its distorted perception – as they maintained – in the subjective words of *human* teaching embodied in much of church dogmatic Tradition. Therein lay the challenge and the crux of the matter.

The changing faces of Ireland

If a Martian had landed in sixteenth-century Ireland, asking who was in charge and to be conducted thence, he might have received very different suggestions. For the land was not an integrated nation, people, kingdom or jurisdiction, like most others in people's imaginations. 'Ireland', somewhat like modern Afghanistan, was largely a geographical expression, and had never really been otherwise. It was a land of 'sundry folks', and was destined at the end of the century to be even more so. Even contemporary political discourse in Ireland has begun to adapt its vocabulary to recognize this partially continuing reality. This is seen in the increasing use of the tantalizing phrase 'island of Ireland' in recent times. There is possibly a link between this and the usage of an Irish historian thirty years ago, Robert Dudley Edwards. In relation to Ireland not just in the sixteenth century, but before and afterwards, he spoke of the 'community' of Ireland or even more neutrally, the 'inhabitants' of Ireland. Edwards urged caution against misleading historical and current perceptions of Ireland conditioned in terms of 'oneness'.[9] Accordingly, no matter which oneness one selects or invents (usually in terms of 'destiny'), one inevitably excludes other sections of the citizenry or 'traditions'.

On the eve of the Reformation, Ireland (like many other areas of Europe) was politically particularist, and so presented a plethora of lordships, that is, territorial units or districts of jurisdiction. According to estimates, there were about sixty different jurisdictions. Technically, the whole of Ireland had been a dominion or lordship of the Norman-English Crown since the Norman Conquest in the twelfth century. The title 'Lord of Ireland' had been allegedly conferred on the English monarchy by Pope Adrian IV. But this lordship was never very effective beyond the central eastern sector of the country. The reality was that although there was an 'Irish Parliament' in Dublin, the country was divided into various dominions or authorities. These were partly old-colonial Anglo-Norman (or Old English or Anglo-Irish), partly Gaelic, especially in the north, the west, and the south-west, and partly a mixture of both in various border or marcher areas. The surviving core of the old Anglo-Norman lordship and colony was the Pale.[10] This was an area bounded by an arc of about forty miles any direction of Dublin (excluding the no-go area of the Wicklow Mountains). Here royal authority was generally effective, and English law was observed. Acting as buffers between the Pale and the Gaelic lordships were the three large Anglo-Norman earldoms, which had become fairly assimilated to Gaeldom, and so were now hybrid. Though they recognized the king as Lord of Ireland, and acted as Crown officials, they were almost autonomous in their own areas. The chief families possessing these earldoms were the Fitzgeralds (two branches), and the Butlers, otherwise known after their territorial earldoms, Kildare, Desmond and Ormond.

To this group can be added various small coastal towns other than Dublin. These were loyalist but effectively self-governing, like Galway and Limerick, Cork and Waterford, Wexford, Drogheda, Carlingford and Carrickfergus near modern Belfast. In the Gaelic territories, the chief rulers were, in the north, the O'Neills, the O'Donnells, the Macdonnells and the McMahons; in the west it was the O'Connors and the O'Briens, in the south the MacCarthys, the O'Sullivans, the MacMurroughs and the Kavanaghs. They usually simply ignored the Dublin government, though occasionally some of them would acknowledge the English lordship out of political expediency and commercial interest. The Gaelic world was united only by language and religion, not having any effective political unity. Hereditary military, bardic and even clerical castes and dynasties dominated it. Actual power lay in the localities and in the potent social control mechanisms of clan and kinship. As in much of Scotland, feuding rather than parleying was the more familiar method of conflict resolution.

The Ulster Gaelic world was also geographically, culturally and politically linked closely to Scottish Gaeldom, united by a common sea and within sight of each other. Successive Tudor and Stewart governments were determined to break this shared identity and communication route over the Sea of Moyle and the North Channel, since potentially they stood in the way of Anglo-British aggrandizement. The strategy or aspiration was to divide, rule and erase by assimilation the cultural unity extending from Deeside, Sutherland and the Hebrides through most of Ireland to the Dingle Peninsula in the far south-west. Obviously this strategy was not a propitious package with which to commend the Reformation.

Overall then, 'Ireland' was pluralistic, balkanized, over-endowed with fault-lines, and so constantly unstable and troubled, because there was no one really dominant power. What happened in the sixteenth century is that the Tudors and the Stewarts committed themselves to making Crown authority in the whole of Ireland a reality. And since the Crown was now wedded to the Reformation, imposing Crown rule more effectively in Ireland entailed introducing the Reformation as well. This policy was not unique to Ireland. It was part of the general Tudor policy of centralizing authority in the Crown dominions, whether the north of England, Wales or Ireland. The appeal to *imperium* entailed policies of uniformity directed from the sovereign top. Just as the Tudors eliminated over-weening magnates in Wales and northern England, they did the same thing in Ireland. This meant eliminating the authority of the Earls of Kildare, and when that was done, by 1534, it resulted in English rule in Ireland being much more interventionist. To ensure maximum protection from likely foreign attack, the new England had to expand its power and authority in Wales and Ireland, as well as its influence in Scotland. Something, for example, that caused anxiety was the flow of Catholic Gaelic Scots into north-east Ulster, seen as foreign intrusion. But even more feared was the prospect of Ireland being occupied by the Spanish or French, especially since certain Gaelic chieftains, not averse to turning to other foreign powers for aid, were making overtures in those directions.

Henry VIII's declaration in 1541 that Ireland was now a kingdom, and not just a lordship in the gift of the Roman papacy, is to be seen in this light.[11] The king claimed to govern the whole island. This resulted in the Tudor policy of anglicization, the extension of common law, subjecting the whole Irish Church to the royal supremacy, and then introducing new settlers or planters from England (initiated by the Catholic Queen Mary). These settlers may be referred to as New English. The policy also involved intermittent military campaigns. The climax of this at the end of the century was the enormously expensive nine-years' war by Elizabeth against the Earl of Tyrone, Hugh O'Neill of Ulster, chief remaining grandee and last bastion of unconquered Gaelic Ireland. His appeal to the old Anglo-Irish (still largely Catholic) element in the country in the name of 'faith and fatherland' evoked no significant response due to residual loyalism. The conquest of the north was completed by 1603, the starting-point of modern Irish history. The immediate outcome was the plantation of Ulster, instituted by Elizabeth's successor, James VI & I, now also King of Ireland. Since the Ulster Gaelic nobles had forfeited their lands in the war and fled the country (1607), their lands were now given to Protestant settlers from England, lowland (largely) Scotland, Wales, and the Isle of Man. With the introduction now of New Scots, etc. one could henceforth refer globally to all new planters and settlers as 'British'.

The general outcome of these policies was that by the early seventeenth century, Ireland had become more tangibly subject to Crown authority. One further result was that the communities of Ireland had become even more complex than seventy-five years before. Now there were not only

Irish Gaels, Old English, others in between, and Scots Gaels, but also New English and New Scots. There was also a new subdivision of religion, represented not just by the minority Protestant episcopalian state Church of Ireland and majority Catholicism, but also by presbyterian dissenters, largely but not exclusively among the New Scots.

All this has cut a long story short. Ireland being a Crown domain, all religious legislation passed in England was also passed in the Anglo-Irish Dublin Parliament. This meant that, officially, what England and Wales experienced under Henry VIII, Edward VI, Mary I, Elizabeth I, and James I was replicated in Ireland by law, such as the dissolution of the monasteries, the introduction of the *Book of Common Prayer*,[12] clerical marriage, and of course the royal supremacy (1534). The monarch was not just the head or supreme governor of the Church of England, but also of the notional 'Church of Ireland'. There was inevitably an element of charade and farce in all this: two parallel Churches, a small statutory and public one, and an unofficial large one, often in the shadows. For until the Stewart era, the new Church could only claim serious reality where Crown authority was effective, like the Pale centred in Dublin. Otherwise the country remained largely Catholic, in defiance partly of unpalatable religious reform and partly of government authority, seen as interfering.

Pre-Reformation religious features

Irrespective of evidence that suggests flourishing popular religiosity at least, and vitality in the ministries of the Observant friars, the pre-Reformation Christianity in Ireland was just as much in need of reform as anywhere else, though possibly more so.[13] However, because of the lack of consensus on what was legitimately 'Christian', the concept of 'de-christianization' remains controversial. The Irish Church was certainly in need of episcopal downsizing, there being thirty-five sees compared to twelve in Scotland and twenty-three in England. Paradoxically, there is little (attested) anticlericalism or church critique of significance. However, one document ascribed to 1515 does report that the sorry state of the country is due to a decline of Christianity, and that responsible for this are the clergy, all of whom, save the mendicant friars, rarely preach the Word of God; material rather than spiritual profit is the order of the day.[14] Such a formulation is characteristic of Christian Humanist criticism anywhere in Europe before the Reformation, and anticipates themes taken up by the Reformers. The general lack of reported anticlericalism in Ireland may well be related to the very limited urban development, and so a sparsity of the artisan classes as well as of the 'middling and industrious sorts'. Among such groups elsewhere in Europe, criticism of clergy was usually vociferous. Anyway, as result of the tight social intertwining between church and locality in an Ireland that was overwhelmingly rural, and its implication for church appointments, denouncing clergy would involve risks.

There does seem to have been a serious dearth of preaching by secular clergy, of catechizing, a liturgical decline, a recession in vocations, and general clerical mediocrity.[15] In the 1520s, the Earl of Kildare, hardly a zealous Lutheran, wrote with gusto to Cardinal Wolsey, Henry VIII's chief minister, that 'if the king do not provide a remedy, there will be no more Christianity [in Tipperary and Kilkenny] than in the middle of Turkey'.[16] Such a lamentation was universal, referring as it does to abuses, degeneration and superstition. Another contemporary Catholic account from about 1515 retells the story of St Brigid asking her guardian angel about the state of religion in Ireland.[17] The reply focused on the 'lapse of the souls of the Christian folk of that land, who were falling down into Hell as fast as any shower of hailstones'. And there was the old medieval story of the Archbishop of Armagh telling the pope how a soothsayer had found out from the Devil that Ireland provided most of the citizens of Hell. This was because everyone there robs everyone else, never making restitution, and so dying outside the state of grace. One did not have to be a Protestant to express such alarm. As elsewhere in late medieval Catholic Europe, there was manifestly more religion than there was Christianity, more uninformed faith, spiritual self-concern and pursuit of the other-worldly than there was of essential Christian knowledge, ethical regeneration and sanctified living.[18]

In-house church or other religious testimonies about developments, if any, in late medieval Irish piety and theologies informing it are exiguous.[19] However, in 1571 there was published in Dublin a broadsheet of a fifteenth-century Gaelic sermon in poetic form – *God's Patience a Portent of Anger* – composed by an Observant Franciscan poet, Pilib Bocht (Ó hUiginn).[20] It does reflect one of the major strains of reformist thinking elsewhere in the Church of the earlier era, as found notably in Geiler of Kaisersberg (1445–1510), the Strasbourg preacher: the path to salvation is that of individual moral reformation and improvement. Bocht's poem declares that ethical renewal is the last chance, the only way to respond to the wrath of God and threat of imminent apocalyptic judgement; charity and social concern, the touchstone of Christian living, are mandatory and must be reactivated to obviate individual or collective doom.

The entire theology and piety of the poem reflects precisely that in which Martin Luther himself was schooled and then rejected. For example: the stress on the angry God, the concept of divine justice and righteousness as orientated to reward and punishment, and a piety grounded in fear and anxiety. As Bocht says: 'His justice it is that is to be feared most',[21] stressing the image of Christ as judge. Further: the exhortation to good works by way of expiation; the understanding of 'conscience' as that which condemns or at least makes aware of the power of sin, and so on. Luther's Augustinianism and interest in the grace theology of Paul helped prepare him turn his back on such a holiness theology of deterrence, characterized variously as 'Occamistic Nominalism', 'New Pelagianism', etc. The exhortation was to exercise as far as possible one's innate ability (*facere quod in se est*). And it was compatible with the perfectionist strain in the old Celtic tradition of Christian endeavour, which at some levels had survived in the Irish Church.

Bocht's complaints, and historians' acknowledgements of the 'deep shadows'[22] over late medieval Irish Christianity, do however suggest that subsequent intense devotion to Catholicism of the majority of people in Ireland is a post-Reformation development. This was derived from a Counter-Reformation religious revival or recatholicization. In other words, early modern Irish Catholicism reveals a diminishing continuum with certain syncretic traditions and deformed pieties of the past.

One systemic problem in the pre-Reformation Church in Ireland was that it was binary or 'divaricate'.[23] There was the Church of the 'English', and that of the 'Irish', divided between native and colonist, Gaelic and Old English, invader and invaded. Consequently there were, culturally, various kinds of clergy: English-speaking clergy, Palesmen or from England, who worked in anglophone areas only; Gaelic clergy who worked in Gaelic areas only; Gaelic clergy who were allowed, providing they were loyal, to work among Gaelic enclaves in English-speaking areas; then, bilingual Gaelic clergy who also worked in English-speaking parishes, providing they too were loyal. There were also some Old English clergy, particularly bishops, who were bilingual such as Richard Creagh (d. 1585). He became Catholic archbishop in the predominantly Gaelic church province of Armagh in Ulster (1564–7). Therefore seeds of conflict were obvious, and often flowered in various contexts. The Reformation did not create that tension, it only exacerbated and politicised it irreversibly. This was ironic in light of the fact that the Henrician reforms, in particular the Act of Supremacy of 1534, had envisaged a unitary Church for the whole of Ireland – *hibernica ecclesia*, to supersede the traditional bifurcated Church.

Another problem worth noting is this: in the Church of Gaelic Ireland, there was striking secularisation of the ecclesiastical patrimony. The repercussion of this was that bishoprics, abbacies and other beneficed church offices were largely dynastic and hereditary. This also meant that such higher clergy (often Oxbridge educated),[24] were at least *de facto* married; further, that the Church *inter Hibernicos* and her assets were effectively controlled by the Gaelic aristocracy – something that was condoned by the papacy, at least before the Council of Trent. Further, direct lay appropriation of church lands in Gaeldom had also been occurring long before the Reformation. This overall situation is important. It helps surely explain why the Reformation provided no significant material inducement for the Gaelic magnates, as it did in England, Scotland and Wales. The Irish Gaelic and Anglo-Gaelic laity already had considerable control of church lands and property, and so exercised patronage. Hence their support for a Protestant Reformation could not be purchased so easily as allegedly elsewhere. This might be interpreted as good news for Catholic solidarity and survival in Ireland. However, historians seem to agree that the consequences of an essentially privatized church of big-family and feudal owners were not enhancing for pastoral, ecclesiastical and monastic life. Local and parochial caesaropapism prevailed. Tridentine papalism aimed to rectify this.

This leads to another related point: As might be expected, the centralizing and line-management policy of Tudor rule in Ireland met with opposition from the old English colonial class there, since their power and status were threatened by it. Therefore they tended to be unco-operative in church reform as well. This led Henry VIII and his successors to send in New English officials and agents to implement policy. They were rewarded with wealth and lands following the dissolution of the Irish monasteries. This then left the Old English gentry aggrieved, since they had benefited less comprehensively from redistribution and impropriation than their equivalent class in Britain. It also meant that they had no overwhelming financial motive to support a Reformation either. Their deprivation in this respect was only relative, nonetheless. The majority of the Old English continuing Catholic landowners profited to some extent from the uncatholic spoliation of church real estate.

Making sense of the Reformation in Ireland

Almost inevitably, research on the (Protestant) Reformation in Ireland is constrained by being largely a reflection on general failure – the extent, definition and explanation of it. The Reformation secured only limited or nominal allegiance from the Old English population. While they were largely prepared to go along with the conservative Henrician Reformation (half of the higher clergy accepted the royal supremacy in the Church),[25] they had a more openly oppositional attitude to the more substantively Protestant Edwardine and Elizabethan Reformations. The Gaelic population showed even less enthusiasm by all accounts, except those closest to English influence. The Reformation, or commitment to it, became confined largely to the privileged new Protestant Ascendancy and their immediate tenants among whom could be converted Old English and Gaels, whether by prudential self-interest or by genuine response to evangelization. Later, the tenants included significant numbers of dissenting Scottish (and some English) Presbyterians too. Many Scots also simply conformed, since not all of them, even in the seventeenth century, were congenitally Presbyterian. The overall paradox was unusual in Europe: a practising Catholic majority, increasingly subject to civil and social exclusion, in a Protestant state.

Why – and how – did the bulk of the people remain Catholic? There are many hypotheses about this. For example, the divinely ordained

Catholicism of the native Irish people; Protestantism only meant English rule and Scottish infiltration; Catholicism meant Irish or national resistance. Other views are that the eventual Calvinist episcopalian Church of Ireland had little mission incentive, since the Gaelic Irish, perceived as wild and uncivilized, were regarded as eschatologically reprobate and so not of the elect, beyond the Covenant of grace, and therefore not worth the effort. Further, that the Catholic faith was the last bulwark and ultimate resort of conscience, never to be surrendered, of a 'defenceless' wronged people in the face of brutish British colonialism and oppression. Such typologies are largely traditional, and mostly sterile.

Modern research has cleared the stale air, and revamped the terms of the discussion. The contentious question is this: 'Did Protestantism fail because Catholicism succeeded, or did Catholicism succeed because Protestantism failed'? Was Catholic survival and perseverance due to the resoluteness of the old and indefectible faith, implanted ineradicably in the 'Irish' psyche; or to the efficacious vigour of revival Catholicism and the Counter-Reformation that operated unopposed in many areas of the country? Or was it explicable by a dream-team marriage with the old language and culture in Gaeldom in particular as well as with the struggle against colonialism and the Crown; the latter reflected in the non-compliance of local barons and magnates with Government policy? Some modern writers are unhappy with variations of the persistent 'two-way sorting'.[26] This is: what happened was that on the whole, Gaelic Irish and Old English, though material losers, remained Catholic, spiritually reinvigorated by the Counter-Reformation, as a kind of separatist, or nationalist or conservative protest and identity badge of 'faith and fatherland'. In contrast, the new colonialists and planters from England and Scotland came as Protestants, material winners, and centralizers determined to retain their status, so that they were umbilically loyal to the Crown.

Against the background of this hypothesis, the disputatious Bottigheimer–Bradshaw exchanges,[27] heightened rather than moderated after thirty years of (revised) study, testify that on the matter of the 'Reformation in Ireland', or the 'Irish Reformation', there is in fact serious dissensus and a conceptual imbroglio about what 'actually happened' or did not happen. Moreover, it is related to abiding misconceptions of what 'Reformation' or 'Counter-Reformation' was (let alone what 'Ireland' was, and who 'the Irish' were). Another circumscribing factor has been the unfortunate convention, not unique to the treatment of Ireland, of tending to consider the intractable circumstances of the Reformation there *in vitro*, and so out of context, the contexts of the Three Kingdoms (England, Ireland, Scotland) and that of wider Europe. Neglect of these can lead to the idiosyncrasy of the situation in Ireland being magnified out of all proportion in relation to the larger picture.

It has been asked whether the general failure of Protestant religious mission was inevitable. Some point out that in fact neither Gaelic nor Old

English rejection was universal or automatic. They also refer to other hindering factors. Cited are government incoherence, lack of resources, sheer incompetence, spiritual inadequacy, lack of stability, the necessary priority given to political domination and military conquest over religious re-education, pre-existing laicization of the Gaelic Church, and the effective Catholic religious mission of Irish priests trained in Continental seminaries. To this one can add that like Wales, Ireland offered very little or less in the way of conditions (putatively) favouring a Reformation success. However, unlike in Wales, no imaginative mythological package with England-friendly or at least pro-Crown overtones to catch the imagination was devised to make up for this. Also, Wales was not being subjected to colonial settlement. In Ireland, this was defended on the grounds that it was civilizing the country.

The inconsistency of reforming strategy on the part of Reformation clergy can be illustrated. Irish-born clergy, whether Gaelic or Old English, opted for a policy of persuasion and evangelization. Such was the activity of a number of mainly Old English compliant, or genuinely converted, bishops like William Casey[28] (d. after 1556), Edward Staples[29] (d. *c.*1560), Nicholas Walsh[30] (d. 1585) Hugh Brady[31] (d. 1584) and Nehemiah Donnellan[32] (d. after 1609). The bishops brought in from England or Scotland tended to be much more assertive, since they were also agents of government policy and so 'only obeying orders'. Examples were Dublin archbishops such as the ex-Augustinian provincial and strictly Erastian George Browne[33] (d. 1556), and Adam Loftus[34] (d. 1605). Their apparently mechanistic 'Crown policy' approach was evidently counter-productive, as was the provocatively Protestant approach of the colourful ex-Carmelite prior, John Bale[35] (1495–1563), also imported from England and Bishop of Ossory for less than a year in 1553. Irrespective of the modern tendency to undervalue Browne's function as being little more than an obedient agent of Tudor religious change, the wider context of his role should be taken account of. His appointment was part of Thomas Cromwell's and Henry VIII's three-pronged strategy for simultaneous church restructuring in the three nations comprising the entire Crown domains – the appointments of Cranmer in England, Barlow in Wales and Browne in Ireland.

There is a school of thought (e.g. Brendan Bradshaw) that the post-Henrician coercive policy, aggressively Protestant, was 'elementally Reformed' due to 'Calvinist predestinarianism' and the linked doctrine of unattenuated original sin.[36] In this theology, coercion means giving a salutary helping hand to irresistible grace. Writers like Canny dismiss this by appealing to obvious transconfessional historical analogies. Anyway, the sources of religious coercion and persecution implemented by the secular arm are Augustine's fateful application of 'compel them to come in' (Luke 14.23), as well as the mandatory 'one state-one church' ideology of the Codes of Theodosius and Justinian. Such concepts were adopted, hallowed and bequeathed by Catholic tradition, and inherited by the mainstream Reformation. Further, the restrictive, Calvinist predestinarian diagnosis also runs into a cul-de-sac when one considers the openly coercive intentions in Ireland (and England) of Lord-Deputy Wentworth and the Canterbury archbishop, William Laud (1573–1645). For something that one could not accuse Laud of being was a 'Calvinist', in the sense that is generally understood.

Crucial in the matter was not so much predestination, as ecclesiology. The unity of the (true) church, the instrument and channel of authentic grace by Word and sacrament, is paramount. Outside her there is no salvation. To secure this 'seamless robe' of unity, recourse to compulsion or enforced persuasion, and chastisement in the framework of church discipline and the divinely instituted secular 'sword' had been the norm in Christianity since the late fourth century. The penal and punitive aspects of it were not understood as merely judicial, but as a form of pastoral care and responsibility, that is, for the spiritual benefit of the obstinate dissident. Though currently blinded by God because of his inscrutable ways, recalcitrant deviants could conceivably be among the elect, so that coercion, even physical, would benefit them. However, due to its near-elimination of free will, 'Calvinist predestinarianism' only intensifies Augustinian and Lutheran tradition in a manner inimical to Catholic consensus in the matter. Yet, paradoxically, the question must be asked: how many religious martyrs were there in Europe as result of action or policy among theologically Calvinist Churches?

It was as a typical Renaissance modernizer rather than an English colonialist that a civil official like Edmund Spenser (*c.*1552–99), the writer, helped propagate perceptions of Ireland as barbaric and in need of civilizing. He urged enforced implementation of reformation or restructuring in the civil domain, but much more tact, or deferral, in the religious domain. In the latter, persuasive preparatory work should be undertaken by 'godly teachers' who are native Irish and of exemplary lives. He deplored the quality of the ordinary clergy sent to Ireland from England, and compared them unfavourably with the commitment of the new generation of post-Tridentine priests active in the country. Spenser seems to represent the predominant Tudor view that serious religious conversion through the medium of the Irish language should only occur after civil peace, order and restructuring has been established.[37] The use of Gaelic would presumably be an *ad hoc* and interim measure in view of the longer game plan of anglicization. To this extent then, the image of Spenser as an advocate of linguistic extermination to safeguard political conquest needs qualification.[38] Were not Wales (and Gaelic Scotland) showing that the old language, the new religion and loyalty to the Crown were compatible?

Another perspective is illustrated in the intransigently confessional attitude rather than policy of the erudite James Ussher (1581–1656), Archbishop of Armagh (1625) and Professor of Theology in the new Dublin College. Largely dismissive of Catholics, whom he reckoned ought to be 'allowed to go Hell their own way',[39] he did concede the value of preaching in Irish. All the same, his interest in the Irish language seems to have been more literary and historical than evangelical, though he did see some potential in it as a medium of conversion to the Reformation faith.[40]

Commentators like Nicholas Canny deny that there evolved a Protestant policy of religious – and supremacist ethnic – apartheid in Ireland reinforced by a predestinarian theology indifferent to mission (Bradshaw).[41] Rather, it was hoped that the reformed Church would attract Catholics magnetically 'to Heaven the State's way' by a process of attrition. This then would have been a kind of slow, trickle-down Reformation, as in Wales, Scotland and much of England. Canny's analysis is plausible. What prevented that from happening was partly the efficacy of the Counter-Reformation, and partly the catalogue of disasters and devastations that afflicted Ireland in the seventeenth century. These factors, and the subsequent pains of pacification, helped polarize the communities of Ireland along confessional lines even further, with overtones of a caste system rather than of apartheid.

Even so, the relatively enlightened and evangelical outreach of some English-born churchmen in the seventeenth century like William Bedell[42] (1571–1642) also belies notions of predictable bullying, comprehensive indifference or airy optimism on the part of the Established Church or imported ministers. Bedell, one-time Provost of Trinity College, and then Bishop of Kilmore and Ardagh from 1629, had after all seen to it that divinity students at Trinity College be required to learn Gaelic in the interest of enhancing their ministry to all the people. As we shall see below, he was also committed to advancing the project of an entire Bible in the Irish language.

In the future, some Presbyterians, too, were to display similar mission concerns in the north of the country after the immigration of 'Protestant' Scots from the early seventeenth century onwards, and who by all accounts were themselves in urgent need of Christian instruction and disciplining. Stereotypically depicted as 'Lowland Scots', they were not necessarily so monochrome. Evidence and recent research suggests that included among them from the beginning were Scots Gaels whose preachers effected conversions in areas like Down, north Antrim, north Derry and east Donegal.[43] Indeed, the request in around 1567 to Rome from an Ulster bishop (possibly the notorious Miler Magrath)[44] to have the Roman Inquisition introduced to Ireland, based in the safe haven of O'Neillite Ulster, suggests a background of successful undercover activity (*tecti*) of Protestant Scots Gaels in the north.[45] It was asserted that 'heretical meetings were increasing so much' (*in tantum augenter ista prava colloquia*) that action was necessary. The particular implication of such a petition is that even priests or monks were being converted. If this analysis is correct, it would put the incursion of Reformation ideas into Ulster about thirty-five years before the conventional date.

Presenting therefore the Reformation in Ireland, particularly among the Gaelic population, as a definite non-starter will always need qualification. After all, the pro-Reformation Anglo-Scottish Treaty of Berwick (1560) included a clause authorizing Archibald Campbell, fifth Earl of Argyll, to play a key role in subjugating Gaelic Ulster to the English Crown.[46] Argyll, chief Gaelic magnate, was one of the original five Scottish 'Lords of the Congregation' covenanted to advance the Protestant religious Reformation (see Chapter 8). His interest in Ulster was just as religious as military. The Scottish religio-political concern with Ireland, therefore, predates the union of the Crowns under the Stewarts. In addition, that the Protestant input to Tudor Ireland was not exclusively 'English', has been exemplified in recent studies in which at least five ethnic Scots holding livings in the Irish reformed Church have been identified, including the Wittenberg-trained activist and emissary in 1548 of Thomas Cranmer, Walter Spalding and Alexander Craik, Bishop of Kildare (1560–4).[47]

Literary religious landmarks

Certain achievements (connected with the foregoing) are noteworthy, even if chiefly literary and of contested significance.[48] The first evangelical foray into the Gaelic world using the technology of the printing press came not from within Ireland, but from John Knox's Scotland. In 1567, around the time of the recorded anxiety of the Ulster bishop about the appearance of heresy in the province, there appeared the first Gaelic book ever to be published, *Foirm na n'urruidheadh*, namely the worship manual of the reformed Church of Scotland, *The Book of Common Order* (sometimes misnamed 'John Knox's Liturgy').[49] The translator was the Church of Scotland superintendent of Argyll, and Bishop of the Isles, John Carswell (Séon Carsuel)[50] (*c.*1520–72). Written in the literary Gaelic common to Scotland and Ireland, Carswell explicitly targeted the entire Gaeltacht, or more realistically, Ulster as well as Scotland. 'To the men of Scotland and Ireland', Carswell writes in his dedication, 'to such of them as desire to receive the faithful words of God in their hearts and minds.' The phrase is more than evangelical jargon. It announces the Reformation reorientation of Christian piety, from sheer devotion to cognitive understanding, from external ritual and observance to internalization and transformation, from priestly mediation of grace to direct appropriation of the proclaimed Word of God and the grace of Christ, from faith in the Church and its inflationary doctrines to faith in the Gospel as preached and sacramentally administered.

Carswell's publication posed a challenge not only to Gaelic Catholicism, but also to Crown and Irish government attitudes. These included not only the hope of severing the links between Ulster and Scotland, but the absurd idea of transmitting the Reformation to the Irish Gaelic Church through the medium of Latin,[51] while urging the English vernacular for the Irish English Church. Further, Carswell's preface reveals the classical reformed appeal to the competence in religious affairs of the godly magistrate or prince, since he sees an analogy between his own patron, Archibald Campbell, fifth Earl of Argyll, and Old Testament monarchs, guardians of the true faith of Israel.[52]

Soon a cultural quantum leap occurred in Ireland. In 1571, John Kearney (Seaán Ó Cearnaigh) (c.1545–c.1587), an office-bearer in St Patrick's Cathedral, Dublin, published in one volume an Irish language primer and an evangelical *Gaelic Catechism*, the first Gaelic book published in Ireland: *Aibidil Gaoidheilge et Caiticiosma*.[53] Two hundred copies were printed, of which none have survived in Ireland, but three in England and one in Scotland. The failure to reprint in later years does suggest a lack of commitment in the state Church in its outreach to Gaeldom. The catechism contained texts of the classical, threefold minimum requirement of Christian knowledge, namely the Lord's Prayer, the Apostles' Creed and the Ten Commandments. It also included some catechetical material from the English *Book of Common Prayer*, as well as prayers from Carswell's translation of the Scottish *Book of Common Order*. Contained in it too is a Gaelic rendering of the Church of Ireland's twelve 'Articles of Religion' of 1566.[54] In the prefatory Epistle of *Aibidil*, the twinning of good religion and good government, subjection to the rule of law, spiritual (the Word of God) and secular (the Crown), is evident: 'We are immersed in blindness and in ignorance, lacking the rule of God and of the world up to now, and we are more savage and more uncouth in our manners and customs than any race of people in this western part of Europe.'[55] The 'glory of God' is explicitly linked with the 'common good'; in other words, right religion with social improvement.

Even more promising was the publication in 1603 of a delayed Irish translation of the New Testament from Erasmus' Greek text, whose very preface or 'Paraclesis' had explicitly cited the Gaels (*Scotti*) as having a right to have the Scriptures translated into their language.[56] Had not the Scottish poet and dramatist, Sir David Lindsay stated in 1554:

> Had Sanct Jerome bene borne in tyll Argyll
> In to the Yrische toung his bukis had done compyle.[57]

There may have been much earlier attempts to translate the Latin Vulgate or parts of it into Irish.[58] One such tradition linked to Richard Fitzralph, Archbishop of Armagh in the fourteenth century, was transmitted by John Bale, John Foxe and James Ussher. And the *Connacht Annals* records that a bard, Urard O'Mulconry (Urard Ó Maolchonaire) (d. 1482), translated scriptural portions into Irish. These examples, even if authentic, were really little more than historical curiosities, and were paralleled elsewhere in Europe.

The 1603 translation – in 'Classical Common Gaelic' – was the culmination of the work of a largely Cambridge-educated circle, a task initiated over a quarter of a century earlier. It was dedicated to James I. Originally involved were the said John Kearney, Bishop Nicholas Walsh and Nehemiah Donnellan (Archbishop of Tuam, 1595–1609). The project was completed by William O'Donnell[59] (Uilliam Ó Domhnaill) (d. 1628), latterly the vigorously reformed Archbishop of Tuam from 1609 in the western province of Connacht. The translation was aided by some notable Gaelic bards, such as, in the province of Munster, Maolin Og Mac Bruaideadha (MacBrady). The work, like that for the *Gaelic Catechism* of 1571, was subsidized by an Old English, Dublin patrician family, the Usshers. Though seen as a 'Protestant' or 'heretical' translation, there is some evidence that in the absence of any alternative, Gaelic writers of Catholic texts later made discreet use of the Irish New Testament.[60] Ironically, the only vernacular translation (from the Vulgate) bearing an imprimatur in accord with (ambiguous) legislation of the Council of Trent, and so permissible for Irish Catholics, was to be the Douai–Rheims English New Testament version (1582–1610). The Bible was not published as a whole until the early nineteenth century.

Interesting in the enterprise of providing appropriate published religious texts in Gaelic was that Queen Elizabeth instigated it early in her reign. She helped materially by providing money to create an Irish letter type for printers,[61] and later made threatening noises to the Irish bishops about lack of progress.[62] It is important to recall that she was opposed to persecution of Catholics on religious grounds, treason or disloyalty being the litmus test; instead, they should be converted, and not necessarily by preaching in English to them. The *Calendar of State Papers, Ireland, 1509–73* reveals that in 1564 Elizabeth intervened to have Robert Daly (d. 1584) appointed as Bishop of Kildare on the grounds that he was an Irish speaker (ibid., pp. ix, 234). In reality, however, the queen's good intentions in this respect were always on the back burner of actual government policy due to military and security preoccupations, national and international. In contrast to Wales, the intention was also hindered by the shortage of native Irish clergy of episcopal potential in the new Church.

In 1608, O'Donnell also published an Irish Gaelic version of the *Book of Common Prayer* (*Leabhar na nVrnaightheadh gComhchoidchiond*), with what Caball in his essay (p. 135) calls an 'obsequious' dedication to the Lord Deputy, although such a posture was standard practice in prefaces and dedications thoughout Europe in this era and beyond. The translation was completed on the basis of earlier preparatory work done by Kearney and Walsh. It is conventionally believed that these publications came too late to advance the Reformation or enhance, crucially, the status and acceptability of the Irish language.[63]

The gaelicization of the Reformation was never effectively realized due to paralysing ambivalence in both the central civil and ecclesiastical authorities in England, Ireland and Scotland. Official government priority given to the advancement of 'civility' and anglicization in Gaeldom[64] was hard to reconcile with the authentically evangelical, pro-Gaelic language instincts of some churchmen and government officials. Such an attitude was grounded in basic Reformation and Christian Humanist principles. In Ireland, among laymen of note (apart from Spenser), one can cite Henry Sydney (1529–86).[65] In April 1576 he commended a proactive mission strategy to the queen that included seeking out university-trained preachers in England who were competent in Irish. Should such be wanting, then Gaelic preachers should be imported from the reformed Church of Scotland. He urged the appointment of Irish-speaking bishops. Thereby 'thousands would be gained for Christ'. Sydney complained that the priority given to civil before religious reformation was like driving a cart with only one wheel, so that 'I work waywardly'. Further, higher English clergy should be reminded of their apostolic vocation and responsibility in the matter of Ireland.[66]

Twenty-five years later, in 1602, when things had changed little due to the government's virtual *laissez-faire* policy in religion consequent on the priority accorded to military subjugation, one no less than Francis Bacon (1561–1626) wrote to Secretary William Cecil in similar vein. Under the rubric of 'Recovery of the hearts of the people', and distinguishing between 'piety' and 'policy', he urges that if in the domain of religion there is to be coercion, then time must be allowed for preliminary re-education as well as provisional indulgence. This should not be deferred: 'There should go hand in hand with [civil reformation] some course of advancing religion, as . . . the sending over some good preachers, especially the sort which are . . . zealous persuaders, scholastically . . . taking care of the versions of Bibles, catechisms, and other books of instruction into the Irish language.'[67] Granted, Bacon also advocates an offensive against the institutions of Gaelic culture. The accommodation therefore is only pragmatic and relative to ulterior motives, like ultimate anglicization, as was also foreseen for Wales and Scotland.

Another twenty-five years saw some more progress. William Bedell (see above) undertook to have the Old Testament translated into Irish. Due to troubles and serious instability from that time onwards, this was not published (in London) until 1685, accompanied with O'Donnell's earlier New Testament translation. Instrumental in its publication was Robert Boyle, the scientist with Irish connections (seventh son of the Earl of Cork) and Christian philanthropist. The 'Irish Bible' did, however, have a positive role outside Ireland. It was used in Gaelic Scotland,[68] especially the region of Argyll, no doubt connected with the historical pro-Reformation identity of the Clan Campbell and its ducal chiefs. These developments only helped defer the ultimate objectives of government policy on language, societal reform and religion in the whole of Gaeldom.

An interesting illustrative link was Andrew Knox (1559–1633). As Bishop of the Isles, he advanced James VI & I's policy on religion, society and culture in the west Highlands and Hebrides by the 'Statutes of Iona'

(1609), 'agreed' with nine clan chiefs.[69] The consistency of such royal policy is reflected in the fact that the same Knox was translated to the Diocese of Raphoe (1611–33) in north-west Ulster.[70] It is clear that he was commissioned to pursue the same royal counter-cultural policies, targeting the ideological sway of chiefs, bards and Catholicism. His remit would also have included discouraging presbyterianism among Scottish immigrants.

Catholic clergy were soon to warn their flocks about religious books and preachers in Gaelic, as they were likely to be heretical. Some works of Catholic teaching and piety did however appear in Irish in 1611, 1616 and 1618. The first, published in Antwerp, was a catechism, *An teagasg críosdaidhe* (The Christian Catechism) composed by Bonaventura O'Hussey (Ó hEodhasa).[71] The second, published in Louvain, was a combination of (Spanish) mystical devotion with rudimentary Catholic apologetics. Entitled *Desiderius* or *Sgáthan an chráibhidh* (The Mirror of Faith), it was assembled by Florence Conry (Flaithrí Ó Maoil Chonaire).[72] The third, Hugh MacCaghwell's (Aodh Mac Aingil) *Scáthán shacramuinte na h-aithridhe* (Mirror of the Sacrament of Penance), was published in Louvain.[73] Apart from the characteristic Western late-medieval stress on penitential theology, this work contains markedly polemical anti-Reformation elements. The Reformers are demonized, so that there are references to 'Luther MacLucifer', and even more implausibly, the 'sensuous Calvin'. The tract was however important for the genre and language style it employed. This was poetic verse, a useful medium for a largely analphabetic populace. The language register was plain, rather than the near-hieratic style of bardic high culture. Missionary concerns took precedence over linguistic finesse.[74]

However, Irish was not to be paramount for the survival or revival of Catholicism in Ireland. This was partly because Tridentine principles reaffirmed that both the Mass and the sole authorized Bible version be in Latin, the compulsory language of international Catholicism. A pre-determined and infrangible interlocking of Catholic faith and Gaelic (language) culture was not ultimately sustainable. Accordingly, while Irish could be effectively employed for edification and indoctrination, it could not be perceived as a sacred language, a medium of the divine Word in worship or of sacramental grace (as in a Gaelic Protestant context), nor used for higher theological discourse – the jealously guarded preserve of the higher clergy or *magisterium* (teaching authority) anyway. Soteriologically, the faith had priority over national or ethnic culture, just as the language was not adequately exploited in the interests of Protestant evangelization either. Catholicism was to remain the people's faith; the same was not to be true of the language. After the battle of Kinsale in 1601, Gaelic Ireland's Culloden, the lamentation of the Gaelic Annalists and its implicit prophecy was not over the *longue durée* to be corroborated as regards religion: 'Manifest was the displeasure of God and misfortune to the Irish . . . devotion and pure religion of the island were lost.'[75]

Confessional and identity formation

The survival and consolidation of the Roman faith was facilitated by a variety of reasons. For example, a response from the Irish Catholic diaspora included the founding of Irish seminaries for priests at Salamanca in 1592, and at Douai in 1594, both named after St Patrick. In 1593 an Irish college was also established at Lisbon. These were all to be training grounds in Tridentine Catholic orthodoxy, spiritual renewal and mission.[76] This led to an influx of Irish priests from abroad trained in the new Catholicism, although they tended to gravitate to Old English communities where there were better prospects of patronage. Throughout the seventeenth century such priests constituted between one-third and one-quarter of all priests, not quite the flood often alluded to. Their short-term impact should not be exaggerated, since a Continental seminarian training did not necessarily mean they were intellectual high fliers.[77] Anyway, the quality of such seminaries needs to be further researched. The main consequence was that the Irish Catholic Church was gradually reintegrated into mainstream (Tridentine) Catholicism, even if it did lose out on the earlier phase of (Erasmian) Catholic Humanism and its irenical, less clericalist disposition.

Moreover, there were occasional fact-finding operations by members of Orders like the Jesuits, for example, David Wolfe (1561 onwards), who also reported on largely urban 'Church papistry', that is, Catholics who out of prudence conformed only externally.[78] In addition, crucial was the actual continuation of traditional structures and institutions such as the hierarchy,[79] episcopal synods and lay confraternities, as well as ongoing sacramental administration, whether out of sight or in public. Further, it would be wrong to think of Catholic revivalist nonconformity in Ireland as being something purely spiritual and detached from mundane perspectives, such as the Reformation association with civility, the common good and socio-economic reform. For along with revitalizing the ordinances of religion and guarding the people against the spread of Protestant ideas of Christianity, advanced Catholic reform also addressed, at least, popular 'superstition', cultural profanity, and excessive, over-indulgent leisure activity. How far this (in Catholic circles) envisaged abolition, or just attenuation, is a matter for debate. In the first half of the seventeenth century, David Rothe, the Anglo-Irish Catholic Bishop of Ossory (1620–50), onetime vicar-apostolic, and firmly Tridentine, maintained that reform Catholicism in Ireland would help 'eliminate barbarous customs, abolish bestial rites, and convert the detestable inter-course of savages into polite manners and a care for maintaining the commonwealth'.[80] Similar views were expressed by Richard Stanihurst. How far was this too an attack on Irish Gaelic 'culture', or on sub-Christian pagan superstitions? Was this a Catholic form of the 'Greater English theory' in Ireland? Tantalizingly, John Bossy has suggested that any Catholic religious revival among Irish Gaels was more of 'a response to Elizabethan Anglophone catholic nationalism [in Ireland] than ... to any action of the Elizabethan or Jacobean governments'.[81] In other words, the tradition of linking the policy of English conceptions of civility exclusively to Protestantism does not correspond to the facts.

In 1592, Ireland's first tertiary education establishment was founded, Trinity College, Dublin, partly modelled on Emmanuel College, Cambridge. An essential aim was to inject much needed intellectual and academic capital into the Reformation Church in Ireland.[82] It was to become ultimately a Protestant institution from which Catholics were excluded, not that most would have wanted to go there anyway. Irish Catholics who could afford a university education either had or opted to attend Catholic institutions on the Continent. Yet some of those who were not doing theology probably continued to study at Oxbridge, just as it is known that some attended Trinity College, Dublin in its early phase. Others, chiefly from Ulster, continued to study at Glasgow University, which regarded Ulster as part of its constituency.[83]

In its early decades, Trinity College was not an exclusively English, British, 'Anglo-Irish', or exclusively Protestant institution, since during that era about one-quarter of its students were Gaelic Irish, and not necessarily converted.[84] In theology, the tone of the College in its first forty years or so was markedly reformed (Calvinist) and broadly puritan. This was because Ireland tended to be the receptacle of English puritans seeking more liberation from the conservative and traditionalist wing of the Church of England. Some of them were (like Ussher himself) Church puritans, and so episcopalian, such as Adam Loftus; others like Thomas Cartwright (1535–1603) and Walter Travers (*c*.1548–1635) were presbyterian.[85] Further, the first two Fellows of Trinity College, Dublin were presbyterians from Glasgow, James Hamilton and James Fullerton,[86] both of whom were resident in Dublin since 1587 as schoolmasters and as Scottish agents seeking Irish (and discreet English) support for the Stewart strategy of claiming the English Crown after Elizabeth. Hamilton – the tutor of the future archbishop, James Ussher – had close links with Andrew Melville (1545–1622),[87] the chief architect of Scottish presbyterianism. One of the new Scottish landowners in Ulster, Hamilton's estates in north Down helped fund the new Dublin College. He was ennobled as Lord Clandeboy. Fullerton was knighted.

And just as not all Englishmen coming into the Church of Ireland in the first three decades of the sixteenth century were episcopalian by conviction, so not all Scottish incoming churchmen were inveterate presbyterians, even if they were, like King James VI & I, firmly Calvinist in theology. The neat paradigms of later eras and availed of still by some historians did not always apply in most of the seventeenth century.[88] One can cite Scottish 'episcopalians' provided with Irish bishoprics, usually in Ulster, like George Montgomery (d. 1621), James Spottiswoode (d. 1645), Andrew Knox (1559–1633), John Leslie (d. 1661), Robert Echlin (d. 1635), or deans like Robert Maxwell in Armagh, John Gibson in Down, etc. Yet some of them had had presbyterian ordination. And as for the sixty-four

Scottish ministers who settled in Ulster in the reign of James, fifty held office in the Church of Ireland.[89] The Scottish bishops in Ireland had a relaxed attitude to the installation of compatriots of apparent presbyterian convictions in Irish parish churches.

Such a *modus vivendi* was not to last very long following the strict conformist policies pursued by Charles I and Archbishop Laud of Canterbury, as well as by their representatives in Ireland, the prelate, John Bramhall (d. 1663), and the Lord Deputy (1633–41), Thomas Wentworth.[90] Consequently, presbyterians by conviction, or more properly, non-conforming ministers, were expelled definitively from the Irish parish churches, notably in Ulster. This, due to the underestimation of presbyterian commitment and the further influx of Scots later, was to handicap seriously the wider religious impact of Protestantism in Ireland. It also undermined the 'comprehensive' aspirations of some Established Church thinkers. Nonetheless, both sides knew that ultimately no merger was seriously viable, given that divine right and sanction could not be accorded to both presbytery and episcopacy simultaneously. Bearing in mind the 'Britishness' of Irish Protestant profiles, the failure to devise a common Reformation Church in Britain was necessarily transposed on to Ireland despite some unionizing, but frustrated plans. Autonomous structural developments could therefore not take place in Ireland.

One might say that in the early seventeenth century, the Church of Ireland was influenced by waves that occurred elsewhere in Christian Europe, referred to as the 'second Reformation' and 'confessionalization'.[91] Among the non-Lutheran reformed Churches, this can be understood as a firming up along 'Calvinist' lines. Accentuation of matters like predestination as well as church and social discipline are characteristic of this development. Of note, then, is that in adopting and utilizing the royally-approved 104 *Irish Articles of Religion* from 1615 to 1634[92] – 'for the avoidance of diversity of opinions and the establishing of consent' – the Church of Ireland in that period was confessionally the most categorically Calvinist anywhere in the British Isles. Also, like the *Scots Confession* of 1560, the *Articles* elevated discipline (the power of the keys) to the rank of being one of the three marks of the church alongside the ministries of the Word and the sacraments.[93] However, unlike any other Reformation confession – including the *Scots Confession* – the *Irish Articles* of 1615 included seven formulations (nos. 11–17) that embodied double predestinarian ideas, derived from the radical Augustinian and the advanced Calvinist tradition. James Ussher must have been involved at some level in the composition of the articles, though there seems to be a tendentious tradition of minimizing his role. Anyway, his double predestinarian credentials are corroborated with his publication of an account of the controversy surrounding Gottschalk, the ninth-century Saxon Benedictine monk.[94] Gottschalk had bequeathed to Christian dogma the very formulation: double predestination (*predestinatio gemina*).[95]

In regard to predestination, the *Irish Articles*' stance on the prior 'eternal decrees of God' corresponds substantially to that articulated at the Synod of Dordrecht, or Dort, (1618–20) in the Netherlands, the international council of Reformed or 'Calvinist' Churches. The Church of England had participated in this, mandated by the king to exercise a temperate influence on radical predestinarianism, and which did not have very much success.[96] The Dublin creed also anticipated in this respect the *Westminster Confession* (1647), a 'scholastic' articulation of reformed orthodoxy intended for all the Churches of Reformation provenance in the British Isles. The development and its theologically partisan outcome reflected emerging and disruptive tensions within broad reformed theology between pessimistic and optimistic views of human nature, on the extent of original sin, on the scope of the atonement and the covenant of grace and so on. The hope of enduring consensus was forlorn. The *Irish Articles* also echoed elements of the doctrinally mediating, but unofficial *Lambeth Articles* (1595) of the Church of England.[97] Unusually in any confession of faith, the evangelical exigency of the Irish situation is perhaps reflected in the Irish article number 4, which states that 'the Scriptures ought to be translated out of the originall tongues into all languages for the common use of all men'.

The theologically advanced situation in Ireland was however soon offset with the adoption by the Established Church in 1634/5 of the English *Thirty-nine Articles* as a co-ordinate, though effectively chief credal standard. These were more dogmatically reticent on divine election. This manoeuvre was due ultimately to Laud in the interest of enhanced English–Irish church uniformity. He also resisted puritan precisionist tendencies and excessive dogmatic curiosity in soteriology.[98]

Further, in the battle for minds in the Reformation era – whether Europe-wide or in Ireland – the Church of Ireland was fortunate to have in the early seventeenth century someone of the scholarly and cosmopolitan status of the home-grown James Ussher, a nephew of another notable Dublin citizen who stood firmly on the other side of the religious fence, Richard Stanihurst.[99] Ussher was the Church's chief spokesman in, among other things, the area of controversial theology.[100] He was well equipped to participate in the response to the Catholic post-Tridentine campaign against the claims of Protestantism. He is also important for the attempt to legitimize and ideologically hibernicize the reformed Church in Ireland. This he attempted by grounding its origins, spiritual and structural, not only in Scripture, but also in Celtic Christian antiquity, perceived as essentially evangelical and Rome-free.[101] This reflects classical Reformation apologetics and its use of the previous 'Golden Age' principle of Renaissance and Christian Humanist historiography. The reformed Churches are not 'new', their teachings are not 'innovations'. Rather, they are restorationist; they have retrieved the purer Christianity of the early Church, the apostolic and patristic eras, bearers of the authentic mind and spirit of Christ (see Chapter 5). In short, St Patrick would be at home in the Church of Ireland.

The issue was not academic. For, a few years before, David Rothe, Catholic Bishop of Ossory, had published a work that was to assist identity formation.[102] This argued that the celestial glue that constitutes and binds the Irish nation and people (Gaelic and Old English) together is the Catholic faith, rooted in Christian and Celtic antiquity. Such a concept posits an essential and indissoluble co-inherence of land, nation, people and faith – of Old Testament proportions! The future trammelling consequence of this influential idea was that just as Irish Catholics were relegated to being second- or third-class citizens by the Ascendancy, so Protestants of all hues were viewed as sub-Irish and so intrinsically alien by the disadvantaged Catholic majority (or at least their spokesmen). Thereby the 'colonial' paradigm was internally appropriated.

Facing up to realities

Lastly, there are two extra considerations of interest. Firstly, as indicated above, there are many hypotheses claiming to explain why the majority in Ireland adhered to Catholicism. The voices of the ordinary people rarely figure in the discussions for lack of evidence. But a surviving fragment does suggest clearly that prudential self-interest and conformity to the dissent prevailing in one's immediate socio-economic context was a factor, and probably remained so. This is in a memorandum (1612) of Thomas Ram (d. 1634), Church of Ireland Bishop of Ferns, in the south-east:

> As for the poorer sort, some of them have not only discovered unto me privately their dislike of Popery and the mass, in regard they understand not what is said or done therein, but also groaned under the burden of many priests in respect of the double tythes and offerings, the one paid by them to us, and the other unto them. Being then demanded of me why they did not forsake the Mass and come to our church, their answer hath been (which I know to be true in some) that if they should be of our religion, no Popish merchant would employ them being sailors, no Popish landlord would let them any lands being husbandmen, nor set them houses in tenantry being artificers; and therefore they just either starve, or do as they do.[103]

The quotation does appear in some of the literature, though somewhat hesitatingly in the context of 'why the Reformation failed'. The reality of the dynamics on the ground would seem to be interpreted with some credibility by Corish. Though tempted by the idea that the people referred to might have been saying what the (gullible) churchman wanted to hear, he comments that 'the propertied Papist could bear down more heavily than the Protestant Bishop'.[104] One does hear a lot about 'Church papistry' and 'prudential conformity', but the phenomenon of prudential nonconformity among dissenting groups is also worth exploring more.

After the Stewart plantations had begun, there was a noticeable drift among the tenantry away from Catholicism to attending the reformed Church; but accompanying it were knee-jerk measures of intimidation to prevent it, as recently illustrated by Canny.[105]

Inversely, the same forces could of course also operate on the immunity of the new British tenantry of Protestant landowners from the Counter-Reformation – in so far as they were ever targeted at all. Ultimately there does seem to be a nice symmetry in Ireland between the Established Church's diffidence about evangelizing the Catholic majority and the Counter-Reformation's inhibition about crusading among the new Protestant settlers.

A second consideration worth highlighting is this: Catholicism survived as a potent force in Reformation-era Ireland partly because of resistance, reform and revival, and partly because it, *qua* religion, was never frontally persecuted by Crown forces with a view to its extirpation by the sword. Penal legislation and official discrimination manifestly existed, but the leap from statute book to general enforcement was usually half-hearted. Treason and Catholicism were not perceived as synonyms, and as long as many Catholics, especially the Old English or Anglo-Irish, continued to profess allegiance to the Crown, indulgence was accorded to closet or discreet Catholicism at least. The Tudor strategy of prioritizing civil reformation helps account for this situation rather than the potency of Irish Catholic resistance and solidarity. This engendered a situation of actual, reluctant, *de facto* tolerance, if seen as only provisional. However, against the background of debates in the wider European scene, there inevitably arose ideas of both pragmatic and principled toleration, religious liberty, and freedom of private conscience. Such notions had been current within European Christianity since the 1550s (though earlier if one recalls the Anabaptist appeal to them) in view of the confessional impasse that was gradually becoming solidified following the failure of Emperor Charles V to restore political and ecclesiastical unity in Germany. The subsequent particular theatres of debate (about religious pluralism within a particular jurisdiction) had been areas of eastern central Europe, France, Scotland and the Netherlands. Inevitably some of the seeds drifted across to the religious situation in Ireland and had an influence. Accordingly, Ireland's religio-political history in this era cannot be regarded as *sui generis*, a miserably perennial squabble in England's backyard divorced from ideas and development from further afield.

Examples of official pragmatic toleration elsewhere (other than the Peace of Augsburg, 1555), and where ideas of 'freedom of conscience' were bandied about during this era were: Scotland, where the Protestant establishment had granted the right of private Mass to Queen Mary and her court (1560–7); France, whose Edict of Nantes (1598) after more than thirty years of religious civil warring granted limited legal rights to the significant Protestant minority (and to Catholics in Huguenot areas); the Netherlands, where, after the revolt against Spanish imperial rule, the Union of Utrecht (1579) granted limited freedom of religion to non-Calvinist groups in the northern Dutch Republic where the reformed Church was established. Yet even here, where Catholicism was 'banned', the civil rulers pursued a policy of non-harassment of continuing Catholic communities, so that religious pluralism in fact prevailed.

Precedents that were less appreciated in the future were ultimately abortive attempts at religious 'consensus toleration'. For example, the religious colloquies in Germany, 1538–41, and later, the *Consensus of Sandomir* (1570) in Greater Poland provided for a while peaceful existence and mutual 'recognition' of the three main confessions. There were even ideas of *laissez-faire* religious freedom based on personal spiritual and civil rights of conscience. This was articulated influentially by the Protestant Humanist, Sebastian Castellio (1515–63) in opposition to the penalty of capital crime adhering to doctrinal heresy.[106]

In all these situations and contexts, official church leaderships, Catholic or Protestant, generally maintained discouraging attitudes. This was in the face of increasing lay utilitarian assertions that political and civil exigencies have precedence over absolutist religious claims. These should be subordinate to civil 'peace', 'mutual accommodation', 'greater advantage', and the 'public good'. Such thinking opened the way to civil quasi-neutrality and legally enshrined confessional co-existence of varying degrees, achieved in many places after the traumas of the later seventeenth century.

There are undoubtedly echoes of this wider situation in Ireland, when one recalls the alternation in government policies between coercion, persuasion, and *de facto* tolerance. Intellectual or ideological hesitations account for this as much as what is usually cited, namely incompetence, lack of resources, endemic disorder and insurgency, etc. While practical religious persecution was not on the Elizabethan agenda in Ireland, James I did try with no great success to tighten the screw. It was with Charles I in 1625 that the religious issue in Ireland achieved a measure of official pragmatic regulation, when in return for much needed revenue he gave certain rights to Catholics by his 'Graces'.[107] This alleviation, even if it was something of a false dawn, obviously helped the Catholic cause in Ireland to stabilize and flourish. Church leaders like James Ussher openly opposed it. He fully appreciated the *realpolitik* that determined royal policy when he complained that the privileges now being offered to Catholics represented 'a toleration for that religion in consideration of the payment of a great sum'.[108] Conviction Protestant opinion decried the 'scandal' of toleration.

Irrespective of impurity of motives, in Ireland there had been some explicit talk of toleration and related concepts since the late Tudor period. From 1595, the Earl of Tyrone, Hugh O'Neill, had made 'free liberty of conscience' a top priority in his negotiations with government authorities, even if the concept he cited was more of a Thomist than a Christian

Humanist kind like in Castellio.[109] Hugh, however, was still sufficiently medieval not to think in terms of vague equal rights, since what he meant by it was comprehensive Catholic restoration, abolishing the Protestant Church of Ireland.

An interesting insight into how the intelligentsia in English government circles were aware of trends elsewhere (especially France), and so argued for the legitimation of pragmatic toleration on not only political, but also religious grounds, is Francis Bacon. In the interests of other benefits, he argues in 1602, provisional toleration should be confirmed, in order (as noted already above) to provide better conditions for a more committed campaign or persuasion and evangelization. To quote Bacon:

> One of the principal pretences whereby the heads of the rebellion have prevailed both with the people and with the foreigner, hath been the defence of the Catholic religion; and it is this that likewise hath made the foreigner reciprocally more plausible with the rebel. Therefore a toleration of religion (for a time not definite) except it be in some principal towns and precincts, after the manner of some French edicts, seemeth to me to be a matter warrantable by religion, and in policy of absolute necessity.[110]

This is anything but – in modern terms – a manifesto of religious freedom. It does, however, help explain the inherent ambiguities of oscillating government policies in Ireland. In 1605, now the Stewart era, Catholic landowners in the Pale asserted the 'right' to the 'private use of their religion and conscience'. They ended up in jail. As mentioned already, however, the 'Graces' – religious concessions to Catholics – were granted by Charles I twenty years later.

A few years after that saw the destruction (1632) of a site of historical significance for European medieval Catholic piety in general, St Patrick's Purgatory at Lough Derg in Co. Donegal, Ireland's chief pilgrimage centre.[111] Superstitious practices associated with the cult had actually led to its condemnation by the pope in 1497, so that it was allowed to run down. However, in the sixteenth century popular demand led to its revival. A question about its destruction in the reign of Charles I could be: why did it not occur much earlier in the Reformation era? Tudor and early Stewart anti-Catholic policy in Ireland fell well short of systematically widespread repression and persecution.

This apparent incoherence of overall policy confirms two things. Firstly, that the overall Anglo-British approach to implementing the Reformation in Ireland was anything but a consistent application of a blunt-edged sword or battering ram. In practice it took second place after civil reform and constitutional restructuring. Secondly, the ultimate reasons for limited progress of the Reformation in Ireland are derived not just from the special problems of Britain–Ireland relations, whether in political or ethnic-cultural terms. Rather, they are also to be related to the overall fissure in Western Christendom, whereby 'accompanying the pan-European echo of the Reformers' message was an equally universal No'.[112] In the event, accordingly, neither the Reformation nor the Counter-Reformation was able to manage a clean sweep in Ireland, so that there obtained in the end what no one in principle wanted: religious and ecclesiastical pluralism, if only in the form of an uncomfortable *modus vivendi*. It was ironical that among the British Isles, it was to be Ireland where the implosion of the ancient and sacrosanct unitary concept of 'one king, one faith, one church' was to be most vivid. This is why 'Ireland', like its religion, is historically better understood in plural rather than singular terms.

CHAPTER 7

Scotland: Accounts Old and New

The impact of history derives largely from how people imagine what happened, especially if information has been packaged and marketed in a certain way – the extreme example of William Cobbett was cited in Chapter 3. Perceptions by the 'public' are inevitably conditioned by what they read or hear, which is often tinted in ways they are not conscious of. Presentations are received on trust, especially by 'constituencies' to which they are directed. Most people simply do not have the time, opportunity or training to ponder over and sift crates of original sources or allegedly objective accounts. Being then dependent on the secondary accounts of historians and the tertiary accounts of others, as in the more popular media, non-specialist readers are vulnerable. The trouble is that the practitioners of historical writing and their imitators can be crafty. Therefore every history book needs to be handled with caution. It should bear a list of essential ingredients on the author's profile, an educational health warning, a sell-by date, etc. In the past, many historians included in their titles phrases like 'A True Account', just as some modern historians or their publishers claim 'impartiality' and offer 'critical accounts'. As suggested earlier in this book, 'True Accounts' often purvey myths, apologetics, propaganda or hidden agendas. Questions need to be asked like: what is the historian's personal provenance? Whose side are they on? How 'critical' is their 'critique'? And ultimately: what is the source of their income?

Perceptions of the Scottish Reformation have been peculiarly susceptible to distortion, caricature and semi-myths at least, such as that it was elementally presbyterian, somehow democratic, and achieved by a crusade of hard-line, card-carrying Calvinists led by John Knox. Alternative views can just be as wide of the mark, such as that Knox was a puppet in the hand of 'robber barons', or that in terms of 'culture and civilization', the Scottish Reformation was a retrograde step, etc. Inside and outside Scotland, older and traditional accounts of the Scottish Reformation have been partisan, though to be fair, usually explicitly. This is not especially unusual; it is not confined to either Scotland or Scottish historians. But since Scotland is a relatively small country, there have never been enough relatively disinterested historians around to challenge some of these traditions in a decisive way. Such challenges as there have been or tend to be are one or another older tradition in disguise, attacking the alternatives. This encourages a certain sterility, barring exit from the vicious circle, and has been endemic in much of Scottish Reformation historiography. Though there has always been some input into the field from outside Scotland, research into the history of the Scottish Reformation, like that of the entire British Isles, requires greater internationalization if it is to break free from the hamstrings of various domestic, cultural predispositions.

Old accounts

As intimated, histories of the Scottish Reformation up to recent times have been largely confessional in a religious or ecclesiastical sense. There has also been an emergence of versions that can be described variously as secular, non-denominational, non-religious and anti-religious. These reflect, brightly or dimly, the variegated competing historiographical philosophies that have staked claims since the eighteenth century onwards. The staunchly Protestant version was of course established by John Knox (*c.*1514–72) in his *History*.[1] This was a virtuoso combination of eyewitness accounts, documentary sources, conviction history, propaganda, prophetic discourse, apocalyptic invocation, dramatic and linguistic talent, and so never a dull moment. Reformations elsewhere never quite produced anything so potentially marketable, except perhaps Foxe's *Book of Martyrs*, which was partly an inspiration for the *History*. Knox's account is a saga about doing fifteen rounds with Satan in the form of the pope, or the Mass, or French magnates like the Guises, or Mary, Queen of Scots, or Reformation carpetbaggers of suspect religious commitment. Knox's spiritual even-handedness has to be acknowledged. He is more than anti-Catholic, as many wish or need to confine him to. For to him, many in the Protestant bandwagon also fostered the wiles of Satan with their self-interest, their pragmatic and prudential 'human' judgements.

Published in London in 1587, fifteen years after his death, the *History* was instantly impounded and banned on the grounds of its inflammatory content – not so much in the religious sphere, as in the political sphere. Knox's thoughts on the extent of right of resistance to rulers were never applauded by English or Scottish governments (nor by Genevan pastors either for that matter).[2] While an edition of the *History* reappeared in 1644 during the Covenant era, it was not until the eighteenth century that the first textually reliable edition of the work was published. By that time, however, the Scottish Reformation, now safe and sound, had begun to slide into the shadows of Enlightenment realms. It became the preserve of historians of tradition and evangelical churchmen. Both used it to condition popular, if incompatible perceptions of the Reformation for subsequent generations. In other words, Knox's *History* was only widely circulated generations later. Unlike Foxe's *Book of Martyrs* in England, it did not help create pro-Reformation public opinion in the sixteenth century. Since it was not therefore a public, primary Scottish Reformation text, it was not initially formative. Accordingly, its importance before the mid-seventeenth century was very limited.

The chief contemporary Roman Catholic counterpoise to Knox's *History* was John Leslie (or Lesley) (1527–96), canonist and nonconforming Bishop of Ross, who left Scotland after Queen Mary's deposition in 1567. His *History of Scotland* (up to 1561), which appeared in London round about 1571, was written originally in Scots. It was subsequently expanded and published (1578) in Latin, nine years before Knox's *History* was abortively published, and was finally translated into English at the end of the sixteenth century.[3] Only the final section deals with the period culminating in the events of 1559–61. A major apologist for Mary Stewart as well, it is no surprise that Lesley's portrayal of the queen is much more positive than Knox's, nor does he share Knox's view of himself as a 'trumpeter of God'. Lesley's Latin account helped shape the mind of Catholic Europe on the matter: the Scottish Reformation was born of rank heresy and sedition. This would not have been a surprise, since such a diagnosis of the Reformation in general was current in Catholic circles anyway since the 1520s, particularly in France where Lesley had received most of his higher education. As traditionally in Catholic formulaic accounts, Lesley downgrades the Reformation in Scotland as 'political'.

Since Knox's *History* was not publicly accessible until the middle of the seventeenth century, much more significant for the Protestant tradition of demonizing Mary, and so emphasizing discontinuity, is George Buchanan's *History of Scotland*.[4] Buchanan (1506–82) belonged to the anti-Mary establishment of James VI, whose preceptor he had become in 1570. That did not, however, prevent him from sharing and advocating the stance of the Knoxian wing of the Scottish Reformation that unjust rulers could be resisted, deposed and even killed if necessary. Buchanan's writings in this respect were of significance for the whole field of European (and future American) political theory and the accountability of monarchs.[5] In Scotland, the immediate effect was to help cement a union between a Scottish tradition of holding the monarch accountable on the one hand, and presbyterian ecclesiology as well as Knoxian oppositionalism on the other (rather than 'Protestantism').

It is no surprise that a contemporary Scottish Catholic abroad like Ninian Winzet (see below), who also worked closely with the expatriate Lesley, should highlight Buchanan's views as irrefutable proof of the inherent link between Protestantism and political subversion. In 1582 he published twin tracts against the political philosophy of Buchanan and

Scottish presbyterian thinkers that obedience to God does not necessitate unqualified obedience to 'divinely instituted' rulers on earth. In Winzet's eyes, this was a recipe for revolt and anarchy. His titles embody the old conservative Catholic view: *A Scourge for the Sectaries who under the Pretext of Religion seek to foment Sedition against the Emperor or other Orthodox Princes with their Ridiculous Question, whether God is to be Obeyed Rather than Princes.*[6] The second title was: *A Challenge to George Buchanan over his Dialogue . . .*[7]

The chief architect of the explicitly presbyterian concept of events was David Calderwood (1575–1650) in the seventeenth century. One version of his *The True History of the Church of Scotland,*[8] posthumously published in 1678, is the canonical historical apologetic of Presbyterianism, and helped prepare the ground for the restoration and legalization of the presbyterian church polity in 1690. In this respect, Calderwood is much more significant than Knox. Interestingly, the General Assembly gave Calderwood an indefinite sabbatical and an annual pension to compose his work. The book is a major source for the history of the Church of Scotland from the Reformation till 1625, and part of its value consists in its use of contemporary sources no longer extant.

Even before Calderwood, the Covenanting minister and historian, John Row (1568–1646), had written a manuscript presbyterian *History of the Kirk* covering the years 1558–1637.[9] This was for the benefit of younger ministers, lest they succumb to Crown and episcopalian propaganda. It was not published as such till the nineteenth century.

Lastly, retrospective apologies for episcopacy, and the pro-episcopalian policies of the Crown were also supplied. As stressed in the chapters on England, it is a famous falsehood to imagine that Presbyterianism and Calvinism are synonyms. English, Welsh, Irish and Scottish episcopalians in the sixteenth century and later were nearly all Calvinists too, just as the Crown in the person of James VI & I was. In Scotland, episcopalian apologetic on the historical plane soon appeared to supplement that on the theoretical plane. This was a work by John Spottiswoode[10] (1565–1639), Church of Scotland minister and successively (nominal) Archbishop of Glasgow and St Andrews, as well as Moderator of the controversial General Assembly at Perth in 1618. He was the chief ecclesiastical instrument of advanced Jacobean policy in the Scottish Church, and so of Anglo-Scottish church uniformity. His *History of the Church of Scotland* (London 1655), reflecting the royal and episcopalian line, was undertaken at the request of James in return for an appropriate honorarium.[11] In the eighteenth century, the Scottish Episcopalian Primus, Robert Keith (1681–1756) reiterated this perspective in his *History of the Affairs of Church and State in Scotland, from the Beginning of the Reformation to the year 1568* (Edinburgh 1734).[12]

Incidentally, the formative Scottish Reformers, being essentially biblicist, did not cite an early Church or 'Celtic Church' ideal prototype to legitimize the Reformation (as we saw above in the case of some churchmen in England, Ireland and Wales). However, later controversies over polity, episcopalian or presbyterian, injected this element, if in a much more subdued way.[13] The historians provided the ammunition. Consequently, Spottiswoode, taking his cue from the Venerable Bede about Christian origins in Scotland, argues that with Ninian, the faith was planted initially by bishops rather than presbyters and monks, though he does not argue for a linear apostolic succession of bishops as such.[14] Calderwood, however, seeing Columba as the more effective missionary to Scotland, urges that since he was a presbyter, and not a bishop, episcopacy is not essential to a viable Christian Church. Not only that, Calderwood boldly argues for continuity between the Reformation, Presbyterianism and the Culdees.[15] The latter were understood as groups of holy men, nonconformist surviving witnesses to the original Rome- and episcopacy-free Christianity of Columban times after the perceived 'takeover' by Rome of Scottish Christianity in the eighth century, an after-effect of the Synod of Whitby (664). The 'presbyterian' Culdees were conceived of as exemplars of the true and pure worship of God, continuing authentic witnesses in the medieval era.

An Enlightenment perspective: Hume

Those are the chief confessional historiographical landmarks determining ways of interpreting the Scottish Reformation: prophetic Protestant, Presbyterian, Episcopalian and Roman Catholic. They still permeate most people's attitudes. However, there has also been a traditional alternative view, very influential, and which has helped shape modern cultural correct-ness. This view has also a long history. Originating in the Enlightenment, it was adopted by a diverse basket of latitudinarian Anglicans, Church of Scotland moderates, rationalists, later Anglo-Catholics, liberal Protestants, civil religionists and modern secularists. Certainly, the most determinative source of this view was a well-known member of the Church of Scotland in the eighteenth century, namely the philosopher David Hume (1711–76). He was a child of British unionism and proponent of anglicization. Since his intellectual status was world class, his perception of the Scottish Reformation was bound then to shape the mind of large sectors of modern opinion at home and abroad. Such a perception is found in Hume's *History of England*, a great and immensely readable work, whose title in the definitive edition changed significantly from the earlier *History of Great Britain*.[16] Hume's view of Scotland, its history and religion, has conditioned that of generations of educated and semi-educated classes, including some historians.

Before illustrating Hume's understanding of the Scottish Reformation, that which determined it should be highlighted. Firstly, despite his personal agnosticism, he had a strong belief in Erastianism, religious practice regulated by the civil authority in the interest of stability and sanity. Secondly, he envisaged the civil power and government as a civilizing agent of improvement, rationality and relative neutrality in theological controversy. Thirdly, he was convinced (not the first) of the inferiority of Scottish traditions and culture. Fourthly, he swallowed the propaganda of Restoration and Enlightenment Anglican apologists of the Reformation. This was, that unlike others, the English Reformation had intrinsically been one of exemplary moderation, civility, decency and virtue. Compared to this, other Reformations were fanatical follies and theocratic tyrannies. In these cases (like Scotland) the rational and urbane civil power had been elbowed aside, or, the particular society was culturally challenged anyway. It is remarkable that Hume, the Delphic oracle of scepticism, was quite credulous when it came to church history.

To be borne in mind is that Hume was also antipathetic to Roman Catholicism. He granted it some aesthetic value, but otherwise it was a religion of superstition, obscurantism, gaoler of the human spirit and manned by bigoted clergy. If religious affairs in sixteenth-century Scotland were unsavoury, Catholics were just as much to blame as Protestants. Hume's even-handedness in this respect is reflected, among other things, in his comment on the burning at St Andrews of the elderly clergyman, Walter Milne (*c.*1476–1558), for heresy as 'the last barbarity the catholics had the power to exercise in Scotland'.[17]

As for the Scottish Reformation movement, it was in Hume's view driven to extremism and violence – a remarkable thesis, in light of the fact that the English Reformation as a whole was far more bloody, and was a martyrs' Reformation in the way the Scottish one was not. In reality, striking in the Scottish Reformation is that despite (between 1558 and 1567) its undoubted rhetoric of violence, intimidation and Old Testament invocation of minatory divine vengeance exercised through any freely selected human agency, bloodshed was not much more widespread. In Scotland, however, says Hume, 'the new sectarians' (by which he means conviction Protestants) 'broke through all the bounds of reason and moderation . . . and led violent invasions of established religion . . . fanaticism concurring with avarice'.[18] This refers to the political revolution accompanying the Scottish Reformation, as it did in Reformations in most places. Anyway, who can seriously exonerate internal political backers of the English Reformation from avarice? To be pointed out, however, is that sixteenth-century Scotland had no wars of religion, unlike contemporary France; nor does she match the religious crime count of contemporary England with its bloody religious revolts, the Pilgrimage of Grace, the Western Rebellion, the Northern Rebellion, its Marian persecution, the execution of Anabaptists, radicals and Catholics for treason, etc. Scotland saw about twenty religious executions before 1560, and a maximum of two religio-political executions of Catholics in the entire post-Reformation era.[19]

Hume's startling picture of John Knox was conditioned by Enlightenment arrogation of moral and aesthetic high ground and by utter bamboozlement at a figure of heightened prophetic utterance. Combined with the denigration found in traditional Roman Catholic accounts,[20] Hume's portrayal is the chief source of the received modern caricatures of the Scottish Reformer as one who blasted Scotland back to a cultural and spiritual Stone Age, 'year Zero'.[21] He likes to call Knox the 'ringleader, or 'rustic apostle',[22] who, he says, 'arrived from Geneva, where he had imbibed from his commerce with Calvin the highest fanaticism of his sect, augmented by his own native ferocity . . . and furious zeal'.[23] Hume discreetly ignores Knox's English background and anglophilia, however, and is unaware that Knox was on occasion ridiculed because of his acquired English accent.[24] Knox then was the chief instigator of the 'outrageous symptoms' of the Reformation in Scotland, with which 'began that cant, hypocrisy and fanaticism which long infested the Kingdom'.[25] Hume continues: 'Knox's politics were as full of sedition as his theology was full of rage and bigotry.'[26] One must however point out that Hume's own politics were 'High Tory', inimical to notions of popular sovereignty and resistance to authority.

Even the bizarre idea of Knox as a misogynist is attributable to Hume. Knox objected only to women in political authority, an anything but unusual view. Like many moderns, Hume garbles this to say that Knox held that neither 'civility nor loyalty is due to any of the female sex'.[27] A strange thing to say of a man who married twice, who confessed to the charm of Mary Stewart, and who had some notable female correspondents.

Further, according to Hume, Knox 'possessed an uncontrollable authority in the Church . . . and even in the civil affairs of the nation'.[28] Such a view of Knox as ultra-Calvinist, theocratic dictator of Reformation Scotland is almost mandatory for some people still. If it had been true, Knox would have been much happier than he was. No seriously informed modern historian subscribes to such an opinion. Knox only enjoyed one year of relative power, 1560–1. Before and after, he was usually in opposition. In the Reformation Church and in politics, any authority he had rested on persuasion not office. It is uncertain if he was ever Moderator of the General Assembly,[29] not that that would give him special authority anyway in the light of the proto-presbyterian principle of ministerial parity, leaders being *primi inter pares* (first among equals). Yet there is evidence he was also reluctant, refusing even to become Church Superintendent of Lothian (just as when a minister of the Church of England he had refused the bishopric of Rochester). That said, as minister of Edinburgh and as a figure of prestige, he was vested (by the Church) with the special power to convene a General Assembly.[30] Some Catholic contemporaries reported that it was not so much Knox who was the leader of the new Church, at least before 1560; rather the 'Primate of their religion'[31] was the ex-Dominican John Willock[32] (d. 1585), returned exile from Germany, Church Superintendent of Glasgow, five times Moderator, and now not well known. Knox was in many ways more of a John the Baptist than Captain of the new Scottish Israel. His role was that of inspirational prophet, Ezekiel the Watchman, catalyst and exhorter. He was a preacher, not (manifestly) a man of affairs or of 'policy', for which he was temperamentally not suited. His spiritual inheritance was, as in Luther and Calvin, belief in the priority of faith and conscience over pragmatism and accommodation, though it translated into a much more radical oppositionalism influencing much of subsequent Scottish Christianity.

Unlike most other mainstream Reformers, who were simultaneously erudite, literary theologians and preachers, Knox was primarily an evangelist, though he also published writings in a variety of genres: polemics, doctrine, liturgy and edification. Direct mission and evangelism on the ground were his medium and forte. His essential vocation was apostolic and prophetic, not ecclesiastical and scholarly. His exilic background had made him one of the most cosmopolitan of all Reformers, a classical 'international Calvinist', having been active in Scotland, England, France, Germany and Switzerland. Unlike other Reformers anywhere, he had engaged in preaching tours at home. His target was the nation, not individuals. He was a man of Jerusalem rather than Athens, of affirmation rather than speculation, a proclaimer rather than a reasoner – though he often did avail himself of scholastic dialectics and rhetorical canons in argument.

The distaste of Hume, the man of reason and empirical verification, is surely rooted in antipathy to these Knoxian 'irrational' characteristics. Knox's self-understanding was this: 'It has pleased [God] to make me not a lord-like Bishop, but a diligent Preacher of his blessed Evangel.'[33] 'Argument and reason are not handmaids [of theology, determining the interpretation of Scripture], but serve to obey it as the Voice of God.'[34] Oral rather than literary confrontation is Knox's priority: 'For considering myself called by God to instruct the ignorant, comfort the sorrowful, strengthen the weak, and rebuke the proud by tongue and living voice in these corrupt days, rather than to write books for a future age, since so much has been written (and by men of great distinction) and yet barely heeded – I decided to confine myself to that vocation to which I have been especially called.'[35]

To conclude with some further Hume judgements illuminating his influential attitude. Two of them would make Scottish patriots see red mist. Firstly, the young Catholic queen's personal reign was burdened by the fact that 'she was left to the society of her own subjects, a people unacquainted with the pleasures of conversation, ignorant of arts and civility, corrupted beyond their usual uncouthness by a dismal fanaticism, incapable of all humanity and improvement'.[36]

Secondly, he quotes from a letter from the English ambassador in Edinburgh in 1560, Thomas Randolph, to William Cecil, Queen Elizabeth's Principal Secretary: 'I think marvellously of the wisdom of God that gave this unruly, inconstant, and cumbersome people no more power and substance, for otherwise they would run wild.'[37] Such a view continues sometimes to be echoed in modern times. Jasper Ridley, for example, remarked that sixteenth-century Scotland was 'the most backward and lawless country of Western Europe'.[38] He did not, however, produce an evidence base.

Further, Hume's sharing of the Georgian and subsequent Church of England's own origins-account is summed up in the following: 'Of all the European churches which shook off the yoke of papal authority, no one proceeded with so much reason and moderation as the Church of England . . . rage and animosity against the catholic religion was little indulged . . . the new religion, by mitigating the genius of the ancient superstition, and rendering it more compatible with the peace and interests of society, has preserved itself in that happy medium.'[39] Of interest in this observation is that it also anticipates by nearly two centuries the modern reductionist interpretation of religious transformation, that it primarily reflects adaptation and accommodation to social and political change.

Lastly, Hume expresses no principled antipathy to presbyterian polity, stating only that certain 'inconveniences' tend to come in its train, notably 'bad habits', such as 'a furious zeal for religion, morose manners, a vulgar and familiar, yet mysterious cant'.[40] Worth noting is that while Hume makes use of Knox's *History*, he finds more ammunition for his critique and judgemental posture in the episcopalian histories of Spottiswoode and Keith. The latter was a contemporary of his in Edinburgh.

Modern approaches

To turn to recent historiography of the Scottish Reformation, and the extent of its revisionism or modernization: an increasing spirit of detachment or defused passion now prevails, at least among most professional historians, even if old pulls and sensitivities still linger. Jenny Wormald, who stated that in the historical approach, 'Protestants and Catholics should never be judged as "right" or "wrong"', has uttered a liberationist credo.[41] This blows the whistle on, among others, the Knoxian and Humian traditions. It also reaffirms the sentiment declared by Maurice Lee seventeen years previously, namely that 'the process of reappraisal . . . makes us sharply aware that the truth is like King Pellinore's questing beast,[42] friendly and elusive and ceaselessly to be pursued and never permanently caught'.[43]

Originating in the late 1950s, the process of revision in Scottish Reformation historiography predates that for most other Reformations. Eight broad reassessments or rediscoveries can be highlighted. Firstly, the view has been advanced that the pre-Reformation Catholic Church was a victim of circumstances and propaganda rather than inherently moribund, since it was sufficiently self-critical to embark on reform from within. Secondly, in respect of the Reformation movement, greater consciousness of primary Lutheran waves and impulses has been awakened. Thirdly, the traditional idea that the ultimate success of the Calvinist–Presbyterian Reformation was inevitable is challenged as a view from hindsight. Fourthly, the traditional precedence granted to 'politics' has been re-assessed. Fifthly, there has been a degree of rehabilitation of Mary Stewart in respect of her religious policy, apparently clearing her of imputed ignominy. Sixth, it is maintained that active popular support for the Reformation was limited not only in rural regions but also in urban contexts, and that, subsequently, the process of protestantization was at best erratic until the seventeenth century. Seventh, it has been shown that commending the Reformation to much of Scottish Gaeldom, half the nation, was more subtle and efficacious than previously believed. Eighth, the Calvinism–Capitalism pairing has been found not relevant to Scotland.

Turning to the *first* reassessment, the volume edited by David McRoberts in 1962 made Catholic perspectives on the Reformation in Scotland more generally accessible for the first time for over half a century.[44] Though it is occasionally and anachronistically punctuated with elements of pre-Vatican I ingenuousness, grandiloquence, nostalgia for a *temps perdu* and irascible references to the 'protestant faction', it embodied impressive erudition and opened up new, or neglected ground. It resumed major Catholic studies or accounts of the Catholic side that had appeared in the late nineteenth and early twentieth century. Notable among these were works or source-editions by Alphons Bellesheim,[45] James Walsh,[46] William Forbes-Leith[47] and John H. Pollen.[48] Since the centre of gravity in these works lies in the 'top-down', church-political domain (pre- and post-1560) and to some extent in that of controversial theology, the actual state of Catholicism among the people of the nation before and after the Reformation was not subject to much analysis.

The essential leitmotiv in the McRoberts volume is that while national religion and the Catholic Church were in serious need of reform, structural and spiritual, the Protestant Reformation, if in the context irresistible, was neither necessary nor desirable. The secularization of the old Church is highlighted. The Crown and the nobility held the Church and much of its patrimony in thrall – a view shared by a Scottish pre-Reformation theologian of eminence like the Sorbonnist, John Mair (or Major) (*c.*1467–1550). In his *History of Greater Britain* (1521), it is recalled, he argued that the munificence of King David I (1085–1153) to the Scottish Church seriously disabled the cause of religion.[49] Equally hostile to lay patronage and committed to church autonomy (like the future Free Church of Scotland) was the Cluniac Abbot of Crossraguel (south Ayrshire) and doctrinal apologist, Quintin Kennedy (1520–64).

The Scottish Catholic reform movement, embodied in three provincial councils[50] of 1549, 1552 and 1559 was frustrated by aristocratic vested interest in the financial *status quo*; the majority of the Scottish episcopate were 'baronial prelates' or indeed pirates, dilapidators of the Church. Reform would have involved some redistribution of wealth, not a realistic prospect at a time of rising inflation. The church councils were presided over by the careerist churchman and moderate, John Hamilton (*c.*1511–

71) Archbishop of St Andrews from 1547, well provided for with benefices and part of the cream of Scottish society – he was half-brother of James Hamilton (1516–75), Earl of of Arran, Duke of Chatelherault, former Governor of Scotland who was later one of the Protestant Lords of the Congregation. Archbishop Hamilton therefore was in no position to enforce radical solutions. Serious damage to Catholic credibility had been done by impious and francophile Catholics like James V (1512–42), Cardinal David Beaton (*c.*1494–1546), and the especially notorious Patrick Hepburn (d. 1573), Augustinian Prior of St Andrews and then Bishop of Moray, despite their anti-heretical and persecuting zeal. On the other hand, the temporizing (or conciliatory) policy of Mary of Guise (or Lorraine) during her regency (1554–59) is criticized since it encouraged Protestants with inflated ideas of what was achievable. She had also denied John Knox a trial for heresy and helped bring about the 'ruin of the church'.[51]

By emphasizing the political and economic factors in Protestant success, the volume reflects essentially the traditional Catholic interpretative paradigm. And if the bishops were generally unworthy, responsible for that is primarily the influence of the Crown, rather than the 'Church'. Also, the marriage of Reformation ideology with Scottish national sentiment enabled the substitution of the Protestant English for the traditional French Catholic alliance or clientage. Once the nobility had redefined its interests and prospects for aggrandizement, their most effective propaganda weapon was secured by hijacking 'demagogues' like the 'neurotic Knox' into the service of political revolution.[52]

Somewhat low-key in the McRoberts volume is recognition of the evangelical and pastoral deficiencies of the Scottish higher clergy in particular, though their collective moral corruption is not toned down. Their 'kerygmatic failure',[53] reflecting that elsewhere, needed more attention, as it has been given subsequently by writers like Ian Cowan.[54] Ironically, contemporary reform Catholics, like the Court-sponsored poet and dramatist, Sir David Lindsay[55] (*c.*1490–1555), Abbot Quintin Kennedy, and the likeable schoolmaster-priest, Ninian Winzet, focused on these aspects in their critiques of the contemporary Church. The latter, speaking up on behalf of the lower clergy and Catholic laity disillusioned with the failure and 'deadly sleep' of the church leadership, identified the evangelical deficit in the old Church when he stated: 'Your dumb doctrine, in exalting ceremonies only, without any declaration of the same, and, far more, keeping in silence the true Word of God, necessary to all men's salvation, and not resisting manifest errors, to the world is known.'[56]

Such a classical indictment was all the more credible in view of Winzet's unimpeachable loyalty to Catholicism and his activity as an apologist of essential Catholic doctrine – his thinking anticipates some of the content of decrees of the Scottish Church reform councils. It does look, then, as if the promising appointment in 1548 of Tridentine preaching and lecturing canons like John Watson in the cathedral of Aberdeen was neither copied much elsewhere nor effective.[57] Also, the plea of Patrick Cockburn (d. 1568) seems to have met with little response: 'What is the point of offering sacrifices of the Mass without the Word?'[58] Anyway, the Scottish hierarchy, committed to the Latin Vulgate, had opposed to a man the legislation in 1543 of the Scottish Parliament during the regency of James Hamilton, Earl of Arran, authorizing the circulation and reading of vernacular Bibles in Scotland.[59] The bishops, inheritors of a long-standing tradition, saw the Bible as the book of the clerical church or 'spiritual estate'. The explanation of Scripture was vested in the apostolically-consecrated teachers, not the people of God, who are not qualified to interpret it. This was the Roman Catholic traditionalist viewpoint.

In the McRoberts volume, the contribution by Anthony Ross on the religious orders highlights the significance of the Observant movement among the friars and other manifestations of 'real vitality', spiritual and intellectual, among monks.[60] Subsequent studies by Cowan[61] as well as more recently Dilworth[62] on the state of Scottish monasticism at the time show that for all the problems flowing from the notorious 'commendation' system, the regular clergy were relatively conscientious, productive and comprised the more literate element of the Scottish Church. A Church that sponsored the establishment of three universities in the fifteenth century, at St Andrews, Glasgow and Aberdeen, and two further colleges at St Andrews in the sixteenth century, cannot be said to have been devoted to the idol of ignorance. Studies by Durkan and others underline the fact that for all Scotland's geographical remoteness, it was anything but untouched by European intellectual mainstreams in theology and Humanism. Rather than at Oxbridge, it was in Continental universities where significant numbers of Scots, Gaelic and Lowland, studied and taught – a situation which continued after the Reformation.

Subsequent work by James Cameron has highlighted the Continental roots and impact of moderate, non-Tridentine, Catholic-reform theology in Scotland. Rich in insight into popular Catholic piety and devotion (and shortage of it) in late medieval Scotland up to the middle of the sixteenth century is a piece by Gordon Donaldson that also discusses the extent to which there was accommodation to superstitious folk-religion and sub-Christian traditions.[63] He also points to a paradox: communities where priests were conscientious and instructive were more likely to respond positively to the Reformation message.

Post-1560 Catholicism was not a primary concern in the McRoberts volume, apart from a study on the early process of protestantization through church discipline and another on formal relations with Rome up to 1625. As long as Mary was still in power, reversal was a possibility, and indeed in 1566 she initiated a discreet recatholicization process that was to be a factor at least in her downfall. By 1567, however, even the papacy had distanced itself from her, partly due to her marriage scandals, and partly due to doubts about her Catholic commitment (lack of persecuting zeal). Her departure from Scotland also terminated indefinitely direct relations between Rome and the Scottish monarchy. This signalled essential marginalization of the Catholic cause in Scotland; it was just not a high priority in the European context. More energy was to be devoted to Counter-Reformation on the Continent as well as in England and Ireland. Anglo-Scottish political amity, religious common interest and the union of the Crowns in 1603 justified this strategy. That is to say, successful targeting of England and Ireland would have inevitable effects on Scotland by association.

Accordingly, after 1567 a seriously organized and popular Counter-Reformation in Scotland was neither on the cards nor undertaken, even though there is evidence of stout local resistance throughout the land for thirty years after 1560, including towns with eminent Reformation pedigrees like Perth.[64] Unlike in Ireland, where not only the traditional spiritual, but also the entire temporal infrastructure was being radically disturbed, mass adhesion to Catholicism in Scotland gradually weakened. It survived mainly in areas of the south-west and north-east (and a few districts in the western Highlands and Islands) where the local recusant gentry or nobility remained loyal to the old faith – all well away from the centres of power. By the seventeenth century, committed Catholics in Scotland had been reduced to an insignificant minority. While modest Jesuit and Irish Franciscan missions (both reluctant) helped survival and local revivals, the priorities of general Catholic missionary strategy definitely lay elsewhere. Scots Colleges abroad, at Paris, Rome, Douai[65] and Madrid were indeed recruiting grounds for Counter-Reformation missioners, but rarely for Scotland. Accordingly, research into post-Reformation Catholic subculture is not so much concerned with reasons for general failure, which are self-evident, as with reportage and documentation of remnant survival manifestations, intermittent recatholicization successes in isolated districts, and heroic labours of individuals, often tartan pimpernels, in adverse circumstances. [66] Unfortunately the focus is usually on clergy and gentry, so that the mentality of ordinary survivalist Catholics is difficult to gauge.

A *second* feature of modern research has been that in considering the sources of the early Reformation movement in Scotland originating in the early 1520s, the tracing of the formative Lutheran impulses and manifestations has, following earlier cues from W. Stanford Reid[67] and John Durkan,[68] seen some progress. This is identified with the names of James Cameron, James McGoldrick, Rainer Haas and again John Durkan, as well as others like Gerhard Müller and Gotthelf Wiedermann. Lutheran theology had penetrated Scotland directly, securing a toe-hold in 'stations of high tension' like St Andrews University (St Leonard's College in particular), the eastern sea ports, some Augustinian and Dominican houses, and in the households of a small number of gentry and burghers. Already by 1525 already, the Scottish Parliament was legislating against the import of Lutheran literature in the interests of retaining Scotland's reputation for being 'heresy free'. In subsequent years, generally effective suppression and persecution backed this up.

Undoubtedly the catalyst that brought the Reformation movement to life in Scotland was the Lutheran theological impulse with its leapfrogging over sacramental grace to the gratuitous promises of God, and its denial of human capacity to sway God. Research shows that the Wittenberg theology penetrated Scotland by different routes: directly from Germany by books (via Frankfurt, Basle and Antwerp) and returning students; from Scandinavia, Denmark in particular; from France, and from England. Certain themes of Luther's theology, apart from justification by faith alone, were particularly relevant for discreet sympathizers in the early decades and who could not easily 'come out'. For example: the theology of the cross, consolation, prayerful compliance with oppressive authority, a sense of membership of the true church that is invisible, and so interior piety. Studies also suggest that like elsewhere, pro-Reformation Scottish religious thinkers, domestic or exilic, revealed a partiality for Melanchthon, the chief spokesman and moderate voice of Lutheranism; his formative *Augsburg Confession* and *Apology* (1530–1) was available in English translation by 1536.[69]

As in the wider 'reformed' world of Europe including Britain, the primary Lutheran layer in Scotland (there is no evidence for early Zwinglian input) became subsumed by two waves. Firstly, there was the south German–Swiss genus of Protestant consensus theology and of comprehensive reformation of church and society. Secondly, there was the more advanced form of this, namely Genevan Calvinism in its various expressions. The Scottish Reformation proper, being the last in Europe, belongs very much to the 'Second Reformation' – one shaped more by broad reformed and Calvinist theology, its biblicism, ecclesiology and social concern in particular, and which superseded the earlier dissemination of the Wittenberg theology in the country. As with Luther before him, however, Calvin's direct involvement with the Reformation in Scotland was negligible.

However, there are interpreters like Heinz Schilling who exclude Scotland from this category. This is because he conceives the 'second Reformation' as functioning in a multi- rather than mono-confessional context, in other words, where Lutheran and reformed Churches existed side by side. In this scenario (in Germany), the 'reformed' Churches embody a second, more advanced phase within the context of an already existing official Reformation. Since Scotland's 'Lutheran' phase was in no way 'official', Schilling reckons that Scotland's Reformation 'history' is simply part of the history of undifferentiated 'Calvinism', and so has no equivalent elsewhere.[70] Such a paradigm needs revisiting.

A *third* re-evaluation, involving some reshuffling of concepts and received orthodoxies, concerns the notion of the Scottish Reformation as Calvinism in presbyterian form as inevitable, virtually by prior divine decree. The received and perpetuated orthodoxy in the world of wider literature and general knowledge is encapsulated in the following recent statement by an historian: 'Thanks to the efforts of John Knox, Calvinism became the sole established religion in the Kingdom of Scotland in 1560, in a form known as Presbyterianism.'[71] Happily, this influential cliché has been subjected to recasting.

This followed an amicable altercation between Gordon Donaldson and James Kirk. Donaldson, who has also stressed that the Scottish Reformation was theologically no more 'Calvinist' than that in the developed English Reformation, proposed the following syllogism: all presbyterians were Calvinist, not all Calvinists were presbyterian. Therefore the church revolution of 1560 was not even proleptically presbyterian. Consequently, seeing continuity rather than discontinuity, and insisting that there was a reflex in the direction of true evangelical episcopacy with the installation of regional church superintendents on the Lutheran model, Donaldson revived the episcopalian interpretation of the early reformed Kirk. Further, he suggested that this was compatible with the model of the Church of England, whose influence in Scotland has been underestimated – a stance derived in part from a study by F. W. Maitland earlier in the century.[72] Not till the late 1570s, under the impact of the Protestant Humanist Andrew Melville (1545–1622), Theodore Beza in Geneva, and English presbyterian theorists like Cartwright and Travers did a doctrinaire presbyterian party emerge in the Kirk. Further, Knox himself assented to the *modus operandi* on the question of episcopacy arrived at between the General Assembly and the Crown at the Convention of Leith in 1572; anyway, he is not on record as ever having expressed antipathy to the office as such. Donaldson considered that later presbyterian churchmen, writing from hindsight, hijacked the mentality of the official Reformation Church in its early decades.

Kirk stoutly negated the implication of these views.[73] He maintained that at least the notions of ministerial parity and presbyterial discipline were central to the thinking of the 1560 Reformers. Committed to a 'radical root and branch Reformation' and not inclined to 'tarry for the magistrate', they were impatient from the start, determined on here-and-now implementation of a truly reformed Kirk in which Presbytery ruled autonomously.[74] In this context, then, the office of superintendent was essentially a transitional expedient, a pragmatic, provisional manoeuvre for the sake of the immediate well-being of the Church. The office was not intended to be permanent, nor to be a prelude to the restoration of a fully reformed historic episcopate (the office still existed in Crown patronage, but its role in ecclesiastical reality was very limited).[75]

A *fourth* mark of revision (relatively speaking) has been a firm qualification at least of the reductionist view that the Scottish Reformation was just 'political', and imposed from the top. Donaldson, Kirk and Cowan combine forces in making this corrective. They have been given discreet support from the more sceptical Michael Lynch. He does concede that the religious impulse was authentic and primary in many key cases, but argues that it was astutely politicized to gain broader immediate support, compensating for the lack of wide spontaneous sympathy.[76] Pierre Janton's works on Knox have re-established the absolute priority of the Reformer's spiritual and theological concerns and analysed them and their potency in a systematic manner.

A *fifth* development has been a degree of rehabilitation of the religious policy of the queen, Mary Stewart, throughout her personal rule (1560–7). Contrary to received tradition, Donaldson and Kirk combine to laud Mary for the appropriateness of her religious policy, one of pragmatic accommodation and compromise (a policy not at all welcomed by Knoxian radicals, who might have profited more from persecution). Mary's policy (or the policy she was advised to follow by both her Protestant Privy Council and French Catholic elements in her Court and in France) produced a situation unparalleled in Europe. This was an effectively Protestant state with a committed Catholic monarch at its head. Not only that, she placed an element of Crown funds derived from church patronage at the disposal of the new Reformed Church, even if payments were desultory. She was even willing to endure a series of personal debates with Knox, whom she infuriated with her astute appeal to 'liberty of conscience' in respect of her right to have Mass said in Holyrood Palace in Edinburgh. That was a concept imported from contemporary France, and one with which she was familiar before she came to Scotland. It was employed previously in Scotland by her mother, Mary of Guise, and very much by her ex-mother-in-law, the French Regent, Catherine de Médicis in contemporary France.[77] Mary also seems to have countenanced irenical 'third way' ideas of reform designed to reintegrate the Church.[78]

In a sense, such a profile of Mary places the alleged ultra-polarization of the early Scottish Reformation in a new light. The air may have been thick with tension. Knox and the General Assembly may have complained about lack of progress and the doldrums in which the Reformation found itself, but at least open, brutal confrontations and ritual violence were avoided. The conceptions of Mary propagated by Knox and Buchanan, making her the victim of a 'black legend' are seen by some as the mythologizing work of the Protestant Scottish Establishment.[79]

Even so, Mary's policy has to be judged by criteria other than utilitarian ones. For she aspired ultimately to have the throne of England as much as to the beatific vision. The former was unconcealed French policy. Further, her commitment to the eventual recatholicization of Scotland was understandably part of her agenda, only possible, as she realized, with foreign aid. This was not forthcoming. Her upping of the ante in a Catholic sense in 1566 seems to corroborate her intentions, justify Knox's pessimistic diagnosis, and seal her fate.[80] In the end, she forfeited the support of Catholic Europe as well, unconvinced as it was about her religious commitment and despondent about her marriage history. In the domain of religion, 'inevitable failure' rather than 'creditable success' has to be the tag put on Mary's policy, since she was pursuing a lost cause.

A *sixth* characteristic of modern study of the Reformation in Scotland has been a challenge to the myth that Reformation legislation commanded wide and popular support throughout the country, so that it was somehow responding primarily to pressure 'from below'. Whatever older Protestant inflationary conceptions were,[81] such a view has not been especially current among more recent historians. It was certainly not the understanding of John Knox. One of his major complaints was that the religious Reformation was so unpopular, engaging only a small minority – 'a little flock'. Correspondingly, writers like Cowan and Lynch have highlighted evidence of both passive and active resistance, apathy, and adhesion to old ways after 1560. The progress of the official Reformation in the first generation among the largely inert populace was tardy, muddled, and often unwelcome.

However, if Cowan and Lynch tended to focus on lack of progress, others like Sanderson and Bardgett have charted positive Reformation growth in contrasting regions of Scotland before and after 1560. There is therefore some incongruity between the official pro-Reformation policy emanating from the centre, albeit hamstrung, and relatively buoyant Reformation manifestations in certain districts and localities that pre-existed for some time.[82]

The cartography of the Reformation movement in Scotland is as follows: in the regional and rural areas, there was inertia, protest or resistance of various kinds such as the south-west, most of Gaeldom except Argyll, and the north-east. The same is true initially of towns like Edinburgh[83] and cathedral cities like Glasgow and Aberdeen, all seats of traditional power, civil or ecclesiastical. Activist Protestantism was more manifest firstly, in regions like Angus in the north-east as well as in parts of Ayrshire, where there were older traditions of religious dissent apparently associated with Lollardy, and secondly, in urban contexts like Stirling, Perth, Dundee and Ayr. Here were located the concentrations of the artisan and rising 'middling' classes who were to be the workhorses of future Protestantism. St Andrews was in a category of it own. An episcopal city and centre of both the Scottish Inquisition and reform-Catholic ideas, its university had been to some extent a platform for Reformation ideas and controversial theology. This had an impact on the tiny local population, but more importantly, the mobile student population.

The broad pattern was that pro-Reformation sympathy, and so a degree of popular commitment, was concentrated in prosperous east central Scotland with its direct links to the Continent, the exception being Ayr, the west of Scotland's chief sea port. This corresponds roughly to the situation in England, where there was a focus in the south-east, with Bristol being the Reformation's *entrée* in the west. Broadly speaking, the further any area was from the centre of power, the longer Catholicism survived. The patterns of compliance, conformity and resistance or indifference are broadly related to this situation, and partly to the predispositions of the local nobility. Yet at the end of the day the fundamental situation in Scotland during its uneven transition to Reformation was the same as elsewhere in Western Christendom, where 'accompanying the pan-European echo of the Reformers' message was an equally universal No'.[84]

Most writers acknowledge that the process of Protestant evangelization was handicapped by the Kirk's underendowment following the nobility's impropriation of two-thirds of the ecclesiastical patrimony at the outset. For this addiction to Mammon they were excoriated by the Reformers. Also, during Mary's rule, the reformed Church found herself becalmed, operating with only a provisional status, and without the support of the full panoply of state authority, the personal royal court being Catholic. Such an unnatural situation hardly encouraged extensive spiritual regeneration campaigns. Further, Keith Brown has made the timely point that more pressing than the sanctification of the commonalty was the moral acculturation and christianization of the nobility. They were often a law unto themselves, settling issues by the *lex talionis* or blood feud, and exercised arbitrary power in the localities. An ultimate achievement of the Reformation was to domesticate them, a (popular) fruit of the Kirk's insistence that church discipline embrace all social classes.[85]

Lastly, all writers grant that one carrot which increasingly helped rouse relatively popular support for the reformation Church was participative laicization. Sanderson emphasizes this in relation to Ayrshire in particular, where she finds the development of a 'People's Church' and urges recognition of 'the layman's history of the Scottish Reformation'.[86] Donaldson and Kirk ground lay activation in the appeal of religious principles (priesthood of all believers, sanctification of secular work, access to Scripture, worship as communal fellowship, heightened Christian social-ethical awareness, etc.), Lynch and Brown more in terms of class interest and politics of kinship. And in identifying post-Reformation priorities, Michael Lynch makes an interesting observation. This is that since most religious historical writing on Scotland in the later sixteenth and seventeenth centuries has been dominated by the Episcopalian–Presbyterian struggle and church–state relations, the process of the comprehensive protestantization of Scotland in those generations has been neglected.[87]

Progress in this respect has now been made in an innovative work by David G. Mullan on the nature and dissemination of broad reformed piety and theology during the two generations between the Melvillian era (*c.*1575–85) and the Covenant of 1638.[88] While not offering a 'bottom-up' perspective', its focus is not so much on high-flying divines, as on the mediators, the preachers, the ministers, the bishops, that is, the inculcators and shapers of increasingly wide public opinion, and not just male. Highlighted also are the increasingly articulate lay respondents. What emerges are polarities and tensions that are only secondarily 'Scottish', but which need to be better appreciated in order to make more sense of the later, much studied struggles connected with Covenant politics. The situation reflected a distant outworking of the ancient Augustinian dichotomies (or dualities associated with the world of late Christian Antiquity and being recycled in Continental and English puritanism). Examples of such tensions cascading through Scottish Protestantism were: the poles of external and internal spirituality, individual and collective, personal and national, subjective and objective, scholastic and experiential, catholic and sectarian, ecclesiastical and voluntary, public and private, militant and irenic, political and quietist, predestination and free-will, sin and grace, sacrament and preaching, church and state, heavenly and earthly cities, election and reprobation, conversion and indoctrination, lay and clerical, extempore and set prayer, exposition of the Word and mystical devotion, evangelical and ritualist, male and female, formal and informal, lofty and familiar, introversion and extroversion, coercion and persuasion, covenant and faith, and so on – all against the background of the Scottish netherworld of 'ineradicable irreligion and anti-clericalism'.[89]

A *seventh* reassessment has ensued from work on the Reformation in Scottish Gaeldom, which has only got off the ground in recent times, by Jane Dawson, James Kirk and Donald Meek. The traditional lack of attention to it has been due largely to the political domination of Scotland by the England-orientated Lowlands, from where nearly all Reformation historians have come. Yet in this era Gaels were more than half the population of Scotland. They also formed part of a wider Gaeldom whose political fracture was not complete until after the subjugation of Gaelic Ulster by 1601–3. As in Ireland, the official attitude of the civil and church authorities to Gaeldom was at best ambivalent. Under James VI, however, the official policy was that evangelization, anglicization and civilization should go hand-in-hand, not – as in Ireland (see Chapter 6) – that the second and the third should precede the first. This strategy was understood as a campaign against what was described in a government policy document of 1615 as 'these unhallowed people, with that unchristian language', echoing a paradigmatic observation by James VI previously that the Gaelic population were 'wild savages devoid of the fear of God'.[90] Notwithstanding, in the face of later Protestant protest about a successful Franciscan Catholic mission in Kintyre directed from north Antrim, James VI responded that he actually regarded it preferable that the people of Kintyre be some sort of Christians, even if Catholic, rather than wild pagans.[91] Does this also provide a clue to the mystery of ambivalent religious policy of the Crown in Gaelic Ireland in the Reformation and post-Tridentine era?

No urgent reconversion strategy was systematically implemented in what was seen as the sub-Christian world of the Highlands and Islands (despite a promising start with Carswell's Gaelic *Book of Common Order*). Yet irrespective of the Scottish Reformers' reputed predestinarian Calvinism, there is no evidence for any sentiment of wanting to abandon the Gaels to a predestined permafrost, *ifrinn* (hell) either. In fact, most of Gaelic Scotland was absorbed into the Kirk over 150 years without precipitous loss of the language and other cultural assets at least. The early adhesion of the politically important Argyll region to the Reformation doubtless helped detach the old faith from the Gaelic half of the country more easily. And the temptation to consider Scottish Gaeldom as bereft culturally, and theologically cut off from European mainstreams must be resisted. After all, why was the Gael and Humanist writer, Roderick MacLean (d. 1553), studying theology in Wittenberg in the 1530s? There he matriculated along with at least one other compatriot as being 'ex Hibernia', even if he subsequently relapsed and became Catholic Bishop of the Isles (1547–53).[92]

Paradoxically, Dawson's work reveals a remarkably pragmatic accommodation of initially benign Calvinism to a boisterous, pastoral Gaeldom of clans, oral and bardic tradition, fairy worlds, ghosts, ancestor veneration and religious art.[93] This occurred even if the long term 'policy', as in Ireland and Wales, was to wean people off this culture and language rather than affirm them. Yet the phenomenon also poses a problem for the Calvinism and Capitalism thesis, and its concept of the new religious man, ascetic and urban, associated with industrial enterprise, the work ethic and bourgeois values.

The *eighth* and last amendment to the understanding of 'Scottish Calvinism' followed from work by Gordon Marshall and James McEwen. They demonstrated that Max Weber's thesis about Calvinism and capitalism breaks down in Scotland, as had been long suspected.[94] If Scotland was super-Calvinist, why was it not prosperous? McEwen pointed out that linking providence and blessings to affluence was not in the theology of Calvin and Knox. Rather God's benevolence is to be discerned in calamity and exigency. Marshall assents to this. The theology of renunciation and this-worldly asceticism was inimical to self-interest, capitalism and enterprise. In practice, however, a balance had to be sought – the use of God-given talents and prosperity should be subordinated to the needs of others and the common good. De Jong's study of John Forbes (of Alford) (*c.*1568–1634) – the presbyterian minister and writer exiled in the Netherlands by James VI after the defiant General Assembly at Perth in 1605, and minister to the Company of Merchant Adventurers in Middelburg and Delft – confirms that there was at least a cognitive dissonance at work. Predestinarian theologians like Forbes preached one thing, whereas assenting Protestant businessmen practised something different. Election, urged Forbes, is consecration to a life conformable to that of Christ; acquisition of wealth and worldly status can subvert, negate, and desanctify such a calling.[95]

In Scotland throughout these centuries the Kirk's economic statements were wholly conservative and restrictionist. There was no Scottish urban middle-class laity sufficiently large, wealthy and independent-minded to defy this in a significant way. The country was, in terms of population, just too small, distant and economically undeveloped until the union with England in the eighteenth century. The Scottish Reformation, usually seen as comprehensively 'successful', was achieved without either a significantly 'rising' or potent middle class. In a future era, and after such religious turbulence had passed, Adam Smith's *Wealth of Nations* was however to unlock the potential.

CHAPTER 8

Reformation in Scotland

The pre-1557[1] era

Phase 1

The date of birth of the Reformation in Scotland is open to discussion, as the year '1560' just refers to its public or quasi-official adoption. There is no obvious beginning for the movement as such, though news at least of Luther's *Ninety-five Theses* conceivably reached Scotland very soon, bearing in mind that copies of the text were circulating in London in 1517. And when the Scottish Parliament ordered a clampdown on Lutheran and designated heretical books in 1525, one can assume that these works had been imported for some years previously. For the period thereafter, rather than map out the evolution of a putative growing 'movement', this section will indicate the main evidence of intermittent pro-Reformation manifestations in a hostile environment.

Such symptoms are usually connected with this or that individual who fell foul of the authorities, or fled the country in order to avoid such an eventuality. While the previous chapter has drawn attention to the fact that the early appearance in Scotland of the revolutionary theology is associated essentially with east coast Lutherans, it is ironic that the earliest known indigenous Lutheran document in Scotland originates in the west, in Ayrshire. Here there was a pre-existing local tradition of religious dissent arguably derived from Wycliffite Lollardy.[2] It expressed itself in anti-clericalism, hostility to sacred images, an interest in vernacular Scripture and lay religious initiative. Understandably the 'Luther affair' evoked responses in such a community, which eventually, like Lollards in England and Waldensians in France and Savoy, aligned itself with the mainstream Reformation.

Associated with these circles was Murdoch Nisbet (d. *c*.1550), who was rediscovered at the end of the nineteenth century. All dates concerning him are insecure, but he seems to have returned to Scotland in the mid-1520s after exile in England or the Continent due to heresy suspicions. While away, he also produced a manuscript scotticized version of the Wycliffe–Purvey English New Testament based on the Vulgate.[3] There are signs of influence of Tyndale's English New Testament in his text. Striking, though, is that the preface to Nisbet's version is an independent translation of Luther's Preface to his German New Testament (1522). It looks then as if this Luther translation was done between 1522 and 1526, after which Tyndale's translation began to circulate in Scotland. In the event, Nisbet's biblical work was to be of no significance for the future since it was only a manuscript and a Vulgate-based text. But it is important for including a modest monument to the earliest Scottish echo of Luther. Further, it would have helped disseminate scriptural knowledge among certain west of Scotland lay groups in the interim.

If the Reformation in general was ultimately a contention over and about the Bible, the situation in Scotland was no exception to this, even if no Bible was actually published in the country till 1579,[4] versions from England having been always readily available. The issue was deadly serious. Involved was the Word of God – accessible and tangible for all or not? Was the Bible a reserved book of the clerical Church, or did it belong to the whole People of God? After all, the not-so-good traditional Catholic, Erasmus, even before Luther, laid down the challenge in the prologue to the Greek New Testament (1516):

> I disagree very much with those who are unwilling that Holy Scripture, translated into the vulgar tongue, be read by the uneducated, as if Christ taught such intricate doctrines that they could scarcely be understood by [only] a very few theologians, or as if the strength of the Christian religion consisted in men's ignorance of it.[5]

To represent such an attitude in Scotland in the early decades of the Reformation movement was life threatening, since in the eyes of the Church Establishment, it was linked (potentially) with the crime of heresy, and had been since the Middle Ages. A principal charge against Patrick Hamilton (see below), Scotland's first Lutheran martyr in 1528, was that he advocated open access to the Word of God by the means of vernacularized Scripture. The Scottish hierarchy proceeded to ban Bible translations in Scotland, similar to an equivalent prohibition on French vernacular Scriptures pronounced by the provincial council of Sens (or Paris) in 1528.[6] One of those who at the time attempted to change Hamilton's mind was Alexander Alesius (or Alane or Allan) (1500–65), like Luther, an Augustinian and a Nominalist. He himself then became converted. The outcome was that he fled Scotland in 1530 in the face of inquisition,[7] having confronted the singularly unaugustinian Augustinian Prior of St Andrews, Patrick Hepburn, eventually becoming a student at Wittenberg. Scotland's loss, he was to have a future distinguished career as writer and professor of theology in Cambridge, Frankfurt-on-Oder and Leipzig.[8]

It was Alesius, writing from Germany, who put the question of Bible translation on the national agenda in Scotland. In 1533 he published an open letter to James V: *Letter against a Certain Decree of the Bishops in Scotland Prohibiting the Reading of the New Testament in the Vernacular.*[9] He uses the argument that the right to Scripture in the language of the people is grounded in the Incarnation, so that God wishes the sacred mysteries to be seen and handled by all, and to reach out to all. Robbing God's people of their inheritance rather than giving it to them is the real source of errors. The implications of such thinking were dramatic, since the notion of the laity putting their hands on the written Word of God and 'understanding' it, was seen as almost as sacrilegious as their fingering of the sacramental body and blood of Christ. Arch-conservative reactions were rooted in this fear.

This led to a polemical exchange between Alesius and the Catholic controversialist in Germany, John Cochlaeus (1479–1552). The latter composed a lengthy response (173 pages), and somewhat inconsistently for a committed Catholic, also addressed it to James V as arbiter. This was: *On the Merits of Lay People Reading the Vernacular New Testament.*[10] One of his essential arguments in this was that making the Bible available in the vernacular opens up a Pandora's box of calamities for church and society. The Peasants' Revolt (1525) and other radical religious disruptions derived from Luther's German New Testament, 'a noxious and deadly pasture'. The debate continued with two further tracts. These were Alesius' *Reply to Cochlaeus' Calumnies*, and then Cochlaeus' counter: *An Explanation for the Kingdom of Scotland . . . in regard to the Pretended Alexander Alesius, a Scot.*[11] This was a mischievous attempt to expose Philipp Melanchthon, Alesius' tutor at Wittenberg, as the real author of Alesius' tracts, and so weaken their credibility.

The Scottish authorities listened more to Cochlaeus than to Alesius. In 1536 Parliament ordered a ban on English Bibles in Scotland. That the law had teeth was exemplified in 1539 when an Augustinian canon and priest in Stirlingshire, Thomas Forret, was 'unmercifully' burned alive (along with others convicted of heresy)[12] at Edinburgh Castle for being in possession of an English New Testament. Objections to him included refusing tithes, teaching parishioners to say the Lord's Prayer, the Creed, and the Ten Commandments in English, preaching every Sunday, and eating meat during Lent.[13] In Glasgow, an Observant Franciscan and a young layman were also burned.[14] And in 1540 Sir John Borthwick (d. 1569), soldier, diplomat and theologically literate was excommunicated in his absence for a range of heresies including possession of the New Testament.[15] Among those arrested and charged on flimsy grounds at the time was George Buchanan (1506–82) who managed to escape and flee the country.[16] Also charged on probably better grounds were the Wedderburn brothers from Dundee (see below), who also fled into exile. Nine recantations are reported in 1539.

A brief pro-English turn in Scottish government policies during the Governorship of James Hamilton, Earl of Arran, led to an official flirtation with Lutheran notions. One symptom of this was legislation in 1543 permitting 'all men and women' to read the Bible in their own language, 'or in the English tongue'. The Scottish bishops opposed this unanimously in vain. Theoretically, the move gave the green light to both Scots and Gaelic Scriptures. Yet even future Reformation Scotland failed to publish such versions – a failure that had serious long-term consequences for the currency and status of both such languages in Scotland. Due to the power of James Beaton (or Betoun) (*c.*1480–1539), Archbishop of St Andrews (1523–39) and his nephew, the career politician and strongly pro-French Cardinal David Beaton (*c.*1494–1546), Archbishop of St Andrews (1539–46), the Church Establishment regained the upper hand. Conservative religious policies prevailed, even if the religio-political opposition could still sometimes do damage. In 1546 the Scottish bishops ruled that only the Latin Vulgate was to be read, and that Bible possession by the laity would remain felonious.

Increasing lay exposure to Scripture and to elementary Christian teaching in the vernacular was reflected in one of the most successful oral, and later printed, media disseminating Lutheran ideas in Scotland, this time in Scots. These were the popular and catechetical *Gude and Godly Ballatis*, devised from composite sources.[17] Their authors originated in Dundee Protestant milieu, notably the Wedderburn brothers, especially John (*c.*1508–56) an ex-priest who had studied in Wittenberg. There he clearly learned some lessons from Luther on mass communication through song and rhyme. In the Ballads, biblical authority is paramount, and functions as the antithesis of church authority and Tradition. Often mimicking the clergy with coarse derision, they can utter:

> The water of lyfe we gave them never to drink
> Bot stinkand pulis of everie rotten synk
> For haly Scripture allutterlie we have mocked
> And with traditions of men we have them yockit.

And proudly echoing lay insubordination, they proclaim:

> For limmar (upstart) lads and litle lassis, lo
> Will argue baith with bischop, priest, and freir.

Yet the keynotes of Reformation soteriology,[18] Christ alone, grace alone, faith (as trust) alone, are expressed in a nutshell:

> Christ, our onlie succour in distres,
> In till his grace quha dois confide
> His grace till him will ay incres
> Quhen warldlie traist will faill at neid.

Some writers question the extent of the *Ballads*' circulation – yet from 1543 to 1556, they were periodically 'banned' or denounced by Church, Parliament and Regent, which suggests a diffusion that was causing concern.

Intermittent persecution continued, and in 1550, a lay tutor, Adam Wallace, of Ayrshire origins, was burned at Edinburgh for heterodox ideas including the holding of Bible classes. One of his accusers had rhetorically asked: 'What then, shall we leave to the bishops and kirkmen to do, if every man shall be a babbler on the Bible?'[19] A few years later a crucial voice in high places was heard urging the availability of translated Scriptures. This was the (protected) Court poet and dramatist, Sir David Lindsay, an Erasmian reform Catholic rather than a Protestant. In one of his writings in particular, *The Monarchie* (1554), he pleads in effect for a Gaelic or 'Irish' Bible, pointing out that if St Jerome had been an Argyll man, such a Bible would have been available long ago.[20]

Lastly, in 1556, before his second departure from Scotland, John Knox circulated his *A most wholsome counsell, how to behave ourselves . . . touching the daily exercise of Gods most holy and sacred worde.*[21] This offered guidelines on the using of the Bible and on principles and methods of scriptural interpretation. It is of great interest, as it indirectly substantiates what Catholic opponents of a common Bible had long argued, that it would lead to an implosion of authority and an explosion of doctrines and errors jeopardizing salvation. Knox, however, warns precisely against that, denouncing individualism, subjectivism, captiousness and selectivity, urging rather family, corporate, and communal reading and exposition in order to arrive at a common mind in accord with the Spirit. Solutions of difficulties should be deferred. In other words he counsels against biblical 'fundamentalism' and alerts Reformation enthusiasts to the dangers of ascribing validity to 'reader responses'.

While it is wrong to imagine that by 1560 Scotland was a nation of Bible readers, or a nation well-versed in biblical knowledge, it is right to affirm that segments of the laity and lower clergy had wrested Scripture and its interpretation from the exclusivist hands of the Church's *magisterium*. The process involved living with the risk of criminalization and making great escapes from it. Core support for the religious revolution of 1558–60 is determined by that background. While from 1557 the struggle obviously and necessarily broadened into the general public and political arena, the primary battle in Scotland had already been won by the small underground resistance, since the religious war was about the possession of the key strategic fortress of Scripture.

The random seeds of religious subversion in Scotland were accordingly watered by the propagation of vernacular Scripture in one form or other. While this definitely encouraged or corroborated criticism of the old Church, its claims and usages, and often ethically challenged office-bearers, the formal articulation of fundamental Reformation doctrines by qualified theologians was a different matter. Though works by foreign 'heretics' circulated clandestinely in the Scottish market, the country did not exactly enjoy a free press or liberty of opinion. Consequently, the domestic formal expression of dissenting theology in the vernacular was usually confined to responses by defenders at heresy trials. The dogmatic content of these statements constitutes the theoretical foundation of future Scottish Protestantism.

One well-known figure of iconic status for the broadcasting of Reformation thought in the country was Patrick Hamilton[22] (*c*.1504–28), roasted alive at St Andrews for the heresy of 'disputing, holding, and maintaining divers heresies of Martin Luther and his followers'.[23] Hamilton is a fine example of the fact that one did not have to be from a deprived or artisan or bourgeois or any other upwardly mobile class to be attracted by Reformation ideas, since he came from the cream of society. A member of the gentry he was also very well-connected to the nobility, firstly the Hamiltons (Arran earls), and the royal Stewarts through his mother. Therefore his execution also involved social and political dimensions of risk.[24]

In his own person Hamilton also embodied part of the Church's problem, since from the age of 13 he had been titular Abbot of Fearn (Premonstratensian) in Ross-shire to secure his income. A typical wandering student Scot, and so intellectually mobile, he studied in Paris and Louvain at the time when the Luther affair occupied the universities there; then he tutored at St Andrews, where he seems to have represented Erasmian Humanist reform ideas; finally he engaged in theological study at the new Protestant university in Marburg. These were all 'stations of high tension'. His teacher in Marburg was the French Protestant exile, the ex-Franciscan Francis Lambert of Avignon. Here Hamilton imbibed the new evangelical theology as represented by Luther, Melanchthon and Lambert, with its focus on the concepts of faith, justification, anthropology and the divine–human relationship.[25] Hamilton's participation in an academic disputation led to Lambert's suggestion that the Scot publish his Theses or *Loci*. This only happened posthumously and in English translation.[26]

On returning to Scotland in 1527, Hamilton married and apparently did some controversial preaching or teaching in the Linlithgow area. Cardinal Beaton initiated proceedings. The false articles he was accused of teaching embody the corrosive Lutheran theology that was lapping on Scottish shores. For example:

> Original sin is undiminished after baptism
> Natural man can do no good by the power of free will
> Even pious Christians live sinfully in this life
> True Christians enjoy the certainty of grace
> Works do not justify before God, rather faith alone
> Works do not make one good, but a good person does good
>   works
> Faith, hope and love are inseparable; lacking one means lacking
>   them all

Scripture alone is the source of belief, and should be accessible
  to everyone
There is no Purgatory
The Pope has no more spiritual power than any priest.

Spurning possibilities of rescue attempts and flight (not so easy anyway
with a wife and baby), Hamilton's fate was sealed by ceremonial excommunication in St Andrews Cathedral and immediate execution. Such
a revolutionary and ultra-Augustinian theology would have turned the
Church on its head. The challenge had, however, now been laid down
from within, where it was firmly resisted as well – not just by hard-line
reactionary Catholics, but also on the theological front by the eminent
Franco-Scottish Nominalist theologian and reformer in the Conciliarist
tradition, John Mair (Major) (*c.*1467–1550). He taught mainly in Paris,
but also had spells at Glasgow as well as at St Andrews, where he spent the
last nineteen years of his career. In an earlier period at St Andrews, Patrick
Hamilton would have been one of his students. In 1529, Mair published
in Paris his *Commentary on the Four Gospels*, a work designed to ground
sound Catholic doctrine in Scripture, and to aid the rebuttal of Protestant
teachings. The preface denounced the Lutheran Reformation,[27] and the
entire volume was dedicated to James Beaton, commending him for
his opposition to heresy (as in the Hamilton case). Works of Catholic
apologists were also acquired by Scottish universities, notably those of
John Fisher (1469–1535), Bishop of Rochester, against Luther and
Oecolampadius.[28]

Hamilton's death, a message of deterrence, had two chief effects. It
helped generate a veiled quasi-church of the Cross at home, edified in
part by martyrs' blood, a discreet community of external conformity and
internal dissent – 'Nicodemites' or 'secret professors', though often with
local lordly protection.[29] Further, among those who could not accept such
an existence or were exposed, it created a Scottish Protestant diaspora
abroad and to a lesser extent in Tudor southern Britain during periods
of more favourable religious weather under Henry VIII after 1534. This
little exodus points to the fact that despite increasingly repressive policies
later, especially when David Beaton was Archbishop of St Andrews (1539–
46), agitation was endemic, even if largely adventitious and unorganized,
confined to lay enclaves and debates among clergy. It is known that
between 1528 and 1546, there were 168 heresy suits resulting in nineteen
executions of which one was a woman, Helen Stirk (Stark) of Perth.[30]

Of the twenty-one people in Scotland known to have been executed
for religious reasons in the previous millennium of Christianity in the
country, this statistic shows that in these years, the Church, as elsewhere,
was afflicted with a serious pathology and that 'all was out of fraim'.[31] Yet
one must not jump to rash conclusions about the relative severity of such
measures. It could evidently have been much worse. With the exception
of Hamilton and George Wishart (see below), high-profile suspects were

not among the victims, since they seem to have been allowed or even encouraged to flee following tip-offs, even from the inquisitors. Social-political and kinship realities in Scotland exercised a restraining influence, or facilitated evasion.

Of interest is the fact that among the accused there was a fair proportion of regular clergy, notably friars and Augustinian canons. If in Ireland, for example, vitality among the friars and Observants is often cited as a key factor which kept Catholicism alive there, in Scotland the itinerant preaching Dominicans and Franciscans as well as other regulars seem to have been less unanimous in their reaction to Lutheran ideas. This was the case elsewhere in Europe. Some notable escapee ex-friars, mostly priors, who became Protestant émigrés in England or on the Continent were: Alexander Seton (d. 1542), Paris graduate and Dominican prior at St Andrews; John Willock (d. 1585), Ayr Dominican; John MacDowell (d. 1555), Cologne graduate and Dominican subprior at Glasgow, then prior at Wigtown; John MacAlpine (d. 1557), Cologne graduate and Dominican prior at Perth; John Craig (c.1512–1600), St Andrews graduate, later becoming a Calvinist in Italy; Thomas Guillaume (*fl.* 1540s), Dominican prior at Inverness who is credited with having initiated Knox's conversion by his preaching in Lothian; John Rough (d. 1577), Stirling Dominican. Craig and Willock were to have leadership roles in the future reformed Church of Scotland, the former as minister of the Canongate Church in Edinburgh, the latter as superintendent of Glasgow. Rough entered the ministry of the Church of England, and was martyred in Mary Tudor's reign. After a spell in England under the patronage of Thomas Cromwell followed by further study at Wittenberg, MacAlpine became involved in the Reformation in Denmark, where he became professor of theology at Copenhagen in 1542, to be known as 'Machabaeus'.[32]

Apart from friars, included among apostates or suspects[33] were a number of Augustinian canons regular (like Alesius and Forret as well as John Gau[34] (d. 1553)), monks from a variety of orders, secular priests, and some lay theologians like Borthwick (see above); Henry Balnaves[35] (1509–70), graduate of St Andrews and Cologne, law lord and diplomat, preacher of Reformation doctrines in the brief Protestant-friendly inter-lude (1542–3) during the Governorship of the Earl of Arran, and author of a treatise on justification by faith (1548), later edited by Knox;[36] George Wishart (c.1513–46), Louvain graduate, who fled Scotland in 1538, a teacher and preacher who on his return to Scotland was called to a high-profile martyrdom at St Andrews in 1546 (see below). One cannot at all speak of a flood, rather a significant oozing of critical spirits out of the old Church. Yet the defection, for example, of at least nineteen Blackfriars and Greyfriars in the early 1530s was enough to occasion a warning from the King about the need to stop heterodox preaching to the common people[37] – even if this was probably often confined to 'criticism of abuses'.

Repeated and expanded legislation by state and church in these decades points to anxiety about the spread of dissident theology among the literate religious nation as well as the effects of this among the illiterate masses. The increasingly long English Protestant shadow over Scotland was also rightly perceived as a problem. The means of transmission and broadcasting, literary and human, were naturally targeted. Yet the existence of theological Jekylls and Hydes even among the inquisitors showed that cast-iron reliability among the defenders of received theology could not be depended upon. A classical example of this was the ambivalent Dr John Winram (*c*.1492–1582), Augustinian subprior at St Andrews and professor of biblical literature there. Despite his long record in heresy cases, he became a superintendent in the reformed Church of Scotland and co-authored the *Scots Confession of Faith* (1560). Another notable act of conformity was the formal recantation in 1560 of the elderly Provincial of the Scottish Dominicans, John Grierson.[38]

As regards the literary appearance and possible clandestine dissemination of Reformation ideas and piety, two small writings in the vernacular published abroad are of significance. Even if they are seen only as small straws in the wind of religious change blowing on the fringes of the wider Reformation, they are no less interesting because of that. The first was a Lutheran catechetical work by John Gau (*c*.1490–1553), a St Andrews graduate, and a religious refugee in Denmark who had fled probably not long after Hamilton's death in 1528. *The Richt Vay to the Kingdom of Hevine* was published in Danish in Sweden (Malmö) by J. H. van Hochstraten,[39] who had earlier published dissident works in Antwerp. Gau's work is not an original composition. Rather it is essentially an anthology of common places from leading Lutheran writers and structured around the Ten Commandments, the Apostles' Creed and the Lord's Prayer. Not only that, it is a translation from a Danish version. It is primarily an aid to the new reformed devotion, free from prayers to the saints and all-manipulative, self-interested intercession. People should be taught the Lord's Prayer in their own language, Gau urges. Significant is that the book is the first Reformation text published in Scots, though this was not to be an earnest of any future important developments in this respect. Although there is yet no evidence that it circulated in Scotland (there is only one copy extant), it was aimed at the country, as the prefixed epistle to the nobles and barons implies. They are warned about the 'false preaching of dreams and fables and traditions of men' in contrast with biblical teaching and the witness of Patrick Hamilton.

The second work with a Scottish link has the very Lutheran title of *An confortable exhortation: of oure mooste holy Christen faith and her frutes Written (unto the Christen bretherne in Scotlande) after the poore* [pure] *worde of God.*[40] Its publication emanated from the same Antwerp–Malmö nexus associated with Hochstraten that handled Gau's *Richt Vay*. Though composed a few years earlier, its date of publication is stated as 1535.[41] The cited place of publication of 'Paris' was probably an attempt to deceive the censors and customs control, 'Paris' signalling Catholic orthodoxy. The author was John Johnsone, and since he gives an eyewitness account of Hamilton's martyrdom, it looks as if he too was as an exilic Scot who fled from St Andrews afterwards. Otherwise nothing is known of him, though speculation associates him with Anglo-Scottish communities in the Baltic or Hanseatic ports. Unlike Gau, he wrote in southern English rather than Scots, suggesting that like Knox, he mixed with predominantly English exiles.

The work projects an emphasis throughout on faith and its relationship to works (fruits), and alludes to inner-Reformation controversy on the matter. There are warnings against self-righteousness and despair, along with stress on the divine promises, assurance, Christian liberty, patience and perseverance in the face of necessary suffering and tribulation (theology of the Cross), as well as ongoing repentance in the face of continuing sin in the believer. This then is a work of spirituality and devotion, and is not a call to external action against the oppressive system – vengeance is to be left to God. Neither Johnsone nor Gau were issuing manifestos of public resistance. Prudential and internal evangelical piety of the hidden church, the real battleground of faith, is the keynote. Such a theology, however transmitted, percolated Scotland with its amorphous network of closet Lutherans.

Phase 2

The Reformation movement in Scotland went up a key in the 1540s and produced some more landmarks. Part of the reason for this was increasing political involvement, if bruising, with the increasingly meddlesome and expansionist Reformation England under both Henry VIII and Edward VI. It was also a symptom of inherent tensions between the pro-French and the pro-English political interests in Scotland. The domination of the former and its blending with the Catholic cause was personified in Cardinal David Beaton, in office from 1539–46. This increasingly encouraged Protestant sympathizers in Scotland to pin hopes of real progress on English support. They experienced a false dawn during the 'godly fit' of Governor Arran in 1543, when circulation of the Bible in the vernacular was sanctioned and some pro-Reformation preaching was tolerated. This encouraged bolder religious agitation and criticism of the Mass, the papacy, intercession of the saints, the seven sacraments, canon law, indulgences and monasticism, and was accompanied with occasional iconoclastic gestures. Following a successful fight-back by Beaton, subsequent punitive military incursions by the English, and eventual defeat of the Scottish army under Arran by the English at Pinkie in 1547, Scotland was forced back into French clientage and Catholic religious governance where it remained until 1559/60. Beaton's assassination in 1546, backed by some Protestant pro-English political activists, did not alter that fact.

In consequence, the Reformation cause was subdued. In 1544, half a dozen Protestant artisans including a woman were executed at Perth as part of a crackdown on 'popular' support for the Reformation at the instigation of Beaton. His authority had been freshly enhanced by his promotion to being papal legate *a latere* (with full powers) that year, and to the office of Chancellor of Scotland the year before. This was the prelude to a dramatic double killing. The first notable victim of the fall-out was the martyr and charismatic George Wishart.[42] He had been expelled from Montrose by the Bishop of Brechin, John Hepburn, in 1538 for giving lessons on the Greek New Testament. His exile was in England – where he preached with some success in Bristol – and possibly in the Upper Rhine German or Swiss region. This is suggested by his English translation,[43] published in 1548, of the *First Helvetic Confession* (1536) that was an attempt by the Swiss Reformers to accommodate to Lutheran concerns. Did the Protestant Reformation party in England send Wishart on a preaching mission to Scotland in 1544? It looks like it.[44] Wishart's itinerary took him to localities with known Protestant enclaves as in Angus, Dundee, Ayrshire and Lothian where he met up with the newly converted John Knox. The conclusion of Wishart's activities was that he was pursued by Cardinal Beaton (who should have been at the Council of Trent), subjected to a show trial, condemned and burned for heresy at St Andrews in 1546.[45] John Winram uneasily preached the sermon at the proceedings.

Arguably, the occasion was one of the last macabre, medieval spectacles of grand format in Scotland. Wishart, however, skilfully used the oppor-tunity to commend a range of Reformation doctrines to a large audience of higher Scottish clergy, academics, priests, government leaders and ordinary laity all in one precinct. The Cardinal's motion to have questions to the accused answered by a simple Yes or No had been frustrated.[46] The elimination of Wishart was with hindsight a pyrrhic victory. He is often cited as having introduced a 'Zwinglian' layer over pre-existing Lutheran theology in Scotland. In his trial, for example, he did use a Zwinglian (or 'sacramentarian') argument in denying the corporal presence of Christ in the sacramental elements as such, so that there is no 'local inclusion': bread, something finite, cannot contain the Deity, something infinite. This does resemble Zwingli's dualist hypothesis that spirit and matter are incompatible, that grace cannot be mediated by physical means, so that the elements are only symbolical. In reality, however, Wishart's views on the matter derive from an earlier mediating Lutheran–Zwinglian position or attempt, embodied in the *First Helvetic Confession* with which he had aligned himself. This text refers to the sacramental elements as 'not mere, empty signs, but consist of sign and substance . . . by which the communion of Christ's body and blood is administered and offered as spiritual food . . . the sacraments *exhibit* (i.e. present and offer) the spiritual realities they signify . . . they are an aid and support to faith'.[47] This accommodating formulation, with its Augustinian echoes, was influenced by the thinking of the conciliation theologians, Melanchthon and Bucer – Bucer in fact participated in the Confession's drafting at Basle.

The process of striving for inner-Protestant harmony was to take another important step in 1549. Calvin, coming from the middle of the road position on the matter, similar to that represented by his friends Bucer and Melanchthon, reached agreement with Zwingli's successor, Henry Bullinger. This issued in the *Zurich Consensus* that established agreed theological parameters for Swiss Protestantism.[48] It constituted the basis of what came to be called 'reformed' theology as distinct from confessional 'Lutheran' theology, though there is much overlapping on fundamentals. Such a reformed consensus is distinct from not only 'Zwinglianism' but also 'Calvinism' as traditionally understood. Wishart is indicative of this process, and after him, Reformation theology in Scotland – as well as in England[49] – adapted to and reflected this evolution. Citing Wishart as introducing 'Zwinglianism' is half a red herring.[50] Similarly, describing Reformation theology in Scotland and England from the mid-1540s onwards as making a transition to 'Calvinism' is equally not wholly true. The transition was to wider 'reformed' synthesis, though ultimately no single label is adequate. The relative pluralism did allow for different accents including ongoing Lutheran ones on matters other than the sacraments. This helps explain why the future orthodox 'Calvinism' of the Synod of Dort and the *Westminster Confession* only had minority appeal in the British Isles, since it ruptured the Reformed consensus which had also embraced the Churches of England and Ireland. The same sort of disruption was occasioned by post-Reformation era 'Anglican' developments represented by Archbishop Laud, the Caroline divines, etc. with their allegedly 'Arminian'[51] and neo-catholicizing tendencies.

After Wishart's death, the second significant mortality was that of Beaton himself, the victim of retributive assassination in the same year, 1546.[52] It was a testimony to the fact that Beaton's real enemies, pro-Reformation Anglophiles in government, among the gentry, among his own tenants, and the English government, were beyond his reach. Since 1544, Henry VIII had been aware of the conspiracy. However, despite continuing struggles, there was no dramatic change in government or religious policy (though belated Catholic internal reform was initiated, see below). Wishart's elimination, like Hamilton's, and like Beaton's, concentrated minds and stimulated a new exodus of committed Protestants. They formed a new exilic generation, among whom were John Willock and John Knox. Knox was involved with the assassins, if not the assassination of Beaton, so that legally his implication was peripheral. It was, however, enough to have him exiled as a galley slave of the French for eighteen months, and so give him that experience of bondage and spiritual testing which helped him discern the implications of his vocation.

Phase 3

For the next dozen years, up to 1559, the Catholic Church in Scotland finally embarked on an effort at self-reform, partly motivated by the concurrent Council of Trent. The removal of David Beaton facilitated this, since he had no testified interest in theology and was very much a Johnny-come-lately to the idea of internal reform, being concerned more with church authority and the integrity of church property. Not that Beaton's successor as archbishop, John Hamilton (*c.*1511–71) was a high-flying theologian, preacher or reformer with a Continental education. He was at least aware that there had to be positive changes in the Church's structure, staffing and teaching if it was to retain credibility. He certainly had had plenty of time to think about the issues, since as a youth he had studied at St Leonard's College in St Andrews when Lutheran theology was being disputed. He had been there, too, at the time of the execution of his kinsman, Patrick Hamilton. Unlike most Scottish bishops, John Hamilton was in a monastic order (Tironensians: Observant Benedictines) at Kilwinning Abbey in Ayrshire, and was there until his appointment as Bishop of Dunkeld in 1546. He also enjoyed the fruits of the abbacy of Paisley *in commendam* (i.e. provisionally in theory, until a proper ministering cleric was appointed, but usually for life without duties). His appointment as bishop had unsurprising political overtones, since he was a kinsman of James Hamilton, Governor Arran (one of the future 'Lords of the Congregation'). At this time, Arran obviously preferred him to the papal nominee, Robert Wauchope (d. 1551), Archbishop of Armagh, the able (and sole) Scottish Tridentine Father. In 1547, Hamilton was catapulted to the top of the ecclesiastical tree by becoming Archbishop of St Andrews. As a moderate, as someone firmly linked to the political establishment, and as a person of genuine religious credentials (he does not seem to have been an object of Protestant invective), the task entrusted to him was the attempt to bring the Scottish Catholic Church into the sixteenth century. He was to be one of a handful of Scottish bishops not to conform after 1560, which says something about his integrity. He was never impugned with moral notoriety, being no Renaissance ecclesiastic.

Hamilton's name is firmly attached to the Scottish Church reform synods in 1549, 1552 and 1559, three essentially abortive attempts inspired by earlier Catholic provincial reform councils in France (1529), in Cologne (1536) and in Mainz (1549).[53] The statutes of the Scottish councils aimed at moral improvement among the clergy, enhancement of the priesthood and ministry, promotion of Christian knowledge and education, and the furtherance of social and economic welfare. Among many other things, the councils deplored poor church attendance and lack of scriptural knowledge among the clergy.

Two concrete achievements are noteworthy. The one was the production of a largely vernacular catechism, *Hamilton's Catechism*[54] as an instruction manual for the clergy – inspired largely by the *Enchiridion* of the moderate Catholic reformer in Cologne, John Gropper. Involved very much in the draft of the catechism was an English Dominican at St Andrews, Richard Marshall.[55] Doctrinally the text echoes a degree of accommodation to Lutheran thinking on faith and justification in accord with pre-Tridentine, but now somewhat redundant, 'third way' theology of conciliation. The second achievement was better provision for education for the priesthood, reflected in the 'refoundation' of St Mary's College in St Andrews.[56] This had been established by James Beaton in 1539, though not actualized until 1546. It had had trilingual Humanist aspirations. The Scottish church council implemented further reform of the College, which got under way in 1554 with a stress on Catholic reform principles, biblical study and Christian character formation in the curriculum. Its Provost since 1547, Paris-educated John Douglas (*c.*1494–1574)[57] was to join the Protestant Reformers in 1560. For a decade or so therefore, St Andrews was a centre of Catholic revival, with a Dominican core in St Mary's.

Since the horses had already bolted, Catholic reform in Scotland was in vain. It was unable to induce the closet church-in-waiting, the 'Privy Kirk', to co-operate or conform. Too many bishops lacked a vocation. The most distinguished Catholic theologian in Scotland, John Major in St Andrews, was too elderly to play a part in the process, dying in 1550. Finally, lack of financial restructuring meant that the severe resource imbalance to the detriment of the parishes was not addressed. Nor does any particular advantage seem to have accrued from a re-catholicized England (1553–8) – on the contrary, some Marian Protestant exiles found Catholic Scotland less life-threatening than England, and so helped boost the Reformation movement among the Scots.

To the pattern of Anglo-Scottish mobility among some Protestant preachers belongs the last milestone of religious significance before the Reformation. This was in 1557 when a decisive politicization occurred with the 'band' between a number of key Scottish nobles and barons, the 'Lords of the Congregation', to set the overthrow of the Catholic Church in train. Some expatriate Scots in England had returned to conduct preaching missions, like Wishart (1543–6), and the ex-Dominican, John Willock (1552). The Church of England's major gift to the Scottish Reformation was John Knox. At the invitation of a group of nobles he returned (rather reluctantly) to Scotland via Geneva where he was a Marian exile. He was active in the country in the year 1555–6.[58]

The significance of this stay was that it served as a kind of trailer for his second and permanent ministry in Scotland from 1559 onwards. It was facilitated to some extent by a relatively relaxed, if politically circumspect, religious policy of the Regent, Mary of Lorraine, at the time. Indeed she went so far as to halt heresy proceedings in 1555 against Knox in Edinburgh, though he was judged and condemned *in absentia*, then burned in effigy after his departure in July 1556. He later published a response to this – *The Appellation*.[59] Echoing Luther in 1520, Knox appeals in this for judgement by the Magistracy – the Christian nobility of the Scottish nation in effect.

Knox's aim during the period was to give more organization, substance and form to the dissident Church as a preliminary to imminent externalization. To this end, like Wishart before him, he engaged in a preaching circuit (with a disconcertingly anglicized accent) in essentially safe territories, like parts of Fife, Angus, Lothian, Ayrshire, Renfrewshire and even once in Edinburgh. This was not just evangelism. It was the beginnings of mobilization, preparation for a new Church, since Knox accompanied his preaching with eucharistic ministrations. He urged a public boycott of the Catholic Mass and sacraments. Significantly his last visit was to Castle Campbell, the seat of the Gaelic magnate, the Earl of Argyll, where he preached for several days. For a crucial facet of Knox's mission was the *de facto* consecration of the select lay apostles and enforcers of the Reformation in Scotland, the Lords of the Congregation. After his departure, Knox sent his *Letter of Wholesome Counsel,* a memorandum laying down guidelines on the use of Scripture and on worship.[60] With his first ministry then, the long *praeparatio evangelica* (preparation for the Gospel) preceding the public Reformation in Scotland was concluded.

The post-1557 decade

Formal Reformation victory in Scotland was achieved by a threefold revolution. First: with a *coup d'état* carried out by largely pro-English and Protestant elements in the political nation against the Regent, Mary of Lorraine, Scotland changed from being within the Catholic French to the Protestant English sphere of influence. This was marketed as being somehow an act of independence and liberation. It was obviously facilitated by the adoption of the Reformation by England following the accession of Elizabeth to the throne in 1558. Second: in 1560, Parliament endorsed the religious revolution with the formal abolition of Catholicism, more specifically the Roman Mass, and papal jurisdiction embodied in canon law (the royal assent of the new monarch, Mary Stewart, was not given until 1567, so that this legislation remained inherently provisional). Third: there was the enforced, though not strategically planned abdication of Mary in 1567. Since many Marian legitimists and loyalists were high-profile Protestants, like the Church General Assembly's first moderator, John Erskine of Dun (see below), that deposition cannot be seen as essential to general Reformation policy.

In this process, there were three vital moments. The *first* was, as mentioned, in 1557. Encouraged by Knox in Geneva, a small, bonded or covenanted group of five Scottish nobles and barons, aristocratic leaders of the evangelical Church, issued a Protestant statement of faith. Declared was the intention to replace the old Church, the 'congregation of Satan', with one grounded in the scriptural Word of God. This was not so much a crusading call to take to the streets as a statement of protection for the scattered 'privy kirks' and an encouragement of them to prepare for change.[61] Association with ecclesiastical developments south of the border is revealed by the Lords' call for the English Edwardine *Book of Common Prayer* (1552) to be adopted by Scottish parish churches to replace the

Latin Mass. There is evidence that for the time being (as in Glasgow, for example),[62] this happened, and that Scottish churchmen were using it much later in the century.[63]

Bearing in mind the nature of Scottish society, ruled by territorial magnates and lairds or barons, the manoeuvre of the group of Lords was hugely more significant than five ordinary subjects doing the same thing. Moreover, these five were not concentrated in one area of the country. Two were from the east, the first being John Erskine of Dun[64] (1509–90) in Angus, near Montrose. He was a long-standing moderate but committed Protestant (some say Lutheran, others say Reformed à la First Helvetic Confession of 1536), later a Reformed Church superintendent as well as the new Church of Scotland's first moderator of the General Assembly (though not ordained). The second from the east was James Douglas, Earl of Morton (*c*.1516–81), future controversial Regent during James VI's minority. His authentic religious credentials are less verifiable.

There were three from the west, the first being Alexander Cunningham, Earl of Glencairn[65] (d. 1574) in the north Ayrshire-Renfrewshire region. Like his father before him, he had been a Protestant by conviction for many years and was a close friend of Knox. The next two were father and son, and their participation was to be of importance for Gaelic Scotland: Archibald Campbell, fourth Earl of Argyll (d. 1558), and his son, also Archibald (1530–73), the fifth earl (previously Lord Lorne).

This then was the aristocratic conclave whose commitment to the new faith and political revolution was decisive. It acted as the Protestant negotiating party with the Regent, and soon other important politico-religious players joined it. Notable among the accessions were James Hamilton (*c*.1516–75), second Earl of Arran; his son, also James (1537–70), the third earl, who had been converted to the Reformation in France; and Lord James Stewart[66] (1531–70), future Earl of Moray, and half-brother of Queen Mary whose chief minister of state he became. Thereby, the Reformation movement was furnished with formidable political and military armoury. This powerful phalanx, taking advantage of wider political changes in England and Europe, neutralized the Regent, and then had her suspended from power in 1559. It invited Knox back to Scotland, who in that year arrived in Edinburgh as the Provincial Council of the Scottish Catholic Church was still in session. The Lords of the Congregation governed the country and managed the legislative Reformation in the Scottish Parliament of 1560 before the new queen's arrival from France. All had been achieved bloodlessly.

Purely Scottish circumstances did not explain the Reformation victory. Obviously the commitment of the new English monarch from 1558, Elizabeth I, to the Reformation was influential. In addition, the strategic intensification of the evangelization of France in the period 1558–61, directed from Geneva, was part of a wider reformed sense of seizing the opportunity. In both Scotland and France, judicial processes against Protestant heretics, and so persecution, had been slowing down in the

1550s.[67] Unlike in Scotland, however, the 'push' in France failed to secure decisive support from a large enough body of leading nobles.

One is tempted to date the beginning of the onslaught of the Reformation with the event of the 'bond' of 1557. Yet soon there were ominous gestures of iconoclasm among the populace, symptomatic of wider agitation, even though one might interpret them in terms of cause and effect. For example, there was the public destruction of the image of St Giles in Edinburgh on 1 September 1558, the day of its annual procession in the town.[68] Or one could cite, as evidence of the people's 'pressure from below', the riots that ensued from Knox's preaching at Perth in 1559,[69] seen by some as the real 'beginning' of the Reformation in Scotland. Or there was the salvo known as the *Beggars' Summons*,[70] a broadsheet affixed to Scottish friaries early in 1559 giving six months' notice of eviction[71] – the nearest Scotland got to an *Affaire des Placards*. The element of social protest in the *Summons* was strong, since it was composed on behalf of 'the blind, the crippled, the bed-bound, widows, orphans, and the poor unable to work'. It demanded the return of the patrimony of the poor. With this action, iconclasm, unlike simple vandalism, was then linked to claims for social justice.

The *second* turning point was the meeting of the Scottish Parliament at Edinburgh in 1560. Under the watchful eyes of English diplomats and the English navy in the Firth of Forth, basic Reformation legislation was enacted abolishing Catholicism and a *Confession of Faith* (see below) adopted. Fairly generous and humane arrangements were made for pensions for priests, monks and friars who did not wish to minister in the new Church; those in possession of benefices were enabled to retain two-thirds of the revenues. The creation of a new Church was authorized, though a blueprint for the reorganization and restructuring of the Church and its finances, backed by the General Assembly, was not adopted. This was the *First Book of Discipline* (see below), concerned not only with structures of ministry, but also general education and poor relief.

This area of the Scottish Reformation was to constitute dissensus for many years. Scotland had no godly, that is, Protestant prince at this time (Mary remained Catholic) to help implement and realize the Reformers' ideals. While withholding her assent from such legislation, Mary, in the name of 'liberty of conscience', cited by her, promised not to undermine it as long as her subjects would not constrain her to worship in the Protestant manner. This quid pro quo enabling Mass to be said in Holyrood Palace was embodied in an 'edict of toleration'.[72] The outcome was that to the chagrin of the Church and those who aspired to 'root and branch' religious reform, the Reformation marked time in Scotland for the next seven years. Some like Knox felt that they had experienced a false dawn. The former Church-in-waiting was now regularized and convened representatively as the General Assembly, but the 'waiting' dimension was to remain indefinite as regards the seriously practical implementation of reforms with teeth.

Anyway, even for two or three years after 1560, the Reformers still had to encounter Catholic controversialists in public or in writing. Therefore, untypical of Reformations elsewhere, the fundamental argument continued.[73] Stiff Catholic dogmatic defence was offered by Quintin Kennedy (1520–64), St Andrews- and Paris-educated, and Abbot of Crossraguel in south Ayrshire. His *Compendious Tractive* (Edinburgh, 1558) discusses the relationship between Scripture and Tradition from a Catholic viewpoint, and was intended to shaft the *scriptura sola* principle and other hermeneutical principles employed by the Reformers.[74] Further, the teacher-priest Ninian Winzet (see also previous chapter), enjoying some measure of patronage at the royal court that included a few Paris theologians like Roche Mammerot (d. 1587), a Dominican, and René Benoist (1525–1608), published a number of writings in 1562 and 1563 opposed to Reformation theology.[75] These were his *Certane Tractatis* (Edinburgh, 1562) including *The Last Blast of the Trompet . . . aganis the usurpit auctoritie of Iohne Knox* (Edinburgh, 1562), and *The Buke of Fourscoir-Thre Questions* (1563, published at Antwerp).[76] Late in 1562, however, Winzet, socially subordinate, had to flee the country. Not so Quintin Kennedy, who as son of the Earl of Cassillis had a local power-base in south-west Scotland. In 1563, Kennedy and Knox had a three-day adversarial disputation at Maybole in Ayrshire, largely on the sacraments, and especially the Mass as sacrifice. Kennedy's arguments at this were assembled in his *Ane Compendious Reasoning*.[77]

For Knox and his colleagues such distractions, along with the conclusion of the work of the Council of Trent, the scandal of the officially sanctioned Mass for the queen at Holyrood Palace in Edinburgh, as well as Reformation inertia and popular Catholic resilience in parts of Scotland including Edinburgh, did not really make 1560 a golden year. It was like the half-hearted Edwardine Reformation all over again, something that might even provoke God's vengeance, as in England with the Marian persecution.

The *third* and final dramatic moment, in terms of the erection of the Reformation political scaffolding, was the enforced abdication of Queen Mary in 1567 in favour of her infant son, James VI (1566–1625). This was brought about partly by 'no confidence' in the monarch's fitness to rule arising from her calamitous marital decisions, partly by anxiety about her foreign Catholic connections, partly by English interests, and partly by an apocalyptic religious imperative articulated by the General Assembly. Yet the ensuing 'civil war' that followed Mary's deposition was obviously not a religious war for everyone. It was primarily a conflict between legitimists and usurpists, since Protestants and surviving Catholics were on both sides.

Bearing in mind Protestant England to the south, and considering her strong claim to the English throne, Mary's religious policy had the following contours. She acknowledged the 1560 Church revolution while retaining a natural but discreet, personal Catholic bias, which only latterly became more pronounced. Her attitude was hardly bullish, despite papal encouragement that she embark on persecution. Her policies resembled those of her mother and former mother-in-law, Mary of Guise and Catherine de Médicis, namely flexibilty and accommodation with the goal of preventing religious war. Yet the atmosphere of provisionality engendered conflicting signs and messages. Protestant doctrine was sanctioned by Parliament, and the Reformed Church was officially permitted, though not established. At the same time, both court and popular Catholicism openly manifested itself, especially in the Edinburgh region, and it can hardly be said that wider rural Catholicism had evaporated overnight.

Mary's strategy did divide the Protestants, at least until 1566. Many of the more *politic* among them were content to live with stagnant nature of the ecclesiastical situation as well as tolerate the queen's domestic Mass – in fact all had agreed to the latter on her arrival in 1561. In defending her practice in this respect against Knox's intransigence in particular, the conceptual cards that she repeatedly played were 'liberty of conscience' and 'freedom of worship', notions which ironically the Edinburgh Protestants had used in 1558 in their negotiations with the Regent. These ideas had been circulating on the Continent after the Peace of Augsburg in 1555, and especially in France.[78] They were, however, no more acceptable to militant Protestants than to militant Catholics. In Scotland, informed (and possibly vaguely Erasmian Humanist) lay Protestants were mindful that the Reformation was originally over a 'conscience' issue, even if the more restrictive sense of 'Christian conscience' may have eluded them. They may even have inherited the early Lutheran *laissez-faire* tradition – no coercion in matters of religious practice. Against this, uncompromising Reformers like Knox considered that Mary was duping the majority of subscribing Protestants in Scotland. Their compliance was betraying the Reformation, and God, with its 'perfidious defection from Christ'.[79]

During the period 1565 to 1566, a crisis was brewing. The General Assembly petitioned the queen (in vain)[80] to discontinue the palace Mass as well as to transmit the funding (a share with the Crown of the 'thirds of benefices')[81] promised to the Church, whose ministers were suffering hardship and abandoning their charges. An unsuccessful revolt by some Protestant nobles against Mary's marriage with Darnley weakened Protestant political solidarity. It was rumoured that the Scottish Parliament due to meet in 1566 would consider restoring limited rights to Catholicism in Scotland. Permission granted to some Dominicans to preach publicly in Edinburgh outraged Protestant opinion. The murder of the queen's secretary, David Riccio, by Protestant zealots might have provoked disorder; instead it engendered a truce and some political reconciliation.

Knox's thinking in this period was deeply pessimistic and he was convinced that the situation was due to divine displeasure with the lack of progress in the Reformation. His analysis was that the Reformation had degenerated since the spring of 1559–61; the bulk of the Protestant nobility was guided more by worldly pragmatism than the Word of God; material gain at the expense of the patrimony of the Church had been an inducement to join the Reformation as a bandwagon; their behaviour was apostasy and the source of current miseries; Catholic restoration was imminent as a divine punishment, along with natural and social afflictions. Knox and the General Assembly embarked upon an extraordinary manoeuvre to redress the situation and in this they were encouraged by elements in the nobility and government which were increasingly disaffected with Mary. This was the calling of a public fast by true believers, the 'little flock', as an act of repentance to stay God's wrath in the face of licensed idolatry and continuing social injustice, and so a manifestation of opposition and protest.

The Assembly proceeded to publish a collectively drafted fasting manifesto along with a detailed explanation and an order on how to exercise it.[82] Much of the text reflects Knox's participation. Rooted in biblical, especially Old Testament fasting concepts, its fundamental argument is this: Scotland, as a form of the new Israel, is bound to God's covenant. Anything inimical to the covenant, like idolatry (the Mass), a Jezebel as monarch, social injustice – especially among the 'poor labourers of the ground', religion without heart (soft Protestantism, pseudo-Christians), ethical degeneration in public and private life, etc. must be eradicated and exigencies of the common good given priority if God is not to unleash disaster on the nation as punishment for 'contempt'. And so an act of divinely mandated amendment and self-humiliation by the faithful remnant would induce the currently 'absent God' to return to the care of Scotland. The eight-day fast took place in Edinburgh from 23 February to 3 March 1566.

Results were not fast. But over a year later, following the murder of Mary's husband and her marriage to a man (Bothwell) implicated in the matter, the queen's domestic and international support was severely depleted, so that she was deposed and sent into exile. This enabled the granting of the royal assent by the new Regent to the religious legislation of 1560, securing at last the Reformation in the country. Scotland could now set about being a truly Protestant kingdom with the active aid (it was believed) of what had been lacking before, the Crown and the government.

The Church of Scotland's foundational texts

The Reformation Church of Scotland was not, even after 1690 when it became established, a 'state Church' in the way the Church of England was continuously since 1534, since it developed largely in opposition to the state Executive. Its claims were rather to be a separate 'national' church, a status it secured after the nation's complete absorption in the united British kingdom after 1707. Consequently, its foundational documents have never had the same juridical, non-negotiable and near-canonical authority as those of the Churches of England and Ireland. Equally, most civil legislation in respect of the Church was from the outset either provisional, conditional or unenforceable. Consequently, only full statutory authority was accorded to one document in particular, and after a seven-year wait. This was the *Scots Confession of Faith*, passed by Parliament in 1560 and assented to by Regent Moray in 1567. No other primary church Reformation text in the country enjoyed such authority. It was ironic then that the Kirk, during a pan-British craze, unilaterally abandoned this Confession in 1647, adopting in its stead the English presbyterian *Westminster Confession.*

Six theologians with a common Christian name, who included Knox and two stalwarts of the old Catholic establishment in St Andrews, John Winram and John Douglas (see above) composed the Scots Confession hurriedly in 1560, at English insistence.[83] Also among them was a canonist recently returned from Padua and Rome, John Row. Significantly, it is the doctrine of the priesthood of all believers that helps account for the later authority of the Confession. For it is composed and presented on behalf of 'the Estates of Scotland, with the inhabitants of the same', even if in reality this is pious rhetoric. The conception, however, is not 'top-down' faith, rather collectivist and covenantal. Nor is the Confession sectarian or only national in its referential framework. Rather it claims for itself the true faith of 'all realms, nations, and tongues', since 'this Kirk is Catholic' (chapter 16). The document is vigorous, clear-headed, and predominantly positive in emphasis. It is only 'militant' or 'polemical' in so far as the demarcation from Roman Catholic (and Anabaptist) doctrine is formally marked. Though there are some occasional allusions to the 'Papistical Kirk', the 'false Kirk', and the 'Roman Kirk', the papacy as such is never mentioned. It is essentially pedagogic and catechetical, under-standably necessary during a phase of transition. And while all affirmations are grounded in 'the infallible truth of God's Word', the preface makes it clear that the Confession itself does not claim infallibility. Rather it is subordinate and subject to correction, so that with scriptural warrant 'we shall alter whatever one proves to be wrong'.

Of the twenty-five chapters or articles, the first eleven are non-controversial, embodying the oecumenical faith in fundamentals articulated in the early Church between the Councils of Nicaea and Chalcedon. Only with the introduction of a pessimistic anthropology at the beginning of chapter 12 is a controversial tone struck: 'Our faith and its assurance do not proceed from flesh and blood, that is to say, from natural powers within us, but are the inspiration of the holy Ghost.' The remainder of the articles mirror the controversial issues of the day, such as faith, justification, sanctification, Scripture and Tradition, the offices of Christ, the authority of the Church, the sacraments and the function of the civil power. Compared with other confessions throughout Europe in the era, there is an unusual stress on the fundamental nature of the Church, on the sacramental eating of Christ's flesh and blood, and on Christian ethics. Overall, the most discernible contemporary voice in the Confession is that of Calvin in his *Institutes*, but not exclusively so. It reflects rather broad reformed consensus with a Calvinist slant, especially on the Eucharist, sanctification, ethics and church discipline. However, it is not explicitly predestinarian, confining itself essentially to the common election theology of Paul. Also, its equivocation on obedience to (unjust or tyrannical) secular authority has been controversial[84] – there is no notion here of viewing the monarch as 'next to God'. Nor, of course, is the Confession in any way 'presbyterian', since it does not deal with church government as such. Accordingly, Scottish Episcopalians were subsequently just as devoted to the creed as Presbyterians were, and indeed often appealed to it against later hard-line Presbyterian radicals.

In 1572, the Confession was belatedly, and slightly tendentiously, translated into Latin by the militantly anti-presbyterian Patrick Adamson (1537–92), who soon became Archbishop of St Andrews. Alongside the *Scots Confession*, the General Assembly was also to sanction 'for profitable use' the *Genevan English Confession* (1566), as well as 'the orthodox faith and Catholic doctrines' of the Swiss *Second Helvetic Confession* (1566), a confession of high authority in the reformed Churches of Europe.

The remainder of subsequent formative documents were church texts only, and so functioned without the parliamentary or royal authority essential to notions of a 'state church'. In the area of worship, practice and procedure in the Church, 'approved' guidelines were provided by the *Book of Common Order* (1564) which also contained a complete metrical psalter.[85] It remained in force until 1645, when the English puritan and liturgically permissive *Westminster Directory of Public Worship* replaced it.

While Protestants in Scotland before the official Reformation had been content to use the Edwardine 1552 *Prayer Book*, the return of many exiled from the Continent around 1560 acted as a fillip for further developments out of which the *Book of Common Order* emerged. Its parent was *The Forme of Prayers and Ministration of the Sacraments used in the Englishe Congregation at Geneva* (1556). Knox had played a part in its drafting, though it is essentially an English translation of Calvin's *La forme des prières* used in the Genevan Church. This in turn was derived from the Strasbourg order for worship which had been adapted and adopted by Calvin at the time of his ministry there (1538–41). The Genevan English formulary was used initially in Scotland, but as changes and additions were made, as in the version published in 1562, it mutated into the *Book of Common Order*. The Knoxian, or Anglo-Genevan, English determining the language is a further illustration of how the Reformation helped hasten the demise of indigenous Scots (though the Confession was in Scots). The other major factor in this respect is that there was no Scots Bible, the adopted version being the generally influential Genevan English Bible (1558).

The fundamental concept of worship in the Strasbourg–Geneva–Scotland nexus was that Word and sacrament were inseparable, so that Communion ought to be held weekly as Bucer and Calvin had urged. In reality, that was not achieved, so that the offer of quarterly Communion, like in Swiss churches, became the norm, as recommended by the *First Book of Discipline* (see below). There was difference of opinion, since the *Book of Common Order* recommended monthly Communion. Conventional Sunday services therefore tended to become didactic preaching occasions, and in many areas of Scotland, only annual Communion obtained – though infrequency undoubtedly heightened the importance of the occasion. The fundamental source of reformed inhibition in this respect was aversion to the pre-Reformation experience of trivialization, commercialization and multiplicity of Masses.

In 1567, Séon Carsuel (John Carswell)[86] (*c.*1520–72), reformed Superintendent of Argyll and Bishop of the Isles published the Scottish service book (with some modifications) in Scottish Gaelic.[87] A graduate of St Andrews, he was also bardically trained. This was a Celtic cultural landmark, being the first printed book in either Scottish or Irish Gaelic. More than that, it embodied the first formal evangelical outreach to the entire cross-border Gaelic world.[88] Composed in the literary Gaelic common to Scotland and Ireland, Carswell specifically targeted the entire Gaeltacht, or more realistically, Ulster as well as Scotland. 'To the men of Scotland and Ireland', Carswell writes in his dedication, 'to such of them as desire to receive the faithful words of God in their hearts and minds'. The phrase is no mere pietistic formula. It echoes the Reformation reorientation of Christian piety, from sheer devotion to cognitive understanding, from external ritual and observance to internalization, from priestly mediation of grace to direct appropriation of the Word of God and the grace of Christ, from faith in the Church and its inflationary doctrines to faith in the Gospel as preached and sacramentally administered. Moreover, Carswell's preface reveals the general Reformation appeal to the competence in religious affairs of a 'godly' magistrate or prince. He sees an analogy between his own patron and a founder 'Lord of the Congregation', Archibald Campbell, fifth Earl of Argyll (whose chaplain Carswell was), and Old Testament monarchs or captains of Israel, guardians of the true faith.[89]

Of great importance for the Scottish Kirk were the practical reform proposals embodied in *The First Book of Discipline*[90] (1560) and the *Second Book of Discipline*[91] (1578). Both texts were multi-authored, though Andrew Melville's name is conventionally associated with the latter due to its firmly presbyterian concepts in relation to church government – every minister is a bishop; a lord bishop, and 'pastors of pastors' have no scriptural warrant; rather there is ministerial parity. Neither *Book* was fully sanctioned in civil law, not just because of government antipathy to a church without bishops, but due to the Kirk's claims on the assets or 'patrimony of the church', the bulk of which had been seized by the Crown and the nobility after 1560.

In the area of church government, the *First Book* is not signally presbyterian, though it does seem to envisage parity among ministers. Its provision for regional superintendents was intended to be a 'temporary expedient'. It is in the *Second Book* that a definite presbyterian polity is advanced, based on the notions of the fourfold ministry of minister, elder, doctor and deacon, and hierarchical government not by individuals like bishops but by church courts, such as the local Kirk Session, the Presbytery and the General Assembly. This concept was accepted by the General Assembly in 1581 and by the Scottish Parliament in 1592, but was never sanctioned by the Crown.

Both *Books* dealt with far more than polity. The entire organization of the ministry and services of the Church was dealt with as was education and social welfare. This was to the extent that they virtually embody national reconstruction programmes in the Swiss and south German urban Reformation traditions with their focus on the *bonum commune* or common weal.[92] However, the *Books* reflect the Church's aspirations rather than any achieved or achievable reality. Its thinking in respect of societal 'reformation' was grounded in Christian moral precepts rather than hard politico-economic analyses. Yet the very utterance of these ideals, along with the policy of 'discipline for all classes' gave the Church a popular appeal – even if this is what revisionist ardour has characterized as 'the more respectable face of Protestantism'.[93] Pertinent indeed were pleas for agricultural labourers (the largest workforce in Scotland), as well as for the redemption of the historical financial deficit in the parishes. However, the nobility and the Crown held on to the bulk of church endowments, and the burgher declined to pay taxes for such ends. The Kirk decried the loss of ecclesiastical 'liberty' that this entailed, in modern terms, loss of financial independence and 'curtailment of services'. Freewill church offerings became the chief mechanism of funding.

Considering that collective public fasting exercises for both religious and political reasons were a regular and important feature of presbyterian life in Scotland and elsewhere until the nineteenth century, of interest is the *Ordour and Doctrine of the General Faste* (1567), which lays down procedures.[94] The context of the *Doctrine* section has been considered above. The entire text was incorporated into the *Book of Common Order* in 1587, and remained there in all subsequent editions until 1901.[95] Private pre-Communion fasting continued to exist in Scotland as did *de facto* abstinence from meat on Wednesdays, Fridays and in Lent. This text foresees procedures on special, *ad hoc* occasions, such as national calamities, foreign threats, war, religious danger, crime waves, etc. all of which called for demonstrations of public repentance (sometimes as a form of 'opposition' to government policies). It is remarkable that the Church of Scotland was the only Reformation Church anywhere to prescribe and publish a set liturgical fasting order, the minister's only latitude being in the content of the sermon.

In the area of catechesis, Christian education, English versions of the *Genevan Catechism* and later of the *Heidelberg Catechism* were used in Scotland (as in England too). However, in 1581, a Scottish primer was sanctioned by the General Assembly, composed by the ex-Dominican, John Craig. This was *A Shorte Summe of the Whole Catechisme . . . for the greater Ease of the Common People and Children.*[96] Structured around a simple question and answer format, it was widely used in the country, and a shorter version was used to prepare people for pre-Communion examinations. It was also kept free of inserted proof references to 'the Scriptures or Fathers', though readers are referred to Calvin's *Institutes* for general corroboration.

It was also Craig who composed the brief *King's Confession*, or *Negative Confession*, or *Second Confession of Faith*, published in 1581.[97] It was designed primarily to flush out alleged or real crypto-Catholics in government at a time of heightened dread of international Catholicism, the Counter-Reformation, Jesuit missions, the Spanish menace, etc. In the previous year, a college for the training of Scots for the priesthood had been established at Douai. Crucially, the *King's Confession* included a declaration of loyalty to the monarch. Much more militantly 'anti-Catholic' than the *Scots Confession*, it status was ambiguous. While it was accepted by the Church and had 'royal approval', it was not approved by Parliament, to which it was not submitted. It was at most a codicil to the official Confession, though it played a major role in the Covenant era in the next century. It embodied a definite hardening of post-Reformation Protestant attitudes to Catholicism that were shared by Presbyterians, Episcopalians and the Church of England alike, so that there is nothing specifically 'Scottish' or 'presbyterian' about it.

Future developments, or lack of them

The evangelization of the nation, as well as the Church's input into social, economic, and educational amelioration was seriously impeded by generations of preoccupation with contention over church government, discipline, liturgy and church–state relations. Since this affected the 'people', such issues in Scotland were in the full sense 'public' ones, as they often agitated local communities. At the local level, the introduction and exercise of discipline by presbyteries and kirk sessions, in which prominent laymen as elders participated, did help impose strict Christian moral values on the recalcitrant populace. Its extension to all classes of society was a key factor in making it acceptable at large, it being transparently obvious that the 'Church' is composed of both 'the godly and hypocrites', as the *Second Book of Discipline*, in the best Augustinian ecclesiological tradition, declared in its first article. The disciplinary model availed of in Scotland was not individualist or private, but corporate and public like that of the Genevan Consistory as devised by Calvin. The institution and its operation were justified with reference to Matthew 18.15–17.[98] Calvin envisaged the Consistory as a kind of Christianized Jewish Sanhedrin, a mixed body of ministers and elders endowed with the power of excommunication.[99] Crucial for Calvin was that such a power should be exercised without appeal to the civil authority, something that was achieved in Geneva by 1555 after a tough struggle, and after it was realized that there was public (though not government) support for such a system. In Scotland, the establishment of Kirk Sessions in the parishes and regional Presbyteries meant that they could exercise, or claim to exercise disciplinary functions in a way analogous to the Genevan Consistory – indeed the *First Book of Discipline* actually uses the word 'consistorie' to describe the prototype Kirk session.[100] By 1569, an *Ordoure of Excommunication and of Public Repentance* was published. Its purpose was not punitive, but corrective and pastoral, even if traditional concomitant civil punishments were still assumed to apply.

Unlike in Geneva, the particular touchstone of church–state relations in Scotland was not so much autonomous discipline (which had been legitimated in the *Scots Confession* as a mark of a true Church) as church polity. Consequently, the energies of the Church's leadership were to be consumed chiefly by a labyrinthine struggle between on the one hand, autonomous presbyterian aspirations of large sections of the Kirk and people, and on the other, Erastian-episcopalian policies of the broadly Calvinist Crown, government, and a party in the Church. The seismic struggles of the Covenant era in the seventeenth century symbolized the failure of conflict resolution.

In 1572, an Act of Uniformity was passed in Scotland.[101] It was designed chiefly to penalize lingering Catholicism by compelling conformity, but on church government and forms of worship it was still vague – in great contrast to the English uniformity Acts. The permanent conflict was epitomized in two famous maxims. James VI insisted: 'No bishop, no king.' Andrew Melville,[102] churchman and Scottish university reformer who had studied or taught in Germany, St Andrews, France and Geneva, was the chief presbyterian ideologue, and riposted with: 'God's silly vassal, the king, is neither lord nor head of the Church, but a member of it' – and so subject to its authority. His thinking was partly influenced by Calvin's thought, but more especially by Calvin's successor in Geneva, Theodore Beza as well as by Travers and Cartwright in England. The *Second Book of Discipline*, which embodied the Kirk's proto-presbyterian church order, signalled the Church's definitive alienation from the compromise solution devised in 1572 – the 'Concordat of Leith' – and condoned by Knox. Not until 1592 was presbyterian church government 'approved', but only by Parliament, and not by the hostile Crown.

Neither party was strong enough in Scotland to impose its will on the other and so resolve the remarkable anachronism, or pragmatic *modus vivendi*, whereby unofficial or semi-official presbytery and official episcopacy in various forms co-existed.[103] Until 1690, Presbyterianism in Scotland functioned essentially as working hypothesis, just as episcopacy functioned as an expedient that was still grounded in law. Following the union of the Scottish and English Crowns in 1603, James, now Supreme

Governor of the English and Irish state churches, and inspired by the notion of ecclesiastical uniformity throughout the British Isles, began to get the upper hand. His Anglican chaplain, William Laud, a strong proponent of mandatory uniformity and royal authority in the Church, guided the king a great deal. Royal policy in respect of polity as such was not substantively different from previous and like-minded Scottish Regents, such as James Douglas, Earl of Morton, and James Stewart, Earl of Arran. In 1610, diocesan pastoral episcopacy was imposed and the General Assembly reduced to consultative importance. James' hopes of ushering in Anglican or 'episcopalian' liturgical features provoked more fundamental opposition. At Perth in 1618, with Melville now exiled in France at the University of Sedan after imprisonment in the Tower of London for five years (1607–11),[104] a managed General Assembly was compelled to accept 'Five Articles' specified by the king himself in addition to liturgical changes that had been adopted before. Though accorded statutory status in 1621, these requirements were not enforced due to the strength of opposition, which was popular as well as ministerial.

The unacceptable articles may not seem to modern eyes to be sufficiently important to warrant dividing nations and kingdoms, but they and the opposition to them were indicators of incompatible concepts on matters of first principle. They dealt with: kneeling at the Lord's Supper, private Communion, private baptism, bishops' participation in confirmation, and observance of major church holy days. Their rejection was related to issues such as authority of Scripture, the nature of Christ's eucharistic presence in relation to the elements, the indissoluble bond between Word and sacrament, the relationship if any between the sacraments and salvation, and equally, between the Gospel and Old Testament ceremonial law in regard to religious festivals, and so the exclusive supremacy of the Sabbath. In addition, there was the question of the authority of the monarch in the Church. General political reaction to centralizing government tendencies in distant London, where the monarch now resided, added to the unpopularity of Jacobean policies in Scotland. Ultimately, both Andrew Melville and James VI & I became symbols of Protestant disunity due to conflicting visions of the institutional Church. The politicized polarization of the issues ought not conceal the fact that there was an erudite school of largely north-eastern Scottish theologians that was broadly Protestant, but non-presbyterian, only mildly Calvinist by conviction, and not sharing the burgeoning covenant theology. They were not agents of the Church of England or its supreme governor. Orientated more to the patristic traditions of theology and spirituality, and episcopal notions of church government on historical and theological grounds, their creative and more irenical outlook was afforded little breathing space in the Scottish ecclesiastical imbroglio.[105]

After years of sterile stalemate, the National Covenant movement in 1638 forced Charles I, James' successor, to allow the banned General Assembly to convene at Glasgow. It excommunicated the bishops, abolished prelacy and alien Anglican practices in worship as 'popish'. This initiated a struggle whereby Scotland was propelled into the initially 'English' Civil War. Subsequently, by means of the radical 'Solemn League and Covenant' (1643), the dominant party in Scotland attempted to establish presbyterian church order throughout the British Isles. That miscarried, and after further subjection to episcopacy following the restoration of the monarchy, the Scots' reward for finally deserting the Stewarts and supporting William of Orange in 1688–90 was an established and exclusive presbyterian Church in Scotland, with a tolerated offshoot in Ireland. If this was a 'failure', then the failure of monarchical episcopacy to establish itself throughout the whole of Britain and Ireland has to be taken into account as well.

Arguably, without the National Covenant, Presbyterianism in Scotland would have sunk into oblivion as in England. Crucial in the Covenant was aristocratic commitment to allegedly urban and bourgeois Presbyterianism. The Covenant was not just about opposition to bishops and English liturgy. It was also welded with political resistance to Crown centralizing and interventionist policies in Church and Nation – perceived by the Scots as 'tyranny' or arbitrary use of the royal prerogative, in the light of their corporatist traditions (often misunderstood as 'democratic'). When diagnosing the opposition, Covenant Presbyterianism (like English Puritanism) saw a sinister association between episcopacy, set liturgy, Erastianism, Arminianism and trends towards monarchical absolutism, all of which would enable papacy in one form or other to re-enter, and so betray the Reformation.[106] As in England, militant Protestant patriotism became the dominant, 'popular' ideology, especially after the death of James VI & I (1625).

Anti-encroachment politics, in the name of church 'freedom', became wedded to Covenant theology, which provided the 'celestial glue' uniting the nation. Only from this point on do Presbyterianism and advanced 'Calvinism' become synonymous in Scotland – a process assisted by the movement of some Anglican and Scottish episcopalian bishops away from strict 'Calvinism' to 'Arminianism'.[107] Add to this the tradition of oppositional Word of God theology bequeathed by Knox and Melville in particular, plus ideas of popular sovereignty, the right of resistance and to depose unworthy rulers, as propounded by Catholics like John Major and Protestants like George Buchanan, then the mix is potent.

The Covenant movement brought Presbyterianism to the verge of great power in the British Isles, but this was not to materialize, as the 'Isles' were fundamentally too disparate on most counts. The episode and the ultimate issues underlying it were part of the universal conflict between traditions of an authoritarian unitary church–state ('caesaropapism', 'Erastianism'), and notions of church–state polarity or dualism, echoed in Melville's 'two kingdoms' theory. If in 1560 Scots sought emancipation from the spiritual supremacy of the papal theocracy, thereafter many of them sought emancipation from subjugation to all-too-theocratic kingship.

A long Reformation?

If the *terminus a quo* of the Reformation in Scotland was a problem, so also is its *terminus ad quem*. Allusion has been made already to distortion that arises from presenting the materialization of the 'Scottish Reformation' as a short, sharp affair in the period from 1558 to 1560, a sudden coup resulting in Calvinist and even presbyterian conquest. Many brief accounts of the Reformation do end around 1560, or do not advance much beyond the 1560s. Such a restricted perception derives understandably from the revolutionary drama of those years. Retrospectively, those years constitute the turning-point in the transition from Reformation movement to process and arduous implementation in church and society. Preoccupation with that period can, however, issue in the same imbalance that follows from an analogous conventional tendency to keep the camera on the years 1517–25 in Germany, and on a handful of high-profile figures. The year 1560 in Scotland was partly the climax of what had been rumbling since the 1520s, and partly the beginning of what only achieved some kind of fulfilment – when? – 1567? (the royal assent accords the Reformation full legal validity) – 1690? (legislative abolition of episcopacy in favour of Presbyterianism) – 1707? (guaranteed security of presbyterian church government in Scotland within the context of the Scoto-English parliamentary union) – 1930? (the achievement of full church autonomy and freedom outside the scope of the civil power).

Or what about the plausibility of 1572? – when the Scottish government during the minority of James VI enacted what was effectively an act of uniformity in religion: 'all subjects shall worship the only true God in the uniformity of religion'.[108] This obliged all Scottish residents, male and female, to submit themselves to the sacraments and discipline of the Church of Scotland. It provided for the naming, registration and formal excommunication (with its civil consequences) of all those who did not conform or comply after due warning. It also provided for the deprivation of clergy who failed to co-operate in any way with the identification of recusants. Thereby citizenship and legal rights were henceforth symbiotically tied to confessing publicly the Reformation faith. This was then a crucial step in the process of creating, however artificially, a Protestant nation (although pockets of the old faith continued to survive in remote places). It represented the restoration of the *cuius regio eius religio* (the religion of the ruler obtains) principle after the defeat of the Marian legitimists (though many of them were Protestant), and so a reversion to the medieval principle of a unitary religio-political kingdom. A generation or so later, by the early seventeenth century, non-Protestants in Scotland were a tiny minority. By that time, the 'Reformation' was basically completed as a national cultural identity at least, even if collective sanctification was still unachieved.

In Scotland, however, 'uniformity' was less manifest in the visible ecclesiastical sense (and on the matter of the demarcation of church–

state relations) than concepts of uniformity in England. Equivalence does not apply. There, acts of uniformity related also to liturgy and church government, and the Church was regulated by the paramount principle of the royal supremacy. As indicated, these matters remained on hold in Scotland. Here, the law only required commitment to the object of true worship, to the two sacraments, and to acceptance of basic Reformation doctrines (embodied notably in the *Scots Confession of Faith* of 1560).[109] In 1574, the Scottish Parliament acknowledged this minimalist situation in deploring the fact that although 'since the alteration of religion, the liberty of the Evangel has been enjoyed in unity of doctrine', church formats and the delivery of its services, so to speak, remained matters of contention.[110]

A major consequence of the Elizabethan Settlement in England was lack of settlement, even though the state Church held its own on the whole. In Scotland, the lack of settlement in the precise ecclesiastical sense was even more prolonged than in England. 'State Church' had no unchangeable profile in Scotland. Scottish disputes were much more continuously open and adversarially politicized up to the end of the seventeenth century, though in both countries there were mutations in theology still within the broad 'reformed' context. Accordingly, the Scottish Reformation in the full sense is a 'Long Reformation', in terms of origins, evolution and accomplishment, since its ecclesiological aspects required many generations to resolve. Ironically, this was achieved at a time when the sovereignty of confessional Reformation theology – be it in the form of general evangelical affirmation rooted in Scripture and in some cases, the Church Fathers as well, or of Calvinist scholasticism, or of Covenant theology, or of puritan, schematic biblicism – became subject to gradual subversion from within.

A regenerate people?

The Scottish Reformers, Knox in particular, conceived of 'sin' in terms of corporate religious and socio-economic disorder, expressed in impiety and injustice, the result of congenital fallen and perverted human nature. Yet they found themselves on the horns of a dilemma when they, but more particularly their successors, set about providing a remedy. On the one hand, the Reformers parted from the traditional Catholic notion that the gradual infusion of grace and acquisition of merit could induce an ontological change for the better in human nature, incomplete in this life, but completed in the purgatorial after-life. Instead, they held to the idea of the undiminishable reality of sin in this life, even among true believers. On the other hand, in a more specifically Calvinist way they were so committed to the idea and necessity of righteousness and sanctification, individual and collective, that they embarked upon achieving this not only through preaching and sacrament, but also by the coercive means of church discipline. Thereby they tried to integrate, at the practical and verifiable level, the moral law and the Gospel. In common with the wider Reformed tradition, in particular its Calvinist wing, they fell into the danger of lapsing into that which precisely had provoked the original reformation, namely, moral perfectionism or works-righteousness. The consequence was that they envisaged the reformed nation or city as a New Jerusalem, living virtuously in near-monastic probity. While some achievements were notable – such as holding the upper classes and rulers accountable to the law of God, by making some church ministerial offices open to the laity, and by restoring fellowship to worship – in general, expectations were too high on the issue of the transformation of society and most individuals. The remedy of the evangelical 'transforming power of grace for sinners' just did not always function within the framework of ecclesiastical structures and management. The claims made for the accessible Bible, that it (with the aid of preaching) would expose the population to the irresistible power of the Word and grace of God, was with many individual exceptions, unsubstantiated.

The failure to create a sanctified and righteous society led to another shift in perception in later generations. As in English Puritanism and in prominent streams of Catholic tradition going back to the early Church (and not just in the West), there developed a strong tendency to trivialize the *essence* of sin as the pleasurable, all too human activities of individuals or groups. The recovery of stoical traditions and the widening of ascetical expectations to include the entire laity, now all 'priests' expected to live in conformity to Christ, encouraged this. Accordingly, sin was in practice depicted primarily as 'sins', like make-up, theatre, sport, dancing, festivities, funeral wakes, sexual peccadilloes, perfume, swearing and even public swimming, though not alcohol till centuries later. A caricature of moralist (puritan) Protestantism developed. Religion became increasingly confined, almost irreversibly, to the *individual* moral and social spheres, and to damage limitation, an idea that would have been alien to the original Reformers. This signalled a defaulting on central Reformation doctrines, like being justified and a confessing sinner simultaneously, or justification by grace alone, or Christian liberty, or the incapacity of human nature to change, even if it can be restrained, subdued, and maybe 'transformed' or 'converted' in individual cases. An escape route was to appeal to the minority of the Elect, the righteous remnant, even if identifying them was hazardous.

Why this happened is understandable, for collective sanctification and a 'Christian society' were ultimately unattainable, even if improvements could be made. The ancient problem for Christianity as such was: how can it balance affirmation of life with a counter-cultural stance? The problem was wholly transconfessional too, even if Christian reform attitudes to the manifestations of sin oscillated and varied from eradication to accommodation.[111] Counter-Reformation Catholicism in Ireland ran up against the same dilemma, as Alison Forrestal's illuminating study of the era amply demonstrates.[112] A statement from the General Assembly of 1596 depicting the state of the nation must – allowing for an ancient Judaeo-Christian tradition of proclivity to sanctimonious hyperbole, though with a genuine concern for social justice – therefore raise the question: if the Reformation in Scotland changed a lot by way of form, what did it change in human behaviour?

> An universal coldness, want of zeal, ignorance, contempt of the Word; prayer, singing of psalms, and the Word of God profaned and abused; superstition and idolatry entertained; blaspheming in God's name; swearing, banning, and cursing; profanation of the Sabbath by working, journeying, trysting, gaming, dancing, drinking, fishing, killing, and milling; inferiors not doing duty to superiors; children taking out law-suits against their parents, and marrying without their consent; breaches of duty between married persons; great blood-shed; deadly feuds and assisting bloodshedders to elude the law; fornication; adultery, incest, unlawful marriages, and divorces; excessive drinking and gluttony; filthy and impure speeches and songs; sacrilege in all estates growing daily, to the utter undoing of the Kirk; cruel oppression of the poor; thraldom in service; oppression by usury; lying; universal neglect of justice; judges ignorant and profane. Through the abusing, delaying, perverting and neglecting of justice ... all horrible crimes abound ... [Due to too many ministerial vacancies] the people perish in ignorance, atheism, and profanity.[113]

Plus ça change, plus ça reste la même chose. Apart perhaps from the reference to 'superstition and idolatry', there is no obvious allusion to the shadow-world of magic arts and witchcraft in the above extract. Yet Reformation Scotland has the unfortunate distinction of representing a uniquely close link between the Reformed Church and the persecution of witches and practitioners of magic, largely female. This inherited and intensified the late medieval Catholic tradition, which the Renaissance, the Reformation and the Counter-Reformation did little to mitigate in much of Europe.

In Scotland, between 1563 (when a Witchcraft Act was passed by Parliament and extended to all magic, whether malign or benign) and 1727, about 1,500 witches were subjected to capital punishment. This was chiefly in the Lowlands, though another 1,000 or so were exonerated. This contrasts with about 1,000 of them executed in the same period in England, though proportionately it is comparable to the numbers killed in largely Catholic regions of France, Germany, Switzerland and Poland.[114] Such a scale of witch-hunting was then not unique to Scotland. What was unique was the solemn sanction and exhortation of both the Reformed Kirk and the monarch, James VI. As an example of princely godliness, the latter's *Daemonologie* (1597) outlined strategy against the machinations of Satan and other demons in a troubled society, all part of the cosmic struggle between God and the Devil.[115] What was distinctive about the Scottish Kirk's active endorsement was that it contrasts markedly to dis-interest in the matter found among reformed consistories and synods on the Continent, as in France, Switzerland, the Rhineland Palatinate, East Frisia and the Netherlands. The relative exception was Geneva, though witch persecution there (unlike Scotland) had a long pre-Reformation history. It was therefore not a universally 'Calvinist' phenomenon.[116]

Received interpretation suggests that 'Scottish Puritanism' was to blame for the scale of the problem in Scotland.[117] 'Scottish radical biblicism', or 'biblical totalitarianism' might be nearer the mark. The blurring of the distinction between the Old and the New Testaments, between the old and the new covenants, led to the attempt to apply literally many of the norms and conventions of old Israelite society to Scotland, even if not essential to Christianity. The ultimate sanction for attempting to impose such a perceived blueprint was claimed to lie with the 'will of God' and his sovereignty, and Scripture, which was equated with his oracles. The Word and the words were seen as identical. Therefore 'sorceresses should not be allowed to live' (Exodus 22.18), 'rebellion (against God) is the sin of divination' (1 Samuel 15.23), sorcerers and soothsayers will be 'cut off' (Micah 5.12), etc. Further, ancient Christian tradition linked magic to idolatry and heresy (Simon Magus).[118]

One could say then that what helped enable the witch craze in Scotland was a certain understanding of the normative role of the whole of Scripture in church and society that prevailed. This had consequences for its contemporary 'application' by zealous presbyteries and Kirk sessions at the local level in the name of obedience to the Word of God, of 'discipline' and the war against 'superstition'. The need for 'results' was grounded in the (signally sub-reformed) urge, more religious than Christian, to placate divine wrath with acts of quasi-sacrificial atonement. Thereby the nation would be 'cleansed'.

While ideas of demonic pact and Satanic leagues pervaded Scottish society in the sixteenth and seventeenth centuries, only two theologians (apart from James VI) touched on witchcraft in their writings. These were William Struther (future Episcopalian Dean of Edinburgh) and John Weemes.[119] Both shared the generally prevalent federal or Covenant theology. Some suggest that in the minds of many, the perceived accompanying counterpoise to the Covenant of Grace was a covenant of diabolical works due to consorting with the Evil One, as in atheism, sorcery, witchcraft, etc.[120] Such dualist and pseudo-Manichaean thinking was also compatible with predestinarian ideas of reprobation. Preaching such notions was counterproductive, since it could be pastorally destabilizing and psychologically damaging.[121] One could also argue that the relatively extraordinary witch craze in Scotland was a symptom of the nation's love–hate relationship with itself and of the overcompensation for this by means of self-admiration and glorification in respect of the 'purity' of its religion.[122] Religious activism was devoted to three things: firstly, identifying and eliminating all traces of putative religious impurity and perversion (superstition and Catholicism); secondly, punishing all verifiable cases of sexual impropriety, that is, sexual activity outside marriage that was its divinely ordained, exclusive framework; thirdly, eliminating the excesses and even harmless manifestations of popular social customs.[123] Religious and 'social control', therefore, became the chief objective of 'reformation within the reformation', and the 'taming of the nation'. Yet while to modern eyes the work of Kirk elders as morals police and enforcers was often shockingly abusive, it was not invariably a bad thing in a social world of cruelty, oppression, hedonistic improvidence and uncivil arbitrariness.[124]

CHAPTER 9

Conclusion

Predictably, a satellite image of the British Isles during the Reformation era would have revealed religio-political atmospheric developments corresponding to those on the Continent, and so an equivalent turbulence. The movements, processes and legislative acts were diverse, as were the perception, reception, and appropriation of Reformation ideas, so that motion and flux rather than definitive settlement are the hallmarks.

The reasons for this are manifest. Firstly, while in the religious domain the Church in the British Isles had previously formed part of an integrated (Western) Christendom and a single, overarching ecclesiastical institution, such a seamless Christian body no longer existed. Secondly, the British Isles itself did not constitute a geographical, political or cultural unity anyway. Thirdly, this was true of the Continent as well. Accordingly, just as the Reformation on the Continent was variable, partial, and asymmetrical, so it was in Ireland and Britain too. From the global perspective therefore, the origins and evolution of the Reformation in the British Isles and its sequel were typically European. Much in modern historiography has tended to obscure this fact due to a preoccupation with 'distinctiveness', 'uniqueness', 'national characteristics', etc. (if somewhat less so in the case of Scotland).

There was therefore no comprehensive success in the ecclesiastical sense for the Reformation in these islands, although there nearly was. Also, what victories occurred were in the context of the times relatively pyrrhic. With the hindsight of 450 years later, the basic reorientation at least seems to have been 'settled' by 1558–60, in a formal legislative sense. Yet for the 130 years or so after that date, the Reformations in Britain and Ireland were manifestly fragile and vulnerable. There were internal fissures that had been papered over, and in the international context, survival became indissolubly linked to issues of national security. This was due largely to the unconcealed strategy and potency of crusading and political Catholicism.

Yet if the ecclesiastical problem remained permanently unresolved, this has to be offset with the emergence of a potent, all-British (and part-Irish), common Protestant 'culture'. In times of stress engendered from without this common factor held good and transcended respective political and ecclesiastical differences. There may have been no common formal creed, but there was a sense of mutual ownership and profession of the Bible as a source of ultimate authority; this was fastened firmly to evolving 'identities' of political, cultural and religious kinds.

However, while the ecclesiastical contrasts among the four nations are conspicuous, and were to remain so, the potential for a monochromatic clean sweep – universal uniformity of religion and church – existed up to the beginning of the eighteenth century. The traditional Constantinian–Theodosian concept of a unitary state and religion, one faith and one church within society, was still axiomatic. Both Catholic and Protestant secular rulers' religious policies during the Reformation era were grounded in such an irrefragable conceptual mandate. The pragmatic, but legal settlement in Germany after 1555 according to the principle of *cuius regio eius religio* (the faith of the ruler obtains) was based on the same premiss, except that that arrangement allowed for relative pluralism, not internally, but in the form of external coexistence among various relatively sovereign territories. A similar situation of 'confessional equity' prevailed in Reformation Switzerland, where canton and confession went hand-in-hand. The increasing political centralization of sovereignty in the British Isles meant, however, that there was no principled legal bridling of confessional imperialism, at least up until 1690.

The *force majeure* of England in the British Isles meant that it was either a matter of strategic policy, or at least aspiration, that its religious settlement be applied to the other nations in so far as they were subject to the same sovereign. The union of the English and Scottish Crowns after 1603, and its momentous implications for Ireland, made such universal uniformity an increasing and technically legitimate possibility. Forceful English (and Anglo-Scottish) attempts in this respect did not succeed in the end. The witness to this was the carnage of the seventeenth century when competing theologies, ecclesiologies, and ideologies caused recourse to arms in order to settle matters in the sadly customary way. While currently there are quite different explanations for such events based on bread-and-butter issues and the socio-economic forces behind them, seventeenth-century revolution, rebellions, civil wars and militarization were still due in part to the unresolved clash between Episcopalian, Erastian, Presbyterian, Separatist and Catholic conceptions of Christianity and Church, and in part to disputed theologies of political sovereignty and government.

Although basic commitment to the Reformation was pledged by the sovereign powers in the British Isles, highly contentious was ecclesiastical form and polity. The Anglo-Welsh Protestant episcopalian state Church, known later as the 'Anglican Church', had to cope with presbyterian and other challenges. This debate was at a level of theological principles rather than utilitarian pragmatism, since both parties' point of departure was that their system had sanction *de iure divino*. That being the case, 'truth' itself was at stake, so that comprehensive vitiation and denigration of the opposite position ensued. In addition, the Scottish Kirk had to balance *de facto* presbytery with official state-sponsored episcopacy, and her principle of church autonomy with government Erastian pretensions. In the English and Scottish Churches, then, everything was at risk for several generations.

In Ireland, the Church of the sovereign authority, the Church of Ireland, became confined essentially to elements in the colonial Old English, and to the new Anglo-Scottish planter minority. Eventually, however, significant presbyterian secession or nonconformity, mainly though not exclusively among the Scottish incomers, diminished crucial Irish Protestant solidarity in both the religious and political spheres. The Scots–Irish presbyterian factor, with its combination of opposition to episcopacy, Crown regulation of religious affairs, explicit predestination, and popular evangelical revivalism from 1625 onwards[1] was to be a permanent thorn in the flesh for the statutory Irish Church. One could therefore argue that the ultimately unresolved episcopalian–presbyterian conflict and the accompanying dissensus over church–state relations significantly undermined any prospects of successfully commending the Protestant Reformation to the Roman Catholic majority in Ireland. The Protestant 'Irish mission' in its disunited forms, and devoid of anything like the expertise of the Society of Jesus, always functioned on the barren ground of indifference rather than open hostility, despite local and isolated successes. Yet the conundrum of continuing outlawed mass Catholicism in Ireland was unique in Europe, where normally Catholic integrity depended on secular real power. At any rate, monocausal explanations of that phenomenon will never suffice, especially those grounded in the 'spirit and devotion of the Irish people'. The frustration for Catholic Ireland was that it never achieved the equivalent of a 'Dutch Revolt'.

Lastly, Protestant theologies became increasingly encased in various prescriptive orthodoxies, whether 'scholastic', or propositional biblicism. This tends to be dismissed as a 'bad thing'. The former reappropriated Aristotelianism, which had been initially proscribed by the Reformation. It was necessitated by the dialectical exigencies of ongoing disputation with Catholic theologians. The second is broadly described as 'Ramism' (after Peter Ramus (1515–72) in Paris). Its systematic and often diagrammatic presentations of doctrines (the original flow-charts) were to enable students, churchmen and others to have recourse to instruments of relatively user-friendly, theological schematic order, in an era of intensifying confusion and relative despair. The atmosphere of dialectical confrontation and set-piece struggles for victory also encouraged these tendencies. It also embodied a reaction to the biblical-commentary mountain, works that by definition were the antithesis of good literature, and so 'handbooks' rather than thought-shapers. Yet older Christian

Humanist (Erasmian) and mystical streams touched by Neoplatonism rather than Aristotelianism, plus the emergence of alternative theologies of God and humanity challenging the Trinity and notions of original sin (Socinianism, Arminianism, Unitarianism), gradually emerged to subvert the monumental edifices of ecclesiastical theology within Protestantism.

Catholic theology, however, was to be disturbed by tendencies of another direction, namely radical neo-Augustinian manifestations and anti-Scholastic attitudes, notably 'Jansenism'.[2] This, with its denial of freewill, its belief that grace could never be resisted, and its suggestion that Christ only died for the Elect was seen as undermining the Church's mediatorial and necessary role in salvation, and so was condemned as heterodox. It had attracted English-speaking theologians like the Irish Franciscan teaching on the Continent, Luke Wadding (1588–1657), who in the end submitted to church judgement on the matter. Ironically, if the Catholic Church rejected the theology of Jansenism, it discreetly adopted Jansenist moralism in the pastoral sphere. The consequence was that from the seventeenth century onwards, coercive righteousness, sanctification, and 'social discipline', vigorously exercised by clergy, became increasingly characteristic of Catholicism in Ireland as well. Therefore, in the social and individual spheres, practical 'puritanism' cannot be convincingly confined to one or other 'Protestant' religious culture.

Notes

Preface

1. This Church was formed in Scotland in 1847, constituting a union between two denominations that had separated from the established Kirk in the eighteenth century, the 'United Secession Church' and the 'Relief Church'. Characterized later by liberalizing theology and mitigated Calvinism, it united with the 'Free Church of Scotland' in 1900. The new 'United Free Church of Scotland' in turn combined with the old Church of Scotland in 1929/30 to form the modern disestablished Church of Scotland.
2. A term emphasizing the traumatic incongruity of time and eternity, humanity and God. Cf. Alister E. McGrath, *Historical Theology. An Introduction to the History of Christian Thought* (Oxford 1998), pp. 238f., 347, 351, 362.
3. J. V. Langmead Casserley, *Providence and History. A Tale of Two Cities* (Signposts 5), Westminster 1940, p. 122.
4. Quotation (anglicized by me) in his *Buke of Four Scoir Thre Questions* (Antwerp 1563), Scottish Text Society, Series 1, Vol. 15, p. 53. Cf. Burns, *Ninian Winzet*, p. 12 (see below, Bibliography V).

Chapter 1: History, Church History and Reformation History

1. Of the 'deconstructionist' kind, whereby texts, primary or secondary, are stripped of ostensible meaning in the search for hidden agendas, like suppression, exclusion, privilege, etc. Cf. Joyce Appleby, Lynn Hunt and Margaret Jacob, *Telling the Truth about History* (New York and London 1994), pp. 198–237.
2. For a very useful survey of mainstream treatments, Protestant and Catholic, of the Reformation from the sixteenth century to the middle of the twentieth century, see John P. Dolan, 'The Reformation in Retrospect', in his *History of the Reformation. A Conciliatory Assessment of Opposite Views* (New York, Toronto and London 1965), pp. 21–63.

3. In the preface to the German original of his *History of the Latin and German Peoples* (1824), but the preface was omitted in the translation by Philip Ashworth (London 1887). The formulation is a reprise of an ancient ideal of historical objectivity, articulated in the second century AD by Lucian of Samosata. Cf. the latter's *How to Write History*, in Kelley, *Versions of History*, pp 67f (NB: All author-short title citations in this chapter will refer to works found in the Bibliography, section I.) See also George G. Iggers and James M. Powell, *Leopold von Ranke and the Shaping of Historical Discipline*, Syracuse 1990.

4. Cf. Peter Novick, *That Noble Dream. The 'Objectivity Question'*, Cambridge 1988.

5. For example, the widely circulated *General History of the Reformation of the Church* by Johann Sleidan (1506–56), an approach that anticipated the Rankian spirit. See extracts in Kelley, *Versions of History*, pp. 321, 325–9. Cf. Dickens, *Contemporary Historians*, pp. 2–5, 19. Sleidan was among the first early modern historians to treat political and religious history as intertwined, though he cites Old Testament histories as obvious precedents.

6. Cf. A. G. Dickens, *Ranke as a Reformation Historian*, Reading 1980.

7. Ironically, modern 'text-books' rarely contain 'texts'!

8. Cf. George P. Gooch, *History and Historians in the Nineteenth Century*, London 1913. Benedetto Croce, *Theory & History of Historiography*, London 1921. David Bebbington, *Patterns in History*, Leicester 1979. B. A. Haddock, *An Introduction to Historical Thought*, London 1980. Ernst Breisach, *Historiography. Ancient, Medieval & Modern*, Chicago and London 1983. Michael Bentley, *Modern Historiography. An Introduction*, London and New York 1999.

9. Cf. Alan Richardson, *History Sacred and Profane,* London 1964.

10. Apparently by the philosopher and man of letters, August-Wilhelm von Schlegel.

11. Associated with Aristotelianism, the idea was mediated to theology chiefly by Thomas Aquinas.

12. Cf. Michael Grant, *Readings in the Classical Historians* (New York, Toronto, etc. 1992), pp. 5f.

13. See his *The Philosophy of History*, trs. by J. Sibree (New York 1956), p. 10.

14. Cf. Williams, *Reformation Views*.

15. *History of Scotland* (Cambridge 1912), Vol. 2, p. 126.

16. Cf. Gordon Donaldson: 'Historians like to be on the winning side . . . consequently the failures of history get a bad press', *All the Queen's Men*, p. 4.

17. Though he had to write a book about history to make the point: *The History of Civilization in England*, 2 vols, London 1857–61.

18. As in, for example, the expressive rather than formative book by Oswald Spengler, *The Decline of the West* (1918), trs. by C. F. Atkinson, New York 1939.

19. Cf. Christopher Hill, *Past & Present* (1965), p. 12.

20. Cf. Abraham Friesen, *Reformation and Utopia. The Marxist Interpretation of the Reformation and its Antecedents*, Wiesbaden 1974.

21. See n. 25 below.

22. See especially his *The Historian's Craft. Reflections on the Nature and Uses of History and the Techniques and Methods of Historical Writing* (1941–4), trs. by Peter Putman, Manchester 1954.

23. Thomas A. Brady, 'Social History', in Ozment, *Reformation Europe*, p. 176. For an influential nineteenth-century statement (1875) of classical simplicity identifying an umbilical cord between the Reformation and the rising middle classes (in England), see the Introduction by J. S. Brewer to *Letters and Papers Foreign and Domestic of the reign of Hernry VIII*, Vol. IV (1524–30), pp. dcxlix–dclxiv.

24. Cf. O'Malley, *Trent and All That*, pp. 98ff.

25. Cf. his 'A new kind of history', in *A New Kind of History from the Writings of Lucien Febvre*, ed. by Peter Burke (London 1973), pp. 36–41.

26. Title of a book (Cambridge 1923) by the Irish biblical scholar, J. Ernest Davey.

27. Cf. his *The Reformation Era, 1500–1650*, 2nd edn, London and New York 1973.

28. See Kyle C. Sessions and Philip N. Bebb, *Pietas et Societas. New Trends in Reformation Social History. Essays in Memory of Harold J. Grimm* (Sixteenth Century Essays & Studies IV), Kirksville, MO 1985, pp. x, 21.

29. Cf. Appleby, Hunt and Jacob, *Telling the Truth* (see n. 1 above), pp. 37–43, 52–90. A notable precursor of the secularization of history was Lord Bolingbroke with his *Letters on the Study and Use of History* (1751).

30. *On the Consolation of Philosophy*, Penguin Classics, 1976. There is now a new edition and translation by Patrick G. Walsh, Oxford 1999.

31. *Preface to Galeatius Capella's History*, in *Luther's Works*, ed. by J. Pelikan and H. Lehmann (Philadelphia 1955–86), Vol. 34, pp. 275ff.

32. Cf. Bebbington (see n. 8 above), 'Christian History', in his *Patterns in History*, pp. 38–67.

33. One influential statement of Christianity as the key to history was Herbert Butterfield, *Christianity and History*, London 1950.

34. Cf. Dickens, *Contemporary Historians*, pp. 2–5.

35. Cf. *Ferdinand Christian Baur on the Writing of Church History*, ed. and trs. by Peter Hodgson (New York 1968), pp. 79–257. Meinhold, *Historiographie*, Vol. 1, pp. 227–343. Gordon, *Protestant History, passim.*

36. Cf. the preface to his novel, *The Magic Mountain*.

37. John Donne, *The Anatomy of the World*.

38. 'A new kind of history' (see n. 25 above), p. 39.

39. In *The German Reformation. The Essential Readings*, ed. C. Scott Dixon (Oxford 1999), p. 90. Cf. n. 41 below.

40. E.g. Brady, Oberman and Tracy, *Handbook of European History 1400–1600*. Andrew Pettegree (ed.), *The Reformation World*, London 2000.

41. Dixon, 'Narratives of the German Reformation', in *The German Reformation* (see n. 39 above), pp. 3, 31. The challenge of attaining a coherent concept of the religio-theological mutations during the Reformation era, in their concrete context, is innovatively presented by Berndt Hamm in his 'Normative centering in the fifteenth and sixteenth centuries:

observations on religiosity, theology and iconology', *Journal of Early Modern History* 3.4 (1999), 307–54.

42. Quoted by Euan Cameron, *The European Reformation* (Oxford 1991), p. viii. Cf. [Brady] in *Handbook of European History*, Vol. 2, 'Introduction', p. xv: 'The . . . extension of the scope of historical knowledge . . . has muted the bold claims to a single, comprehensive and indeed inclusive Grand Narrative.'

43. Professor at the (United) Free Church College of Glasgow (later 'Trinity College Glasgow'). Cf. *Dictionary of Scottish Church History & Theology*, pp. 486f. He was also the first modern scholar to write in English on the Strasbourg Reformer, Martin Bucer: 'Martin Bucer and the Reformation', *Quarterly Review* 220 (1914), 116–33.

44. Excluded without apology were Wales and Ireland.

45. Similar concerns lie behind his contribution on the Reformation era to *Religious Life in Scotland from the Reformation to the Present Day*, ed. by T. M. Lindsay, London 1888.

46. Cf. his *Catalogue of the Witnesses of Truth*, Basle 1556.

47. Vol. 2, p. 104.

48. Cf. Paul's Letter to the Romans 11.1–5.

Chapter 2: Introducing the British Isles and their Reformations

1. *An Address*, in Kelley, *Versions of History*, p. 470.

2. Cf. John Guy, on the reconstructionist agenda of Renaissance monarchy, in MacCulloch, *The Reign of Henry VIII*, pp. 36–9 (see below, Bibliography II.)

3. For a refreshing example of presenting the history of the British Isles in its complex totality, representing a welcome departure from the distortions of both the old anglocentric and the subsequent 'national' historiographical approaches, cf. Kearney, *The British Isles* (see below, Bibliography I).

4. Cf. Mason, 'Scotching the Brut', esp. pp. 55ff. (see below, Bibliography V).

5. For various approaches to this general theme see, for example, Stuart Mews, *Religion and National Identity* (see below, Bibliography I). Gordon, *Protestant History*, passim.

6. His *History of Greater Britain* (1521) helped set the tone of ancient legitimacy.

7. Cf. Kearney: 'What provided an additional impulse towards the assertion of full cultural dominance by the south over the rest of England and Wales and in due course Ireland and Scotland was the impact of the Reformation', *The British Isles*, p. 145.

8. Brendan Smith, in *Atlas of Irish History* (ed. Duffy), p. 42 (see below, Bibliography I).

9. The 'Rough Wooing'.

10. *History*, new rev. edn by Nicholas Pocock (Oxford 1865), Vol. 1, part 1, p. 482.

11. Although after the 'Augsburg Interim' (1548) and the reconvening of the Council of Trent in 1551, which put Protestant Reformations on the defensive, the English model, even if still largely academic, aroused stronger interest on the Continent. Cf. Gotthelf Wiedermann, 'The First Latin *Book of Common Prayer*', *Reformation & Renaissance Review* 4 (2002), esp. pp. 205ff.

12. Cf. Frederick M. Powicke, *The Reformation in England* (London 1941), p. 1. Stanley T. Bindoff, *Tudor England* (Pelican History of England 5) (Harmondsworth 1950), p. 99.

13. Cf. Arthur C. Cochrane (ed.), *Reformed Confessions of the 16th Century*, Philadelphia 1961. 'Anything like a universal Confession imposed on all congregations and Churches is foreign to the genius of Reformed Churches', p. 17.

Chapter 3: England: Modern Accounts

1. See Dickens, *The English Reformation*, p. 9.
2. *The Debate on the English Reformation.*
3. Cf. Herbert Butterfield, *The Whig Interpretation of History* (London 1931).
4. *History of England from the Fall of Wolsey to the Defeat of the Spanish Armada*, 12 vols, London 1856–70. Cf. Jeffrey P. von Arx, *Progress and Pessimism. Religion Politics and History in Late Nineteenth Century Britain* (Harvard Historical Studies 104), Cambridge, MA 1985.
5. *Social Evolution*, London 1894, 1906. Not to be confused with the Church historian, B. J. Kidd.
6. *A History of the Protestant Reformation in England and Ireland, showing how that event has impoverished the main body of the people in due course*, 2 vols, London 1829.
7. O'Day, *The Debate*, p. 82.
8. 'Everything is good when it springs from the hands of our Creator; everything degenerates when shaped by the hand of man.' *Émile*, opening line.
9. *History of England during the Reign of George III*, 2nd edn (London 1865), Vol. 2, p. 40.
10. J. Huizinga, *The Waning of the Middle Ages* (Penguin; Peregrine Books 1965), pp. 26–9.
11. Cf. Max Weber, *Protestant Ethic and the Spirit of Capitalism* (1904–5). For a classical restatement of the notion, see Patrick C. Gordon Walker, 'Capitalism and the Reformation' (1937), in Lewis W. Spitz (ed.), *The Reformation. Material or Spiritual?* (Problems in European Civilization) (Lexington, MA 1962), pp. 28–36. See also Chapter 1 above, n. 23.
12. E.g. Ogier, *Reformation and Society in Guernsey*, esp. pp. 173–7.
13. Cf. his *Policy and Police*.
14. Cf. Paul Ayris, 'Continuity and Change in Diocese and Province: the Role of a Tudor Bishop', *Historical Journal* 39 (1996), 291–313.
15. Andrew Pettegree, 'Afterword' to G. R. Elton, *Reformation Europe 1517–1559, Second Edition* (Oxford and Malden, MA 1999), p. 241.

16. See his *Reform and Reformation*, pp. 354, 359, 361, 376, 382.
17. See her *Reformation in London*, where John Willock is characterized as a 'rabid Scottish Reformer', and Alexander Alesius, later professor of theology in a German university and translator of the *Book of Common Prayer* into Latin, a 'rabid Scot', pp. 286, 330. On Willock and Alesius, see Chapter 8 below.
18. A similar perception underlies Claire Cross, *Church and People*.
19. Cf. the remarks on T. M. Lindsay in Chapter 1 above.
20. See Dickens, *The English Reformation*, p. 11.
21. See *English Reformations*, p. 13.
22. See *The English Reformation Revised*, p. 210.
23. See his *Stripping the Altars*, pp. 4–6.
24. See Seymour Baker House, 'Literature, Drama and Politics', and Robert Whiting, 'Local Responses to the Henrician Reformation', both in MacCulloch (ed.), *The Reign of Henry VIII*, pp. 181–202, 203–26. See also Whiting's book, *Local Responses*.
25. *The Voices of Morebath.*
26. See his *Early Tudor Church and Society*, p. 4.
27. Cf. Ramsey MacMullen: 'Nothing said about the mentalities, behaviour, norms, or proclivities of millions of people can be taken seriously without proofs proportionate to the size of the sample. One individual from the past, one single thing said or done, no matter how striking or evocative, can support no general truth', in *Christianity and Paganism in the Fourth to Eighth Centuries* (New Haven and London 1997), p. 161.
28. Cf. *The Religion of the Protestants.*
29. Cf. *The Later Reformation.* Idem 'The Myth of the English Reformation', *Journal of British Studies* 30 (1991), 1–19.
30. Named after the Dutch reformed theologian, Jacob Arminius (1560–1609), who attacked predestination grounded in prior divine decrees. See Chapter 4, n. 162.
31. The Confession of Augsburg (1530) in particular had 'ecumenical' intent. In 1534/5, the French King, Francis I, pursued church reunion policies involving, on the Protestant side, theologians like Philipp Melanchthon and Martin Bucer; between 1539 and 1541, there were church reunion colloquies at Hagenau, Worms and Regensburg (Ratisbon), some of which Calvin, too, attended.
32. Cf. Tadataka Maruyama, *The Ecclesiology of Theodore Beza. The Reform of the True Church* (Travaux d'Humanisme et Renaissance 166) Geneva 1978, esp. pp. 80–106. Philippe Denis and Jean Rott, *Jean Morély et l'utopie d'une democratie dans l'église* (Travaux d'Humanisme et Renaissance 278), Geneva 1993.
33. Cf. Rex, *Theology of John Fisher.*
34. Cf. Redworth, *In Defence of the Church Catholic.*
35. Cf. MacCulloch, *Thomas Cranmer.* Ayris and Selwyn, *Thomas Cranmer.* On earlier portrayals of Cranmer, see O'Day, *The Debate*, pp. 74–6.
36. Cf. Jasper Ridley, *Nicholas Ridley*, London 1957.
37. Cf. Hunt, *Life and Times of John Hooper.*
38. Cf. Collinson, *Archbishop Grindal.*

39. Cf. Victor J. K. Brook, *Life of Archbishop Parker*, Oxford 1962.
40. Cf. Brown, *Robert Ferrar*.
41. *Bishops and Reform.*
42. Cf. Collinson and Craig, *The Reformation in English Towns*.
43. See *Birthpangs*, pp. 28–93.
44. *Tudor Histories*, p. 218.
45. See *Reformation Europe*, p. 2.
46. See Bindoff, *Tudor England*, p. 100.
47. Cf. Loades, *Revolution in Religion*, p. 55.
48. See his *Wolsey. Church and State in Sixteenth-Century England* (1929), here quoted from the London and New York 1966 edn, p. 187. Cf. Powicke, op. cit. and Bindoff, op. cit., both at n. 12 of the previous chapter. See also O'Day, *The Reformation Debate*, p. 106.
49. Cf. *Assertio septem sacramentorum adversus Martinum Lutherum* [Vindication of the seven sacraments against Martin Luther], ed. Pierre Fraenkel (Corpus Catholicorum 43), Münster i. Westf. 1992. An English translation by John Webster was published in Dublin in 1766.
50. Cf. Chapter 1 above, notes 5 and 34.
51. *De origine et progressu schismatis Anglicani libri tres* [On the Origin and Course of the English Schism], Cologne 1585. Engl. trs. 1587, reprinted at Paris in 1676. It was also translated into French. New English edn (London 1877) introduced and annotated by David Lewis.
52. *History*, rev. edn by Nicholas Pocock (Oxford 1865), Vol. 1, Preface, p. 4.
53. Ibid. p. 6. Cf. O'Day, *The Debate*, pp. 39f.
54. *History*, Vol. 1, p. 583.
55. His preface to Robert Barnes' *Confession of Faith* at the latter's execution in London, published in German at Wittenberg (1540), in *Martin Luthers Werke*, Vol. 51 (Weimar 1914), p. 450, lines 30–1. English version of preface in Erwin Doernberg, *Henry VIII and Luther* (London 1961), pp. 124–6.
56. Table Talk, no. 4198, in *Martin Luthers Werke. Tischreden*, Vol. 4 (Weimar 1916), p. 194.

Chapter 4: Reformation in England

1. *Confutation of the Pope's Bull*, published in Latin, German and English (London 1572).
2. Cf. Helmut Kressner, *Schweizer Ursprünge des anglikanischen Staatskirchentums* (Schriften des Vereins für Reformationsgeschichte 170) Gütersloh 1953. David J. Keep, *Henry Bullinger and the Elizabethan Church*, doctoral thesis, University of Sheffield, 1970. Elton sometimes characterizes the Church of England as 'Helvetic'. See his 'Luther in England', p. 129.
3. Cf. Bray, *Documents*, pp. 113f.
4. Rex, *Henry VIII*, p. 56.
5. Cf. Robert Kingdom, in Chaunu (see below, Bibliography I), *The Reformation*, pp. 216f. See also Steven Ozment, *The Age of Reform 1250–*

1550. An Intellectual and Religious History of Late Medieval and Reformation Europe (New Haven and London 1980), pp. 149–55. Dickens, *The English Reformation*, pp. 106–8.

6. Cf. Carleton, *Bishops*, p. 192.
7. Ibid., pp. 192f.
8. English edn by Alan Gerwith, Vol. 2 (Records of Civilization. Sources and Studies 46), New York 1951–60.
9. By William Marshall. Cf. James McConica, *English Humanists and Reformation Politics under Henry VIII and Edward VI* (Oxford 1965), pp. 133–7.
10. Cf. Carleton, *Bishops*, p. 191. Davies, *Religion of the Word*, pp. 237f.
11. Carleton, *Bishops*, p. 192.
12. On the views of the Reformers on the matter, see Selderhuis, *Marriage and Divorce*, pp. 137–48. Cf. Guy Bedouelle, 'The Consultations of the Universities and Scholars concerning the "Great Matter" of King Henry VIII', in David Steinmetz (ed.), *The Bible in the Sixteenth Century* (Durham, NC 1990), pp. 21–36.
13. See previous chapter, n. 49.
14. Cf. Carleton, *Bishops*, p. 191. Davies, *Religion of the Word*, p. 237. Dickens, *The English Reformation*, pp.151–4. He was brother-in-law of the Scottish Reformer in Denmark, John Macalpine (see below, Chapter 8).
15. Modern-spelling editions of Tyndale's New Testament and (incomplete) Old Testament have been published by David Daniell, London and New Haven 1989 and 1992 respectively. For Tyndale's New Testament Prefaces, see Bray, *Documents*, pp. 18–31. For Preface and Prologues to his publication of the Old Testament Pentateuch, see ibid., pp. 32–40.
16. Cf. Bray, *Documents*, pp. 234–43.
17. Cf. Scott H. Hendrix, *Tradition and Authority in the Reformation*, (Variorum Collected Studies Series 535), Aldershot and Brookfield, VT 1996. MacCulloch, *Cranmer*, pp. 462–9.
18. Cf. Bray, *Documents*, pp. 162–75. Conventionally believed to have been drafted by Cranmer, one biographer, Jasper Ridley, reckons the author was more likely to have been Edward Foxe, Bishop of Hereford. The 'authorship' was in reality much more complicated, see MacCulloch, *Cranmer*, pp. 161–5.
19. Extracts in A. G. Dickens and D. Carr, *The Reformation in England* (London 1967), pp. 85–9. The complete text, along with that of the later *King's Book* (see n. 25 below) is in Charles Lloyd (ed.), *Formularies of Faith Put Forth During the Reign of Henry VIII*, Oxford 1856.
20. Cf. Bray, *Documents*, pp. 118–61. English trs. also in N. S. Tjernagel, *Henry VIII and the Lutherans. A Study in Anglo-Lutheran Relations from 1521 to 1547* (St Louis 1965), pp. 161–5. Text critical edn of German and Latin parallel texts by Georg Mentz, *Die Wittenberger Artikel von 1536* (Leipzig 1905). Repr. Darmstadt 1968.
21. Cf. Carleton, *Bishops*, pp. 193f.
22. Cf. Bray, *Documents*, p. 163.
23. See below, to n. 54, and Chapter 8, n. 8.

24. Cf. Bray, *Documents*, pp. 222–32. Two bishops, Shaxton of Salisbury, and Latimer of Worcester resigned because of them.

25. Otherwise known as *The Necessary Doctrine and Erudition for any Christian Man*, it was composed by the bishops and had a preface written by the king. It reaffirmed Masses for the dead and rejected Lutheran views on justification and free will. Extracts in Dickens and Carr (see n. 19 above), pp. 114–18.

26. Cf. MacCulloch, *The Reign of Henry VIII*, pp. 177ff.

27. The word was first used this way in the seventeenth century. By the eighteenth century, members of the Church of England came to be called Anglicans. Only in the nineteenth century does the word 'Anglicanism' appear.

28. Cf. W. H. Frere and W. M. Kennedy, *Visitation Articles and Injunctions* 1 (Alcuin Club 14) 1910, p. 143.

29. See MacCulloch, *Tudor Church Militant*, p. 105.

30. Cf. Hudson, *The Cambridge Connection*, pp. 69f., 73–5.

31. Cf. Davies, *Religion of the Word*, pp. 236f.

32. Cf. Carleton, *Bishops*, p. 195. Davies, *Religion of the Word*, p. 242. See Rosemary O'Day, 'Hugh Latimer: Prophet of the Kingdom', *Historical Research* 65 (1992), 258–76.

33. Cf. Geoffrey Elton, 'Reform and the "Commonwealth Men" of Edward VI's England', in Peter Clark *et al.*, *The English Commonwealth 1547–1640* (Leicester 1978), pp. 3–11. See also n. 48 below.

34. Cf. Elton, *Reform and Renewal*, p. 1: 'Commonwealth, Protestantism, and Christian humanism have been jumbled together in a splendid porridge of reformist yearning.'

35. *Altercatio luciferani et orthodoxi*, 19, in Migne, *Patrologia latina* 23, col. 155. There: on the sanctioning of an unorthodox creed by Emperor Constantius in AD 359, Jerome wrote: 'The whole world groaned and was astonished to find itself Arian.'

36. See Ridley, *John Knox*, pp. 106–29.

37. Cf. Carleton, *Bishops*, p. 194. Davies, *Religion of the Word*, pp. 240f.

38. Cf. Carleton, *Bishops*, pp. 47f.

39. Ibid., p. 197. Cf. Jasper Ridley, *Nicholas Ridley. A Biography*, London 1957.

40. Cf. Ayris, 'The Relationship between the Crown and the Archbishopric', in Ayris and Selwyn, *Thomas Cranmer*, pp. 143–8. Loades, 'Thomas Cranmer and John Dudley', ibid., pp. 166ff.

41. Cf. Constantin Hope, *Martin Bucer and the English Reformation*, Oxford 1947. Harry C. Porter, *Reformation and Reaction in Tudor Cambridge*, Cambridge 1958. Basil Hall, 'Martin Bucer in England', in David F. Wright (ed.), *Martin Bucer. Reforming Church and Community* (Cambridge 1994), pp. 144–60. Collinson, *Archbishop Grindal*, pp. 49ff. David Wright, 'Martin Bucer in England – and Scotland' (see below, Bibliography V). Burnett, *The Yoke of Christ*, p. 208, n. 1 (there: further bibliography).

42. Cf. Victor J. K. Brook, *A Life of Archbishop Parker*, Oxford 1962.

43. First published in 1557, it was composed in Latin, and within a few years translated into French and German. Not translated into English until 1969, by Wilhelm Pauck, *Library of Christian Classics*, Vol. 19, pp.

155–394. Its impact in England was limited due to the deaths of Bucer and Edward VI soon after.

44. See Burnett, *The Yoke of Christ*, pp. 208–16.

45. See text in E. C. Whitaker (ed.), *Censura English and Latin. Martin Bucer and the Book of Common Prayer* (Alcuin Club Collections 35), Great Wakering 1974.

46. See n. 52 below.

47. *Florilegium patristicum*, ed. Pierre Fraenkel, *Martini Buceri opera latina* 3 (Studies in Medieval and Reformation Thought XLI), Leiden 1988.

48. 'England und die oberdeutsche Reform', p. 7.

49. See MacCulloch, *Cranmer*, 351–516. Idem *Tudor Church Militant*.

50. Cf. A. Krieder, *The English Chantries. The Road to Dissolution*, London and New Haven 1979.

51. Cf. Aston, *England's Iconoclasts*. MacCulloch, *Tudor Church Militant*, pp. 14f., 57–156.

52. On the literary debate shortly before on this issue between Stephen Gardiner (Catholic) Bishop of Winchester, and Martin Bucer, the Strasbourg Reformer, cf. Selderhuis, *Marriage and Divorce*, pp. 343–8. Cf. also Hope, *Bucer and the English Reformation* (see n. 41 above), pp. 183–98.

53. Cf. excellent edn by Bond, *Certain Sermons or Homilies*.

54. See above, to n. 23.

55. See Gotthelf Wiedermann, 'The First Latin *Book of Common Prayer:* English Reformation in a Continental Perspective', *Reformation & Renaissance Review* 4 (2002), 190–216. Cf. Chapter 2, n. 11. In the Henrician era, Alesius had translated though not published the *Ten Articles*, see MacCulloch, *Cranmer*, p. 164.

56. See Bray, *Documents*, pp. 284–311.

57. Cf. Duffy, 'Cranmer and Popular Religion', in Ayris and Selwyn, *Thomas Cranmer*, pp. 205–7. MacCulloch, *Cranmer*, pp. 429ff.

58. Cf. Davies, *A Religion of the Word*, pp. 140–76, 197–219.

59. For both letters, cf. *Original Letters relative to the Reformation in England*, ed. H. Robinson (Parker Society 1847), Vol. 2, pp. 542–8.

60. Davies, *A Religion of the Word*.

61. Cf. John A. F. Thomson, *The Later Lollards*, Oxford 1965.

62. See especially Horst, *The Radical Brethren*. Also David Loades, 'Anabaptism and English Sectarianism in the mid-sixteenth century', in Baker (ed.), *Reform and Reformation*, pp. 59ff. Sheils, *The English Reformation*, pp. 95f.

63. *The English Reformation*, p. 12.

64. *The Early Tudor Church*.

65. For example, Gerald Strauss, *Luther's House of Learning*, Baltimore and London 1978.

66. *The English Reformation*, pp. 326, 332.

67. From 1541–8, he was a refugee at Strasbourg. Cf. Ernst Staehelin, *Briefe und Akten zum Leben Oekolampads* (Leipzig 1927–34), Vol. 2, p. 832.

68. Cf. Carleton, *Bishops*, pp. 143–7, 196–7. He was ordained priest on the day of Cranmer's execution, and consecrated as archbishop the

next day – he had been a 'Cardinal Deacon' since 1536. See also Loades, art. 'Pole, Cardinal Reginald', in Fritze, *Historical Dictionary*, pp. 374–7.

69. Cf. Carleton, *Bishops*, pp. 192f.
70. Ibid., p. 190.
71. See Bray, *Documents*, pp. 315–17.
72. Cf. Carleton, *Bishops*, pp. 148–55.
73. See Brown, *Robert Ferrar*, pp. 221 ff. Carleton, *Bishops*, p. 192.
74. Cf. Davies, *Religion of the Word*, p. 236.
75. Cf. Carleton, *Bishops*, p. 197. Davies, *Religion of the Word*, p. 244.
76. See also Ayris, 'The relationship between the Crown and the Archbishopric', in Ayris and Selwyn, *Thomas Cranmer*, pp. 148–52. Ayris also points out that the prosecution of heterodox radicals in Edward's reign was undertaken not by the 'Church', but by the Crown and according to common law.
77. See particularly Loades, *The Reign of Mary Tudor*.
78. Cf. Acheson, *Radical Puritans*, pp. 5–9. J. Martin, 'The Protestant Underground in Mary's Reign', *Journal of Ecclesiastical History* 35 (1984), 519–30. Collinson, *The Religion of the Protestants*, pp. 252–6.
79. *The Zurich Letters, Comprising the Correspondence of Several English Bishops and Others*, Publications of the Parker Society, Vol. 50 (Cambridge 1842), pp. 44f.
80. *Livre des Prières Communes*, trs. by François Philippe.
81. Cf. Hudson, *The Cambridge Connection*, pp. 131–5.
82. Text in Mason (ed.), *On Rebellion*, pp. 43f (see below, Bibliography V).
83. Cf. Hazlett, 'Jihad'. For further literature, see there. Also Mason, op. cit., pp. xxviii–xxx.
84. John Aylmer's *An Harborowe for faithfull and trewe subiectes*, 'Strasbourg' [London] 1559.
85. Cf. Loades, 'The Origins of English Protestant Nationalism', in Mews, *Religion and National Identity*, pp. 297–307.
86. *An Harborowe*, sig. P 4v.
87. Cf. Collinson, *Birthpangs*, pp. 4f., 7, 156.
88. Ibid., p. 1.
89. Art. cit., p. 307.
90. Cf. MacCulloch, *The Later Reformation*, p. 33.
91. *The Elizabethan Religious Settlement* (Bangor, Gwynedd 1992), p. 20.
92. Cf. Hudson, *The Cambridge Connection, passim*.
93. Quoted in Stanley T. Bindoff, *Tudor England* (Harmondsworth 1950), p. 203. See also Hudson, *The Cambridge Connection*, p. 100.
94. Cf. Bray, *Documents*, pp. 318–28.
95. Ibid., pp. 329–34.
96. Modern edn by John E. Booty, Charlottesville, VA 1976.
97. Bray, *Documents*, pp. 285–309 (Latin and English). For a solid exposition of the Articles, see E. J. Bicknell, *A Theological Introduction to the Thirty-Nine Articles of the Church of England* (3rd edn, rev. by H. J. Carpenter), London 1955.

98. Only one English bishop raised objections to the Helvetic and south German tenor of the eucharistic articles, see MacCulloch, *The Later Reformation*, p. 75.

99. E.g., John Neale, *Elizabeth I and her Parliaments*, London 1953.

100. See Hudson, *The Cambridge Connection*, and Jones, *Faith by Statute*.

101. Cf. Bray, *Documents*, pp. 35–48.

102. For background to this issue, see W. Ian P. Hazlett, 'Was Bucer an Aérian? The Question of Praying for the Dead', *Reformation & Renaissance Review* 4 (2002), 135–51.

103. Cf. Victor J. K. Brook, *Whitgift and the English Church*, London 1964. Powel M. Dawley, *John Whitgift and the English Reformation*, London 1955.

104. Bray, *Documents*, pp. 397f.

105. For memoranda by Hooper and Laski on the matter see Iain H. Murray (ed.), *The Reformation of the Church. A collection of Reformed and Puritan documents on Church issues* (Edinburgh and Carlisle, PA 1967), pp. 53–69.

106. Cf. MacCulloch, *The Later Reformation*, pp. 34f.

107. See Bond, *Certain Sermons*, pp. 7–9.

108. Latin and Greek translations of the Catechism by William Whitaker, a Calvinist theologian at Cambridge, were published in 1573. See also Burke, *Popular Culture*, p. 320, n. 43 (see below, Bibliography I).

109. Cf. Ayris, 'Canon Law Studies', in Ayris and Selwyn, *Thomas Cranmer*, pp. 316–22.

110. Modern English translation by J. C. Spalding, *The Reformation of the Ecclesiastical Laws of England, 1552* (Sixteenth Century Essays & Studies XIX), Kirksville, MO 1992.

111. Edn by John E. Booty, *Apology or Answer in Defence of the Church of England* (Folger Documents of Tudor and Stuart Civilisation), Ithaca 1963.

112. Cf. W. M. Southgate, *John Jewel and the Problem of Doctrinal Authority* (Harvard Historical Monographs) (Cambridge, MA 1962), p. 62.

113. See Sheils, *The English Reformation*, p. 58.

114. Cf. Arthur Pollard (ed.), *Richard Hooker. Laws of Ecclesiastical Polity. Selections*, Manchester 1990.

115. Cf. MacCulloch, *The Later Reformation*, pp. 44–61.

116. Cf. Nijenhuis, *Adrianus Saravia*. Also his 'Adrianus Saravia as an irenical churchman', in Baker, *Reform and Reformation*, pp. 149–63.

117. For quick overview, see Richard Greaves, art. 'Presbyterianism', in Fritze, *Historical Dictionary*. Cf. O'Day, *The Debate*, pp. 197–9.

118. His major work on presbyterian polity was *Ecclesiasticae disciplinae . . . explicatio* (1574). In the same year it was translated into English by Cartwright: *A full and plain declaration of ecclesiastical discipline out of the Word of God, and on the declining of the Church of England from the same.* Cf. S. J. Knox, *Walter Travers: Paradox of Elizabethan Puritanism*, London 1962.

119. Cf. Leland H. Carlson and Albert Peel (eds), *Cartwrightiana*, (Elizabethan Nonconformist Texts 1), London 1951.

120. Cf. Collinson, *Godly People*, ch. 13.

121. Cf. *Dictionary of Scottish Church History & Theology*, pp. 556–7.

122. First part (by Wilcox) in Murray (see n. 105 above), *The Reformation of the Church*, pp. 85–94.

123. Whitgift also had Travers dismissed from a post in Trinity College, Cambridge. Travers later became Provost of Trinity College, Dublin.

124. Cf. Christianson, *Reformers and Babylon*, pp. 66–72.

125. See to n. 5 above.

126. *Explicatio.* For English trs., see R. Lee (ed.), *The Theses of Erastus concerning Excommunication*, Edinburgh and London 1844.

127. *Tractatus de vera excommunicatione.*

128. Cf. Davies, *Religion of the Word*, p. 238.

129. Extracts in Kelley, *Versions of History*, pp. 334–40 (see below, Bibliography I). A Latin translation was also made by Foxe in collaboration with John Aylmer when both were still in exile.

130. Cf. Collinson, *The Birthpangs*, pp. 12–17.

131. See especially Elton, 'Luther in England', pp. 126–9.

132. For its preface (to the queen) see Bray, *Documents*, pp. 356–63.

133. Ibid., pp. 364–96. For the preface to the Old Testament, see ibid., pp. 402–12.

134. Cf. David J. Keep, 'Bullinger's Defence of Queen Elizabeth', in *Zürcher Beiträge zur Kirchengeschichte*, Vol. 8.2 (Zurich 1975), pp. 231–42, and Robert C. Walton, in ibid., pp. 243–6.

135. Text in Dures, *English Catholicism*, pp. 98f.

136. For a good overview, see Dures, *English Catholicism*, pp. 1–39.

137. A ruling of the fourth session of the Council of Trent in 1546 was ambiguous about the use of vernacular translations from the Vulgate, leaving the matter open to permissive interpretation. Among the council bishops there was sharp division of opinion. Cf. *Canons and Decrees*, p. 19 (see below, Bibliography I). Hubert Jedin, *A History of the Council of Trent*, trs. by Ernest Graf (London 1961), Vol. 2, pp. 67–85.

138. Cf. Davies, *Religion of the Word*, p. 245. E. Macek, 'Richard Smith: Tudor cleric in defence of traditional belief and practice', *Catholic Historical Review* 72(3) (1986), 383–402.

139. Cf. John Durkan, 'Cultural Background', in McRoberts (see below, Bibliography V), *Essays*, pp. 301f.

140. Cf. J. Andreas Löwe, '*Facite, quod fieri*: biblical exegesis at Douai in the mid-sixteenth century', *Reformation & Renaissance Review* 3, no. 1/2 (2001), 9–35.

141. On both Smiths, cf. Hugo Hurter, *Nomenclator literarius recentioris theologiae catholicae* (Oeniponti [Innsbruck] 1873), Vol. 1, p. 860.

142. Cf. Edwards, *The Jesuits in England*. McCoog, *The Society of Jesus*. Reynolds, *Campion and Parsons.*

143. A near-contemporary history of the English Jesuit mission was composed by Henry More: *Historia missionae anglicanae Societatis Jesu/ The Elizabethan Jesuits* (1560), ed. and trs. by Francis Edwards, London 1981.

144. Cf. Dures, *English Catholicism*, pp. 67f.

145. See P. J. Holmes, art. 'Seminary Priests', in Fritze, *Historical Dictionary*, p. 455.

146. Ibid., pp. 454f.

147. Dures, *English Catholicism*, pp. 66–9.
148. So-called also in the Netherlands, they were equivalent to Scottish presbyteries, French colloquies or South German synods.
149. Cf. Collinson, *Archbishop Grindal*, pp. 233ff.
150. Cf. Acheson, *Radical Puritans*, pp. 10ff. Barrington Raymond White, *The English Separatist Tradition*, Oxford 1971. J. W. Martin, 'The first that made separation from the reformed Church of England', *Archiv für Reformationsgeshchichte* 77 (1986), 281–312.
151. Cf. Christianson, *Reformers and Babylon*, pp. 58–65.
152. Ibid., pp. 58–64. Cf. Albert Peel and Leland-Carlson, *The Writings of Robert Harrison and Robert Browne* (English Nonconformist Texts 2), London 1953.
153. Cf. Leland H. Carlson (ed.), *The Writings of Henry Barrow* (Elizabethan Nonconformist Texts 3, 5), London 1951. See also Murray (cf. n. 105 above), *The Reformation of the Church*, pp. 193–202.
154. Cf. Leland H. Carlson, *The Writings of John Greenwood, together with the Joint Writings of Henry Barrow and John Greenwood* (Elizabethan Nonconformist Texts 4, 6), London 1962–70.
155. See Chapter 5, notes 32 and 33.
156. Cf. David Loades: 'The evidence for genuine separatism in England in the first twenty years of Elizabeth's reign is fragmentary . . . sectarianism in the sense of "gathered" churches hardly existed', in 'Anabaptism and English sectarianism in the mid-sixteenth century', in Baker, *Reform and Reformation*, pp. 69f.
157. See Christianson, *Reformers and Babylon*, p. 92, n. 62.
158. Thus the Donatist schismatic in Carthage, Donatus, in the fourth century AD. In Optatus, *On the Schism of the Donatists* III, 3; English trs. by Mark J. Edwards, *Against the Donatists* (Translated Texts for Historians 27), Liverpool 1997.
159. On Barrow's stance in this respect, cf. Carlson, *The Writings* (see n. 154 above), pp. 73–92.
160. Walsham, *Church Papists*, p. 107.
161. Cf. MacCulloch, *The Later Reformation*, pp. 94–100.
162. A theological stance derived from a Dutch reformed theologian in Leiden, Jacob Arminius (1560–1609). A moderate Calvinist with an irenical attitude, Arminius dissented from the double predestinarianism of advanced Calvinism, from the notion of limited atonement, and from the idea that grace is irresistible. In Britain, other ideas were often wrongly attached to him, such as Pelagianism, Socinianism and Erastianism, suggesting that he was truly heterodox. Cf. Carl Bangs, *Arminius. A Study in the Dutch Reformation* (Nashville and New York 1971), pp. 332–55.
163. Cf. Tyacke, *Anti-Calvinists, passim*.
164. Text in Bray, *Documents*, pp. 399f., drafted by William Whitaker, Professor of Divinity at Cambridge.
165. Cf. Heiko A. Oberman, *Archbishop Thomas Bradwardine, a Fourteenth-Century Augustinian. A Study of his Theology in its Historical Context*, Utrecht 1957. Gordon Leff, *Bradwardine and the Pelagians. A Study of his 'De causa Dei' and its opponents*, Cambridge 1957.

166. Cf. Paul A. Welsby, *George Abbot, the Unwanted Archbishop*, London 1962. Abbot was otherwise famed for his involvement in a *cause célèbre* of manslaughter, accidentally killing a gamekeeper whilst hunting; see R. E. Head, *Royal Supremacy and the Trials of Bishops 1558–1725* (London 1962), pp. 37ff.

167. Cf. Anthony Fletcher, 'English protestantism and national identity', in Mews, *Religion and National Identity*, esp. pp. 314–17. Abroad, anti-Church of England polemic went up a gear with the publication in 1613 of Francisco de Suarez's *Defence of the Catholic and Apostolic Faith against the Error of the English Sect.*

Chapter 5: Reformation in Wales

1. See Davies, *History of Wales*, pp. 117ff.
2. Ibid., p. 288. Williams, *Wales and the Reformation*, p. 143.
3. See Williams, *Recovery*, p. ix.
4. Ibid., p. 327.
5. Quoted in Herbert and Jones, *Tudor Wales*, p. 111. Cf. Williams, *Wales and the Reformation*, pp. 178f.
6. Cf. Williams, *Recovery*, p. 300. Idem, *Welsh Reformation Essays*, p. 49. Idem, *Wales and the Reformation*, p. 180.
7. See T. Roberts, *Bulletin Board of Celtic Studies* 16 (1954–6), 251–3. Williams, *Wales and the Reformation*, pp. 175f.
8. Davies, *A History of Wales*, p. 239.
9. Cf. Williams, *Recovery*, pp. 283–301. Idem, *Welsh Reformation Essays*, pp. 39–47.
10. Quoted in Jones, *Early Modern Wales*, p. 158.
11. On him, an exemplary survivalist, and later Edwardine Bishop of Bath and Wells, and then Elizabethan Bishop of Chicester, see Williams, *Welsh Reformation Essays*, pp. 111–24. Idem, *The Reformation in Wales*, pp. 11f. Idem, *Wales and the Reformation*, pp. 62–4, 118–20, 122–5, 142–4. Jones, *Early Modern Wales*, pp. 130–4. E. Gordon Rupp, *Studies in the English Protestant Tradition* (Cambridge 1949), pp. 62–72. Carleton, *Bishops* (see below, Bibliography II), p. 189. And especially Brown, *Robert Ferrar*, pp. 265–83.
12. Cf. Williams, *Wales and the Reformation*, p. 143.
13. Cf. D. R. Thomas, *The Life and Work of Bishop Davies and William Salesbury*, Oswestry 1892. More recently, see R. B. Jones, *William Salesbury*.
14. Text in A. O. Evans (ed.), *A Memorandum on the Legality of the Welsh Bible* (Cardiff 1925), pp. 83–124.
15. Cf. Williams, 'Some Protestant views of early British church history', *Welsh Reformation Essays*, p. 207–19. Idem, *The Welsh and their Religion*, pp. 40f. Meek, *The Quest*, pp. 110f. (see below, Bibliography I).
16. His *A Testament of Antiquity* strove to establish the pedigree of the Elizabethan Church in the Anglo-Saxon Church, and his *De antiquitate britannicae ecclesiae* attempted to authenticate further derivation from the ancient Romano-British Church.

17. Cf. Booty, *John Jewel as Apologist*, ch. 6 (see below, Bibliography II).
18. Cf. Davies, *Religion of the Word*, pp. 180–3, 235 (see below, Bibliography II). See also Chapter 6 below, n. 35.
19. Meek, op. cit., p. 110.
20. Cf. Walker, *A History*, p. 68.
21. Cf. Chapter 6, n. 56.
22. Quoted by Williams, *The Reformation in Wales*, p. 16.
23. Cf. Ivor Bowen (ed.), *Statutes of Wales* (London 1908), pp. 149–51.
24. *Recovery*, p. x.
25. On the entire process, see idem, *The Reformation in Wales*, pp. 26–31. Idem, *Wales and the Reformation*, pp. 177f., 235–44, 338–60, 383f., 404–6.
26. Cf. R. Geraint Gruffydd, 'The earliest Welsh printed book', *Bulletin of the Board of Celtic Studies* 23 (1968–70), 105–16.
27. Cf. G. Williams, 'William Salesbury's *Baterie . . .*', *Bulletin of the Board of Celtic Studies* 13 (1949), 146–50.
28. See Thomas, *Salesbury and his Testament*.
29. Edn by M. Richards and G. Williams, Cardiff 1965.
30. Cf. W. Hughes, *Life and Times of William Morgan*, London 1891. G. Williams, 'Bishop William Morgan and the first Welsh Bible', *Journal of the Merioneth Historical and Record Society* 7, 347–72. Thomas, *William Morgan and his Bible*. Gruffydd, *The Translation of the Bible*.
31. Davies, *History of Wales*, p. 245.
32. Ibid., pp. 246f. Jones, *Early Modern Wales*, pp. 159–63.
33. *Three Treatises concerning Wales* (ed. D. Williams), Cardiff 1960.
34. Cf. Williams, *Wales and the Reformation*, pp. 382f.
35. See G. Williams, 'Edward James a Llyfr yr Homilïau', in *Grym Tafodau Tân* (Llandysul 1982), pp. 180–98.
36. Idem, *Wales and the Reformation*, pp. 383f.
37. See Davies, *History of Wales*, pp. 249f.
38. See Brown, *Robert Ferrar*. Carleton, *Bishops* (see below, Bibliography II), p. 192.
39. See Williams, *Wales and the Reformation*, p. 205.
40. Ibid., pp. 206f.
41. Ibid., pp. 248–79.
42. Later first (controversial) Rector of the English College at Rome. Cf. Williams, op. cit., pp. 252f, 266f.
43. Ibid., pp. 259, 286.
44. See Thomas, *Welsh Elizabethan Martyrs*. This also contains the transcripts of the trials. Cf. Williams, *Wales and the Reformation*, pp. 269f., 368f.
45. Cf. Jones, *Early Modern Wales*, pp. 163–6.
46. Cf. Davies, *History of Wales*, pp. 247–9. Thomas, op. cit., pp. 19–46.
47. Cf. Williams, *Recovery*, pp. 315–31. Roberts, art. 'Wales', in Fritze, *Historical Dictionary*, p. 530.

Chapter 6: Reformation in Ireland

1. *The Reformation in Dublin, 1536–58. From Original Sources,* London 1926.
2. In *History of the Church of Ireland from the Earliest Times to the Present Day,* ed. W. Alison Phillips (London 1934), Vol. 2, pp. 169–291.
3. *The Reformation in Ireland. A Study in Ecclesiastical Legislation,* London 1919.
4. Ed. by Theodore W. Moody and Francis X. Martin, Cork 1967.
5. Meigs, *The Reformations,* pp. 160f., n. 21.
6. The author was subsequently assured that the editorial preface's unfair reference to the '*usual* scanty treatment accorded to . . . Ireland and Wales' (p. ix) would be excised from the second edition, which did happen.
7. In his rev. edn of *Mosheim's Institutes of Ecclesiastical History* (London and Belfast 1848), p. 599, n.1.
8. Raymond Gillespie, *Devoted People,* pp. 1–15.
9. *A New History of Ireland* (Dublin and London 1972), pp. viii–ix.
10. Late Middle English, 'enclosure', and then an area subject to a particular jurisdiction. It had also been applied to English Calais.
11. The concept was later endorsed by the papacy with a declaratory Bull to this effect in 1555, and so enhanced the authority of Queen Mary I.
12. An edition published in Dublin in 1551 was the first book printed in Ireland. For a convenient overview of the Reformation process in Ireland, see Ellis, *Ireland in the Age of the Tudors,* pp. 218–42.
13. Cf. Lennon, *Sixteenth-Century Ireland,* pp. 115–34. See also Jeffries, *Priests and Prelates;* Ellis, *Ireland in the Age of the Tudors,* pp. 193–201; Meigs, *The Reformations,* pp. 41–53; Mooney, *The Church in Gaelic Ireland.*
14. 'State of Ireland and Plan for Reformation', in *State Papers. King Henry the Eighth,* vol. II, pt III, 1: *Correspondence between the Governments of England and Ireland, 1515–1538,* pp. 1–15. Cf. Constantia Maxwell, *Irish History from Contemporary Sources (1509–1610)* (London 1923), pp. 79–87.
15. See Mooney, *The First Impact,* pp. 7f.
16. *State Papers* II (see n. 14), p. 123; Maxwell, *Irish History,* p. 88.
17. *State Papers* II (see n. 14), p. 123; Maxwell, *Irish History,* p. 83.
18. Cf. Forrestal, *Catholic Synods,* pp. 25f. By 1600, the situation was much the same, ibid., pp. 31f.
19. Cf. David Quinn in *A New History* (ed. Moody *et al.*), Vol. 3, p. 30: 'the actual religious life of later medieval Ireland has been little studied'.
20. *Tuar feirge foighide Dhé.* Republished and translated in 1994 by B. Ó Cuív in the Appendix of his edition of John Kearney's *Aibidil,* pp. 199–208.
21. Ibid., p. 199.
22. Alphons Bellesheim, *Geschichte der katholischen Kirche in Irland* (Mainz 1890), Vol. 2, p. 29.
23. Cf. Lennon, *Sixteenth-century Ireland,* p. 115.
24. Cf. Mooney, *Church in Gaelic Ireland,* pp. 25f.
25. Others who declined continued to pledge loyalty to the Crown, such as Archbishop Richard Creagh.

26. See Clarke, 'Bibliographical Supplement', p. 699 (*ad fin.*).
27. Cf. their perspectives in their essays on 'Revisionism and the Irish Reformation'.
28. Bishop of Limerick, 1551–6, 1571–91.
29. Bishop of Meath, 1529–54.
30. Bishop of Ossory, 1578–85.
31. Bishop of Meath, 1563–84.
32. Archbishop of Tuam, 1595–1609.
33. Archbishop of Dublin, 1536–54. Cf. Bradshaw, 'George Browne'. Bradshaw cites the brief hagiographic life of Browne, apparently with the title of *The Reformation of the Church of Ireland*, by Robert Ware, published in Dublin [?] in 1681. Is this the same as the work distributed in London entitled *Historical Collections of the Church of Ireland . . . set forth in the life of G. Browne?* This was republished in the *Harleian Miscellany*, ed. Samuel Johnson, Vol. V (London 1745), no. lxxiii. It was later translated into Latin and published by Daniel Gerdes, *Scrinium Antiquarium sive Miscellanea Groningana nova ad historiam Reformationis*, Groningen and Bremen 1749–65. The work constituted the old Protestant view of Browne as the patriarch of the reformed Church of Ireland and its pseudo-Cranmer.
34. Archbishop of Dublin, 1567–1605. Cf. Knox, *James Ussher*, pp. 14f.
35. Cf. Davies, *Religion of the Word*, p. 235 (see below, Bibliography II). See also Bradshaw, 'George Browne', pp. 321f. He (Bale) has been characterized by Dickens as 'one of the stranger human creatures of early academic Protestantism', *The English Reformation*, pp. 194f.
36. See his 'Sword, Word, and Strategy'. Cf. Lennon, *Sixteenth-century Ireland*, p. 318.
37. See his posthumously published (1633) *A View of the Present State of Ireland*, ed. W. L. Renwick (Oxford 1970), pp. 161ff. See also Canny, *Making Ireland British*, pp. 53–5.
38. See Thomas O'Fee, 'The Language and Political History', in Brian Ó Cuív (ed.), *A View of the Irish Language* (Dublin 1969), p. 104.
39. Cf. Ford, *The Protestant Reformation*, p. 228.
40. Cf. Ford, 'James Ussher and the creation of Irish Protestant identity', pp. 206f.
41. Bradshaw's views lead to his claim that Irish Protestantism became spiritually moribund and ethically bankrupt. See art. 'Irland', in *Theologische Realenzyklopädie*, ed. G. Müller (Berlin and New York 1976–), Vol. 16, p. 278, lines 39–44. Anyway, an association of predestinarianism with a lack of missionary concern is not necessary, cf. Gillian R. Evans (ed.), *The Medieval Theologians* (Oxford 2001), p. 77.
42. Cf. E. Gordon Rupp, *William Bedell, 1571–1642*, Cambridge 1972; Terence McCaughey, *Dr Bedell and Mr King: the making of the Irish Bible*, Dublin 2001.
43. See Roger Blayney, *Presbyterians and the Irish Language* (Belfast 1996), pp. 6–8.
44. Cf. Robert Wyse Jackson, *Archbishop Magrath – The Scoundrel of Cashel*, Dublin and Cork 1974.

45. Text in Vatican Archives, and reproduced in Bellesheim, *Geschichte* (see n. 22 above), pp. 696f.
46. Cf. Dawson, *Campbell Letters* (see below, Bibliography V).
47. Cf. Durkan, 'Heresy in Scotland', pp. 347–53. Idem in McRoberts (ed.), *Essays on the Scottish Reformation*, pp. 297, 313f. (for both, see below, Bibliography V). Spalding is the 'Walter the Scot' cited by Bradshaw, 'George Browne', p. 318, and whose vigorously Protestant preaching apparently upset the Dublin archbishop.
48. Cf. Ó Cuív, *A View* (see n. 38 above), pp. 146–8. Ellis, *Ireland in the Age of the Tudors*, pp. 257–9.
49. The Gaelic title alludes to Calvin's liturgy in Geneva, *La forme des prières*, or its English version '*The Forme of Prayers*', the core of the *Book of Common Order*. Edn of Gaelic text by Thompson (see below, Bibliography V).
50. See especially Kirk, *Patterns of Reform*, pp. 280–304 (see below, Bibliography V). See also Chapter 8 below, n. 86.
51. See Edwards, *Church and State*, pp. 134f.
52. Cf. Meek, *The Quest*, p. 112 (see below, Bibliography I).
53. Modern text-critical edn by Ó Cuív. On John Kearney, see there, pp. 3–6.
54. Ibid., pp. 128–55; for English original, see ibid., Appendix II, pp. 185–9. See also William D. Killen, *The Ecclesiastical History of Ireland* (London 1875), Vol. 1, Book III, pp. 515–20. See also below, n. 61.
55. Ó Cuív, *Aibidil*, pp. 13, 53–5. This Epistle has been translated into English by the editor, pp. 12f.
56. See John C. Olin (ed.), *Christian Humanism and the Reformation. Selected Writings of Erasmus* (New York 1987), p. 101.
57. In *The Monarchie*. See David Laing (ed.), *The Poetical Works of Sir David Lindsay* (Edinburgh 1879), Vol. 2, lines 627–8.
58. See Mooney, *The Church in Gaelic Ireland*, pp. 37f.
59. Also known as 'Daniel'.
60. Cf. Williams, *The Printed Book*, pp. 131–3.
61. Kearney acknowledges this in the dedicatory Epistle of his *Catechism*, see Ó Cuív, *Aibidil*, pp. 13, 55.
62. Ibid., p. 2.
63. For some discussion of the Reformation and Gaeldom, see Ellis, *Ireland in the Age of the Tudors*, pp. 235–6, 257–9. Meigs, *The Reformations*.
64. Cf. Meek, 'Gaelic Bible', p. 10 (see below, Bibliography V).
65. Chief Governor of Ireland for various spells between 1558 and 1578. He also brought Christopher Goodman to Ireland in 1572 as his chaplain. Professor of Divinity at the University of Oxford in the Edwardine era, Goodman was a close English associate of John Knox in the Marian exiles' churches at Frankfurt and Geneva (1553–8) as well as in Scotland, where he had been minister at Ayr and St Andrews. See also Quintin Skinner, *The Foundations of Modern Political Thought* (Cambridge 1978), Vol. 2, pp. 221–38.
66. See *Letters and Memorials of State*, ed. Arthur Collins (London 1746), Vol. 1, pp. 113f., 127f.

67. *The Letters and the Life of Francis Bacon*, ed. James Spedding *et al.* (London 1857–74), Vol. 3, p. 49.
68. Cf. Meek, art. cit. (see n. 64 above).
69. Cf. Kirk, *Patterns of Reform*, pp. 485–7 (see below, Bibliography V).
70. Cf. Canny, *Making Ireland British*, pp. 198f.
71. Edn by F. Mac Raighnaill, Dublin 1976.
72. Edn by T. F. O'Rahilly, Dublin 1941.
73. Edn by C. Ó Maonaigh [Mooney], Dublin 1952. On all three writers see Meigs, *The Reformations*, pp. 81–4. MacCaghwell was Rector of St Anthony's Irish Franciscan College in Louvain, a centre of Gaelic Irish Catholicism abroad, and helped instigate a Catholic mission to Gaelic Scotland in 1618. See also Caball, 'Faith, culture and sovereignty', pp. 131–7.
74. Cf. Canny, *Making Ireland British*, pp. 422–4.
75. *Annals of the Four Masters, anno* 1601.
76. See esp. John J. Silke's chapter in Moody *et al.* (eds), *A New History*, Vol. 3: 'The Irish Abroad in the Age of the Counter-Reformation, 1534–1691'.
77. Cf. Gillespie, *Devoted People*, p. 152.
78. Cf. Lennon, *Sixteenth-century Ireland*, pp. 312f. Ellis, *Ireland in the Age of the Tudors*, p. 239. Mooney, *The First Impact*, pp. 30–8. Jones, *The Counter-Reformation*, pp. 8–12.
79. Though after 1588 the appointment of residential bishops often had to be supplemented with a system of 'vicars apostolic' or 'vicars general'. See *Handbook of British Chronology*, pp. 509f.
80. *Analecta sacra*, ed. P. F. Moran (Dublin 1884), p. 100 (cf. n. 102 below). Cf. Moody *et al.* (eds), *A New History*, Vol. 3, p. 225. Forrestal, *Catholic Synods, passim.* Burke, *Popular Culture*, 229–43 (see below, Bibliography I).
81. 'Catholicity and Nationality in the Northern Counter-Reformation', in Mews, *Religion and National Identity*, pp. 294f. (see below, Bibliography II).
82. Cf. Robinson-Hammerstein, *European Universities*, pp. 1–134 (articles by J. Murray, H. Robinson-Hammerstein, A. Ford and E. Boran).
83. Cf. Kirk and Durkan, *The University of Glasgow* (see below, Bibliography V), pp. 11, 186. Some of the Irish students speaking 'Irish and Latin' might have been Gaelic Protestant converts, ibid., p. 383. Others seem to have been Catholic, causing concern among the authorities in 1595 at a time of anti-Catholic fervour, ibid., p. 361.
84. See Ford, 'Who went to Trinity?', ibid., pp. 59ff.
85. See Chapter 4, notes 118 and 119.
86. Cf. Kirk and Durkan, *The University of Glasgow*, p. 304.
87. Cf. Thomas McCrie, *Life of Andrew Melville*, 2nd edn (Edinburgh 1824), Vol. 2, pp. 405–8.
88. The presbyterian polity of the Church of Scotland was not legally established until 1690 – until then, episcopacy in one form or other was still in place as the legal or preferred option of the Crown, government and some churchmen, so that an uneasy dualist system prevailed from

1560 to 1690. Cf. Gordon Donaldson, *Scotland. Church and Nation through Sixteen Centuries* (London 1960), p. 75. Foster, *The Church before the Covenants*, and Mullan, *Episcopacy in Scotland, passim* (see below, Bibliography V).

89. Cf. John M. Barkley, 'Some Scottish bishops and ministers in the Irish Church, 1605–35', in Duncan Shaw (ed.), *Reformation and Revolution. Essays* (Edinburgh 1967), pp. 141–59. M. Perceval Maxwell, *The Scottish Migration to Ulster in the Reign of James I* (London 1973), p. 268, and Appendix F.

90. For an introduction to presbyterian origins in Ireland, see Finlay Holmes, *The Presbyterian Church in Ireland. A Popular History* (Dublin 2000), pp. 9–25.

91. 'Confessionalization' includes Tridentine Roman Catholicism. See also Chapter 7, n. 70. For a good summary of the process, cf. Heinz Schilling, 'Confessional Europe', in Brady, Oberman and Tracy, *Handbook of European History*, Vol. 2, pp. 341–70 (see below, Bibliography I).

92. Previously the confessional standard of the Church of Ireland had been very basic, twelve articles enshrined in *A Brief Declaration of certain Principal Articles of Religion* (1566), see above, n. 54. For a modern accessible text of the 1615 *Irish Articles*, cf. Bray, *Documents*, pp. 437–52 (see below, Bibliography II).

93. Discipline as a third mark derives not so much from Calvin, who regarded it as belonging more to the well-being rather than to the essence of the Church. The 'high' view of discipline derives more from the Strasbourg and Cambridge Reformer, the ex-Dominican Martin Bucer. Cf. François Wendel, *Calvin. The Sources and development of his Religious Thought* (London 1963), pp. 300f.

94. *Gotteschalci, et predestinatianae controversiae ab eo motae, historia: una cum duplice ejusdem confessione* (Dublin 1621).

95. Cf. Gillian R. Evans (ed.), *The Medieval Theologians* (Oxford 2001), pp. 76–80.

96. Cf. John Platt, 'Eirenical Anglicans at the Synod of Dort', in Baker *Reform and Reformation*, pp. 221–43 (see below, Bibliography II).

97. King James did not approve of them.

98. Laud rejected double predestination anyway, preferring election based on divine prescience rather than on prior arbitrary divine decrees. Thereby free will is allocated some role in salvation. Such a position is broadly characterized as 'semi-Pelagian' or 'Arminian' or 'sacramentalist' and with other labels, though it essentially reflects that of Catholic orthodoxy.

99. Cf. Lennon, *Lords of Dublin, passim*.

100. See especially Ford, 'James Ussher'.

101. See his *Discourse of the Religion Antiently Professed*, Dublin 1622. Cf. Lotz-Heumann, 'The Protestant Interpretation of the History of Ireland'. Meek, *The Quest*, pp. 113f. (see below, Bibliography I). See also Williams, 'Some Protestant views of early British church history', *Welsh Reformation Essays*, pp. 207–19 (see below, Bibliography III). Davies, *Religion of the Word*, pp. 180–3 (see below Bibliography II).

102. *Analecta sacra*, Cologne 1617.
103. Quoted in Meigs, *The Reformations*, p. 71; her cited source is P. J. Corish, *The Catholic Communities in Seventeenth and Eighteenth Century Ireland* (Dublin 1981), pp. 31f. who refers to P. H. Hore, *History of Wexford* (1910–11), Vol. 6, p. 259. James Seaton Reid quotes Ram in his *History of the Presbyterian Church in Ireland*, 3rd edn (London 1853), Vol. 1, pp. 61f. The source there cited is 'Reports of [the] Com[mission] of Pub[lic] Rec[ords] in Ireland, vol. i, p. 264'. I have not yet been able to track this down.
104. *Catholic Communities*, p. 32.
105. *Making Ireland British*, pp. 434–6.
106. Cf. Ian Hazlett, 'Scripture, Tradition and Intolerance', *Irish Biblical Studies* 6 (1983), 104–19.
107. Cf. Aidan Clarke, *The Old English in Ireland, 1525–1642* (London 1966), pp. 60–5. Moody *et al.*, *A New History*, vol. 3, pp. 233–42.
108. Quoted in Canny, *Making Ireland British*, p. 267. For rising Catholic public self-confidence at the time, see ibid., pp. 443ff. Forrestal, *Catholic Synods*, pp. 136ff.
109. See Constantia Maxwell (ed.), *Irish History from Contemporary Sources (1509–1610)* (London 1923), p. 182.
110. Letter to Mr Secretary Cecil in 1602, op. cit. (see n. 67 above), p. 49.
111. Cf. Jacques le Goff, *The Birth of Purgatory*, trs. by Arthur Goldhammer (London 1984), pp. 198–200.
112. Pierre Fraenkel, 'Johann Eck und Sir Thomas More 1525 bis 1526', in Remigius Bäumer (ed.), *Von Konstanz nach Trient* (Munich 1972), p. 486.

Chapter 7: Scotland: Accounts Old and New

1. Modern edn by William C. Dickinson, *John Knox's History of the Reformation in Scotland*, 2 vols (London 1949, New York 1950). A new critical edition is currently being prepared by James Kirk and Margaret Sanderson.
2. See Greaves, 'John Knox, the Reformed tradition, and the development of resistance theory'. Cf. Jane Dawson, 'Resistance and Revolution in the sixteenth century: the case of Christopher Goodman', in J. van den Berg and Paul G. Hoftijzer (eds), *The Church, Change and Revolution* (Publications of the Sir Thomas Browne Institute, n.s. 12) (Leiden 1991), pp. 69–79. Idem 'Goodman and Knox', in Mason, *John Knox and the British Reformations*, pp. 131–53.
3. *The History of Scotland* (London, *c.*1571), Part II [1437–1561], ed. by Thomas Thompson (Bannatyne Club Publications 38), Edinburgh 1830; *De origine, moribus, et rebus gestis Scotorum libri decem*, Rome 1578; *The Historie of Scotland* (1596), trs. by James Dalrymple, ed. E. G. Cody and William Murison, 4 vols. in 2 (Scottish Text Society, Old Series, nos. 5, 14, 19, 34), Edinburgh 1888–95.
4. Trs. by James Aikman, 6 vols (Glasgow and Edinburgh 1827–9). Original: *Rerum Scoticarum historia*, 1584ff. A more recent translation of Books

17–19, *The Tyrannous Reign of Mary Stewart*, is by W. A. Gatherer (Edinburgh University Publications: History, Philosophy and Economics 10), Edinburgh 1959.

5. Notably his dialogue, *De Jure Regni apud Scotos* (1579) [*On the Right of Kingship among the Scots*] – a modern English translation was done by Duncan H. MacNeill, *The Art and Science of Government among the Scots*, s.l. 1964.

6. *Flagellum Sectariorum, qui religionis praetextu seditio . . .*

7. *Velitatio in Georgium Buchananum circa Dialogum* . . . Both published at Ingolstadt in 1582. Two copies are in Glasgow University Library.

8. Another MS. version was edited by Thomas N. Thompson, 8 vols. (Wodrow Society 7), Edinburgh 1842–9. In his Dutch exile Calderwood also published a major critique of English episcopacy, in English and then Latin, *The Altar of Damascus*, 1621–3.

9. (Maitland Club 55/Wodrow Society 4), Edinburgh 1842.

10. Cf. A. Ian Dunlop, 'John Spottiswoode', in R. Selby Wright (ed.), *Fathers of the Kirk* (London and Glasgow 1960), pp. 48–61. J. H. S. Burleigh, 'The Scottish Reformation seen in 1660 and 1760', *Records of the Scottish Church History Society* 13 (1959), pp. 241–56. A tract by Spottiswoode against exclusive presbyterian claims and targeted at Calderwood was edited by James Maidment, *Spottiswoode Miscellany*, Vol. 1 (Spottiswoode Society 3) Edinburgh 1844.

11. Ed. by Mark Napier and Michael Russell, 3 vols. (Bannatyne Club 93/ Spottiswoode Society 6), Edinburgh 1847–51.

12. Ed. by John P. Lawson and Charles J. Lyon, 3 vols (Spottiswoode Society 1), Edinburgh 1844–50.

13. Cf. Meek, *The Quest*, pp. 112f. (see below, Bibliography I).

14. See Kirk, 'The King's Bishop. Archbishop Spottiswoode and the See of Glasgow', in idem *Patterns of Reform*, p. 428.

15. Céli Dé (clients of God). On them see Ian B. Cowan, art. 'Culdees', *Dictionary of Scottish Church History & Theology*, pp. 226f.

16. 1778 edn reprinted, slightly revised, in Liberty *Classics* (directed by W. B. Todd), Indianapolis 1983–85, 6 vols.

17. Op. cit., Vol. 4, p. 21.

18. Ibid., pp. 19, 20.

19. See *Dictionary of Scottish Church History & Theology*, art. 'Martyrs' (Archbishop Hamilton and John Ogilvie).

20. An example of an influential Catholic historian appealing to Hume for corroboration is Alphons Bellesheim, *History of the Catholic Church of Scotland*, trs. from German (1883) by D. O. H. Blair, Vol. 3 (Edinburgh and London 1889), pp. 227f.

21. The strictures against Knox and the Reformation by some prominent figures in contemporary Scottish high culture derive from this pedigree, e.g. the composer, James MacMillan, and the Glasgow poet, Edwin Muir.

22. *History*, Vol. 4, pp. 40, 41.

23. Ibid., pp. 22, 26.

24. For example, by Ninian Winzet in a letter to Knox of 27 October 1563: 'If through zeal for innovations you have forgotten our old plain Scots

which your mother taught you in the past, in future I shall communicate with you in Latin, for I am not familiar with your Southern (English)', in *Certane tractatis*, ed. David Laing (Maitland Club 33), Edinburgh 1835, *Certain tractates*, ed. J. King Hewison (Scottish Text Society, Old Series 15) (Edinburgh 1888), Vol. 1, p. 138, lines 8–11.

25. *History* 4, pp. 24f.
26. Ibid., p. 41.
27. Loc. cit.
28. Ibid., p. 40.
29. See Shaw, *General Assemblies*, p. 134.
30. Ibid., pp. 157f.
31. Ibid., p. 135. The remark was made by Abbot Quintin Kennedy of Crossraguel, cf. *Wodrow Miscellany*, p. 267 (see below, Chapter 8, n. 74).
32. Cf. Duncan Shaw (ed.), *Reformation and Revolution. Essays presented to Hugh Watt* (Edinburgh 1967), pp. 42–69. Kirkwood Hewat, *Makers of the Scottish Church at the Reformation* (Edinburgh 1920), pp. 130–65.
33. See *The Works of John Knox*, ed. David Laing (Bannatyne Club 112) (Edinburgh 1846–64), Vol. 6, p. 559. This and the next two quotations have been modernized.
34. Op. cit., Vol. 5, p. 61.
35. Op. cit., Vol. 6, p. 229.
36. *History*, Vol. 4, p. 42.
37. Ibid., p. 44.
38. *John Knox*, p. 102.
39. Ibid., pp. 119f.
40. Ibid., p. 45.
41. *Court, Kirk and Community*, p. viii.
42. Cf. Thomas Malory's *Le Morte d'Arthur*.
43. 'The Scottish Reformation after 400 years', p. 147.
44. For a comprehensive bibliographical survey, see Dilworth, 'The Counter-Reformation in Scotland'. A work by Donald Maclean, *The Counter-Reformation in Scotland 1560–1930* (London 1931) is written 'from a definite Protestant viewpoint' and is polemical, but has some introductory value.
45. See n. 20 above. Vols 2 and 3 cover the fifteenth and sixteenth centuries.
46. *History of the Catholic Church in Scotland from the Introduction of Christianity to the Present Time*, Glasgow 1874.
47. *Narratives of Scottish Catholics under Mary Stuart and James VI* (1885), new edn, London 1889.
48. *Papal Negotiations with Mary Queen of Scots during her Reign in Scotland 1560–1567* (Scottish History Society 37), Edinburgh 1901.
49. See Latin original, *Historia Maioris Britanniae* (Paris 1521), p. cxxxiii. English edn. by Archibald Constable (Scottish History Society 10), Edinburgh 1892.
50. Cf. David Patrick (ed.), *Statutes of the Scottish Church 1225–1559* (Scottish History Society 54), Edinburgh 1907.
51. *Essays*, p. 345.
52. See McRoberts (ed.), *Essays*, pp. 199, 345.

53. Mullan, *Episcopacy in Scotland*, p. 12. For similar complaints in England, see Carleton, *Bishops*, pp. 89ff. (see below, Bibliography II).

54. *The Medieval Church*, pp. 29, 191f.

55. Cf. *The Works of Sir David Lindsay of the Mount*, ed. Douglas Hamer (Scottish Text Society, 3rd series, 1, 2, 6, 8), Edinburgh 1931–6. Notably effective was the *Satire of the Three Estates* which alludes to the clergy being better at games than at preaching. See also Kirk, 'Early Scottish Protestants', pp. 384–6; Brother Kenneth, in McRoberts (ed.), *Essays*, pp. 171ff.

56. *The Last Blast of the Trompet of God's Word* (Edinburgh 1563), in idem *Certain Tractates*, 5 (see n. 24 above). Cf. Bellesheim, op. cit., 3, pp. 38ff. Burns, *Ninian Winzet*, pp. 18–21, 24.

57. McRoberts (ed.), *Essays*, pp. 369f.

58. *De utilitate et excellentia Verbi Dei* (Paris 1551), sig. Dviii. Cf. John Durkan, 'Cultural Background', in McRoberts (ed.), *Essays*, pp. 311f.

59. Ibid., pp. 308f. Wright, *The Bible in Scottish Life*, pp. 167f.

60. McRoberts (ed.), *Essays*, p. 227.

61. *The Scottish Reformation*, pp. 27–48.

62. *Scottish Monasteries*.

63. *The Faith of the Scots* (London 1990), pp. 37–60.

64. Cf. Cowan, *Regional Aspects*, pp. 30–3. Sanderson, 'Catholic Recusancy'.

65. Cf. James H. Baxter, 'The Scots College at Douai'. *Scottish Historical Review* 24 (1927), 251–7. H. Chadwick, 'The Scots College, Douai, 1580–1613', *English Historical Review* 56 (1941), 571–85.

66. See Dilworth, *Counter-Reformation*, pp. 88ff. Idem, 'Dunfermline'.

67. 'Lutheranism in the Scottish Reformation', *Westminster Theological Journal* 7 (1945), 91–111.

68. 'Cultural Background', in McRoberts, *Essays*, pp. 295ff. Cf. also his 'Scottish Evangelicals', and 'Heresy in Scotland'.

69. See Chapter 4, p. 42.

70. Cf. Heinz Schilling (ed.), *Die reformierte Konfessionalisierung in Deutschland – Das Problem der 'Zweiten Reformation'* (Schriften des Vereins für Reformationsgeschichte 195) (Gütersloh 1986), pp. 387–438, esp. pp. 389n. 5, 400. Cf. Chapter 6 above, n. 91.

71. Norman Davis, *Europe. A History* (Oxford and New York 1966), p. 494.

72. Cf. his *The Scottish Reformation*. See also F. W. Maitland, 'The Anglican Settlement and the Scottish Reformation', in *The Cambridge Modern History* (Cambridge 1904), Vol. 2, 550–98.

73. See especially his 'Superintendent: Myth and Reality', in *Patterns of Reform*, pp. 154–231.

74. See his 'Reformation and Revolution, Kirk and Crown 1560–1690', in Wormald (ed.), *Scotland Revisited*, p. 90.

75. For a view of the strengths, limitations and distinctiveness of Donaldson's interpretation of the Reformation in Scotland as well as the importance of his contribution, see also James Kirk's *Her Majesty's Historiographer. Gordon Donaldson 1913–1993* (Edinburgh 1996), pp. 97ff.

76. See his 'Calvinism in Scotland 1559–1638', in Menna Prestwich (ed.), *International Calvinism 1541–1715* (Oxford 1985), pp. 225–55. Cf. Hazlett, 'Knox and Fasting', p. 195.

77. The idea that the reformers ought to grant liberty of conscience was also broached in a letter of Archbishop Hamilton to the Archbishop of Glasgow in 1560. Text in Keith, *History of the Affairs*, Vol. 3, 7–10 (see n. 12 above).

78. Cf. Hazlett, 'Prophecy and Politics', pp. 184ff. Idem, 'Marie, reine des écossais', pp. 32ff.

79. See John Guy, 'Dangerous Liaisons', in *BBC History Magazine* 3, nr. 2 (2002), pp. 12–14.

80. See Julian Goodare, 'Queen Mary's Catholic Interlude', in Lynch (ed.), *Mary Stewart*, pp. 154–70.

81. Based on works such as William Robertson's *History of Scotland*, and Thomas McCrie's *Life of John Knox*, the notion that in 1558 the Reformers had 'half the nation' behind them was accorded universal circulation in works such as *Mosheim's Institutes of Ecclesiastical History*, trs. James Murdoch, rev. edn with supplementary notes by James S. Reid (London and Belfast 1848), p. 668, n. 1. By the early decades of the twentieth century, this view began to be modified at least. See Alexander R. MacEwen, *A History of the Church in Scotland* (London and New York 1918), Vol. 2, pp. 146ff.

82. See also Michael Yellowlees, *Dunkeld and the Reformation*, doctoral thesis, University of Edinburgh 1990. Alan White, *Religion, Society and Politics in Aberdeen, 1543–1593*, doctoral thesis, University of Edinburgh.

83. Where there was in 1562 nearly a communal 'war of religion', cf. Lynch, 'John Knox, Minister of Edinburgh and Commissioner of the Kirk', in Mason, *John Knox*, pp. 261f.

84. Pierre Fraenkel, in Remigius Bäumer (ed.), *Von Konstanz nach Trient* (Munich 1972), pp. 486f.

85. Cf. Brown, *Bloodfeud*. Idem 'The Nobility of Jacobean Scotland', in Wormald, *Revisiting Scotland*, pp. 61–71.

86. *Ayrshire and the Reformation*, pp. 11–22, 120–44 (quotation at p. 144). Cf. Lynch., art. cit., pp. 258, 260f.

87. 'Preaching to the Converted? Perspectives on the Scottish Reformation', in Alasdair MacDonald *et al.*, *The Renaissance in Scotland*, pp. 301ff.

88. *Scottish Puritanism*.

89. Ibid., p. 2. The 'rhetoric of contrariety', practised so effectively by Knox earlier, flourished in such a thought-world; see Euan Cameron, 'The European Dimensions of Knox's Reformation', in Mason, *John Knox*, p. 72.

90. Cf. Donald Meek, art. 'Gaelic', in *Dictionary of Scottish Church History & Theology*, 345, col. 2 (first quotation); Dawson, 'Calvinism in the Gaidhealtachd', p. 223.

91. See Giblin, *Irish Franciscan Mission*, pp. 46f.

92. See Durkan, in McRoberts (ed.), *Essays*, pp. xvi, 317, 320.

93. See her 'Calvinism and the Gaidhealtachd'.

94. *The Protestant Ethic and the Spirit of Capitalism* (Eng. 1930), trs. by Talcott Parsons, revised introduction by Randall Collins (Los Angeles 1998).

95. Cf. De Jong, *John Forbes*, p. 169.

Chapter 8: Reformation in Scotland

1. December 1557 was when the Reformation avant-garde in Scotland finally mobilized in the form of a 'band' or 'covenant' sworn by a small but influential number of nobles and gentry, 'Lords of the Congregation' (i.e. high-profile Protestant nobles), to overthrow Catholicism and its political stanchions.

2. See Sanderson, *Ayrshire and the Reformation*, pp. 36–47.

3. Ibid., pp. 42f. 46f. Cf. Wright, 'The Bible in the Scottish Reformation', in idem, *The Bible in Scottish Life*, pp. 156f. See both for further literature, as well as art. 'Nisbet, Murdoch', in *Dictionary of Scottish Church History & Theology*, p. 629. Nisbet's entire text was published by Thomas G. Law (ed.), *The New Testament in Scots* (Scottish Text Society, Old Series, Vols. 46, 49, 52), Edinburgh 1901–5.

4. The 'Bassendyne Bible', see s.v., *Dictionary of Scottish Church History & Theology*, pp. 64f. This was a reimpression of the English Geneva Bible.

5. In John C. Olin (ed.), *Christian Humanism and the Reformation. Selected Writings of Erasmus* (New York 1987), p. 101.

6. Cf. J. D. Mansi, *Sacrorum conciliorum nova et amplissima collectio* (Paris 1901–27), Vol. 32, col. 1161ff.

7. See Sanderson, *Cardinal of Scotland*, Appendix 3, no. 3.

8. See John T. McNeill, 'Alexander Alesius, Scottish Lutheran', *Archiv für Reformationsgeschichte* 55 (1964), 161–91. See also art. 'Alesius', *Dictionary of Scottish Church History & Theology* 8 (there: further literature). See also Chapter 4 above, notes 23, 54 and 55.

9. *Epistola contra decretum quoddam episcoporum in Scotia quod prohibet legere novi Testamenti libros lingua vernacula*, s. l. 1533.

10. *An expediat laiciis, legere novi testamenti libros lingua vernacula?* [Basle] 1533.

11. *Pro Scotia regno apologia . . . ad personatum Alexandrum Alesium Scotum*, Leipzig 1534. Cochlaeus outlines his involvement in Scottish religious affairs in his Latin biography of Luther: *Commentary on the Deeds and Writings of Dr. Martin Luther* (Mainz 1549), translated and annotated by Elizabeth Vandiver and Ralph Keen, in: *Luther's Lives. Two Contemporary Accounts of Martin Luther* (Manchester and New York 2002), pp. 294–7, 316–17.

12. A Dominican, a Franciscan, a priest and a layman. Cf. James M. Aitken, *The Trial of George Buchanan before the Lisbon Inquisition* (Edinburgh and London 1939), pp. 120f. Sanderson, *Cardinal of Scotland*, Appendix 3, nos. 16, 63, 64, 89, 142.

13. For contemporary accounts of the trial, see Robert Pitcairn (ed.), *Ancient Criminal Trials in Scotland*, Vol. 1, part 1 (Bannatyne Club 42)/(Maitland Club 19) (Edinburgh 1833), pp. *211–*215.

14. Cf. Sanderson, op. cit., Appendix 3, nos. 90, 136.

15. Cf. Calderwood, *True History of the Church of Scotland*, Vol. 1, pp. 114–23. Sanderson, op. cit., Appendix 3, no. 19.

16. Sanderson, op. cit., Appendix 3, no. 26. Aitken (see n. 12 above), p. 60.

17. Text edn by Alexander F. Mitchell, *A Compendious Book of Godly and Spiritual Songs commonly known as 'The Gude and Godly Ballatis'*, (Scottish

Text Society, Old Series 39), Edinburgh 1897. Brother Kenneth, 'Popular Literature', in McRoberts, *Essays*, pp. 173–7.

18. Brother Kenneth refers to the *Ballads'* 'tedious repetition of justification by faith' and their 'marring by a depressing note on our corrupt nature', ibid., pp. 175f.

19. Knox, *Works* (ed. Laing), Vol. 1, pp. 297ff.

20. See Wright, 'The Bible in the Scottish Reformation', pp. 166f. Cf. Chapter 6 above, to n. 56.

21. Published abroad in the same year. In Laing (ed.), *Works* 4, pp. 133–40.

22. Cf. Peter Lorimer, *Patrick Hamilton, the first Preacher and Martyr of the Scottish Reformation*, Edinburgh 1857.

23. An old account of the trial and martyrdom is found in a work by Robert Lindsay of Pitscottie (1532–80), *The historie and chronicles of Scotland* (first published 1604), ed. Aeneas J. G. Mackay, Vol. 1 (Scottish Text Society, Old Series 42) (Edinburgh 1899), pp. 133–5. There are also two brief eyewitness accounts extant, by Alesius and John Johnsone, see Cameron, 'An early example of Scots Lutheran piety', pp. 138–40. See also Foxe's *Book of Martyrs*, ch. 15.

24. Cf. Sanderson, *Cardinal of Scotland*, pp. 75–7.

25. For analysis of the Marburg theological environment, see Müller, 'Protestant Theology in Scotland and Germany'.

26. By the Cambridge Lutheran, John Frith (*c.*1503–33) in 1532 with the title: *Diverse fruitful gatherings of Scripture concerning faith and works*, and later known as *Patrick's Places*. Also republished both by Foxe in his edition (1572) of the works of Tyndale, Frith and Barnes, and by Knox in his *History* (ed. Dickinson), Vol. 2, pp. 219–29. Frith also had been at Marburg, see Dickens, *The English Reformation*, p. 101.

27. See Major's *Prefaces*, ed. Thomas G. Law, *Publications of the Scottish History Society* 10 (1892), pp. 447f.

28. Cf. Rex, *Theology of John Fisher* (see below, Bibliography II). David V. N. Bagchi, *Luther's Earliest Opponents. Catholic Controversialists 1518–1525*, Minneapolis 1991, *passim.*

29. Cf. James Kirk, 'The 'Privy Kirks' and their antecedents: the hidden face of Scottish Protestantism', in idem *Patterns of Reform*, pp. 1ff.

30. See Sanderson, *Cardinal of Scotland*, pp. 270–83 (a catalogue).

31. See John Maxwell of Terregles (Baron or Lord Herries) (1502–82), *Historical Memoirs*, ed. Robert Pitcairn (Abbotsford Club 6) Edinburgh 1836, p. 14.

32. His wife was a sister-in-law of Myles Coverdale, the English Bible translator, cf. Dickens, *The English Reformation*, p. 153. See also Leif Grane and Kai Hørby (eds), *Die Dänische Reformation vor ihrem internationalen Hintergrund/The Danish Reformation against its International Background* (Forschungen zur Kirchen-und Dogmengeschichte 46) (Göttingen 1990), p. 167. Leif Grane, *Københavns Universitet 1479–1979*, Vol. 5 (Copenhagen 1980), *passim* (see index under 'Machabaeus, Johannes'). Martin Schwarz Lausten, *Die Reformation in Dänemark*, ed. by Johannes Schilling (Schriften des Vereins für Reformationsgeschichte 201), Gütersloh 2003.

33. Cf. Sanderson, *Cardinal of Scotland*, pp. 81–4. Idem *Ayrshire and the Reformation*, pp. 52–4. Kirk, 'Early Scottish Protestants', pp. 376–83. Durkan, 'Early Scottish "Evangelicals"', *passim*. A. Ross, 'Notes on the Religious Orders', in McRoberts, *Essays*, pp. 185–240, *passim*.

34. See below.

35. See Sanderson, *Cardinal of Scotland*, Appendix 3, no. 14.

36. Published in 1584. In *Knox's Works* (ed. D. Laing), Vol. 3, pp. 405–543.

37. Cf. Sanderson, *Ayrshire and the Reformation*, p. 53.

38. Text in George Grubb, *Ecclesiastical History of Scotland*, Vol. 2 (Edinburgh 1861), pp. 77f. Cf. McRoberts, *Essays*, pp. 197f., 400.

39. Text edn by Arthur F. Mitchell (Scottish Text Society, Old Series 12), Edinburgh 1888.

40. Cf. Cameron, 'An early example of Scots Lutheran piety'.

41. See reproduction of title page in McRoberts, *Essays*, p. 241.

42. Cf. Knox, *History* (ed. Dickinson), Vol. 1, pp. 60–74; Vol. 2, pp. 233–45. See also Sanderson, *Cardinal of Scotland*, pp. 192–4, 214–20. Durkan, 'Scottish "Evangelicals"'.

43. Text in David Laing (ed.), *The Miscellany of the Wodrow Society* (Wodrow Society 11), Edinburgh 1844. Also printed in Charles Rogers, *Life of George Wishart* (Grampian Club 11), London 1876.

44. The association of politics and evangelism was not unknown elsewhere, e.g. the Bernese arranged for William Farel to preach in French-speaking western Switzerland, including Geneva.

45. Cf. Knox's *History* (ed. Dickinson), Vol. 1, pp. 60–74; Vol. 2, pp. 234–45. Foxe's *Book of Martyrs*, ch. 15.

46. Cf. Sanderson, *Cardinal of Scotland*.

47. See Arthur C. Cochrane (ed.), *Reformed Confessions of the 16th Century* (Philadelphia 1966), pp. 107–9.

48. Cf. Bruce Gordon, 'Calvin and the Swiss Reformed Churches', in Andrew Pettegree, Alastair Duke and Gilian Lewis (eds), *Calvinism in Europe, 1540–1629* (Cambridge 1994), pp. 64–81. Wulfert de Greef, *The Writings of John Calvin. An Introductory Guide* (Grand Rapids, MI and Leicester 1989), pp. 184–90. For an English translation of the *Zurich Consensus*, see Ian D. Bunting, *Journal of Presbyterian History* 44 (1966), pp. 45–61.

49. Cf. MacCulloch (see below, Bibliography II), *Tudor Church Militant*, pp. 167–70, 172f.

50. E.g. McRoberts himself, *Essays*, p. 252.

51. See Chapter 4, at notes 161 and 162. Chapter 6, n. 98.

52. Cf. Sanderson, *Cardinal of Scotland*, pp. 223–30.

53. Cf. Thomas Winning, 'Church Councils in sixteenth-century Scotland', in McRoberts, *Essays*, pp. 332–58. Cameron, 'The Cologne Reformation and the Church of Scotland'. Patrick, *Statutes of the Scottish Church* (see previous chapter, n. 50).

54. Text edn by Thomas G. Law, *The Catechism of John Hamilton*, Oxford 1884. Facsimile edn by Alexander F. Mitchell, *The Catechism set forth by Archbishop Hamilton* (1551) . . . *together with the Twopenny faith, 1559*, Edinburgh 1882.

55. On him, see Durkan, 'Cultural Background', in McRoberts, *Essays*, pp. 326–9. Also McRoberts himself, op. cit., p. 253.
56. On the history of St Mary's at this time, cf. James K. Cameron, in D. William D. Shaw, *In Diverse Manners. A St Mary's Miscellany* (St Andrews 1990), pp. 29–57.
57. Ibid., pp. 43ff.
58. On his activity during this visit, see Ridley, *John Knox*, pp. 224–40.
59. *The appellation of John Knoxe from the cruell and most unjust sentence pronounced against him by the false bishoppes and clergie of Scotland* (Geneva 1558). In Laing (ed.), *Knox Works* 4, pp. 465–520.
60. See above, n. 21.
61. See Sanderson, *The Reformation in Ayrshire*, pp. 84f. Kirk, 'The 'Privy Kirks'', in idem *Patterns of Reform*, pp. 12–15.
62. *Calendar of Scottish State Papers*, Vol. I, p. 367.
63. Cf. Donaldson, 'Reformation to Covenant', p. 39, and n. 6 there. See also William McMillan, *The Worship of the Scottish Reformed Church, 1560–1638* (Dunfermline, Edinburgh and London 1931), pp. 29–47.
64. Cf. Bardgett, *Scotland Reformed, passim*. James McEwen, 'John Erskine of Dun', in R. Selby Wright (ed.), *Fathers of the Kirk* (London and Glasgow 1960), pp. 17–27. T. Crockett, *The Life of John Erskine of Dun*, doctoral thesis, University of Edinburgh 1924. Some minor writings are extant: 'Appendix to the Dun Papers', in John Stuart (ed.), *Miscellany of the Spalding Club*, Vol. 4 (Spalding Club 20), Aberdeen 1849.
65. Cf. Charles Rogers (ed.), *Three Scottish Reformers* (Grampian Club 11), London 1876. Sanderson, *The Reformation in Ayrshire, passim*.
66. Cf. Maurice du Pont Lee, *James Stewart, Earl of Moray*, New York 1953.
67. Cf. William Monter, *Judging the French Reformation*, Cambridge, MA and London 1999.
68. See anon., *A Historie of the Estate of Scotland*, ed. David Laing, *Miscellany of the Wodrow Society* (Wodrow Society 11) (Edinburgh 1844), pp. 54f.
69. Cf. Gordon Donaldson, '*Flitting Friday*: The Beggars Summons and Knox's Sermon at Perth', *Scottish Historical Review* 39 (1960), 175f.
70. Text in Knox's *History* (ed. Dickinson), Vol. 2, pp. 255f.
71. Cf. Cowan, *The Scottish Reformation*, pp. 44–8, 111–20.
72. See *The Register of the Privy Council of Scotland 1545–1625*, ed. John H. Burton *et al.*, series I (Edinburgh 1877–), Vol. 1, pp. 266–7. Cf. Knox's *History* (ed. Dickinson), Vol. 2, pp. 9f. See also Hazlett, 'Prophecy and Politics', and 'Marie, reine des écossais'.
73. Cf. Maurice Taylor, 'Conflicting Doctrines', in McRoberts, *Essays*, pp. 259–71.
74. Text in David Laing (ed.), *Miscellany of the Wodrow Society*, Vol. 1 (Wodrow Society 11), Edinburgh 1844. John Davidson, the ex-Dominican colleague of Knox in Edinburgh, published a reply to this in 1563, see ibid.
75. Cf. Burns, *Ninian Winzet, passim*.
76. Ed. Hewison, see previous chapter, n. 24.
77. Text edn by Cornelis H. Kuipers, *Quintin Kennedy (1520–1564). Two Eucharistic Tracts*, Nijmegen 1964. Cf. Knox, *Works* (ed. Laing), Vol. 6, pp. 166–220.

78. Cf. Hazlett, 'Prophecy and Politics', pp. 187ff.
79. See his letter to Calvin, in *Works* (ed. Laing), Vol. 6, p. 134. Also in *Corpus Reformatorum. Opera Calvini*, Vol. 47, col. 73. Cf. Janton, *John Knox*, pp. 177f.
80. Cf. Knox's *History*, Vol. 2, pp. 151f.
81. Cf. Kirk, *Books of Assumption*. Before 1560, the Church's annual income was ten times that of the Crown. For the Crown and the nobility, 'Reformation', as in England, involved ecclesiastical asset stripping.
82. Text in Knox, *Works* (ed. Laing), Vol. 6, pp. 391–426. See also Hazlett, 'Playing God's card'.
83. Text edn by Theodor Hesse, in *Bekenntnisschriften und Kirchenordnungen der nach Gottes Wort reformierten Kirche*, gen. ed. Wilhelm Niesel (Zollikon-Zurich 1938), pp. 82–117 (Scots and Latin). In 1937, a non text-critical edition was published by George D. Henderson, *Scots Confession, 1560 (Confession Scoticana) and Negative Confession, 1581 (Confession negativa) with Introduction* (Edinburgh and Glasgow), pp. [33]–99. The Scots original and a modern English translation were published later by George D. Henderson and James Bulloch, *The Scots Confession 1560*, Edinburgh 1960. This modern version is also in *Reformed Confessions of the 16th Century*, ed. Arthur C. Cochrane (Philadelphia and London, 1966), pp. 159–84.
84. Cf. Hazlett, 'The Scots Confession', pp. 315–19.
85. It was often referred to as the 'Psalm-Book'. It was also often misleadingly called '*John Knox's Liturgy*'. Text edn by George W. Sprott, *The Book of Common Order of the Church of Scotland, Commonly Known as John Knox's Liturgy*, Church Service Society, Edinburgh 1901.
86. See especially Kirk, *Patterns of Reform*, pp. 280–304, and Thompson (next note), pp. lxxvii–lxxix. See also Chapter 6 above, to n. 50.
87. Text edn by Robert Thompson, *Foirm na n-Urrnuidheadh*.
88. It was used by Sean Kearney in his Gaelic Irish Catechism of 1571 (see Chapter 6 above); cf. Ó Cuív, *Aibidil* (see below, Bibliography IV), pp. 11, 15f., 181–4.
89. Cf. Meek, *The Quest*, p. 112 (see below, Bibliography I).
90. Text edn by James Cameron (1972).
91. Text edn by James Kirk (1980).
92. Cf. Heiko A. Oberman, *Masters of the Reformation. The Emergence of a New Intellectual Climate in Europe*, trs. D. Martin (Cambridge 1981), pp. 276, 294f.
93. Lynch, *Edinburgh and the Reformation*, p. 103.
94. Text in Knox, *Works* (ed. Laing), Vol. 6, pp. 391–426.
95. A more anglicized version was published by George W. Sprott and Thomas Leishman (eds), *The Book of Common Order* (Edinburgh and London 1868), pp. 150–91.
96. Text in Thomas F. Torrance (ed.), *The School of Faith. The Catechisms of the Reformed Church* (London 1959), pp. 99–165.
97. Text, Latin and English, in Henderson, *The Scots Confession* (see above, n. 83), pp. 102–11. See also ibid. pp. 25–30.

 98. See Robert M. Kingdom, 'La discipline ecclésiastique vue de Zurich et
     Genève au temps de la Réformation: l'usage de Matthieu 18, 15–17 par
     les réformateurs', *Revue de théologie et de philosophie* 113 (2001), 343–55.
 99. For Calvin's theological basis, see *Institutes* (Latin 1559), IV.12.2, and
     Institutes (French 1560), IV.8.15. More extensive discussion is found in
     Calvin's collective New Testament commentary, *Harmony of the Gospels*
     (1555), to Matt. 18, 15–17. See also Kirk, *The Second Book of Discipline*,
     pp. 165f.
100. See Cameron (ed.), p. 169.
101. *Anent the trew and haly Kirk,* in *The Acts of the Parliaments of Scotland,* ed.
     Cosmo Innes and Thomas Thomson (Edinburgh 1814–75), Vol. 2, pp.
     71–3.
102. For a good outline, see James Kirk, art. 'Melville, Andrew', in *Dictionary
     of Scottish Church History & Theology*, pp. 556f. Cf. his '"Melvillian" Reform
     in the Scottish Universities'*, in Alasdair MacDonald *et al.* (eds), *The
     Renaissance in Scotland*, pp. 276–300. Cf. Thomas McCrie, *Andrew Melville.
     A Life*, new edn, Edinburgh 1899.
103. See especially Foster, *The Church before the Covenants*. Cf. George D.
     Henderson, *Presbyterianism* (Edinburgh 1954), pp. 32–52.
104. See the fresh study by Doelman, *King James I and the Religious Culture of
     England*, pp. 63–72 (see below, Bibliography II).
105. Cf. Donald Macmillan, *The Aberdeen Doctors*, London 1909. George D.
     Henderson, 'The Aberdeen Doctors', in idem *The Burning Bush. Studies
     in Scottish Church History* (Edinburgh 1957), pp. 75–93. Torrance, *Scottish
     Theology*, pp. 79–92.
106. Cf. Mullan, *Scottish Puritanism*, pp. 262f. See also Chapter 4 above, at
     notes 162 and 167.
107. See Chapter 4, at n. 161 and 162; Chapter 6, n. 98.
108. *Acts of the Parliament of Scotland* (see above, n. 101).
109. Ibid.
110. Ibid., p. 89, col. 1.
111. Cf. Burke, *Popular Culture*, pp. 208ff. (see below, Bibliography I).
112. *Catholic Synods*, p. 193, and index: 'morality of laity' (see below,
     Bibliography IV).
113. In John Row, *History of the Kirk*, pp. 172–4 (see above, Chapter 7, n. 9).
114. Cf. Brian P. Levack, *The Witch-hunt in Early Modern Europe*, 2nd edn
     London 1995.
115. See recent new edition by Normand and Roberts.
116. Cf. E. William Monter, *Witchcraft in France and Switzerland. The Borderlands
     during the Reformation*, Ithaca and London 1976.
117. See Larner, *Enemies of God*.
118. Cf. Acts 8.9.
119. See Mullan, *Scottish Puritanism*, pp. 24f., 198f.
120. Cf. Louise A. Yeoman, 'The Devil as Doctor. Witchcraft, Wodrow and
     the Wider World', *Scottish Archives* 1 (1995), 94f.
121. See the example of 'Mistress Rutherford' given by Mullan, *Scottish
     Puritanism*, pp. 92–5.
122. Ibid. pp. 265ff.

123. Cf. Graham, *The Uses of Reform.* For an alternative viewpoint, especially on the issue of sexual discipline, see Parker, 'The "Kirk by Law Established"'.
124. Cf. Raymond Mentzer (ed.), *Sin and the Calvinists. Moral Control and the Consistory in the Reformed Tradition* (Sixteenth Century Essays & Studies 32), Kirksville, MO 1994.

Chapter 9: Conclusion

1. Cf. John McKee, 'Revivals, revivalism, and Calvinism with special reference to Ireland', in Donald Patton (ed.), *Ebb and Flow. Essays in church history in honour of R. Finlay G. Holmes* (Belfast 2002), pp. 87, 90–93.
2. Named after the Netherlands theologian and Bishop of Ypres, Cornelius Jansen (1585–1638).

Select Bibliography

I: General and reference works

Baker, Derek (ed.), *The Materials, Sources and Methods of Ecclesiastical History*, (Studies in Church History 11) Oxford 1975 [notably the articles by W. D. G. Cargill Thompson, W. B. Patterson, D. J. Keep, C. Cross and K. Robbins].

Black, Jeremy, *A History of the British Isles*, Basingstoke 1996.

Bradley, James E., and Muller, Richard A., *Church History. An Introduction to Research, Reference Works and Methods*, Grand Rapids 1995.

Brady, Thomas A., Oberman, Heiko A., and Tracy, James D. (eds), *Handbook of European History 1400–1600. Late Middle Ages, Renaissance and Reformation*, 2 vols., Leiden, etc. 1995.

Burke, Peter, *Popular Culture in Early Modern Europe* (1978), rev. edn, Aldershot and Brookfield, VT 1994.

Cameron, Nigel M. de S. *et al.* (eds), *Dictionary of Scottish Church History and Theology*, Edinburgh 1993.

Canons and Decrees of the Council of Trent, trs. H. J. Schroeder, Rockford, IL 1978.

Chaunu, Pierre (ed.), *The Reformation*, Gloucester 1989.

Dickens, A. Geoffrey, *Contemporary Historians of the German Reformation* (The 1978 Bithell Memorial Lecture) Institute of Germanic Studies, University of London 1978.

Dickens, A. Geoffrey, and Tonkin, John M., *The Reformation in Historical Thought*, Oxford 1985.

Donaldson, Gordon, and Morpeth, Robert S., *Who's Who in Scottish History* [1973], Cardiff 1996.

Donaldson, Gordon, and Morpeth, Robert S., *A Dictionary of Scottish History*, Edinburgh 1977.

Donnachie, Ian, and Hewitt, George (eds), *A Companion to Scottish History: from the Reformation to the present*, Edinburgh 1989.

Duffy, Seán (gen. ed.) *et al.*, *Atlas of Irish History*, Dublin 1997.

Elton, Geoffrey, *Return to Essentials. Some Reflections on the Present State of Historical Study*, Cambridge 1991.

Fritze, Ronald H. (ed.-in-chief), *Historical Dictionary of Tudor England* (New York, etc. 1991) [misnamed, it includes much material on Ireland, Scotland and Wales].

Fryde, E. B. *et al.* (eds), *Handbook of British Chronology*, 3rd edn (Royal Historical Society Guides and Handbooks 2) (London 1986) [includes Ireland].

Gordon, Bruce (ed.), *Protestant History and Identity in Sixteenth-century Europe*, Vol. 2: *The Later Reformation* (St Andrews Studies in Reformation History), Aldershot 1996.

Greengrass, Mark, *The Longman Companion to the European Reformation c.1500–1618*, London and New York 1998.

Hamilton, Bernard, *Religion in the Medieval West*, London 1986.

Hillerbrand, Hans J., *Historical Dictionary of the Reformation and Counter-Reformation*, Chicago and London 2000.

Hillerbrand, Hans J. (ed.-in-chief), *The Oxford Encyclopedia of the Reformation*, 4 vols, New York and Oxford 1996.

Johnson, Dale A., *Women and Religion in Britain and Ireland from the Reformation to 1993* (ATLA Bibliography series, 39), Lanham, MD and London 1995.

Kamen, Henry, *Who's Who in Europe 1450–1750*, London and New York 2000.

Kearney, Hugh, *The British Isles. A History of Four Nations* (1989), Canto edn, 1995.

Kelley, Donald R., *Versions of History from Antiquity to the Enlightenment*, New Haven and London 1991.

Maltby, William S., *Reformation Europe. A Guide to Research* (Reformation Guides to Research 3), St Louis, MO 1992.

McNeill, Peter G. B., MacQueen, Hector L., and Lyons, Anona (eds), *An Atlas of Scottish History to 1707*, Edinburgh 1996.

Meek, Donald E., *The Quest for Celtic Spirituality*, Edinburgh 2000.

Meinhold, Peter, *Geschichte der kirchlichen Historiographie*, 2 vols (Orbis Academicus III/5), Freiburg/Munich 1967.

Morris, Terry A., *Europe and England in the Sixteenth Century* (London and New York 1998). [Sets greater England in its European context, and so embraces Wales, Ireland and Scotland.]

Mullett, Michael, *Catholics in Britain and Ireland, 1558–1829*, Basingstoke 1998.

O'Malley, John W., *Trent and All That. Renaming Catholicism in the Early Modern Era*, Cambridge, MA and London 2000.

Ozment, Steven (ed.), *Reformation Europe. A Guide to Research*, St Louis, MO 1982.

Pelikan, Jaroslav, *The Christian Tradition. A History of the Development of Doctrine.* Vol. 4: *Reformation of Church and Dogma (1300–1700)*, Chicago and London 1984.

Rees, William, *An Historical Atlas of Wales from Early to Modern Times* (1951), new edn, London 1972.
Reventlow, Henning G., *The Authority of the Bible and the Rise of the Modern World* (London 1984), pp. 73–146.

Stevenson, David, and Stevenson, Wendy B., *Scottish Texts and Calendars. An Analytical Guide to Serial Publications* (Royal Historical Society. Guides and Handbooks 14/Scottish History Society, Fourth Series, 23) (London and Edinburgh 1987).
Stöve, Eckehart, art. 'Kirchengeschichtsschreibung', in Gerhard Müller (ed.), *Theologische Realenzyklopädie* (Berlin and New York 1989), Vol. 18, pp. 535–60.

Williams, Glanmor, *Reformation Views of Church History* (Ecumenical Studies in History 11), London and Richmond, VA 1970.

II: England

Acheson, Robert. J., *Radical Puritans in England 1550–1660* (Seminar Studies in History), Harlow 1990.
Amos, N. Scott, Pettegree, Andrew, and van Nierop, Henk, *The Education of a Christian Society. Humanism and the Reformation in Britain and the Netherlands* (St Andrews Studies in Reformation History), Aldershot 1999.
Aston, Margaret, *England's Iconoclasts*, Vol. 1: *Laws against Images*, Oxford 1989.
Ayris, Paul, and Selwyn, David G. (eds), *Thomas Cranmer. Churchman and Scholar*, Woodbridge, Suffolk 1993.

Backus, Irena D., *The Reformed Roots of the English New Testament. The Influence of Theodore Beza on the English New Testament* (Pittsburgh Theological Monograph Series, 28), Pittsburgh 1980.
Baker, Derek (ed.), *Reform and Reformation. England and the Continent c.1500–c.1750* (Studies in Church History, Subsidia 2), Oxford 1979.
Bauckham, Richard, *Tudor Apocalypse. Sixteenth Century Apocalypticism, Millenarianism and the English Reformation* (Courtenay Library of Reformation Classics 8), Abingdon 1978.
Bedouelle, Guy, and le Gal, Patrick (eds), *Le 'Divorce' du Roi Henry VIII: Études et Documents* (Travaux d'Humanisme et Renaissance 221), Geneva 1987.

Betteridge, Thomas, *Tudor Histories of the English Reformation, 1530–1583* (St Andrews Studies in Reformation History), Aldershot 1999.

Bond, Ronald B. (ed.), *Certain Sermons or Homilies* (1547) and *A Homily against Disobedience and Wilful Rebellion* (1570), Toronto 1987.

Booty, John E., *John Jewel as Apologist of the Church of England*, London 1963.

Booty, John E. (ed.), *The Godly Kingdom of Tudor England. Great Books of the English Reformation*, Wilton, CT 1981.

Bossy, John, *The English Catholic Community, 1570–1850*, London 1983.

Brachelow, Stephen, *The Communion of Saints. Radical Puritan Thought and Separatist Ecclesiology, 1570–1625*, Oxford 1988.

Bradshaw, Brendan, and Duffy, Eamon (eds), *Humanism, Reform and the Reformation. The Career of Bishop John Fisher*, Cambridge 1989.

Bray, Gerald, *Documents of the English Reformation*, Cambridge 1994 [extends to the year 1700].

Brigden, Susan, *London and the Reformation*, Oxford 1989.

Brooks, Peter N., *Thomas Cranmer's Doctrine of the Eucharist. An Essay in Historical Development*, 2nd rev. edn, Basingstoke 1992.

Bryant, James C., *Tudor Drama and Religious Controversy*, Macon, GA 1984.

Burnett, Amy Nelson, *The Yoke of Christ. Martin Bucer and Christian Discipline* (Sixteenth Century Essays and Studies 26), Kirksville, MO 1994.

Cargill Thompson, W. D. J., *Studies in the Reformation. Luther to Hooker* (ed. C. W. Dugmore), London 1980.

Carleton, Kenneth, *Bishops and Reform in the English Church, 1520–1559* (Studies in Modern British Religious History 3), Woodbridge, Suffolk and Rochester, NY 2001.

Carlson, Eric J., *Marriage and the English Reformation*, Oxford 1994.

Christianson, Paul, *Reformers and Babylon. English Apocalyptic Visions from the Reformation to the Eve of the Civil War*, Toronto, Buffalo and London 1978.

Clay, Christopher, *Economic Expansion and Social Change. England 1500–1700*, Cambridge 1984.

Collinson, Patrick, *Archbishop Grindal 1519–1583. The Struggle for a Reformed Church*, London 1979.

Collinson, Patrick, *The Religion of the Protestants. The Church in English Society 1559–1625*, Oxford 1982.

Collinson, Patrick, *Godly People. Essays on English Protestantism and Puritanism*, London 1983.

Collinson, Patrick, *The Birthpangs of Protestant England. Religious and Cultural Changes in the Sixteenth and Seventeenth Centuries*, Basingstoke 1988.

Collinson, Patrick, and Craig, John (eds), *The Reformation in English Towns, 1500–1640*, Basingstoke 1998.

Cressy, David, and Ferrell, Lori Anne, *Religion and Society in Early Modern England. A Sourcebook*, London 1996.

Cross, Claire, *Church and People 1450–1660. The Triumph of the Laity in the English Church*, London 1976.

Cummings, Brian, *The Literary Culture of the Reformation. Grammar and Grace*, Oxford 2000.

Daniell, David, *William Tyndale. A Biography*, London and New Haven 1994.

Danner, Dan G., *Pilgrimage to Puritanism. History and Theology of the Marian Exiles at Geneva, 1555 to 1560* (Studies in Church History 9), New York 1999.

Davies, Catharine, *A Religion of the Word. The Defence of the Reformation in the Reign of Edward VI*, Manchester 2002.

Davies, Horton, *Worship and Theology in England from Cranmer to Baxter and Fox, 1534–1690*, Grand Rapids, MI and Cambridge 1996.

Davis, John F., *Heresy and Reformation in the South-East of England 1520–1559* (Royal Historical Society in History 34), London 1983.

Dent, Christopher M., *Protestant Reformers in Elizabethan Oxford*, Oxford 1983.

Dickens, A. Geoffrey, *Reformation Studies*, London 1982.

Dickens, A. Geoffrey, *Lollards and Protestants in the Diocese of York 1509–1558* [1959], rev. edn, London 1982.

Dickens, A. Geoffrey, *The English Reformation* (1964), 2nd edn, London 1989.

Dickens, A. Geoffrey, *Later Monasticism and the Reformation*, London and Rio Grande 1994.

Doelman, James, *King James I and the Religious Culture of England* (Studies in Renaissance Literature 4), Cambridge 2000.

Dowling, Maria, *Humanism in the Age of Henry VIII*, London 1986.

Duffy, Eamon, *The Stripping of the Altars. Traditional Religion in England, c.1400–c.1580*, New Haven and London 1992.

Duffy, Eamon, *The Voices of Morebath. Reformation and Rebellion in an English Village*, New Haven and London 2001.

Dures, Alan, *English Catholicism 1558–1642. Continuity and Change* (Seminar Studies in History), Harlow 1983.

Edwards, Francis, *The Jesuits in England. From 1500 to the Present Day*, Tunbridge Wells 1985.

Elton, Geoffrey, *Policy and Police. The Enforcement of the Reformation in the Age of Thomas Cromwell*, Cambridge 1972.

Elton, Geoffrey, *Reform and Renewal: Thomas Cromwell and the Commonweal*, Cambridge 1973.

Elton, Geoffrey, *Reform and Reformation. England 1509–1558* (New History of England 2), London 1977.

Elton, Geoffrey, 'England und die oberdeutsche Reform', *Zeitschrift für Kirchengeschichte*, 89 (1978), 3–11.

Elton, Geoffrey, 'Reform and the "Commonwealth Men" of Edward VI's Reign', in Peter Clark *et al.* (eds), *The English Commonwealth 1547–1640* (Leicester 1979), pp. 23–38.

Elton, Geoffrey, 'Luther in England', in Bernd Moeller (ed.), *Luther in der Neuzeit* (Gütersloh 1983), pp. 121–34.

Fairfield, Leslie P., *John Bale. Mythmaker for the English Reformation*, West Lafayette, IN 1976.

Fincham, Kenneth, *Prelate as Pastor. The Episcopate of James I*, Oxford 1990.

Fines, John, *A Biographical Register of Early English Protestants and Others Opposed to the Roman Catholic Church 1525–1558: Part 1, A–C* (Courtenay Studies in Reformation Theology 3), Abingdon 1981.

Firth, Katherine R., *The Apocalyptic Tradition in Reformation Britain, 1530–1645*, Oxford 1979.

Fox, Alistair, and Guy, John A., *Reassessing the Henrician Age. Humanism, Politics and Reform 1500–1550*, Oxford 1986.

Gaßmann, Günther, 'Die Lehrentwicklung im Anglikanismus', in *Handbuch der Dogmen- und Theologiegeschichte*, ed. Carl Andresen (Göttingen 1988), Vol. 2, pp. 353–83.

Gilman, Ernest B., *Iconoclasm and Poetry in the English Reformation. Down went Dagon*, Chicago 1986.

Greaves, Richard L., *Society and Religion in Elizabethan England*, Minneapolis 1981.

Guy, John A., *Tudor England*, Oxford 1988.

Haigh, Christopher, *The English Reformation Revised*, Cambridge 1987.

Haigh, Christopher, *English Reformations. Religion, Politics and Society under the Tudors*, Oxford 1993.

Hannay, Margaret P. (ed.), *Silent but for the Word. Tudor Women as Patrons, Translators, and Writers of Religious Works*, Kent, OH 1985.

Heal, Felicity, *Of Prelates and Princes. A Study of the Economic and Social Position of the Tudor Episcopate*, Cambridge 1980.

Helmholz, Richard H., *Roman Canon Law in Reformation England*, Cambridge 1990.

Holmes, Peter J., *Resistance and Compromise. The Political Thought of the Elizabethan Catholics*, Cambridge 1982.

Horie, H., 'The Lutheran Influence on the Elizabethan Settlement, 1558–1563', *Historical Journal*, 34 (1991), 519–38.

Horst, Irvin B., *The Radical Brethren. Anabaptism and the English Reformation to 1558* (Bibliotheca humanistica et reformatorica 2), Nieuwkoop 1972.

Houlbrooke, Ralph A., *The English Family, 1450–1700*, New York 1984.

Hudson, Winthrop S., *The Cambridge Connection and the Elizabethan Settlement of 1559*, Durham, NC 1980.

Hunt, E. W., *The Life and Times of John Hooper (c.1500–1555), Bishop of Gloucester*, Lewiston 1992.

Ingram, Martin, *Church Courts, Sex and Marriage in England, 1570–1640*, Cambridge 1987.

Jones, Norman L., *Faith by Statute. Parliament and the Settlement of Religion 1559*, London 1982.

Jones, Norman L., *The English Reformation*, Oxford 2001.

Kendall, Robert T., *Calvin and English Calvinism to 1649* [1979], new edn, Carlisle 1997.

King, John N., *English Reformation Literature. The Tudor Origins of the Protestant Tradition*, Princeton 1982.

Lake, Peter, *Moderate Puritans and the Elizabethan Church*, Cambridge 1982.

Lake, Peter, *Anglicans and Puritans. Presbyterianism and English Conformist Thought from Whitgift to Hooker*, London 1988.

Lake, Peter, and Questier, Michael (eds), *Conformity and Orthodoxy in the English Church, c.1560–1660* (Studies in Modern British Religious History 2), Woodbridge 2000.

Loades, David, *The Oxford Martyrs*, London 1970.

Loades, David, *The Reign of Mary Tudor*, 2nd edn, London and New York 1991.

Loades, David, *Politics, Censorship and the English Reformation 1530–1570*, London 1991.

Loades, David, *Revolution in Religion. The English Reformation 1530–1570*, Cardiff 1992.

Loades, David (ed.), *John Foxe and the English Reformation*, Aldershot and Brookfield, VT 1997.

MacCulloch, Diarmaid, *Thomas Cranmer. A Life*, New Haven and London 1996.

MacCulloch, Diarmaid, *Tudor Church Militant. Edward VI and the Protestant Reformation*, Penguin Books, 1999.

MacCulloch, Diarmaid, *The Later Reformation in England 1547–1603*, Basingstoke (1990), 2nd edn, 2001.

MacCulloch, Diarmaid (ed.), *The Reign of Henry VIII. Politics, Policy and Piety*, Basingstoke 1995.

Macek, Ellen A., *The Loyal Opposition. Tudor Traditionalist Polemics, 1535–1550* (Studies in Church History 7), New York 1996.

Maltby, Judith D., *Prayer Book and People in Elizabethan and Early Stuart England*, Cambridge 1998.

Marsh, Christopher, *Popular Religion in Sixteenth-Century England. Holding Their Peace*, Basingstoke 1998.

Marshall, Peter, *The Catholic Priesthood and the English Reformation*, Oxford 1994.

Marshall, Peter, *Beliefs and the Dead in Reformation England*, Oxford 2002.

Martin, Joseph W., *Religious Radicals in Tudor England*, London 1988.

Mayer, Thomas F., *Thomas Starkey and the Commonweal. Humanist Politics and Religion in the Age of Henry VIII*, Cambridge 1989.

Mayer, Thomas F., *Cardinal Pole in European Context* (Collected Studies series, 686), Aldershot 2000.

McClendon, Muriel C., *The Quiet Reformation. Magistrates and the Emergence of Protestantism in Tudor Norwich*, Stanford, CA 1999.

McEntegart, Rory, *Henry VIII, the League of Schmalkalden, and the English Reformation* (Royal Historical Society Studies in History), Woodbridge and Rochester, NY 2002.

Mews, Stuart, *Religion and National Identity* (Studies in Church History 18), Oxford 1982.

Morcau, Jean-Picrrc, *Rome ou L'Angleterre? Les Réactions Politiques des Catholiques Anglais au Moment du Schisme (1529–1553)*, Paris 1984.

Morgan, John P., *Godly Learning. Puritan Attitudes to Reason, Learning and Education*, Cambridge 1986.

Nijenhuis, Willem, *Adrianus Saravia (c.1532–1613)* (Studies in the History of Christian Thought 21), Leiden 1980.

Null, Ashley, *Thomas Cranmer's Doctrine of Repentance. Renewing the Power of Love*, Oxford 2000.

O'Day, Rosemary, *The Debate on the English Reformation*, London 1986.

Ogier, Darryl M., *Reformation and Society in Guernsey*, Woodbridge, Suffolk 1996.

Pallister, David M., *The Age of Elizabeth. England under the Tudors 1547–1603*, London and New York 1984.

Parish, Helen, *Clerical Marriage and the English Reformation. Precedent, Policy and Practice*, Aldershot 2000.

Parker, Kenneth L., *The English Sabbath. A Study of Doctrine and Discipline from the Reformation to the Civil War*, Cambridge 1988.

Parker, Thomas H. L. (ed.), *The English Reformers* (Library of Christian Classics 26) Philadelphia 1966.

Pettegree, Andrew, *Foreign Protestant Communities in Sixteenth-Century London*, Oxford 1986.

Pettegree, Andrew, *Marian Protestantism. Six Studies*, Aldershot 1996.

Redworth, Glyn, 'Whatever happened to the English Reformation?', *History Today* 37 (1986), 29–36.

Redworth, Glyn, *In Defence of the Church Catholic. The Life of Stephen Gardiner*, Oxford 1990.

Reynolds, Ernest E., *Campion and Parsons. The Jesuit Mission of 1580–1*, London 1980.

Rex, Richard, *The Theology of John Fisher*, Cambridge, etc. 1991.

Rex, Richard, *Henry VIII and the English Reformation*, Basingstoke 1993.

Scarisbrick, John J., *The Reformation and the English People*, Oxford 1984.

Selderhuis, Hermann J., *Marriage and Divorce in the Thought of Martin Bucer* (Sixteenth Century Essays and Studies 48), Kirksville, MO 1999.

Selwyn, David G., *The Library of Thomas Cranmer* (Oxford Biographical Society Publications, 3rd ser., Vol. 1), Oxford 1996.

Sheils, William J., *The English Reformation 1530–1570* (Seminar Studies in History), Harlow 1989.

Skeeters, Martha C., *Community and Clergy. Bristol and the Reformation, c.1520–1570*, Oxford 1993.

Smeeton, Donald D., *Lollard Themes in the Reformation Theology of William Tyndale* (Sixteenth Century Essays and Studies 6), Kirksville, MO 1986.

Solt, Leo F., *Church and State in Early Modern England, 1509–1640*, Oxford 1990.

Targoff, Ramia, *Common Prayer. The Language of Public Devotion in Early Modern England*, Chicago and London 2001.

Thomson, John A. F., *The Early Tudor Church and Society, 1485–1529*, London and New York 1993.

Trueman, Carl R., *Luther's Legacy. Salvation and English Reformers 1525–1556*, Oxford and New York 1994.

Tyacke, Nicholas, *Anti-Calvinists. The Rise of English Arminianism, c.1590–1640*, rev. edn, Oxford 1990.

Tyacke, Nicholas (ed.), *England's Long Reformation, 1500–1800*, London 1998.

Verkamp, Bernard J., *The Indifferent Mean. Adiaphorism in the English Reformation to 1554*, Athens, OH 1977.

Wallace, Dewey D., *Puritans and Predestination. Grace in English Protestant Theology, 1525–1695*, Chapel Hill, NC, 1982.

Walsham, Alexandra, *Church Papists. Catholicism, Conformity and Confessional Polemic in Early Modern England* (Royal Historical Society Publications 68), Woodbridge, Suffolk 1993.

Warnicke, Retha, *Women of the English Renaissance and Reformation*, Westport, CT 1983.

Watt, Tessa, *Cheap Print and Popular Piety, 1550–1640*, Cambridge 1991.

White, Peter O. G., *Predestination, Policy and Polemic. Conflict and Consensus in the English Church from the Reformation to the Civil War*, Cambridge 1992.

Whiting, Robert, *The Blind Devotion of the People. Popular Religion and the Elizabethan Reformation*, Cambridge 1989.

Whiting, Robert, *Local Responses to the English Reformation*, Basingstoke 1998.

Wooding, Lucy E. E., *Rethinking Catholicism in Reformation England*, Oxford 2000.

Zahl, Paul F. M., *Five Women of the English Reformation*, Grand Rapids and Cambridge 2001.

Zaret, David, *The Heavenly Contract. Ideology and Organization in Pre-Revolutionary Puritanism*, Chicago 1985.

III: Wales

Bradshaw, Brendan, 'The English Reformation and identity formation in Ireland and Wales', in Brendan Bradshaw and Peter Roberts (eds),

British Consciousness and Identity: the making of Britain, 1533–1707
(Cambridge 1998), pp. 43–111.

Brown, Andrew J., *Robert Ferrar. Yorkshire Monk, Reformation Bishop, and Martyr in Wales (c.1500–1555)*, London 1997.

Cleary, John M., 'Catholic Resistance in Wales, 1568–1678', *Blackfriars*, 38 (1957), 111–25.

Cleary, John M., *A Checklist of Welsh Students in the Seminaries 1568–1603*, Cardiff 1958.

Davies, John, *A History of Wales*, trs. from Welsh by Allen Lane (London 1990), pp. 224–318.

Griffith, William P., *Learning, Law and Religion. Higher Education and Welsh Society, c.1540–1642* (Studies in Welsh History 10), Cardiff 1996.

Gruffydd, R. Geraint, *The Translation of the Bible into the Welsh Tongue*, Cardiff 1988.

Gruffydd, R. Geraint, 'The Renaissance and Welsh Literature', in Glanmor Williams and Robert O. Jones (eds), *The Celts and the Renaissance. Tradition and Innovation* (Cardiff 1990), pp. 41–56.

Herbert, Trevor, and Jones, Gareth E. (eds), *Tudor Wales*, Cardiff 1988.

Jenkins, Philip, *The History of Modern Wales, 1536–1990*, London 1992.

Jenkins, Philip, 'The Anglican Church and the unity of Britain: the Welsh experience, 1560–1714', in Steven G. Ellis and Sarah Barber (eds), *Conquest and Union. Fashioning a British State, 1485–1725* (London and New York 1995), pp. 115ff.

Jones, J. Gwynfor, *Wales and the Tudor State. Government, Religious Change and the Social Order, 1534–1603*, Cardiff 1989.

Jones, J. Gwynfor, *Early Modern Wales, c.1525–1640*, Basingstoke 1994.

Jones, J. Gwynfor (ed.), *Class, Community and Culture in Tudor Wales*, Cardiff 1989.

Jones, Robert B., *William Salesbury* (Writers of Wales), Cardiff 1994.

Roberts, Peter R., 'The Union with England and the Identity of "Anglican" Wales', *Transactions of the Royal Historical Society*, 22 (1972), 49–70.

Roberts, Peter R., 'Tudor Wales, national identity and British inheritance', in Brendan Bradshaw and Peter Roberts (eds), *British Consciousness and Identity: the making of Britain, 1533–1707* (Cambridge 1998), pp. 8–42.

Rogers, D. M., ' "Popishe Thackwell" and Early Printing in Wales', *Biographical Studies 1534–1829*, 11/1 (1953), 37–54.

Thomas, D. Aneurin (ed.), *The Welsh Elizabethan Catholic Martyrs. The Trial Documents of Saint Richard Gwyn and of the Venerable William Davies*, Cardiff 1971.

Thomas, Isaac, *William Salesbury and his Testament*, Cardiff 1967.

Thomas, Isaac, *Y Testament Newydd Cymraeg* [The Welsh New Testament], *1551–1620*, Cardiff 1976.

Thomas, Isaac, *William Morgan a'i Feibl: William Morgan and his Bible*, Cardiff 1988.

Walker, David (ed.), *A History of the Church in Wales*, Penarth 1976.

Whitebrook, J. C., *The Consecration of . . . Matthew Parker, Archbishop of Canterbury effected by . . . Anthony Kitchen . . . Bishop of Llandaff*, London, Oxford and New York 1945.

Williams, Glanmor, 'John Penry: Marprelate and Patriot?', *Welsh History Reviews*, 3 (1967), 361–80.

Williams, Glanmor, *Welsh Reformation Essays*, Cardiff 1967.

Williams, Glanmor, *The Welsh Church from Conquest to Reformation*, rev. edn, Cardiff 1976.

Williams, Glanmor, *Recovery, Reorientation and Reformation. Wales c.1415–1642*, Oxford 1987.

Williams, Glanmor, 'Medieval Wales and the Reformation', in James P. Mackey (ed.), *An Introduction to Celtic Christianity* (Edinburgh 1989), pp. 206–37.

Williams, Glanmor, *The Reformation in Wales* (Headstart History Papers) Bangor 1991.

Williams, Glanmor, *The Welsh and their Religion. Historical Essays*, Cardiff 1993.

Williams, Glanmor, *Wales and the Reformation*, Cardiff (1997), 2nd edn, 1999.

IV: Ireland

Boran, Elizabethanne, 'Reading theology within the community of believers: James Ussher's *Directions*', in Bernadette Cunningham and Máire Kennedy (eds), *The Experience of Reading. Irish Historical Perspectives* (Dublin 1999), pp. 39–59.

Bossy, John, 'The Counter-Reformation and the People of Catholic Ireland', in *Historical Studies*, 7 (ed. T. D. Williams), 1971.

Bottigheimer, Karl S., 'The Reformation in Ireland', *Journal of British Studies*, 15 (1976), 140–9.

Bottigheimer, Karl S., 'The Failure of the Reformation in Ireland: une question bien posée', *Journal of Ecclesiastical History*, 36 (1985), 196–207.

Bottigheimer, Karl S., and Lotz-Heumann, Ute, 'The Irish Reformation in European Perspective, *Archiv für Reformationsgeschichte*, 89 (1998), 268–309.

Bottigheimer, Karl S., 'Revisionism and the Irish Reformation', *Journal of Ecclesiastical History*, 51 (2000), 581–16.

Bradshaw, Brendan, 'George Browne, first Reformation Archbishop of Dublin, 1526–1554', *Journal of Ecclesiastical History*, 21 (1970), 301–26.

Bradshaw, Brendan, *The Dissolution of the Religious Orders in Ireland under Henry VIII*, London 1974.

Bradshaw, Brendan, 'The Edwardian Reformation in Ireland', *Archivum Hibernicum*, 34 (1977), 83–99.

Bradshaw, Brendan, 'Sword, Word and Strategy in the Reformation in Ireland', *Historical Journal*, 21 (1978), 475–502.

Bradshaw, Brendan, 'The Reformation in the Cities: Cork, Limerick, and Galway, 1534–1603', in John Bradley (ed.), *Settlement and Society in Medieval Ireland* (Kilkenny 1988), pp. 445–76.

Bradshaw, Brendan, 'The English Reformation and identity formation in Ireland and Wales', in Brendan Bradshaw and Peter Roberts (eds), *British Consciousness and Identity: the making of Britain, 1533–1707* (Cambridge 1998), pp. 43–111.

Bradshaw, Brendan, 'Revisionism and the Irish Reformation. A Rejoinder', *Journal of Ecclesiastical History*, 51 (2000), 587–91.

Bradshaw, Brendan, and Peter Roberts (eds), *British Consciousness and Identity: the making of Britain, 1533–1707*, Cambridge 1998.

Bradshaw, Brendan, Hadfield, Andrew and Maley, Willy (eds), *Representing Ireland. Literature and the Origins of Conflict, 1534–1660*, Cambridge 1993.

Brady, Ciáran, and Gillespie, Raymond (eds), *Natives and Newcomers. Essays on the making of Irish Colonial Society 1534–1641*, Dublin 1986.

Brady, Ciáran *et al.* (eds), *Politics, Religion and Society in Ireland, 1515–1641*, Dublin 1992.

Caball, Marc, 'Faith, culture and sovereignty: Irish nationality and its development, 1558–1625', in Brendan Bradshaw and Peter Roberts (eds), *British Consciousness and Identity: the making of Britain, 1533–1707* (Cambridge 1998), pp. 112–39.

Canny, Nicholas P., *The Elizabethan Conquest of Ireland: A Pattern Established, 1565–1576*, Hassocks 1976.

Canny, Nicholas P., 'Why the Reformation Failed in Ireland: Une Question Mal Posée', *Journal of Ecclesiastical History*, 39 (1979), 432–50.

Canny, Nicholas P., 'Protestants, Planters and Apartheid in Early Modern Ireland', *Irish Historical Studies*, 25 (1986), 105–15.

Canny, Nicholas P., *From Reformation to Restoration in Ireland 1534–1660*, Dublin 1987.

Canny, Nicholas P., *Making Ireland British 1580–1650*, Oxford 2001.

Clarke, Aidan, 'Varieties of Uniformity: The First Century of the Church of Ireland', in William J. Sheils and Diana Wood (eds), *Churches, Ireland and the Irish* (Studies in Church History 25) (Oxford 1989), pp. 105–22.

Clarke, Aidan, 'Bibliographical Supplement. Introduction', in Moody *et al.* (eds), *A New History of Ireland (1976–)*, Vol. 3: *Early Modern Ireland, 1534–1691*, rev. edn (Oxford 1991), v. 3, pp. 69ff.

Cunningham, Bernadette, *The World of Geoffrey Keating. History, Myth and Religion in Seventeenth-century Ireland*, Dublin 2000.

Cunningham, Bernadette, and Kennedy, Máire (eds), *The Experience of Reading. Irish Historical Perspectives*, Dublin 1999.

Dawson, Jane E. A., 'Two Kingdoms or Three? Ireland in Anglo-Scottish Relations in the Middle of the Sixteenth Century', in Roger Mason (ed.), *Scotland and England, 1286–1815* (Edinburgh 1987), pp. 113–38.

Edwards, Robert Dudley, *Ireland in the Age of the Tudors. The Destruction of Hiberno-Norman Civilization*, London 1977.

Ellis, Steven G., 'John Bale, Bishop of Ossory, 1552–3', *Journal of the Butler Society*, 2, 1984.

Ellis, Steven G., 'Economic Problems of the Church: Why the Reformation Failed in Ireland', *Journal of Ecclesiastical History*, 41 (1990), 239–65.

Ellis, Steven G., *Ireland in the Age of the Tudors 1447–1603. English Expansion and the End of Gaelic Rule*, London and New York, 1998.

Fletcher, Alan J., and Gillespie, Raymond, *Irish Preaching 700–1700*, 2nd edn, Dublin 2001.

Flynn, Thomas, *The Irish Dominicans, 1536–1641*, Dublin 1993.

Ford, Alan, *The Protestant Reformation in Ireland* (Studien zur Interkulturellen Geschichte des Christentums 34), Frankfurt a. M. (1987), 2nd edn, Dublin 1997.

Ford, Alan, 'James Ussher and the creation of an Irish Protestant identity', in Brendan Bradshaw and Peter Roberts (eds), *British Consciousness and Identity: the making of Britain, 1533–1707* (Cambridge 1998), pp. 185–212.

Ford, Alan, 'James Ussher and the Godly Prince in seventeenth-century Ireland', in Hiram Morgan (ed.), *Political Ideology in Ireland, 1541–1641* (Dublin 1999), pp. 203–29.

Ford, Alan, McGuire, James I. and Milne, Kenneth (eds), *'As by Law Established'. The Church of Ireland since the Reformation*, Dublin 1995.

Forrestal, Alison, *Catholic Synods in Ireland, 1600–1690*, Dublin 1998.

Gillespie, Raymond, *Devoted People. Belief and Religion in Early Modern Ireland*, Manchester 1997.

Gillespie, Raymond, 'Reading the Bible in seventeenth-century Ireland', in Bernadette Cunningham and Máire Kennedy (eds), *The Experience of Reading. Irish Historical Perspectives* (Dublin 1999), pp. 10–38.

Jeffries, Henry A., 'The Irish Parliament of 1560: the Anglican reforms authorized', *Irish Historical Studies*, 26 (1988), 128–41.

Jeffries, Henry A., *Priests and Prelates of Armagh in the Age of Reformation, 1518–1558*, Dublin 1997.

Jones, Frederick M., *The Counter-Reformation* (*A History of Irish Catholicism*, ed. P. J. Corish, Vol. 3, section III), Dublin 1967, pp. 1–53.

Kelly, James, and Keogh, Daire (eds), *History of the Catholic Diocese of Dublin*, Dublin 1999.

Knox, R. Buick, *James Ussher, Archbishop of Armagh*, Cardiff 1967.

Leersen, Joseph, 'Archbishop Ussher and Gaelic culture', *Studia Hibernica*, 22/23 (1982/3), 50–8.

Lennon, Colm, *The Lords of Dublin in the Age of Reformation*, Blackrock 1989.

Lennon, Colm, *Sixteenth-Century Ireland. The Incomplete Conquest* (New Gill History of Ireland 2), Dublin 1994.

Lennon, Colm, *Archbishop Robert Creagh of Armagh, 1523–1586. An Irish Prisoner of Conscience of the Tudor Era*, Dublin 2000.

Lotz-Heumann, Ute, 'The Protestant Interpretation of the History of Ireland: The Case of James Ussher's *Discourse*', in Bruce Gordon (ed.), *Protestant History and Identity in Sixteenth-century Europe*, Vol. 2: *The Later Reformation* (St Andrews Studies in Reformation History), Aldershot 1996, pp. 107–20.

Lotz-Heumann, Ute, 'Social Control and Church Discipline in Ireland during the sixteenth and seventeenth centuries', in Heinz Schilling (ed.), *Institutionen, Instrumente und Akteure sozialler Kontrolle und Diziplinierung im frühneuzeitlichen Europa* (Frankfurt a. M. 1999), pp. 275–304.

Mac Craith, Micháel, 'Gaelic Ireland and the Renaissance', in Glanmor Williams and Robert O. Jones (eds), *The Celts and the Renaissance. Tradition and Innovation* (Cardiff 1990), pp. 57–89.

Mac Craith, Michaél, 'The Gaelic reaction to the Reformation', in Steven G. Ellis and Sarah Barber, *Conquest and Union. Fashioning a British State, 1485–1725* (London and New York 1995), pp. 139–61.

McCaughey, Terence P., *Dr Bedell and Mr King. The Making of the Irish Bible*, Dublin 2001.

McCoog, Thomas M., *The Society of Jesus in Ireland, Scotland, and England 1541–1588. 'Our way of proceeding'* (Studies in Medieval and Reformation Thought 60), Leiden and New York 1996.

McDowell, Robert B., and Webb, D. A., *Trinity College Dublin, 1592–1952. An Academic History*, Cambridge 1982.

Maddison, R. E. W., 'Robert Boyle and the Irish Bible', *Bulletin of the John Rylands Library*, 31 (1958), 81–101.

Martin, Francis X., *Friar Nugent. A Study of Francis Lavalin Nugent (1569–1635), Agent of the Counter-Reformation* (Bibliotheca Seraphico-Capuccina 21), Rome and London 1962.

Meigs, Samantha A., *The Reformations in Ireland. Tradition and Confessionalism, 1400–1690*, Basingstoke and New York 1997.

Moody, Theodore W. *et al.*, *A New History of Ireland* (1976–), Vol. 3: *Early Modern Ireland, 1534–1691*, rev. edn, Oxford 1991.

Mooney, Canice, *The First Impact of the Reformation* (*A History of Irish Catholicism*, ed. P. J. Corish, Vol. 3, section II), Dublin 1967, pp. 1–40.

Mooney, Canice, *The Church in Gaelic Ireland. Thirteenth to Fifteenth Centuries* (*A History of Irish Catholicism*, ed. P. J. Corish, Vol. 2), Dublin 1969.

Ó Cuív, Brian (ed.), *Aibidil Gaoidheilge and Caiticiosma. Seaán Ó Cearnaigh's Irish Primer of Religion published in 1571*, Dublin 1994.

O'Sullivan, William, 'The Correspondence of David Rothe and James Ussher, 1619–1623', in *Collectanea Hibernica* (1993), 7–49.

Robinson-Hammerstein, Helga (ed.), *European Universities in the Age of Reformation and Counter Reformation*, Dublin 1998.

Trevor-Roper, Hugh, 'James Ussher, Archbishop of Armagh', in idem (ed.), *Catholics, Anglicans and Puritans* (London 1989), pp. 120–65.

Walshe, Helen C., 'Enforcing the Elizabethan Settlement: The Vicissitudes of Hugh Brady, Bishop of Meath, 1563–1584', *Irish Historical Studies*, 26 (1989), 352–76.

Williams, Nicholas, *Í bprionta í leabhar: na Protastúin agus prós na Gaelige* [The Printed Book: Protestantism and literature in Irish], *1567–1724*, Baile atha Cliath [Dublin] 1986.

V: Scotland

Barclay, William R., *The Role of Sir David Lyndsay in the Scottish Reformation*, doctoral thesis, University of Wisconsin [1956], University Microfilms International, London 1981.

Bardgett, Frank D., *Scotland Reformed. The Reformation in Angus and the Mearns*, Edinburgh 1992.

Blake, William, *William Maitland of Lethington 1528–1573. A Study of the Policy of Moderation in the Scottish Reformation* (Studies in British History 17), Lewiston 1990.

Broadie, Alexander, *George Lokert. Late-Scholastic Theologian*, Edinburgh 1983.

Broadie, Alexander, *The Circle of John Mair. Logic and Logicians in pre-Reformation Scotland*, Oxford 1985.

Brown, Keith M., *Bloodfeud in Scotland 1573–1625. Violence, Justice and Politics in an Early Modern Society*, Edinburgh 1986.

Brown, Keith M., 'In Search of the Godly Magistrate in Reformation Scotland', *Journal of Ecclesiastical History*, 40 (1989), 553–81.

Burns, John H., *Ninian Winzet* (The Catholic Truth Society for Scotland), Glasgow 1959.

Burns, John H., 'Catholicism in defeat: Ninian Winzet 1519–1592', *History Today*, 16 (1966), 788–95.

Cameron, James K., 'The Cologne Reformation and the Church of Scotland', *Journal of Ecclesiastical History*, 30 (1979), 39–64.

Cameron, James K., 'John Johnsone's *An confortable exhortation of our mooste holy christen faith and her frutes:* an early example of Scots Lutheran piety', in Derek Baker (ed.), *Reform and Reformation. England and the Continent c.1500–c.1750* (Studies in Church History, Subsidia 2) (Oxford 1979), pp. 133–47.

Cameron, James K., 'Aspects of the Lutheran Contribution to the Scottish Reformation, 1528–1552', in *Records of the Scottish Church History Society*, 22 (1984), 1–12.

Cameron, James K., art. 'Knox, John', in *Theologische Realenzyklopädie*, ed. Gerhard Müller (Berlin and New York 1990), Vol. 19, pp. 281–7 (there: further Knox bibliography).

Cameron, James K. (ed.) *The First Book of Discipline*, Edinburgh 1972.

Cowan, Ian B., *Blast and Counterblast. Contemporary Writings on the Scottish Reformation*, Edinburgh 1960.

Cowan, Ian B., *Regional Aspects of the Scottish Reformation* (Historical Association, General Series 92), London 1978.

Cowan, Ian B., *The Scottish Reformation. Church and Society in Sixteenth Century Scotland*, London 1982.

Cowan, Ian B., *The Medieval Church in Scotland* (ed. James Kirk), Edinburgh 1995.

Cowan, Ian B., and Shaw, Duncan (eds), *The Renaissance and Reformation in Scotland*, Edinburgh 1983.

Dawson, Jane E. A., 'The Two John Knoxes: England, Scotland and the 1558 Tracts', *Journal of Ecclesiastical History*, 42 (1991), 555–76.

Dawson, Jane E. A., 'The Scottish Reformation and the theatre of martyrdom', in: D. Wood (ed.), *Martyrs and Martyrologies* (Studies in Church History 30), Oxford 1993, pp. 259–70.

Dawson, Jane E. A., 'Calvinism and the Gaidhealtachd in Scotland', in Andrew Pettegree, Alastair Duke and Gilian Lewis (eds), *Calvinism in Europe 1540–1620* (Cambridge 1994), pp. 231–53.

Dawson, Jane E. A., 'Anglo-Scottish protestant culture and integration in sixteenth-century Britain', in Steven G. Ellis and Sarah Barber (eds), *Conquest and Union. Fashioning a British State, 1485–1725* (London and New York 1995), pp. 87–114.

Dawson, Jane E. A. (ed.), *Clan Campbell Letters, 1559–1583* (Scottish History Society, series 5, Vol. 10), Edinburgh 1997.

De Jong, Christiaan G. F., *John Forbes (ca.1568–1634)*, published thesis, University of Groningen, 1987.

De Jong, Christiaan G. F., 'John Forbes', *Nederlands archief voor kerk geschiedenis*, 69 (1989), 17–53.

Dilworth, Mark, 'Monks and Ministers after 1560', *Records of the Scottish Church History Society*, 18 (1974), 216ff.

Dilworth, Mark, 'The Counter-Reformation in Scotland: A Select Critical Bibliography', *Records of the Scottish Church History Society*, 12 (1984), 85–100.

Dilworth, Mark, 'Archbishop James Beaton II: A Career in Scotland and France', *Records of the Scottish Church History Society*, 23 (1989), 301–16.

Dilworth, Mark, *Scottish Monasteries in the Late Middle Ages*, Edinburgh 1995.

Dilworth, Mark, 'Dunfermline, Duries and the Reformation', *Records of the Scottish Church History Society*, 31 (2002), 37–67.

Donaldson, Gordon, *The Scottish Reformation*, Cambridge 1960.

Donaldson, Gordon, 'John Knox: victim of Puritan mythology', in *New Edinburgh Review Anthology*, ed. James Campbell (Edinburgh 1982), pp. 44–52 (= *New Edinburgh Review*, 3 (1969), 20–3).

Donaldson, Gordon, *All the Queen's Men. Power and Politics in Mary Stewart's Scotland*, London 1983.

Donaldson, Gordon, *Scottish Church History*, Edinburgh 1985.

Donaldson, Gordon, 'Reformation to Covenant', in Duncan Forrester and Douglas Murray (eds), *Studies in the History of Worship in Scotland*, 2nd edn (Edinburgh 1996), pp. 37–57.

Doughty, D. W., 'The Library of James Stewart, earl of Moray', *Innes Review* (1970–1), 21–2.

Dunbar, Linda, 'Synods and Superintendence. John Winram and Fife, 1561–72', *Records of the Scottish Church History Society*, 26 (1997), 97–126.

Dunbar, Linda J., *Reforming the Scottish Kirk. John Winram (c.1492–1582) and the example of Fife* (St Andrews Studies in Reformation History) Aldershot 2002.

Durkan, John, 'The Cultural Background in Sixteenth-Century Scotland', *Innes Review*, 10 (1959), 382–439 (reprinted in David McRoberts (ed.), *Essays on the Scottish Reformation 1513–1625* (Glasgow 1962), pp. 274–331).

Durkan, John, 'Scottish "Evangelicals" in the Patronage of Thomas Cromwell', *Records of the Scottish Church History Society*, 21 (1982), 127–56.

Durkan, John, 'Heresy in Scotland: The Second Phase, 1546–1558', *Records of the Scottish Church History Society*, 24 (1992), 320–65.

Durkan, John, *Bibliography of John Buchanan*, Glasgow 1994.

Felch, Susan, 'The Rhetoric of Biblical Authority. John Knox and the Question of Women', *Sixteenth Century Journal*, 26 (1995), 805–22.

Finlayson, Charles P., *Clement Littill and his Library. The Origins of Edinburgh University Library* (Edinburgh Bibliographical Society) Edinburgh 1980.

Foster, Walter R., *The Church before the Covenants. The Church of Scotland 1596–1638*, Edinburgh 1975.

Giblin, Cathaldus, *Irish Franciscan Mission to Scotland 1619–1646. Documents from Roman Archives*, Dublin 1964.

Goodare, Julian, 'Scotland', in Bob Scribner, Roy Porter and Mikuláš Teich (eds), *The Reformation in National Context* (Cambridge 1994), pp. 95–110.

Gordon, Bruce, 'Zurich and the Scottish Reformation: Rudolf Gwalther's *Homilies on Galatians* of 1576', in James Kirk (ed.), *Humanism and Reform. The Church in Europe, England and Scotland 1400–1643* (Studies in Church History, Subsidia 8) (Oxford 1991), pp. 207–19.

Graham, Michael F., *The Uses of Reform. 'Godly Discipline' and Popular Behaviour in Scotland and France, 1560–1610* (Studies in Medieval and Reformation Thought 56), Leiden 1996.

Graham, Roderick, *John Knox, Democrat*, London 2001.

Graham, W. Fred., 'The Reformation in Scotland', in William S. Maltby, *Reformation Europe. A Guide to Research* (Reformation Guides to Research 3) (St Louis, MO 1992), pp. 235–51.

Greaves, Richard L., 'John Knox, the Reformed tradition and the development of resistance theory', *Journal of Modern History*, 58 (1976), 1–31.

Greaves, Richard L., *Theology and Revolution in the Scottish Reformation. Studies in the Thought of John Knox*, Grand Rapids, MI 1980.

Haas, Rainer, *Franz Lambert von Avignon und Patrick Hamilton in ihrer Bedeutung für die Evangelische Bewegung auf den Britischen Inseln*, published thesis, University of Marburg, 1973.

Haws, Charles H., *Scottish Parish Clergy at the Reformation, 1540–1574* (Scottish Record Society, New Series, Vol. 3) Edinburgh 1972.

Hazlett, W. Ian P., 'The Scots Confession 1560: Context, Complexion and Critique', *Archiv für Reformationsgeschichte*, 78 (1987), 287–320.

Hazlett, W. Ian P., 'A Working Bibliography of the Writings of John Knox', in Robert V. Schnucker (ed.), *Calviniana. Ideas and Influence of John Calvin* (Sixteenth Century Essays and Studies 10) (Kirksville, MO 1988), pp. 185–93.

Hazlett, W. Ian P., ' *"Jihad"* against Female Infidels and Satan: John Knox's First Blast of the Trumpet', in Willem van 't Spijker (ed.), *Calvin. Erbe und Auftrag* (Kampen 1991), pp. 279–90.

Hazlett, W. Ian P., 'Playing God's Card: Knox and Fasting, 1565–66', in Roger A. Mason (ed.), *John Knox and the British Reformations* (St Andrews Studies in Reformation History) (Aldershot and Brookfield, VT 1998), pp. 176–98.

Hazlett, W. Ian P., 'Marie, reine des écossais, et la liberté de conscience: la mise au monde d'une idée mort-née', in Thierry Wanegffelen (gen. ed.), *De Michel de l'Hospital à l'Édit de Nantes. Politique et religion face aux Églises* (Clermont-Ferrand 2002), pp. 32–49.

Hazlett, W. Ian P., 'Prophecy and politics. The exchanges between John Knox and Mary, Queen of Scots, on religious freedom', in Martin Rose (ed.), *Histoire et Herméneutique. Mélanges offerts à Gottfried Hammann* (Geneva 2002), pp. 184–96.

Hewitt, George D., *Scotland under Morton 1572–80*, Edinburgh 1982.

Janton, Pierre, *John Knox (ca.1513–1572). L'homme et l'oeuvre* (Études anglaises 26) Clermont-Ferrand 1967.

Janton, Pierre, *Concept et sentiment de l'Eglise chez John Knox, le réformateur écossais*, Paris 1972.

Jordan, Constance, 'Women's Rule in Sixteenth Century Political Thought', *Renaissance Quarterly*, 40 (1987), 421–51.

Kirk, James, *The Second Book of Discipline*, Edinburgh 1980.

Kirk, James, 'The Scottish Reformation and the Reign of James VI: A Select Critical Bibliography', *Records of the Scottish Church History Society*, 23 (1987), 113–55.

Kirk, James, *Patterns of Reform. Continuity and Change in the Reformation Kirk*, Edinburgh 1989.

Kirk, James, 'Early Scottish Protestants', in idem (ed.), *Humanism and Reform. The Church in Europe, England and Scotland 1400–1643* (Studies in Church History, Subsidia 8) Oxford 1991, pp. 361–411.

Kirk, James, 'Reformation, Scottish', in *Dictionary of Scottish Church History & Theology*, in Nigel Cameron *et al.* (eds) (Edinburgh 1993), pp. 693–98.

Kirk, James, *The Books of Assumption of the Rentals of the Thirds of Benefices. Scottish Ecclesiastical Rentals at the Reformation* (Records of Social and Economic History, New Series 21), Oxford 1995.

Kirk, James, 'John Knox and the Historians', in Roger A. Mason (ed.), *Knox and the British Reformations* (St Andrews Studies in Reformation History) (Aldershot and Brookfield, VT 1998), pp. 7–26 (updated Knox bibli-ography at n. 4; many other recent studies on aspects of the Scottish Reformation cited in other notes).

Kirk, James (ed.), *Visitation of the diocese of Dunblane and other churches, 1586–1589* (Scottish Record Society, New Series, 11), Edinburgh 1984.

Kirk, James, and Durkan, John, *The University of Glasgow 1451–1577*, Glasgow 1977.

Kyle, Richard G., *The Mind of John Knox*, Lawrence, KS 1984.

Larner, Christine, *Enemies of God. The Witch-hunt in Scotland* (1983), Edinburgh 2000.

Lee, Maurice Du P., 'The Scottish Reformation after 400 years. Revision article', *Scottish Historical Review*, 44 (1965), 135–47.

Lee, Maurice Du P., *Government by Pen. Scotland under James VI and I*, Urbana and London 1980.

Lee, Maurice Du P., *Great Britain's Solomon. James VI and I in his Three Kingdoms*, Urbana and London 1990.

Lynch, Michael, *Edinburgh and the Reformation*, Edinburgh 1981.

Lynch, Michael, *Scotland: A New History* (London 1992), pp. 171–244.

Lynch, Michael (ed.), *The Early Modern Town in Scotland*, Scotland 1987.

Lynch, Michael (ed.), *Mary Stewart. Queen in Three Kingdoms*, Oxford 1988.

Lynch, Michael, and Goodare, Julian (eds), *The Reign of James VI*, East Linton 2000.

Lythe, Samuel G. E., *The Economy of Scotland in its European Setting 1550–1625*, Edinburgh 1960.

MacDonald, Alasdair A., Lynch, Michael, and Cowan, Ian B. (eds), *The Renaissance in Scotland. Studies in Literature, Religion, History and Culture offered to John Durkan* (Brill's Studies in Intellectual History 54) Leiden, etc. 1994.

MacDonald, Alan R., *The Jacobean Kirk, 1567–1625. Sovereignty, Polity and Liturgy* (St Andrews Studies in Reformation History), Aldershot and Brookfield, VT 1998.

Macdougall, Norman (ed.), *Church, Politics and Society. Scotland, 1408–1929*, Edinburgh 1983.

McFarlane, Ian, *Buchanan*, London 1991.

McGoldrick, James E., *Luther's Scottish Connection*, Rutherford, NJ, 1989.

McRoberts, David (ed.), *Essays on the Scottish Reformation 1513–1625*, Glasgow 1962.

Marshall, Gordon, *Presbyteries and Profits. Calvinism and the Development of Capitalism, 1560–1707*, Oxford 1980.

Mason, Roger A., '"Scotching the Brut". The Early History of Britain', in Jenny Wormald (ed.), *Scotland Revisited* (London 1991), pp. 49–60.

Mason, Roger A., 'The Scottish Reformation and the Origins of Anglo-British Imperialism', in idem (ed.), *Scots and Britons. Scottish Political Thought and the Union of 1603* (Cambridge 1994), pp. 161–86.

Mason, Roger A., 'Mary Queen of Scots and George Buchanan', *Records of the Scottish Church History Society* 29 (2000), 1–27.

Mason, Roger A. (ed.), *John Knox. On Rebellion*, Cambridge 1994.

Mason, Roger A. (ed.), *John Knox and the British Reformations* (St Andrews Studies in Reformation History) Aldershot and Brookfield, VT 1998.

Meek, Donald E., 'The Reformation and Gaelic culture: Perspectives on Patronage, Language and Literature in John Carswell's Translation of *The Book of Common Order*', in James Kirk (ed.), *The Church in the Highlands* (Edinburgh 1998), pp. 37–62.

Meek, Donald E., 'The Gaelic Bible', in David F. Wright, *The Bible in Scottish Life and Literature* (Edinburgh 1988), pp. 9–23.

Müller, Gerhard, 'Protestant Theology in Scotland and Germany in the Early Days of the Reformation', *Records of the Scottish Church History Society*, 22 (1986), 103–17.

Mullan, David G., *Episcopacy in Scotland. The History of an Idea, 1560–1638*, Edinburgh 1986.

Mullan, David G., *Scottish Puritanism, 1590–1638*, Oxford 2000.

Normand, Lawrence, and Roberts, Gareth (eds), *Witchcraft in Early Modern Scotland. James VI's Demonology and the North Berwick Witches*, Exeter 2000.

Parker, Geoffrey, 'The "Kirk by Law Established" and the "Taming of Scotland", 1559–1600', in idem, *Empire, War and Faith in Early Modern Europe* (London 2002), pp. 253–87.

Reid, W. Stanford, *Trumpeter of God. A Biography of John Knox*, Grand Rapids, MI 1982.

Robinson, Mairi, 'Language choice in the Reformation: The Scots Confession of 1560', in J. D. Maclure (ed.), *Scotland and the Lowland Tongue* (Aberdeen 1983), pp. 59–78.

Sanderson, Margaret H. B., 'Catholic Recusancy in Scotland in the Sixteenth Century', *Innes Review*, 21 (1970), 87–107.

Sanderson, Margaret H. B., *Scottish Rural Society in the Sixteenth Century*, Edinburgh 1982.

Sanderson, Margaret H. B., *Cardinal of Scotland. David Beaton, c. 1494–1546*, Edinburgh 1986.

Sanderson, Margaret H. B., *Ayrshire and the Reformation. People and Change, 1490–1600,* East Linton 1997.

Shaw, Duncan, *The General Assemblies of the Church of Scotland, 1560–1600. Their Origins and Development,* Edinburgh 1964.

Shaw, Duncan, 'Zwinglian Influences on the Scottish Reformation', in *Records of the Scottish Church History Society,* 22 (1985), 119–39 (German trs. in *Zwingliana,* 17 (1988), 375–400).

Shaw, Duncan, 'Action, Remembrance and Covenant. Zwinglian Contributions to the Scottish Reformation Understanding of the Lord's Supper', in Alfred Schindler and Hans Stickelberger (eds), *Die Zürcher Reformation. Ausstrahlungen und Rückwirkungen* (Berne 2001), pp. 303–16.

Shaw, Duncan (ed.), *John Knox. A Quatercentenary Reappraisal,* Edinburgh 1975.

Spinks, Bryan D., *Sacraments, Ceremonies and the Stuart Divines. Sacramental Theology and Liturgy in England and Scotland 1603–1662,* Ashgate, 2002.

Thompson, Robert L. (ed.), *Foirm na n'urruidheadh: John Carswell's Gaelic Translation of the Book of Common Order* (Scottish Gaelic Texts 11), Edinburgh 1970.

Todd, Margo, *The Culture of Protestantism in Early Modern Scotland,* New Haven and London 2002.

Torrance, Thomas F. (ed.), *The School of Faith. The Catechisms of the Reformed Church,* London 1959.

Torrance, Thomas F., *Scottish Theology from John Knox to John McLeod Campbell,* Edinburgh 1996.

Tulloch, Graham, *A History of the Scots Bible. With Selected Texts,* Aberdeen 1989.

Vershuur, Mary B., 'Perth Craftsmen's Book: The Interpretation and Utilization of Protestant Thought by Sixteenth-Century Scottish Townsmen', *Records of the Scottish Church History Society,* 23 (1988), 157–74.

Wiedermann, Gotthelf, 'Martin Luther versus John Fisher: Some Ideas Concerning the Debate on Lutheran Theology at the University of St Andrews, 1525–30', *Records of the Scottish Church History Society,* 22 (1984), 1–34.

Wilkinson, John, 'The Medical History of John Knox', in *Proceedings of the Royal College of Physicians of Edinburgh,* 28 (1998), 81–101.

Wormald, Jenny, *Court, Kirk, and Community. Scotland 1470–1625* (New History of Scotland 4), London 1981.

Wormald, Jenny, *Mary Queen of Scots. Politics, Passion and a Kingdom Lost,* London 2001 (rev. edn of *A Study in Failure,* London 1988).

Wormald, Jenny (ed.), *Scotland Revisited,* London 1991.

Wright, David, F., '"The commoun buke of the kirke": the Bible in the Scottish Reformation', in idem (ed.), *The Bible in Scottish Life and Literature* (Edinburgh 1988), pp. 155–78.

Wright, David F., 'Martin Bucer in England – and Scotland', in Christian Krieger and Marc Lienhard (eds), *Martin Bucer and Sixteenth Century Europe* (Studies in Medieval and Reformation Thought 53) (Leiden 1993), Vol. 2, pp. 523–32.

Wright, David F., 'John Knox and the Early Church Fathers', in Roger A. Mason (ed.), *John Knox and the British Reformations* (Aldershot 1998), pp. 99–116.

Wright, David F., 'The Fathers in the Scottish Reformation', *Reformation & Renaissance Review*, 3, 1/2 (2001), 78–95.

Index

Index of Historical Names

Index of Places

Index of Authors

Index of Select Topics and Terms